Reaching out to
bright minds of the world.

MVC|CAPITAL

www.mvccapital.com
Traded on the NYSE; Ticker Symbol MVC

BIP Business Institution Program

Northwestern's minor program in business institutions is based
the assumption that the study of business can be approached
through a thoughtful investigation of the cultural, political,
philosophical, literary, and social sources and consequences o
business institutions. Therefore the program is not intended to
preprofessional training or to function as a business concentra
within any single departmental major. It is conceived as a broa
multidisciplinary perspective on a significant area of inquiry.
Students who wish to pursue the minor in business institutions
should be open to the intellectual approaches of many disciplin

Business Institutions Program
University Hall 001, Evanston, IL 60208
Phone: (847) 491-2706 Fax: (847) 467-4141
E-mail: bip@northwestern.edu

CHICAGO FIELD STUDIES

ACADEMIC INTERNSHIP PROGRAMS

Learn more about your peers who worked at **United Airlines, Chicago Climate Exchange, Goldman Sachs, Center on Wrongful Convictions, Starcom Entertainment and many others** by visiting:

www.wcas.northwestern.edu/cfs

Gain experience and explore fields in over 30 industries

"CFS allowed me an invaluable opportunity to gain real world work experience while exploring a field which I might not have otherwise had the opportunity to explore."
- Student, Winter Quarter 2008, Walgreens Market Strategies

Leads to future professional success

"My CFS internship offered me highly substantive work at a legal aid organization, in which I encountered real social issues and interacted with clients of my own on a daily basis... I believe these types of professional skills cannot be acquired through classroom education alone, and make the CFS experience both unique and valuable."
- Student, Summer Quarter 2007, Legal Assistance Foundation or Metropolitan Chicago

Integrate academic learning with real world

"Chicago Field Studies offers a truly unique opportunity to obtain an internship during the school year and still incorporate important academic strategies. It should be known that a Northwestern University education can step far beyond a classroom on the North Shore of Chicago."
- Student, Winter Quarter 2006

Flexible to meet your interests and career goals

"CFS has been one of my most positive experiences at Northwestern. I was impressed by the professors' commitment to the program and their accessibility to students. After a long day at work, I was pleasantly surprised that I didn't dread going to class. The discussions were always extremely interesting."
- Student, Winter Quarter 2008, Smith Barney

Chicago Field Studies University Hall 001, Evanston , IL 60208
Phone: (847) 467-0605   Fax: (847) 467-4141
Email: cfs@northwestern.edu

Want to start the next facebook ?

Northwestern Center for Entrepeneurship & Innovat

- One-stop source to start your own business
- Great classes:
  - Principles of Entrepreneurship
  - Engineering Entrepreneurship
  - NUvention Medical Innovation
- Network of alumni and other resources

CEI CENTER for ENTREPRENEURSHIP and INNOVATION

headquartered in the Ford Motor Company Engineering Design Center
2133 Sheridan Road, Room 2.325   www.cei.northwestern.edu

Your connection to success —
the Northwestern Alumni Association.

NORTHWESTERN.
Alumni Association

Why the Northwestern Alumni Association? Because the NAA connects you
to a network of 200,000 successful alumni around the world. From externships to
etiquette banquets, the NAA offers on-campus and online programs and services
especially for students to help you now and in the real world. Find out how to
make the most of your connections — visit **www.alumni.northwestern.edu**.

MBA or IMC?

If marketing and commun... tio...
Medill's IMC Graduate Pro...am...
There's even a part-time p...ogra...

At Medill, you'll learn...
To manage in a time of customer control.
To find real insights in user data.
... to brand communications that truly connect and
...h the multi-media, multi-tasking customer.
... stand how to interact with audience-created
... pass-along messaging.

To lead the integrated marketing process.

To learn more about Medill IMC, register for an
...mation s... ... apply online.

Please visit ww... ...ill.northwestern.edu/imc

MEDILL
Integrated Marketing Communicat...
www.medill.northwestern.edu/...

CHICAGO UNZIPPED
the city guide for new urbanists

EDITOR-IN-CHIEF Nicholas Jackson
PUBLISHER Rena Behar

HEAD OF DESIGN Vinhfield Ta
HEAD OF PHOTOGRAPHY Kristyn Armour

COPY EDITOR Laura Biagi
ASSISTANT EDITOR Jenny An

FEATURES EDITOR Matthew Streib
FAR NORTH EDITOR Sara Abadi
NORTH EDITOR Leona Liu
NORTHWEST EDITOR Nina Kim
CENTRAL EDITOR Meredith Laitor
WEST EDITOR Veronica Crews
SOUTHWEST EDITOR Carley Ribet
SOUTH EDITOR Kasia Galazka

WRITERS Jessica Abels, Christina Amoroso, Amy Anderson, Laura Ashbaugh, Jim Badsing, Jennifer Barnes, Michelle Bejar, Chloe Benoist, EB Blass, Cassandra Blohowiak, Charlie Brottmiller, Nate Brown, Thea Brown, Nisha Chandran, Robyn Chang, James Chapin, Rachel Cicurel, Libby Clark, Liz Coffin-Karlin, Jennifer Crespo, Cristina Cu, Lily Cunningham, Jesse Curti, Alison Deffner, Janna Dons, Nicole Dornbusch, Tara Dubbs, Brenna Ehrlich, Chelsea Ely, Leah Fabel, Andrea Fjeld, Gaby Fleischman, Becky Freking, Julie French, Kevin Garvey, Perry Gattegno, Samantha Goldstein, Liz Granger, Tiffanie Green, Whitney Greenberg, Jenny Gross, Telma Guzman, Matthew Haas, Stacy Jacobson, Marisa Johnson, Niema Jordan, Jeanette Kang, Ross Karp, Aynsley Karps, Lynn Kasanuki, Jessica Kelmon, Sara Kenigsberg, Sarah Kessler, Ryan King, Lucas Koppel. Tracy Lee, Jourdann Lubliner, Dan Macsai, Yvonne Man, Kathrina Manalac, Ron Marek, Ania Markiewicz, Katreva Martin, Sarah McCann, Mikal McLendon, Angela Mears, Oscar Melendrez, Blanca Mendez, Katherine Merriam, Angela Munoz, Amanda Nyren, Emre Parker, Naomi Pescovitz, Ashley Polikoff, Caroline Porter, Lauren Redding, AJ Rudin, Katey Rusch, John Scacco, Sarah Schmidt, Julie Shen, Shane Singh, Caroline Smith, Nicky Smith, Alexandra Squitieri, Lisa Tibbetts, Delena Turman, Melissa Tussing, Anne Valauri, Evan White, Jessica Wiener, Jenna Williams, Nina Yun

PHOTOGRAPHERS Amanda Adlesick, Dan Branca, Kaitlyn Ellison, Clayton Flynn, Daniel Honigman, Nick Infusino, Lydia Merrill, Lindsey Mineff, Wenhong Neoh, Elizabeth Neurauter, Heather Olker, Christina Quintana, Dave Schrimpf, Nick Schweiger, Christopher Starbody, Sara Stubblefield, Rachel Swenie, Colette Tam, Katherine Villamin, Nicky Watts

PRESIDENT Matt Cohlmia
VICE-PRESIDENT Josh Brower

BUSINESS & SALES TEAM Alexis Cordova, Simon Han, Louise Huterstein, Naveen Kumar, Lisa Wang, Eden Yamaguchi

CHICAGO UNZIPPED

third edition

Nicholas Jackson
EDITOR-IN-CHIEF

Matt Cohlmia
PRESIDENT

Chicago Unzipped, a Northwestern Student Holdings publication.

Northwestern Student Holdings dedicates this edition to the memory of **Stuart A. Blankstein**, a board member whose encouragement to student entrepreneurs was unending and who passed away on September 29, 2007. Stuart's dedication to NSH was surpassed only by his insightful sense of humor and excellent judgment. His motivation and guidance will be missed by all.

Chicago Unzipped would like to thank the following people and organizations. Without their support, this book could not have been possible.

Northwestern Student Holdings Sean Caffery • Chief Executive Officer, Matt Dabrowski • Chief Financial Officer, Chad Frontz • Chief Operating Officer **NSH Board & Staff** Thomas Anderman, Majid Boroujerdi, Jeff Coney, Adam Goodman, Michael Marasco, William White, Ethelbert Williams, Mark Witte and Flo Scarfone **Northwestern University** President Henry Bienen, Dean Julio Ottino, Marc Skjervem, Wendy Metter, McCormick Center for Entrepreneurship and Innovation, Business Institutions Program, Mathematical Methods in the Social Sciences, Chicago Field Studies, Wildcat Welcome Committee, Northwestern Alumni Association, Northwestern Club of Chicago and Institute for Student Business Education **Our Sponsors** MVC Capital, Huterstein family, Broadway in Chicago **Special Thank You** Eric Tammes, Roosevelt University and Gary Crews, Colorado Printing Company

contents

features

ARAGON BALLROOM

The Aragon Ballroom [1106 W. Lawrence Ave.], designed to resemble a Spanish village and named for a province of Spain, opened in 1926. Over the years this Uptown venue has hosted Frank Sinatra, Duke Ellington, Glenn Miller and other significant names from the big band era, operated as a roller skating rink and boxing venue, and been used as a traditional ballroom. In its current state of evolution, the Aragon hosts a variety of English language rock concerts and Spanish language shows.

Photograph by Nick Infusino

FAR NORTH

EVANSTON

AN ODD MIX OF RIGHT NOW AND WAY BACK WHEN

One part college students, one part young married couples with strollers, one part retired white-collar workers and one part lower-income minorities, Evanston is an odd mix of right now and way back when with plenty of gems in between. The Chicago suburb is home to Northwestern University and, with one of the best theater departments in the U.S., you can catch a quality student show nearly every weekend for only five dollars. On a warm day, take a walk along the lakefront for beautiful views of the Chicago skyline. The area around campus caters mostly to the student population with cheap eateries. Davis St., which also serves as the downtown drag, has plenty of clothing stores, beauty salons and coffee shops. Known as the dining capital of the North Shore, food alone makes the town worthy of a visit. Further north is Central St., with boutiques best described as quaint. The demographic is significantly older but plenty of shops and restaurants hold their appeal for all ages. The developing Dempster and Main St. areas play host to plenty of oft-overlooked shops and delicious cuisine.

TO EAT

Great Harvest Bread

Carb lover, rejoice. This bakery makes everything from scratch, and the end result is fantastic. The owner and his staff start milling at 4 a.m. and bake warm, delicious bread that stays fresh for about a week. For those with a sweet tooth, the bakery also makes fresh treats — I highly recommend the cookies. The freshly-baked goods will surely satisfy you, making the somewhat far trip from campus worthwhile. **A-**

2126 Central St
847.866.8609
PURPLE LINE to CENTRAL

Mustard's Last Stand

Right by Northwestern's Ryan Field sits a small hot dog joint full of sports photos and, on game days, hungry sports fans. Whether you grab a dog to go or sit at the counter, Mustard's Last Stand offers game day food for a lot cheaper than you'll find at the concession stands. It's the perfect place for a cheap meal or a quick snack, even when it's not football season. **B**

1613 Central St
857.864.2700
PURPLE LINE to CENTRAL

Kafein

1621 Chicago Ave.
847.491.1621
PURPLE LINE to DAVIS

From the kitschy customized Michelangelo painting on the wall to the amusingly lewd menu descriptions, Kaffein is an experience in itself. After one visit, you won't be able to stay away but you'll never be bored with beverage options that include Mexican hot chocolate, chai milkshakes, hot cider, and something called a 'lard-ass latte.' Be sure to pick up some reading material from the piles and piles of postcard-sized flyers advertising student- and family-friendly events going on around Evanston and Chicago, or challenge your friends to a game of Trivial Pursuit since the question cards come stacked on the tables.

Argo Tea

1569 Sherman Ave
847.864.6038
PURPLE LINE to DAVIS

Although it doesn't stick out among the offerings of Sherman Ave., you've got to be impressed by the attempt at fun and quirky menu choices including yummy chocolate mint and hibiscus iced teas. There is also a pleasing array of loose tea you can scoop yourself. It's pretty cool if you don't mind the Starbucks-like atmosphere of this Chicago chain. **A-**

Bar Louie

1520 Sherman Ave
847.733.8300
PURPLE LINE to DAVIS

As a chain, if you've been to a Bar Louie elsewhere, you know what to expect food-wise: sandwiches, burgers, steaks, macaroni and cheese and a few fish dishes. At the location in Evanston, the relatively standard layout, standard decorum and standard drink selection make this a pretty standard bar. But, hey, Tuesdays are one dollar burger nights. **B**

Bennison's Bakeries Inc.

1000 Davis St
847.328.9434
PURPLE LINE to DAVIS

Tell mom to have your birthday cake sent from Bennison's — you'll make dorm friends instantly. Gold Medalist of the 2005 World Cup of Baking, Bennison's is a hotspot for Wildcats with a sweet tooth. From V-day chocolate marzipan hearts to yummy petit fours, the path to the freshman fifteen is oh-so delicious. **A**

Café Ambrosia

1620 Orrington St
847.328.0081
PURPLE LINE to DAVIS

Delicious coffee drinks and over 30 teas to choose from make Café Ambrosia a great place to get your caffeine fix. The café also carries a wide variety of specialty

Benefit Boutique,
1625 Sherman Ave.
KAITLYN ELLISON

EVANSTON

RIGHT: La Petit Amelia, 618 Church St. KAITLYN ELLISON • **BELOW:** Sabai Thai Cuisine, 724 Clark St. KAITLYN ELLISON

sodas, as well as pastries, breads and cakes. While there are plenty of coffee places in Evanston, its live performances set Ambrosia apart. Poetry readings, plays, a cappella shows and even local concerts are performed in the basement. Entertainment and gourmet soda, what's not to love? **A-**

Café Mozart

You might have noticed this cozy corner café while walking down Davis St.

600 Davis St
847.492.8056
PURPLE LINE to DAVIS

– the cheetah-covered love seats are unmistakable. This warm little coffee joint offers free Wi-Fi, making it a good place for getting some work done. Come for a caffeine fix, stay for the chance to finish your paper on animal print. There are a plethora of Evanston establishments to choose from as an alternative to Starbucks, but who else sells Mozart-themed chocolates? **A**

Chipotle Mexican Grill

Mouth-watering combinations of always-fresh ingredients make Chipotle

711 Church St
847.425.3959
PURPLE LINE to DAVIS

a security blanket for countless Wildcats. If there is a group of people making a Chipotle run, I beg you to join. If not, you will only be sorry later when the aroma of burrito permeates the air and reaches your nostrils. If you then politely ask your buddy for a bite, do not be surprised to get a panicked response. **A**

Clarke's Diner

The Clarke's combination of dependably high-calorific breakfast-food dishes

720 Clark St
847.864.1610
PURPLE LINE to DAVIS

and never-perky servers make it an ideal location for hangover mornings, or anytime you yearn for a low-priced, cheesy retro diner atmosphere [and I know you do]. As soon as you slide into a booth, open a menu and eye the words 'chocolate chip pancakes,' you just get it. **A**

Dixie Kitchen and Bait Shop

Zydeco music and décor that looks like a yard sale threw up on the walls cer-

825 Church St
847.733.9030
PURPLE LINE to DAVIS

tainly help Dixie Kitchen stand out. Despite the quirky interior, friendly staff and great food make the experience worthwhile. While the food is a little more Cajun than Dixie, reasonably-priced southern dishes are served in large portions. The pulled pork sandwiches don't exactly rival the authentic Carolina Barbecue I'm used to, but it's certainly some of the best southern cuisine you'll find in Evanston. **B+**

Ethel's Chocolate Lounge

After growing up with the beloved and dependable Bruno's Chocolate Factory in Florida, I was excited to see a chocolate mecca accessible halfway across the country in Evanston. The walk inside, however, was a disappointing one. The prices are shocking, and the quality is ok at best. Take a trip downtown to visit Ghirardelli if you get the urge for chocolate. Ethel's can't satisfy. **C**

527 Church St
847.424.0790
PURPLE LINE to DAVIS

Flat Top Grill

This create-your-own stir-fry restaurant is a staple for Northwestern students, who often develop a love for the deliciously fresh food and friendly service. The exciting hands-on, all-you-can-eat experience will keep you coming back for more. One piece of advice: before you hand over your bowl to the chefs, add the blue stick [for roti prata, or Indian flat bread]. You won't be sorry. **A**

707 Church St
847.570.0100
PURPLE LINE to DAVIS

Jamba Juice

Despite the initial confusion over whether or not grass is an available ingredient [as it turns out, it's only for decoration], Jamba Juice is a refreshing break from walking

630 Davis St
847.425.1740
PURPLE LINE to DAVIS

around downtown Evanston during those fleeting days of warmth. With a complimentary 'boost' to stuff protein, vitamins or energy into your humongous portion, you almost won't feel any guilt at all guzzling such a delicious monstrosity. **A**

Joy Yee Noodle

You're not a true Northwestern student if you haven't yet stuffed your belly with Joy Yee. The tapioca teas and freezes are a favorite among locals, as are the many reasonably priced entrées. With huge portions and beautiful displays, no one can deny the magic that Joy Yee dishes up, as evidenced by its always-packed tables. **A**

521 Davis St
847.733.1900
PURPLE LINE to DAVIS

Phoenix Inn

Phoenix Inn is probably exactly what you would expect from an economical American-Chinese fast-food restaurant, except maybe a little greasier depending on the dish. Cheaper than Joy Yee, Phoenix is a popular delivery choice for those hip Friday night study parties. May I suggest a safe layer of paper towels before chowing down over your twin XL – things could get messy. **B-**

608 Davis St
847.475.7782
PURPLE LINE to DAVIS

Pita Pete's

Tired of BK and the same old fast food choices? Give Pita Pete's a try. With a wide range of meat and dozens of cheeses,

1571 Sherman Ave
847.905.1455
PURPLE LINE to DAVIS

Merle's Boutiques

1727 Benson Ave.
847.475.7766
PURPLE LINE to DAVIS

Merle's claims to be the best in barbecue, and it puts its wings where its mouth is - and so do the customers. Merle's barbecue draws from a variety of southern styles, including the famous tastes of Texas and North Carolina by coupling a slow hickory wood smoking technique with top quality meats and a one-of-a-kind sauce. The diverse menu isn't limited to wings and includes a variety of other southern style salads and sea foods. With cheap wings, a game room, drink specials and even a kids menu, Merle's in Evanston appeals to any crowd craving good barbecue and a good time.

EVANSTON

vegetables and condiments to top your pita with, you won't be lacking in options. The fun, colorful store is great for eating in, but if you're feeling lazy, it also delivers. With endless choices and reasonable prices, Pita Pete's is a nutritious, yet delicious alternative to typically greasy food. **B⁺**

TOP Unicorn Cafe, 1723 Sherman Ave. KAITLYN ELLISON • MIDDLE Dixie Kitchen & Bait Shop, 825 Church St. KAITLYN ELLISON • BOTTOM Bar Louie, 1520 Sherman Ave. KAITLYN ELLISON

Sashimi Sashimi

This trendy mecca for sushi lovers serves up fresh finds from the sea,

640 Church St
847.475.7274
PURPLE LINE to DAVIS

along with Japanese salads and soups, mochi ice cream [rice flour shells stuffed with ice cream balls] and fruity smoothies with tapioca. You can pick from party trays and lunch combos, or order individual pieces of sushi or sashimi. **A**

Tacos del Lago

Tacos del Lago is a cheery Mexican restaurant and a student's dream: you

822 Clark St
847.475.1234
PURPLE LINE to DAVIS

get a whole lot of bang for a very small buck. It's comfy, bright and colorful on the inside and offers personable service. Whether for dinner or a quick snack, it has tasty food served fresh and fast. It's cheap, too. A fat, cover-the-plate burrito costs a mere $4.75. **A**

Tapas Barcelona

Colorful posters and art on the walls give this restaurant a genuine,

1615 Chicago Ave
847.866.9900
PURPLE LINE to DAVIS

Spanish feel. Dining inside allows you to enjoy the lively atmosphere, but when the weather is nice, venture out to the patio. Sit and watch a soccer game at the bar or come with friends and sample a variety of Spanish appetizers [tapas]. Hot and cold dishes alike will surely satisfy your taste buds, plus you can practice your Spanish when you order off the extensive menu. **A⁻**

Unicorn Café

Unicorn Café would be indistinguishable if it weren't for the poetry

1723 Sherman Ave
847.332.2312
PURPLE LINE to DAVIS

readings – a thing most students have only heard about in bad jokes and bad movies – and other regular events. This welcoming and warm environment encompasses what a college community coffee shop can offer. You can indulge your urge to jump onstage, or stay cool and order a mediocre mocha. **B⁺**

Vive Le Crepe

This cute, potentially romantic restaurant offers a multitude of moderately-priced crepes, as well as killer omelets and a few

1565 Sherman Ave
847.570.0600
PURPLE LINE to DAVIS

entrees. Art on the walls and small, closely-clustered tables provide a cozy, intimate environment perfect for a date or any meal full of deep conversation. Some crepes are more filling than others, so an appetizer might behoove a hungry diner. Whatever your reason for going, be sure to order any desert crepe that includes chocolate. **B**

Wild Dogz

With affordable food and a relaxed interior, Wild Dogz is the perfect ad-

1625 Chicago Ave
847.869.9453
PURPLE LINE to DAVIS

dition to Chicago Ave. As the name implies, hot dogs are the specialty here, but don't discount the burgers, chicken and gyros, as well as a surprisingly decent breakfast selection. The big screen in the corner makes Wild Dogz the perfect place to chill out and watch the game, yet the interior is definitely neater and cleaner than your typical sports bar. **B+**

Blind Faith Café

For Whole Food's shoppers, vegetarians, vegans, and people just looking

525 Dempster St
847.328.6875
PURPLE LINE to DEMPSTER

for a more organic or healthy meal, Blind Faith Café offers a 'natural alternative' to the greasier foods of Evanston. The menu jumps from Italian to Mexican to Asian to New Orleans fare, all in one panel. Vegan baked goods like cornbread, cakes, cookies and muffins line the display case in the restaurant's self-service section, which sits adjacent to its normal dining room. You can also buy a neat t-shirt. **B**

Dozika Pan-Asian Cooking and Sushi Bar

Evanston definitely doesn't have a shortage of Asian restaurants, and

601 Dempster St
847.869.9740
PURPLE LINE to DEMPSTER

this joint fails to stand out from the crowd. While the food proves to be satisfactory, there is not much in the restaurant to go crazy over. Inside its quaint quarters, a small sushi bar lines the back of the room directly across from a very modestly-sized bar. The décor is far from stylish, and the

Lulu's, 804 Davis St. KAITLYN ELLISON

easy listening dripping from the speakers does not help the atmosphere. **B⁻**

Homemade Pizza Company

While most pizza restaurants put what you want on a pizza and then bake

1301 Chicago Ave
847.425.1200
PURPLE LINE to DEMPSTER

it for you, Homemade Pizza Company takes a step back: They put what you want on the pizza and then let you cook it at home. So if you feel like you'll want pizza in the future but not right at the moment, and you don't want a frozen pizza, then this is the place for you. I'm calling Pizza Hut. **C⁺**

Prairie Moon

Families, business professionals, students and alcoholics alike can all

1502 Sherman Ave
847.864.8328
PURPLE LINE to DEMPSTER

join together at Prairie Moon's fine establishment for 'All American Dining.' With a bar just inside the door and a quite lovely dining room past that, all ages and types can enjoy what the restaurant has to offer. Popular dishes include the Blackened Salmon Club and the Moon Burger. If you're looking for the more stylish, trendy bar scene though, Prairie Moon might not be your joint. **B⁺**

Sea Ranch Fish Market

A Japanese market and small Sushi restaurant in one, the Sea Ranch Fish

518 Dempster Ave
847.492.8340
PURPLE LINE to DEMPSTER

Market offers a unique experience. After chowing down on some Nigiri sushi or maybe some Maki rolls, customers can conveniently shop for hard-to-find Japanese groceries for home. Come in for the popular lunch specials like the Sushi Deluxe or the cooked caterpillar rolls [eel and avocado sushi]. **B**

Siam Pasta

Siam Pasta offers many of the standard Thai dishes such as Pad Thai and Pad

809 Dempster Ave
847.328.4614
PURPLE LINE to DEMPSTER

See Ew in a nontraditional environment. The strange set-up of the restaurant – three small floors, each with walls covered in intriguing Thai artwork – gives the location a unique feel and makes it worthy of a try. On the third floor a patio hangs over the street, which, while useless in the winter, makes for an excellent dining experience during a warmer season. **B⁺**

ABOVE: Kuni's Japanese Restaurant, 511 Main St. KAITLYN ELLISON • **RIGHT:** Bennison's Bakery, 1000 Davis St. KAITLYN ELLISON

Spice House

1941 Central St.
847.328.3711
PURPLE LINE to CENTRAL

Walk into Spice House, and you will undoubtedly be struck by the strong, but delicious smells coming from the store. Everything is ground fresh, leaving customers with a top-quality product bought at supermarket prices. From baking spices to barbecue seasoning and Thai spices to Scandinavian ones, I would be genuinely shocked to hear of someone who could not find the spice they were looking for at Spice House. The knowledgeable, friendly staff can help the most cooking-challenged customer and even let you taste spices in the store. Spice house also offers pre-wrapped gifts, or you can create your own for a more personal touch. These spices will add tons of fresh flavor to any kitchen.

The Italian Coffee Bar

1549 Sherman Ave
847.328.7164
PURPLE LINE to DEMPSTER

For those looking for an alternative to Starbucks, The Italian Coffee Bar proves to be a worthy choice. The small corner joint serves the standard Italian hot and iced drinks like cappuccinos and espressos, while offering multiple flavors of gelato ranging from chocolate to pistachio, and an assortment of baked goods. Customers can also create their own Panini or order one of the bar's recommendations. Half pound and pound bags of whole bean coffee are available for purchase. **B**

Tommy Nevin's Pub

1450-58 Sherman Ave
847.869.0450
PURPLE LINE to DEMPSTER

While the menu is filled with traditional fare like corned beef and cabbage, fish and chips and shepherd's pie, what truly makes Tommy Nevin's an Irish pub is the bar covered in Guinness advertisements. A dining room and private party room with a pool table and multiple flat-screen televisions supplement the bar nicely, leaving plenty of space for crowds of Evanstonians that rush in on St. Patrick's Day. Brilliant. **B**

Café Mud

1936 Maple Ave
847.773.9904
PURPLE LINE to FOSTER

As a huge Scrabble nerd myself, the first things I was drawn to here were the board games, which make time with friends silly and fun. The coffee is decent, the couches are comfy and the atmosphere is relaxing. The café has Wi-Fi, allowing you to escape the dorms to study. The open space in the middle is used for performances, sort of solidifying Café Mud's standard college coffee shop status. **B⁺**

Hecky's Barbeque

1902 Green Bay Rd
847.492.1182
PURPLE LINE to FOSTER

Known for its famous barbecue sauce, Hecky's always pleases students with its killer wings as well as its ribs, fried chicken and other sandwiches. Whether you have your food delivered or you pick it up yourself, you'll be licking the sauce off your fingers in delight. Perfect for games or just hanging out in the dorms, Hecky's is a must try. Just be ready to get messy, and be sure to have plenty of napkins. **B⁺**

Hunan Spring

635 Chicago Ave
847.328.8082
PURPLE LINE to MAIN

This is a casual restaurant a level above fast food status. Customers are offered Hunan, Szechuan and Catonese cooking, as well as healthy food options, and the prices and quantities of these orders cater to either individual or larger group needs. Dining in the restaurant is an option, but Hunan Spring definitely works better for picking up orders. Four small tables and a large, imposing front window lacking shades or curtains do not offer much of a comfortable setting. **B**

EVANSTON

Lucky Platter

An amazing aroma greets you before you ask yourself, 'What the hell did I just walk into?' The food is great, and the prices are even better. Lucky Platter has an eclectic and eccentric character it seems to wear with pride. The décor is far past interesting. No one thing matches another, except for maybe the plates lined along the edge of the ceiling. **A**

514 Main St
847.869.4064
PURPLE LINE to MAIN

Lupita's

Lupita's does not have much of a selection or any novelty; it can all be found elsewhere for a cheaper price. The dining conditions do not even provide adequate compensation for the lack of character here. There are no interesting decorative pieces, the music is too quiet and the setup and arrangement of tables is bland. **C+**

700 Main St
847.328.2255
PURPLE LINE to MAIN

Oceanique

Oceanique is somewhat of a local secret. This expensive restaurant is quite exclusive, requiring rigorous reservation appointments. The restaurant's interior emphasizes its value of sophistication and modernity, with private dining areas curtained off by thick dark cloth, chandeliers dangling from the ceiling and framed posters tastefully arranged on the walls.

505 Main St
847.864.3435
PURPLE LINE to MAIN

Oceanique has a very popular wine list and possibly serves the best seafood in Chicago. **A**

S-Paragon

S-Paragon is fairly new, but everything inside is comfortable, and prices are reasonable. Noon to 2 p.m. is typically the busiest time of day, but even then the dining experience is pleasurable. A quiet water fountain trickles in one corner, while tall bamboo shoots line the entryway. A well-kept sushi bar is stationed at one end of the dining area, and the wall next to it displays elegant artifacts. **B+**

503 Main St
847.332.2302
PURPLE LINE to MAIN

D. & D. Dogs

It's cheap. It's casual. It's greasy. And for a quick pit stop on the way to a game or class, it's perfect. The typical college burger joint, D&D Dogs sells onion rings, mozzarella sticks and other fried classics, but offer salads, omelets and pulled pork sandwiches for the less greasy appetite. **B**

825 Noyes St
847.864.1909
PURPLE LINE to NOYES

Kim's Kitchen

This cute gourmet shop serves affordable lunches, bakery items and coffees, and offers deluxe take-home or eat-in dinners. Everything is homemade. They serve standard sandwiches, but also alternate specials every week to keep things interesting. Some of their

518 Noyes St
847.475.5467
PURPLE LINE to NOYES

La Cucina di Donatella

2221 W. Howard St.
773.262.6533
RED LINE to HOWARD

The outside of La Cucina di Donatella isn't flashy, and the restaurant is easy to miss. But go back and make the effort to find this Italian gem in Rogers Park. The food at this BYOB restaurant is fresh, homemade and incredibly delicious. Italian banter echoes from the kitchen, adding to the lively atmosphere. The portions are just right, and prices are reasonable. The staff is extremely friendly, knowledgeable and helpful. The décor is a little odd and somewhat mismatched, but if that's the biggest complaint, you don't have much of a reason not to try this place. Great for a date or a family dinner.

South Beach.
KAITLYN ELLISON

specialty sandwiches include apple sausage with caramelized onions and ham and bacon with pico de gallo. **A**

Linz and Vail Espresso Bar and Gelateria

Whether you're craving hot and bitter or cold and sweet, this café has

9222 Noyes St
847.491.1381
PURPLE LINE to NOYES

something for you. They make their own creamy gelato in flavors ranging from pistachio to plain chocolate and offer an array of coffee drinks. Equally popular with kids, adults and college students, it's a good place to hang out, do some homework or hook up to free Wi-Fi. **A-**

Noyes Street Café

A Greek and Italian restaurant with a hint of funky beat, the Noyes

828 Noyes St
847.475.8683
PURPLE LINE to NOYES

Street Café offers everything from Greek Burgers to Vermicelli. Dinner entrées may be a bit expensive for a college budget, but the restaurant could make for a fun, casual date. If splurging on dinner isn't really your thing, they also serve brunch on weekends. **B**

Rollin' To Go

'Pizza, Pasta, Soup, etc…' reads the menu at Rollin' to Go. It's a good place to

910 Noyes St
847.332.1000
PURPLE LINE to NOYES

grab a quick Italian meal in a casual atmosphere

with menu prices pretty friendly to the college budget. Try a Paulie Walnuts sandwich for $6.95: Steak on ciabatta bread with pesto sauce, roasted red peppers, portabella mushrooms, red onions, plum tomatoes, provolone and fresh mozzarella. **B-**

TO PLAY

Peter N. Jans Community Golf Course

Tucked away in the residential area of Evanston, the Peter Jans Community

1031 Chicago Ave
847.475.9173
PURPLE LINE to CENTRAL

Golf Course provides a short, but challenging 18 holes of fun to the public for a reasonable price. A Pro Shop sits at the end of the 18th hole, and private lessons are available for the avid golfer. The course is definitely unique; it takes golfers through a part of Evanston not normally seen and offers an alternative to going to the movies with friends. **A-**

1800 Club

Walk into Hundo any Thursday night, and the place will be packed with

1800 Sherman Ave
847.733.7900
COLOR LINE to STOP

Northwestern Students. The relatively small club has some booth and table seating, but, more importantly, the club has plenty of drink specials. Come with your friends for a fun night out – es-

EVANSTON

pecially karaoke nights. Besides, where else will you get a veggie wrap at 2 in the morning? **A-**

Bill's Blues

Yes, Bill's Blues has a small sandwich menu and a bar with great drink

1029 Davis St
847.424.9800
PURPLE LINE to DAVIS

specials, but the focus here is music. Owner Bill Gilmore is devoted to providing live music every day and hosts blues, rock and folk musicians – though you can guess by the name which one the venue focuses on. The staff is friendly, the beer is cheap and the music is live – what more will it take to convince you to come? **B+**

The Keg of Evanston

The Keg is interesting in that the crowd is always changing. Sometimes the

810 Grove St
847.869.9987
PURPLE LINE to DAVIS

atmosphere is that of a pub, then on Monday nights it's like a giant frat party. On those nights, Northwestern students head out and fill this local favorite. The Keg has everything you need for a great Monday night: cheap beer, a slack carding policy, pool tables and a dancing area. I've never tried the food sober, but no one really goes for the food. **A-**

Dave's Down to Earth Rock Shop

The store owner travels all over the world and brings minerals, fossils and

704 Main St
847.866.7374
PURPLE LINE to MAIN

jewelry back to Evanston, making these wonders available to residents at reasonable prices. If you wander into the museum downstairs you won't be coming back up for a while. Comprised of what the owner has personally compiled from his archaeological digs, the museum takes you back 230 million years and chronologically orders display cases and exhibitions of entire fossils, re-assembled skeletons, and huge dinosaur bones. **A**

TO SHOP

Beadazzled

This bead store may be small, but it packs a lot into one space. Beads,

2002 Central Ave
847.864.9494
PURPLE LINE to CENTRAL

books, tools and work space make this place perfect for someone looking to make something original with a personal touch. Whether you want something that's fancy and a little pricey or something smaller but still fun, Beadazzled helps

ABOVE: Corner of Davis St. and Orrington St. KAITLYN ELLISON • **RIGHT:** Blick, 1755 Maple Ave. KAITLYN ELLISON

City Newsstand

860 Chicago Ave.
847.425.8900
PURPLE LINE to MAIN

A sprawling, impressive building and a landmark of Chicago architecture, the K.A.M. Temple is the oldest synagogue in Chicago and claims to be the oldest in the Midwest. You can't help noticing its massive scale right away, but the winding structure begs to be explored for you to appreciate its details. The three huge oak doors at the main entrance are flanked by beautiful and intricately woven iron lamp-posts, Louis Sullivan-esque in their fusion of function and elegance. Even its gate-like series of front doors is rather inviting upon closer examination, capped with expert stone-carved Old-Testament iconography and flowering long hinges. The worship spaces inside are utterly breathtaking.

you make it all. If you don't feel confident in your artistic abilities, classes are available for both advanced and beginning beaders alike. **B+**

Amaranth Books

828 Davis St
847.328.2939
PURPLE LINE to DAVIS

Specialized in scholarly and collectible books, this cozy, intellectual store offers inexpensive used books to the avid reader. Books are in good condition and sold at prices as low as one and two dollars. You'll get a good deal at Amaranth, and the books are definitely unique, but be weary of the slightly snobby vibe the store gives off. **B**

Art + Science Salon

811 Church St
847.864.4247
PURPLE LINE to DAVIS

Though some services can be a bit pricy, everyone I know who has gotten their hair cut at Art + Science has loved it. Top salon products and a fresh, talented staff make Art + Science the go-to place for a great new hair color or a stellar new hair style. **A-**

Ayla's Originals

1511 Sherman Ave
847.328.4040
PURPLE LINE to DAVIS

Walk into Ayla's Originals, and corals, turquoises, purples, yellows and dozens of bold colors will catch your eye. With one of the largest selections of beads in the area, you leave Ayla's with something far more unique and more personal than you could find in a typical store. Ayla's offers a variety of jewelry-making classes that are great for beginners, but if none appeal to you or there isn't much flexibility in your schedule, private lessons are available. **B+**

Blick Art Supplies

1755 Maple Ave
847.425.9100
PURPLE LINE to DAVIS

Blick not only generously serves the Northwestern art major, but also anyone with a touch of creativity. Everything from scrap-booking supplies to fine oil paints are sold here in a multitude of brands and prices. Sale prices are not only reasonable, but cater to students too. Random tip: At the beginning of the school year, when Target's out of those Pull-and-Release hooks, Blick has a ton. **B+**

Bookman's Alley: Fine Used Books

1712 Sherman Ave
847.869.6999
PURPLE LINE to DAVIS

Inside Bookman's Alley warm rooms laid out like home libraries are full of treasures to discover if you have the time to search. Among the 40,000 used and rare books is a first edition Mark Twain book for $12,500. Other unique items include a collection of used yellowing postcards offering access to strangers' private lives for a buck each and a document from the French Revolution. **A**

Comix Revolution

606 Davis St
847.866.8659
PURPLE LINE to DAVIS

With Hollywood's recent obsession with comic book stories turned screenplays, you're partially out of the loop if you don't read in strip form. This place is welcoming to newcomers and offers a great variety of the popular and the obscure. Go ahead, it's time get over your sophomoric embarrassment. Go in. **A**

Crossroads Trading Company

1730 Sherman Ave
847.492.9400
PURPLE LINE to DAVIS

In between Starbucks and Cosí, this trendy thrift store is a fresh and funky spot – if you don't mind the slightly sour old-clothes smell lingering in the air. The styles change so you never know what you might find on the tightly-stuffed clothes lines, and the garments are divided into sections based on color, which could be a good or a bad thing. **B+**

Dr. Wax

1615 Sherman Ave
847.475.8848
PURPLE LINE to DAVIS

This used record store is a little piece of Lakeview in the NU backyard of Evanston. Some complain the prices are a bit high for used items, but there's a good chance you'll fall in love with something in the sea of goodies from Death Cab's latest pop album to a hard-to-find Against Me LP. The workers are unimposing, and the atmosphere is so chill that you may just forget about that afternoon appointment. **A–**

Dream About Tea

1011 Davis St
847.864.7464
PURPLE LINE to DAVIS

Does liver peace tea entice you? What about hairy crab oolong or gunpowder green tea? While holding the widest and most interesting tea assortment in Evanston, the owner of this 'authentic Chinese tea shop' also teaches a 13-week Chinese language course for Evanston residents. Give this place a second glance. Then go inside. **A**

Fashion Tomato

1631 Sherman Ave
847.328.1681
PURPLE LINE to DAVIS

The clothes are cute and trendy, but the prices can be a bit high. With a rack of pretty dresses, a wide selection of jeans and plenty of funky accessories, it's definitely not hard to find something you like. Plus, the store often has great sales, making it even easier to find that perfect belt or cool new top. For a hot night out or a special day, Fashion Tomato offers Evanston shoppers a fresh alternative to the Gap. **B**

Omni Salon

1729 Sherman Ave
847.475.3632
PURPLE LINE to DAVIS

Located close to campus, Omni Salon offers reason-ably-priced services as well as some student discounts. The small, friendly staff provides hair, nail and waxing treatments to both men and women. One of the more popular features for female clientele is Omni's good, yet cheap manicures. The salon is often full of girls getting last-minute manicures on Fridays

Viva Vintage

1043 Chicago Ave.
847.465.5025
PURPLE LINE to MAIN

Looking for a retro concert shirt? A ridiculous, yet fabulous, poofy prom gown? Jewelry from the 1950s? Stocked with a multitude of funky clothes, shoes and accessories, Viva Vintage makes shopping a bit like playing dress-up mom or playing in a grandma's closet. Men and women shoppers of all ages and sizes can sort through the store and leave with a fantastic new – or should I say old – outfit without breaking the bank. Dresses run around $35, and pants and tops cost even less. The next time you're looking for a great new hand bag or a pair of heels that will set you apart, skip Urban and check out Viva Vintage.

before formals. Omni isn't the best salon in Evanston, but it's not the worst either. **B‑**

Uncle Dan's

If just moving into the area and at a loss for where to start shopping

700 Church St
847.475.7100
PURPLE LINE to DAVIS

for winter gear, I suggest starting here. The workers are incredibly nice and will help you understand the answers to bewildering questions like 'What does '700 fill' mean?' or 'Why might I need a zipper across the armpit of my parka?' **A**

Urban Outfitters

A staple for hip college populations, Urban has its negatives: though

921 Church St
847.492.8542
PURPLE LINE to DAVIS

most of the clothing is very fashion-forward, that doesn't mean it always looks good. With prices comparable to the average affluent department store, it's almost ridiculous to pay that much for clothing that sometimes literally looks trashy. Its positives: amazing clearance racks with cute finds and uber-cheap, uber-chic house wares. **B**

Williams Shoes

Apart from a hit-or-miss clearance section, most of what Williams carries

710 Church St
847.328.5868
PURPLE LINE to DAVIS

will hit you with department store prices, but only because it carries top quality merchandise like Merrell and Haflinger. For those of you not native to the tundra – when you realize your flip-flops and mesh sneakers won't cut it for a Northwestern U. winter, Williams is only a short walk away. **B+**

World Market

Perfect for a last-min-ute birthday present or unique hor'dourves, World

1725 Maple Ave
847.424.1022
PURPLE LINE to DAVIS

Market is like an upscale, international Target, minus the toilet paper. Towels, jewelry, cards, cookies – it's all here, in vivid African colors or elegant Asian style. Prices are a little high, but it's preferable to plane ticket prices to India or

Koi Chinese & Sushi, 624 Davis St. KAITLYN ELLISON

Chile. World Market provides hip, foreign imports without having to leave Evanston. **A‑**

Another Time Another Place

Jewelry, vintage clothes, old photographs, antique furniture and so much

1243 Chicago Ave
847.866.7170
PURPLE LINE to DEMPSTER

more are packed into this store. Plus, the most adorable ladies comprise the incredibly helpful staff. Whether you're looking for an old poster to decorate your wall or furniture for your house, you'll find it here. Prices are definitely reason-able, and the store offers a variety of unique things for young and old shoppers alike. Be sure to allot plenty of time to browse every corner of this fun store. **B+**

Close Knit Inc.

As yarn stores go, Close Knit is pretty fantastic. The selection is vast, and

622 Grove St
847.328.6760
COLOR LINE to STOP

the store has practically every color imaginable; they even have yarn with sparkles in it. The store also provides binders full of possible projects for scarves, hats, blankets and sweaters. Close Knit even holds knitting classes in the back of the store multiple times a month. If you're looking to

EVANSTON

get involved in the Chicago yarn community, this exceptional niche store offers an easy gateway. **A**

Crowded Closet

This boutique has a wide variety of upscale women's clothing to choose from. With brands like Prada, Jimmy Choo, Coach, Chanel and Fendi, prices are a bit high for typical college shoppers just looking for a new top. If you're looking for something special or are willing to drop some serious cash, then Crowded Closet can save you a trip to Michigan Ave. **B**

> 824 Dempster St
> 847.475.1135
> **PURPLE LINE to DEMPSTER**

North Shore Coins

North Shore Coins is not your typical store in Evanston. The store offers rolls, proofs and mint sets of coins, as well as currency from all over the world. Even if you're not an avid collector, it's definitely worth a stop inside to check out the ancient coins. The store is very customer focused, so expect a friendly, helpful and courteous staff to help you find something special. **B+**

> 1501 Chicago Ave
> 847.492.9588
> **PURPLE LINE to DEMPSTER**

Possibilities

Looking for a one-of-a-kind gift? Possibilities is the place for you. You've all seen those quirky shops that offer unique things that you probably don't need but buy anyway, and Possibilities is Evanston's such store. From Curious George clocks to Elvis tote bags, the friendly staff will help you sort through it all. The store also carries not-so-quirky jewelry made by Nepalese women who receive fair wages [similar to the idea of fair-trade coffee]. **A-**

> 1235 Chicago Ave
> 847.328.1235
> **PURPLE LINE to DEMPSTER**

Second Hand Tunes

Offering an alternative to the more mainstream record stores, Second Hand Tunes focuses on stocking quality used and new vinyl, CDs, DVDs and even VHS tapes and record players. The atmosphere of the store, with

> 800 Dempster St
> 847.491.1690
> **PURPLE LINE to DEMPSTER**

its slightly ramshackle displays and indie music soundtrack, seems a bit hipster-ish; nevertheless, Second Hand's environment feels open to anyone interested in finding something a bit different in music and film. They will buy your old music and movies as well. **A-**

Secret Treasure Antiques

This cute little shop is constantly getting new things from auctions, yard sales, moving sales and other stores. With lots to choose from, shoppers can easily find a cool piece of jewelry or a unique gift for someone – maybe mom? Prices can be a bit high, but if you hunt, you can find a great deal. **B**

> 611 Dempster St
> 847.866.6889
> **PURPLE LINE to DEMPSTER**

Casita Azul

This is a great place to go if you're looking for an exotic, unique gift. Even if a tight budget takes precedence over exoticism and uniqueness, it would still be worthwhile to visit Casita Azul for its excitingly different and friendly atmosphere. The store offers an array of tiny ornaments, statues, intricately embroidered dresses and accessories and various types of artwork pertaining to Mexican folklore, all hand-crafted by families, individuals and cooperatives in Mexico. **B**

> 817 Chicago Ave
> 847.424.8180
> **PURPLE LINE to MAIN**

Classy Closet

Classy Closet offers higher-end designer labels and contemporary styles. Tucked away within a neighborhood near the 'El,' this treasure trove is a great place to have some fun with personalized service. If you call before arriving, enthusiastic employees will accompany you and navigate you through the store as they cater to your specific needs. **A**

> 701 Washington St
> 847.475.0072
> **PURPLE LINE to MAIN**

Eureka Antiques and Collectibles

Looking for something fun and different to do on a weekend afternoon? Try browsing around Eureka Antiques

> 705 Washington St
> 847.869.9090
> **PURPLE LINE to MAIN**

and Collectibles. From political memorabilia to vintage Valentines, you won't be bored sorting through the crowded store's small antiques. You won't find much furniture here, but the friendly and helpful staff will recommend different stores if you're in need of a new armoire. Whether you're looking for costume jewelry or leftovers from the Chicago World's Fair, you'll surely find something unique. **A-**

Healthy Green Goods

Looking to decorate your house or apartment but stay environmentally

702 Main St
847.864.9098
PURPLE LINE to MAIN

friendly at the same time? By offering eco-friendly, toxin-free products, Healthy Green Goods allows you to kill two birds with one stone. The body and hair care products are a great place to start, but the furniture, paint and bedding might be good to hold off on until you've settled out of the dorms. Buy new soap or a new mattress and help save the Earth in the process. **B+**

Marie Parie Boutique

The shop is cute, but the expensive prices are disappointing. Some of

512 Main St
847.492.9094
PURPLE LINE to MAIN

the boutique's products hail from Paris, New York and Los Angeles, while others were crafted by local artists. Perfumes, jewelry, skirts, purses and tiny trinkets all look fragile and reinforce a 'look, but don't touch' atmosphere. Claustrophobia is a danger of spending too much time inside the boutique at once, so make sure to avoid the stress. **C+**

Ten Thousand Villages

Ten Thousand Villages is a miniature bazaar alive with enthusiastic

719 Main St
847.733.8258
PURPLE LINE to MAIN

employees and volunteers who greet customers by offering a cup of an international blend coffee while telling stories of villages in third world countries. Vibrant colors, music, furniture and pottery from over thirty countries fill the store. The atmosphere here is incomparable to anything else, and the elimination of middlemen assures

third world artisans will benefit and keeps prices for these international handicrafts low. **A**

Toys Et Cetera

Toys Et Cetera will make you want to be a kid again. With hundreds of

711 Main St
847.475.7172
PURPLE LINE to MAIN

toys that foster learning and promote creativity, Toys Et Cetera is the perfect place to find a gift for any child … or any child at heart. Though spending every day hanging out at a toy store with friends might be a little weird, perusing for an afternoon and channeling your inner child is a lot of fun. **A**

Howard's Books

The only décor in this quaint used bookstore is, well, books. Bookshelves

2000 Maple St
847.475.3445
PURPLE LINE to NOYES

line the walls from floor to ceiling. There's a sign on the door that encourages people to find what they're not looking for, and by the looks of the wide range of topics and genres, they will. Go if you love books. If you don't, go anyway — just looking around the place is entertaining. **A-**

Corner of Chicago Ave. and Main St. KAITLYN ELLISON

ROGERS PARK

FILL YOUR SENSES WITH SOMETHING EXOTIC

The northernmost neighborhood of Chicago proper, Rogers Park is collegiate, ethnic and urban, all at the same time. Proud of its racial and economic diversity, it boasts populations speaking more than 80 languages and the most recent census found it to be one of the most diverse areas in the country. Its residents also range in income and age. This shows in the areas diverse shops and restaurants, catering to both college students and the retired community. It also shows in other area attractions; Rogers Park hosts churches of a wide variety of denominations and religions. Must see sites include the Madonna Della Strada Chapel and the lakefront beaches. Loyola University's Lake Shore Campus dominates the neighborhood and brings in students and faculty. Plenty of late night eateries cater to the students, but they aren't just the usual greasy spoons, though those can be found too. In the west, along Devon Ave. between Ravenswood and California, is 'Little India.' One of the largest Desi areas in the country, a walk down these streets will fill your senses with something exotic – from the sight of elephant knickknacks to the smells of authentic Indian food.

TO EAT

Caribbean American Baking Company

Located in not the best neighborhood with no in-house seating, Caribbean American Baking Company may not seem worth the trip just for take out. However, if you try the jerk chicken, you will soon change your mind. The food is incredible, the prices are reasonable and the staff is very friendly. If you love spices and don't mind going a little out of your way for

1539 W Howard Ave
773.761.0700
RED LINE to HOWARD

the sake of food, then definitely give this place a try. **B**

Jamaica Jerk

The first thing I noticed at Jamaica Jerk was how long the food took to come out. The jerk sauce is delicious and worth the wait, but many of the dishes aren't great enough to warrant such slow service. Jamiaca Jerk has a variety of foods on the menu and offers everything from fried plantains to goat soup. Give Jamaica Jerk a try, just don't rush it. **B-**

1631 W Howard St
773.764.1546
RED LINE to HOWARD

ROGERS PARK

Café Suron

1146 N. Pratt Blvd.
773.465.6500
RED LINE to LOYOLA

This elegant Persian/Mediterranean-inspired restaurant is right off busy Sheridan Rd. Adobe tiled floors, orange-painted fresco walls and colored tile tables make for a light and pleasant setting. The cuisine is relatively cheap as well, with appetizers ranging from $4 to $7 and entrees averaging about $14. The menu is extensive and eclectic, offering items such as the Feta Cheese Plate, Sea Scallop Salad, and Broiled Mahi Mahi. Whether you're taking someone special out on a date or just enjoying a peaceful meal by yourself, this is the perfect place. It's open Tuesdays through Saturdays for dinner and Sundays for lunch and dinner.

Tickie's Belizean Cuisine

7605 N Paulina St
773.973.3919
RED LINE to HOWARD

This tiny, colorful restaurant off the Howard 'El' blends Caribbean and Latin flavors. Dukunuisas, tamales made with fresh corn filled with pork and steamed in foil, are highly recommended by the staff. Entrées range from stewed chicken to oxtail and are served with vegetables. The homemade hot cross buns are a must for dessert. The food may sound strange, but the adventurous eater won't break the bank trying Tickie's. **B**

Charmers Café

1500 W Jarvis Ave
773.743.2233
RED LINE to JARVIS

This homey café is a quiet little refuge in Rogers Park. The storefront snack bar seats about 30 and is populated with gilded Romanesque statues. If the décor is any indication, Charmers serves up drinks with an attitude. Milkshake flavors vary from Funky Monkey to Ooga Booga, and for those watching their health, seasonal fruit smoothies are on the menu too. A standout is the loose-leaf tea, which the barista prepares to order. **B**

Gruppo di Amici

1508 W Jarvis Ave
773.508.5565
RED LINE to JARVIS

Even Chicago-style deep-dish buffs will love this restaurant's Old World toppings and crispy, paper-thin crust. Located right off the Jarvis 'El' stop, this pizzeria is decorated to the hilt with warm colors and an open kitchen featuring a wood-burning oven.

TOP Loyola Park, Pratt Ave. NICK SCHWEIGER
• **MIDDLE** 1137 N. Columbia Ave. NICK SCHWEIGER
• **BOTTOM** Rogers Park. NICK SCHWEIGER

ROGERS PARK

Gruppo di Amici offers a small, simple menu with rotating daily specials. Friendly service and a full bar round out the deal. **A**

shrimp teriyaki, nothing here is more than $10. For a cheap meal at a place with plenty of options, try Jarvis Grill and Wok. **B**

Jarvis Grill & Wok

1505 W Jarvis St
773.274.4117
RED LINE to JARVIS

The grill and wok sections of the menu don't seem like they would go together, but somehow they work. This small, casual restaurant seats about 30 and offers over 20 sandwiches, as well as traditional Japanese dishes. From the BLT sandwich with fries to the

Poitin Stil

1502 W Jarvis St
773.338.3285
RED LINE to JARVIS

The name of this Irish pub means 'moonshine' in Gaelic, and a picture of the owner's father and grandfather making some proudly sits inside. The inside is maroon and gold, the colors of an Irish soccer team. Poitin Stin offers drink specials on imports, as

DEVON: THE SUBCONTINENT STRIP
BY BECKIE SUPIANO

Walking down Devon Ave. in West Rogers Park is supposed to make you feel like you're in India. Local tour companies take groups on 'Indian' tours of the area, which is full of businesses catering to the Indian and Pakistani immigrant community. But is it really like being in another country?

I decided to check it out, but quickly realized there was a huge problem – I have never been to India. How would I know if it felt like I was there? So I grabbed my Indian friend Mrinalini, who was willing to come along as my de facto tour guide, and we hit the pavement.

Everyone in Chicago knows Devon Ave. as the place to go for South Asian culture, as it is mainly inhabited by people from India, Pakistan and Bangladesh. Even the streets have a South Asian flair, given honorifics such as Gandhi Marg and Mohammed Ali Jinnah Way.

First built in the 1850s as Church Rd., Devon Ave. was renamed by English settlers from the county of Devonshire. Later, Devon became the main shopping area for Chicago's Jewish community, but today, the Jewish community has largely been replaced by the Indo-Pakistani community.

Mrinalini and I visited Devon on a Monday. It's much busier on the weekends because families drive in from the suburbs to do their shopping, but it was still bustling with people, and the smells of cardamom and incense let me know I was on the right track.

We first stopped at the Patel Brothers grocery store on the 2600 block of W. Devon. In India, you would buy most groceries from outdoor stands, but the most of the products at Patel Brothers are authentic. One whole aisle was devoted to various Indian spices, packed tightly in large, almost bursting bags. There were vegetables I had never heard of before, [karela, anyone?] and snack foods that were so spicy I knew they'd send my weak stomach for a rollercoaster ride.

Patel Brothers also sells puja [prayer] coconuts, which are smashed in temples to make an offering. The store even had its own small shrine, complete with burning incense. Like a brightly painted dollhouse-sized temple, the shrine sat on top of a shelf of merchandise, and its presence didn't appear to be out of the ordinary to any of the other shoppers. It's gorgeous, with three domes on top and

well as $2 domestic drafts on Mondays and $2.50 Coronas on Thursdays. A bar that carries Guinness, Smithwick's and Murphy's on tap is worth the trip. **A-**

Blue Elephant

Thai food and literally whatever alcoholic beverage you can buy. Does it get any better? This BYOB Asian restaurant is as relaxing as the pale blue that covers its plain walls. Bring a bottle of wine and watch them

1235 W Devon Ave
773.252.5216
RED LINE to LOYOLA

prepare your dish in the open kitchen. Hang out all afternoon if you have the time. **A**

El Chorrito

Get an authentic Mexican-dish-fix 24 hours a day. The Taqueria El Chorrito

6404 N Clark St
773.381.0902
RED LINE to LOYOLA

is a small restaurant with a mostly Hispanic clientele. It has a friendly and comfortable atmosphere, and provides quick, cheap, and authentic food. Taqueria El Chorrito is great for all hours of the day, whether you dine-in or take-out. **A**

three arched doors revealing statues of multi-limbed gods and a yet-unsmashed prayer coconut.

Not quite everything in the store was Indian, though. The incense used in Hindu worship shared shelf space with votive candles decorated with plaintive pictures of Jesus. The store also carried Kraft cheese spread, but Mrinalini said that it wasn't as out of place as I thought – kids loved the stuff back in India.

We later stopped in at Sahiba Boutique a few shops down to scope out their selection of bangles, shoes and embroidered clothing in bright colors. The store offers tailoring so that the saris can be custom-fit for the wearer, just as is the custom in India. Mrinalini, however, was nonplussed by the gaudy selection, and described the store as 'kind of tacky' and overpriced.

She then took me to Sahil, a more upscale clothing store that carries trendy midriff-bearing tops that some Indian women wear with jeans – something Mrinalini also calls 'tacky.' But what drew Mrinalini's attention was the large upstairs devoted to elaborate bridal wear. She showed me an intricately beaded deep purple-blue dress she would pick for her own wedding. Holding it in my hands, I

was impressed by the unexpected weight that the beads gave the dress.

India Book House, our next stop, carries popular fiction by Indian writers and comic books of Hindu myths, which Mrinalini read growing up. 'If I had kids, I'd buy them these,' she said. 'It's a good way to learn.' The store also has bridal and film magazines, Bollywood soundtracks and bindis, the decorated dots worn on many Indian women's heads. Mrinalini said the store's inventory was a little dated, but it was definitely authentic.

The Indian portion of Devon also has a number of electronics stores, which specialize in kitchen appliances like rice cookers. Many of them also carry luggage, which seemed out of place to me. Mrinalini pointed out that people would buy it for trips to India, as they would need space to bring back gifts. International calling cards are another popular item, a testament to the newness of the immigrant community.

For lunch, we went to Uoupi Palace. The menu is all vegetarian, which Mrinalini said is typical for South Indian food. Many Hindus are vegetarians for religious reasons, while the Muslims who live in other parts of the country eat more meat. Our waiter brought us water without ice, which Mrinalini said made

ROGERS PARK

Clark St. Banner. NICK SCHWEIGER

Everyday Thai

The name says it all: it's good for an everyday lunch place. The restaurant is mainly takeout and delivery, but there are a few tables. The entrées tend to hover around $6.00, making this the perfect place to call if you have a casual Thai craving but aren't ready to commit to a large check. **B⁺**

1509 W Devon Ave
773.262.7797
RED LINE to LOYOLA

Gold Coast Dogs

Gold Coast Dogs is a Chicago fast food staple. The delicious, traditional Chicago-style-hot dogs make any day just a little more special. If you're lame and don't want to try a dog with everything, you can order fewer condiments [but I don't suggest that]. As if a Chicago dog alone isn't fantastic enough, Gold Coast Dogs offers delicious french fries and extra thick shakes to top off your meal. **A**

6604 N Sheridan Rd
773.465.6760
RED LINE to LOYOLA

Grande Noodles & Sushi Bar

With a ton of items on the menu, it's hard to choose what to order. Prices are cheap and the quantities are huge. There are almost 20 appetizers, over 30 different sushi

6632 N Clark St
773.761.6666
RED LINE to LOYOLA

---

her feel at home more than anything else. Mrinalini always asks for water without ice when we go out to eat: 'It's too cold on my teeth,' she says, 'It's fantastic that I don't even have to put in a special request here.'

Mrinalini ordered for us: rice and lentil patties called iddly and a giant crepe called dosai. The iddly were small and white and we ate them with a spicy lentil soup and a coconut chutney. The dosai was a spongy, flat bread wrapped around a filling of rice, lentils, potatoes and onions. We would rip a piece of bread and use it to scoop out some of the filling, and then dip the whole bite into sauce. I commented that the food was different from that at other Indian places I had eaten. Mrinalini told me that many places serve these vegetarian dishes as appetizers, but people don't think to order them.

As we drank filtered coffee with milk after dinner, Mrinalini said that a lot on Devon was authentic, and a big reason it felt like home came from what wasn't there. 'There is no Walgreens, no Taco Bell,' she pointed out. Not even Starbucks has made much progress there. The simple absence of American chains made Devon seem more like India to her.

As we walked outside, Mrinalini said 'the smell is just so strong here,' and she was right. It smelled of spices and of meat. 'It's a Muslim restaurant,' Mrinalini told me. I asked how she knew, before noticing an inscription to God in Arabic over the door. That wasn't what clued her in, she corrected me: it was the smell, a scent she recognized from India. And I noticed she had been right – there was not an American store to be seen. For a moment, I imagined I was halfway around the world. Then we got in the car, drove around the corner and found ourselves back in what I knew to be Chicago.

Morseland

1218 W. Morse Ave.
773.764.8900
RED LINE to MORSE

The next time you want a jazzy night out on the town, try Morseland. The soft lighting and velvet curtains add a vintage elegance to the restaurant, which caters to a mix of diners including students, neighborhood locals and young professionals. Morseland recently shifted from a local bar to more of a restaurant/bar/club, but no worries, the bar is still here and fully stocked. With a variety of salads and sandwiches as well as entrée dishes to choose from, this place caters to all sorts of taste buds, though meat lovers will be happiest here. Live jazz will accompany your dinner on certain nights during the week, making Morseland a great place to entertain out-of-town friends.

choices and a wide variety of vegetarian dishes. The open and welcoming environment make for a relaxed dining experience. **B**

Kaffeccino

6441 N Sheridan Rd
773.508.1888
RED LINE to LOYOLA

This is pretty much your run-of-the-mill college area café. The coffee flavors are pretty standard, but the sandwich and salad menus are surprisingly extensive. In the mood for something sweet? Be sure to try one of Kaffeccino's delicious smoothies or anything it makes with ice cream – and there is a lot to choose from. When the weather is warm, Kaffeccino isn't that special, but its winter drinks, like the Turtle Mocha, are definitely worth stopping in for. **B**

La Bella Café & Internet

6624 N Clark St
773.856.7000
RED LINE to LOYOLA

Crisp, clean and modern, this café is new to Clark St., and you can tell. Better yet, the café is furnished with computers from this era, which [for a price] you can enjoy with a standard sandwich or coffee drink. The owner did, however, know when to stick with the 'old, but good.' The chicken noodle soup is made with her mother's recipe. **A-**

Panini Panini

6764 N Sheridan Rd
773.761.4110
RED LINE to LOYOLA

Complete with an outside patio, this café is more than just a spot in which to grab a cup of coffee. Choose from a separate breakfast menu or from a selection of salads,

Rogers Park.
NICK SCHWEIGER

Sweet Magic Studio

6960 N. Sheridan Rd.
773.764.6488
RED LINE to MORSE

Move over, Shakira. After belly dancing classes at Sweet Magic Studio, your hips won't lie either. The studio also teaches yoga and tai chi for the dance floor impaired. The lead instructor, who also has the confidence to go only by one name: Kareena, has over 40 years of yoga experience and the flexibility to prove it. Classes are usually held in the mid-morning or evenings, but the schedules change monthly, so keep your eyes open and be sure to call ahead. Try one class, and if you love it, buy an unlimited monthly pass because you'll probably enjoy the others as well.

soups, sandwiches, desserts and hot and cold drinks. The menu has an ethnic flair, with items like the Greek Salad, the French dessert Marjolaine and Morrocan Iced Tea. **B+**

Rice Thai Café and Sushi

6744 N Sheridan Rd
773.338.1717
RED LINE to LOYOLA

This Asian restaurant serves appetizers, soups, salads, entrées, fried rice and Thai curry selections, sushi, noodle dishes and desserts. Interesting dishes include the Beef Salad, Pineapple Fried Rice and Thai Custard. The food is cheap [entrées range from $6 to $8]. It's

located right next to the Village North Theatres, though it's small in size. **B**

Toham African Restaurant

1422 W Devon Ave
773.973.4602
RED LINE to LOYOLA

Not fancy, but genuine, this family restaurant sports folding tables and a few silk flowers as decoration. They're open every day for dinner and ordering from their menu would be a guess for anyone not familiar with African food. If you're feeling adventurous you should try Jute Leaf Soup: cut jute leaf, melon and seasoning boiled 'until slimy.' **B+**

ABOVE: Grande Noodles and Sushi Bar, 6632 N. Clark St. NICK SCHWEIGER • **RIGHT:** Dulce Landia, 6718 N. Clark St. NICK SCHWEIGER

Vince's Pizza and Taqueria

This Mexican/Italian restaurant happily satisfies an array of cravings.	1527 W Devon Ave 773.274.7018 RED LINE to LOYOLA

It's more of a takeout and delivery place than a sit-down restaurant, but it's the perfect place to order from if you and your ordering partner have different tastes. Tacos and pizza? No problem. Want a shrimp dinner with that? Sure. How about some BBQ ribs to finish off the smorgasbord? **B**

A & T Grill

When people use the term 'greasy spoon,' they're probably talking about	7036 N Clark St 773.274.0036 RED LINE to MORSE

A&T Grill. The décor is a bit drab and screams 1980s pastel flowers, but let's face it, no one comes here for the décor. The huge and very filling portions served at cheap prices are what keep the customers coming, as does the extremely wide selection of dishes. A&T Grill isn't worth a special trip, but if you're in the neighborhood, stop in for a killer omelet. **B⁻**

Athens Café

Located at the owner's home, Athens Café is a fun, friendly, family-run	6757 N Ridge Blvd 773.743.5900 RED LINE to MORSE

restaurant. Athens Café serves its amazing Greek food in very large portions, but does not charge very large prices. Reasonably-priced, authentic Greek food, what more could you want? I'll tell you, some of the best pita in Chicago. **A⁻**

Café Salamera

The best part of this Peruvian restaurant is that the sandwiches are under	6653 N Clark St 773.764.7210 RED LINE to MORSE

$6. Don't think that because the prices are cheap Café Salamera skimps out on ingredients. These sandwiches are loaded with meat. A sandwich makes a great light meal or heavy snack, but if you're very hungry, order some empanadas or ceviche for a full meal. **B⁺**

J.B. Albertos Pizza

Pizzas at J.B. Alberto's include thin, deep, double deck and stuffed, and they	1324 W Morse Ave 773.973.1700 RED LINE to MORSE

can be made with just about anything from jalapenos to Canadian bacon or any of the other 18 toppings. J.B. Alberto's also offers burgers, ribs and wings, but with so many pizza options, why bother? Standing room only gives J.B. Alberto's a bit of a New York feel, but one bite of that pizza will remind you you're in Chicago. **B⁺**

Leona's

The good news about Leona's is that the food is reasonably priced and	6935 N Sheridan Rd 773.764.5757 RED LINE to MORSE

you'll always have leftovers. The bad news is you might not want the leftovers. The food isn't particularly bad, just not particularly great. The pasta and most chicken dishes are good, but the pizza leaves a lot to be desired. Even if the food isn't fantastic, at least you don't have to pay a lot for it. **B⁻**

Lost Eras

1511 W. Howard Ave.
773.764.7800
RED LINE to HOWARD

They bill themselves as an antique store, but every day is Halloween at Lost Eras. With a huge selection of costumes, props and make up, Lost Eras has it all. From Michael Jackson to Michael Meyers, you can put together any costume you can think of with the help of the friendly and creative staff at this funky, eclectic boutique in Rogers Park. The thousands of costumes and props in the store are available to buy and some to rent, but call ahead if you're looking for something specific because a lot of material moves in and out throughout October.

No Exit Café

No Exit Café prides itself on being one of the oldest coffeehouse/performance venues in the country, having opened in the late 1950s. Grab a seat at one of the old wooden tables to hear great music some nights of the week and watch theater the others. The intimate atmosphere makes No Exit Café perfect for deep conversations. Talk, listen to music, play chess or just sit and have a cup of coffee. **A-**

6970 N Glenwood Ave
773.743.3355
RED LINE to MORSE

TO PLAY

The Side Project

This very small venue is doing big things in Chicago theater. Seating about 40 people, The Side Project produces avant-garde plays written and directed by Chicagoans. The venue also features staged readings, an annual one-act festival and a Visiting Artist Series. If you're looking for great, original theater without breaking the bank on tickets, be sure to check out The Side Project. **A**

1520 W Jarvis St
773.973.2150
RED LINE to JARVIS

The Speakeasy Supper Club

The wait can be a bit long, but customers swear the food if worth waiting for. The small but high quality menu offers dishes ranging from the conventional – steak – to the adventurous – ostrich meat. The sleek interior and contemporary American cuisine help this BYOB restaurant stand out on Devon Ave, typically known for its Indian food. **A**

401 W Devon Ave
773.338.0600
RED LINE to LOYOLA

Village North Theater

This theater is a little sketchy, but in an endearing way – it kind of adds to the experience. The letters showing the names of movies playing in Village North's four theaters are often falling off. The small theater lobby is lined with old movie posters and assorted artwork. So why bother with this tiny movie the-

6746 N Sheridan Rd
773.764.9100
RED LINE to LOYOLA

ater, which only holds about 600 people? Cheap Movies. Village North may not be fancy, but for $5 student tickets, who cares? **B**

Lifeline Theatre

This small theater brings stories to life. The ensemble of writers, directors and actors produce theatrical adaptations of literary classics. Seating about 100 people, Lifeline has produced many plays since its founding in the 1980s, including The Jungle Book, Jayne Eyre and Dracula. Student tickets run around $15, making Lifeline an affordable alternative to the movies. **B+**

6912 N Glenwood Ave
773.761.4477
RED LINE to MORSE

Loyola Park

For the most part, Loyola Park is pretty standard, with baseball fields, tennis courts and jogging paths. While the park itself doesn't stand out, the events held there do. Summer festivals, jazz concerts and the annual Artists of the Wall Festival make the park worthwhile to visit. Stop by and relax one afternoon if you're in the neighborhood, but don't go out of your way to visit the park unless you're attending one of the unique events held there. **B**

1230 W Greenleaf Ave
773.262.8605
RED LINE to MORSE

TO SHOP

Armadillo's Pillow

Spend an afternoon browsing in this quaint, used bookstore. With categories such as Philosophy, Design, Music and 'Read the Book if you Hated the Movie,' this place has it all. It also sells random trinkets, like old keys and postcards. Come exchange your own books for store credit. Seating areas are included. **A-**

6753 N Sheridan Rd
773.761.2558
RED LINE to LOYOLA

Flatts & Sharpe Music Co.

Everything the music enthusiast could want. This shop sells instruments

6749 N Sheridan Rd
773.465.5233
RED LINE to LOYOLA

LEFT: Rogers Park. NICK SCHWEIGER
• **BELOW:** Rogers Park. NICK SCHWEIGER

and a wide selection of sheet music in addition to offering repairs and lessons. Come in for lessons Monday through Saturday at $72 for four lessons. Instructors teach the guitar, bass, piano, fiddle, banjo, mandolin and cello. We won't even mention the store's cute and catchy name. **B+**

M.O. Food Store

If you have any use for rice-shrimp, custard powder, bags of whole dried fish, or bulk beans and rice, you should definitely stop by this African grocery store. They also rent African movies and sell African clothing. If you aren't sure what rice-shrimp are, it might be worth the stop to find out. **B+**

1245 W Devon Ave
773.274.8618
RED LINE to LOYOLA

Maquan Royal Fabrics

Bright colors everywhere. The walls and shelves of this store are lined with beautiful fabric in every shade and sequin intensity that's bound to wake you up as you walk through the door. Shoes and jewelry are also sold in equally stunning hues. This place is perfect if you have a good tailor ready to make a traditional

1408 W Devon Ave
773.761.7779
RED LINE to LOYOLA

African dress, but it's still interesting to see and worth wandering around if you don't. **A-**

Policia's Resale

A garage sale moved indoors, Pollicia's Resale features disheveled piles of cups and kitchenware, computers and radios far past their prime decade, and an array of knickknacks and used furniture. If you're looking to furnish an apartment cheaply, this is a great place to go. If you're hunting for treasures, you should try somewhere else. **C-**

1406 W Devon Ave
773.465.3150
RED LINE to LOYOLA

Smokey's Place

Smokey's is an empty square. Along one wall stands every type of pipe and hookah imaginable and on another hangs novelty t-shirts. The only other thing between the two walls is a stand of adult videos in one corner. It's unlikely that anyone who isn't searching for such a place will enjoy it very much, and communicating what you want over the angry music might be tricky. **C**

1217 W Devon Ave
773.552.3678
RED LINE to LOYOLA

EDGEWATER

ENJOY FIRE-SPINNING EVERY SUMMER

Edgewater is the most densely populated neighborhood in Chicago, but underneath the rows of high rise apartment buildings and condominium complexes are sites, shops and attractions less cookie-cutter. The relatively inexpensive housing of the area has attracted a diverse demographic which is mirrored in the wide variety of restaurant types available to diners. It's not a five-star food destination, but you will find everything from Caribbean to Thai to Ethiopian. A flourishing gay population can also be found in Edgewater. Browse through the Gerber/Hart Library, the largest collection of gay and lesbian literature in the Midwest, or wade along Hollywood Beach. Farther north on Foster Beach you can enjoy fire-spinning every summer. Andersonville is Edgewater's hippest community. Originally a Swedish enclave, over the years it has attracted many residents of various backgrounds. Swedish bakeries and delis still abound in the area but a heavy Middle Eastern and Hispanic influence can also be seen. You won't find big box stores on Clark St., the main commercial strip of the area. Instead, independent shops and boutiques, restaurants and bars spice up the area.

TO EAT

Angel's Restaurant

Though the diner has a heavier Mexican focus, Angel's serves everything from huevos rancheros to blueberry pancakes. Breakfast lovers should try the French toast grilled with almonds, while meat lovers will rejoice over the quarter-pound burgers. Almost everything on its rather extensive menu is under $10, making Angel's the perfect place to go in a large group – there's something for everyone. **B**

5403 N Clark St
773.271.1138
RED LINE to BERWYN

Augie's Restaurant

Augie's is your standard diner. Open for breakfast, lunch and dinner, Augie's serves a wide variety of food in decent-sized portions for a low price. The omelets are good and the Monte Cristo sandwiches are even better. The staff is friendly, and the food is decent, but Augie's is nothing that stands out. **B–**

5346 N Clark St
773.271.7868
RED LINE to BERWYN

Hamburger Mary's

5400 N. Clark St.
773.784.6969
RED LINE to BERWYN

Come here immediately and bring all of your friends with you. Mary's fantastic burgers come complete with cheesy [no pun intended] names like 'Buffy the Hamburger Slayer' – a burger cooked to perfection and topped with garlic, red wine and Swiss cheese and the 'Barbra-Q Bacon Cheeseburger' – a patty topped with spicy-sweet Western BBQ sauce, bacon, onion rings and more. You'll find all sorts of moderately-priced burgers with unique toppings in the downstairs dining area, but the upstairs lounge, dubbed 'Mary's Attic,' is where the fun is at. Cabaret and karaoke singers are extremely entertaining and add to the fun time you will surely have.

Bon Bon

5410 N Clark St
773.784.9882
RED LINE to BERWYN

This shop seems right out of the movie Chocolat. Gourmet flavors range from rum flavored dark chocolate to karma sutra truffles, making Bon Bon the perfect place to indulge your sweet tooth. The delectable sweets come at a price, however. One small piece costs around $2, and one pound of chocolate sets you back $60. The chocolate is also incredibly rich, so while I wouldn't eat at Bon Bon every day, coming here is a special treat. **B⁺**

Charlie's Ale House

5308 N Clark St
773.751.0140
RED LINE to BERWYN

Fireplaces illuminate the dining area, adding a little warmth and a little class to this fun, casual restaurant. Charlie's Ale House has a pretty extensive menu, with dishes ranging from 'My Big Fat Greek Salad' to pizzas. Wine lovers will love the 20 by-the-glass choices the restaurant has to offer. With great food that's moderately priced, Charlie's Ale House is worth a try. **B**

ABOVE: Seagulls, Granville Beach. NICK SCH-WEIGER • **LEFT:** Lakeside Buildings, Granville Ave. and Sheridan Rd. NICK SCHWEIGER

Coffee Chicago

Complete with free wireless internet, Coffee Chicago has everything

5256 N Broadway St
773.784.1305
RED LINE to BERWYN

you could imagine at a café. Coffee, ice cream, pastries, soups and sandwiches, calzones and fruit smoothies, just to name a few. There's plenty of seating here and it's a short block away from the Berwyn 'El' stop so there's no reason not to stop by. **B+**

TOP Antique Mall, 6314 N. Broadway St. NICK SCHWEIGER • **MIDDLE** Antique Mall, 6314 N. Broadway St. NICK SCHWEIGER • **BOTTOM** Marrakech Treasures, 5416 N. Clark St. LINDSEY MINEFF

Farragut's Tavern

Two dollars won't even get you a round-trip ride on the 'El,' but it can get

5240 N Clark St
773.728.4903
RED LINE to BERWYN

you a beer on some nights at Farragut's Tavern. While the bar itself isn't anything special, the free pool, beer nuts and cheap drinks are what make it so appealing to the local crowd. **B**

Huey's Hot Dogs

The mustard yellow and ketchup red walls seem a little cheesy consider-

1507 W Balmoral Ave
773.293.4800
RED LINE to BERWYN

ing this is a hot dog place, but if you want some serious cheese, order Kali's Killer Chili Cheese Dog – that thing is loaded. From specialty dogs to the traditional Chicago dog, Huey's seems like a necessary neighborhood fast food place. If you're not craving dogs, try the bleu cheese burger or a chicken sandwich. Huey's is perfect for great, greasy food that doesn't cost much. **B+**

Icosium Kafe

This Algerian café features almost 20 different types of crepes. From the

5200 N Clark St
773.271.5233
RED LINE to BERWYN

signature crepe made with roasted peppers, goat cheese, onions, tomatoes, pine nuts and spinach to some unique crepes, such as ones with pineapple, cilantro, olives and ricotta, Icosium Kafe aims to please all pallets. The café also serves soups and salads, as well as scrumptious dessert crepes. Crepes run in the $7 to $8 range, offering satisfying meals that won't set you back too much. **A-**

Jin Ju

The trade off for great food in the $15 range is that the restaurant

5203 N Clark St
773.334.6377
RED LINE to BERWYN

is small and can get pretty crowded. If a tight, packed space doesn't bother you, then definitely come to this Korean restaurant. The incredibly friendly staff often suggests the Bi Bim Bop, a beef dish that has a vegetarian counterpart if you so choose. It's fun to say and incredibly tasty. **B**

Ole Ole

For some of the best Latin food in Edgewater, come to Ole Ole. Red walls and

5413 N Clark St
773.293.2222
RED LINE to BERWYN

funky lamps make for a sleek, yet elegant interior. The friendly staff is happy to help you choose any one of its delicious items off the large menu. The arroz con pollo is especially tasty, as are the empañadas. Refreshing margaritas make a great addition to any meal. The dishes are a tad pricey, but well worth a few extra dollars. **A-**

Renalli's of Andersonville

This family-owned restaurant offers great food at low prices kept

1512 W Berwyn Ave
773.334.1300
RED LINE to BERWYN

cheap by the BYOB policy. Sandwiches and pasta dishes range from $7 to $10, while entrees range from $12 to $16. The made-to-order pizza is to die for, so definitely give it a try. Come with friends, come with family, even come with a date. The casual atmosphere makes this restaurant perfect for any occasion. **B+**

Reza's Restaurant

Reza's has a friendly staff, a pleasant atmosphere and a wide selection of

5255 N Clark St
773.561.1898
RED LINE to BERWYN

food. The food is served in large portions and at reasonable prices, but there's still something missing. Its meals are good but not great, especially in comparison to other Middle Eastern

Thorndale 'El' Stop. NICK SCHWEIGER

restaurants in the area. I won't say to never eat at Reza's, but I wouldn't rush to try it either. **B**

Star Gaze

Everything in this spacious bar is split down the middle. One half of the

5419 N Clark St
773.561.7363
RED LINE to BERWYN

bar features a dance floor, while the other half is

M Henry

5707 N. Clark St.
773.561.1600
RED LINE to BRYN MAWR

Brick walls and eye-catching art work make for a sleek interior in this warm, friendly restaurant. The staff is very welcoming and extremely helpful in choosing from the many dishes. Gourmet salads and sandwiches look tempting, but many personal favorites come from the breakfast menu served all day. The fried egg sandwich comes highly recommended by customers, and the fluffy pancakes – perfect after a night of drinking – just might be better than Mom's. With food this good and reasonable prices, people were bound to notice. Sunday brunch lines are out the door. To skip the wait, try the bakery section next door, which sells fresh breads and pastries as well as pre-packaged salads and sandwiches.

where people sit and play pool. One part of the menu offers simple bar food, like chicken wings or mozzarella sticks, while another section of the menu features fancier entrees, like broiled salmon or linguini alfredo. No matter which half you choose, be sure to come on Friday nights when salsa dancing is the main event. **B**

Svea

For a not so typical, but incredibly delicious meal, try this Swedish diner/café.

5236 N Clark St
773.275.7738
RED LINE to BERWYN

Dishes like Falukorv sausage or the Swedish fruit soup make this place stand out. Additionally, the personable staff and occasional serenade by the owner Glenn make Svea a must try. Come in the winter and order lutfisk, a traditional Swedish Christmas dish of boiled fish served with cream sauce – that's when Glenn does the singing. **B+**

Swedish Bakery

With cases along three walls full of cookies, cakes, breads and other pastries, it's difficult to decide what to get at Swedish Bakery. The lines here are always long, giving you some time to decide. No matter what you get, it's bound to be delicious, and with loaves of bread running around $3 and yummy bite-sized deserts starting at 88 cents each, your dollar goes further, meaning more food to try. **A**

5348 N Clark St
773.561.8919
RED LINE to BERWYN

LITERACY WORKS: TRAINING CHICAGO TO READ BETWEEN THE LINES
BY FLORA LERENMAN

In Chicago, half a million adults cannot read or write well enough to meet the demands of today's society. While often ignored, the problem is particularly problematic, as it creates an underclass of people who do not have access to the same services, rights, and abilities than many of us enjoy.

One such adult, Andrew Jn Louis, a recent immigrant from St. Lucia, needs to learn English in order to earn a promotion at work and to reunite his family. Nevertheless, he could not meet the literacy criteria of his first class at Truman College, and needed extra tutoring in reading fluency and comprehension. Jn Louis found his way to the Jane Addams Resource Corporation at 4432 N. Ravenswood Ave, where he was paired with tutor Jeannette Mihalek. Every Tuesday, the two meet for a few hours to strengthen Jn Louis's English skills.

The literacy program at Jane Addams is a part of a city-wide initiative, Literacy Works. Partnering with over 50 literacy organizations in over 30 communities throughout Chicago, Literacy Works trains volunteers in convenient locations and at convenient times each month. Since its inception ten years ago, the organization has trained thousands of volunteers to work with all types of learners with various achievement goals. Some are looking to improve basic reading skills or to learn English as a Second Language, while others are looking to pass standardized exams such as the GED and the U.S. citizenship exam. Most importantly, however, they are all looking for the improvement in quality of life that a better command of the English language offers.

Concerned with the socio-economic conditions and policies of this country, Mihalek views furthering literacy as a means of economic empowerment. While thoughtfully twisting a lock of hair, Jn Louis discussed his current situation.

Sweet Occasions

5306 N Clark St
773.275.5190
RED LINE to BERWYN

Candy displays and big comfy booths give the interior here an old-fashioned feel. But with ice cream this rich, sweet and tasty, who cares about the interior? With flavors like Espresso Oreo [which I highly recommend] or Blue Moon, it is apparent that Sweet Occasions is not your typical ice cream shop. Prices are reasonable, and the food is great, making this place a 'sweet' deal. **A**

Taste of Lebanon

1509 W Foster St
773.334.1600
RED LINE to BERWYN

A neon sign outside the restaurant boasts 'Famous Falafel,' and Taste of Lebanon definitely earns the right to keep that sign up. Additionally, Taste of Lebanon serves delicious pita, hummus, soups, kabobs and shawarma. The most expensive item on the menu is $6.99, so come hungry because your money goes far here. Plastic utensils and the smell of grease from the kitchen may encourage you to take out rather than dine in. **B+**

Tomboy

5402 N Clark St
773.907.0636
RED LINE to BERWYN

The art on the walls is funky, the pace is hectic and this restaurant gets downright raucous toward the end of the night. Amidst all the chaos, Tomboy offers upscale dishes including roast duck and escargot. This

---

When he worked as a home health caregiver, Jn Louis worried that his patients could not comprehend him and would look down on him, especially the retired teachers and professors he helped. As a worker in a candy factory now, Jn Louis is working on his math skills to earn a promotion all the while also working on getting his two children into the states.

Jn Louis said that, above all, he is learning English so that he can bring his children to live with him. He said he is frustrated with the petition system, filling out paperwork, and dealing with lawyers — which all take a substantial amount of English language knowledge. 'I adopted them when they were pretty young and they're growing up now and you miss them and they want to see you all the time,' he said of his children with a wistful smile.

'Back in St. Lucia, Andrew was unable to read and write in his native language, so Andrew is basically learning to read and write in a second language, so it's not intuitive,' Mihalek said. 'It's slow going, but it's coming along.'

After working closely with a Peace Corps volunteer in St. Lucia and getting to meet President Clinton, Jn Louis was offered the opportunity to obtain a U.S. Visa and seized it. One of Jn Louis's life dreams — attaining his U.S. citizenship — came to fruition with the help of Mihalek. 'I had to learn all of the constitution laws and she showed me all of the tricks and all of the learning of the constitution,' Jn Louis said of Mihalek. 'I think she's doing a good job.'

A native Creole French speaker, Jn Louis attributes his enhanced English vocabulary to Mihalek's persistence and creative approach. On any given Tuesday, one could hear their lively conversations about current events, history, and Jn Louis's anecdotes from his time in St. Lucia. On some days, they'll take a trip to the local grocery store and discuss products and money management.

Mihalek learned about Literacy Works while getting her Masters in Public Policy at the University of Chicago, and felt that it fit well with her desire to effect positive change in class systems. 'You can really mold your volunteer experience to the interests that you have and the

Standee's Coffee Shop, 1039 W. Granville Ave. NICK SCHWEIGER

food is not for the timid eater, but if your taste buds are feeling adventurous, you won't be disappointed. The only downside is that gourmet food comes at a gourmet price. **A-**

Edgewater Lounge

The inside looks like any other college town bar and smells like one too.

| 5600 N Ashland Ave |
| 773.878.3343 |
| **RED LINE to BRYN MAWR** |

The food and beer, however, are not your standard bar finds. Sandwiches are served on whole-grain bread and come with fried sweet potatoes if you so choose. Edgewater Lounge has a wide variety of beers on tap, from Kalamazoo Ale to Rogue Dead Guy, and it also serves reasonably-priced cocktails. **B**

community you want to serve,' Mihalek said. 'It's an ongoing relationship here and it feels like a community of people with a greater common goal.'

After one and a half years of tutoring, Mihalek attributes part of her success as a citizenship and literacy coach to the trainings she received from Literacy Works. Meeting tutors from other locations during the trainings was an additional highlight of Mihalek's initial volunteer experience.

Literacy Works specializes in training volunteer tutors, with regular 12-hour trainings, usually split between two Saturdays. Each month it holds English as a Second Language trainings in two different parts of the city — Rogers Park and Pilsen — and adult basic education for native English speakers are held in Uptown and West Loop.

'I believe that by helping someone with their literacy skills we are improving not only the lives of the learner, but of his or her family, the community, and ultimately the world,' says Christine Kenny, director of Literacy Works. 'I

personally have a true passion to work with adult learners, and truly believe in our mission: Literacy Works' mission is to fulfill the promise of a basic human right: the right to read, write and interpret the world.'

The program has gained critical mass throughout Chicago as word of mouth about the volunteer opportunities has heightened the program's popularity. Kenny said that Literacy Works trained more than 600 tutors in 2006.

'Tutors very much enjoy Literacy Works' training,' Kenny said. 'They leave feeling much more prepared for tutoring and are often much less anxious about where to begin. ... The tutors often comment that they feel like they are now a part of literacy movement.'

Literacy Works also offers a variety of programs such as the Writer's Circle, where participants get to share their personal stories through compositions based on their life experiences. Participants engage in peer editing, enhancing interpersonal dialogue and exchanging ideas to improve their writing.

Metropolis Coffee Company

1039 W. Granville Ave.
773.764.0400
RED LINE to GRANVILLE

You may have tasted Metropolis coffee at any one of the 50 stores in the city it supplies, but you haven't tasted it like this. Staff is literally roasting beans in the back room as well-trained baristas pour designs to top off cappuccinos. There aren't too many places that care this much about, as the manager put it, 'making traditional coffee drinks beautifully.' Part of the Metropolis philosophy says that a coffee house should be a neighborhood center and the owners here work to keep that idea alive by frequently hosting local musicians and artists. Plus, it's trendy enough to sell its own t-shirt.

Leonardo's Ristorante Tuscan Bistro

5657 N Clark St
773.561.5028
RED LINE to BRYN MAWR

Tired of plain old overpriced and overrated spaghetti? Leonardo's offers upscale entrees for moderate prices. The pappardelle alla fungi – house-made pasta with smoked chicken, mushrooms and oven-dried tomatoes – has been recommended by several customers. The best part about Leonardo's is that the food is fantastic and the tables are beautifully set, yet nothing is over $20 and the restaurant has an inviting feel. **A-**

Noodle Zone

5427 N Clark St
773.293.1089
RED LINE to BRYN MAWR

The biggest complaint I hear about Noodle Zone is that no matter where you sit all the tables are ridiculously wobbly. Tables aside, Noodle Zone offers a wide selection of Japanese and Thai dishes at cheap prices [decent portions for $7-$9]. The food, however, is nothing spectacular. Though not bad, it doesn't stand out. **B-**

Hamilton's Bar and Grill

6341 N Broadway St
773.764.8133
RED LINE to GRANVILLE

Every college has its bar, and Hamilton's is Loyola's. If you aren't enrolled, be warned that you'll be surrounded by college students. Hamilton's serves typical bar food and keeps its big screen plasma televisions tuned onto Chicago games, but – except for hoards of Loyola students – there's nothing here you can't find at most every other bar in Chicago. **B**

Sam's Chicken and Ribs

1102 W Granville Ave
773.764.0803
RED LINE to GRANVILLE

Imagine any non-franchise burger joint in Chicago. Now, eliminate all of the burgers and replace them with ribs and chicken wings. Ta-dah. You've just created Sam's. It's not classy by any means, but it's a great way to get meat cheap. And, if its sign can be trusted, one option will be 'the best rib tips in Chicago.' **B**

Edgewater. NICK SCHWEIGER

Banadir Restaurant

6221 N. Clark St.
773.443.2778
RED LINE to LOYOLA

For the vast majority of us who are not familiar with Somalian Cuisine, eating at the Banadir Restaurant may be somewhat of an adventure. You'll be hard-pressed to find a menu here; act like a regular and head straight to the buffet. The breakfast menu at this small establishment includes goat liver, but the less courageous needn't worry – there is also an egg dish. For dinner they offer goat cooked with their secret family recipe, among other interesting dishes including pasta with red sauce and multiple spicy rice items. The friendly, welcoming, mostly family staff completes a pleasant experience.

Standee's Restaurant

1133 W Granville Ave
773.743.5013
RED LINE to GRANVILLE

Walking into Standee's, you get the subtle impression that you've just intruded on a neighborhood party. Most of the customers of the diner are daily regulars, and Betty the server has a following. Its proximity to both Loyola U. and the Halfway house allows interruptions to the everyday clientele to be made with some interesting variety. Sure, it's an average, greasy diner, but where else are you going to get a fresh hamburger in Chicago for only $4.35? **B-**

Trivoli Café

1147 W Granville Ave
773.338.4840
RED LINE to GRANVILLE

Orange walls speckled with souvenirs collected throughout Europe encase the laidback atmosphere of the Trivoli Café, which takes its name from a café the owner spotted in Capri. Trivoli hosts knitting circles, book clubs and open poetry readings. A few of its tabletops hold checkerboards. Coffee is coffee, tea is tea and the food is average, but the atmosphere makes it one of the most pleasant places to hang out in Edgewater. **A**

Caracas Grill

6340 N Clark St
773.262.9900
RED LINE to LOYOLA

The Caracas' self-described mission is to serve 'South American cuisine with Caribbean taste.' There are quite a few dishes from Venezuela, where the owner is from. Their menu is navigable but not boring and their atmosphere is dark but not drab. If you're looking for authentic, no-frills South American food, here it is. **A-**

Blue Nile Restaurant, 6120 N. Ravenswood Dr.
NICK SCHWEIGER

Deluxe Diner

Get anything, any time. This is a classic diner, right down to the alumi-

6349 N Clark St
773.749.9900
RED LINE to LOYOLA

num-plated walls and swiveling café stools, and it's open 24 hours a day. They serve sandwiches, cheeseburgers, typical breakfast foods and other diner classics. With the diverse menu and low prices, you could probably eat lunch here every day, and some people do. But in a neighborhood packed full of unique ethnic restaurants, eating here as a tourist seems like a cop-out. **B+**

La Mexicana Restaurante, Bakery & Café

This is about as authentic as you're going to get. In fact, you might have

6241 N Clark St
773.338.3417
RED LINE to LOYOLA

trouble finding a staff member who speaks English. They sell beautiful homemade Mexican bread in a variety of flavors as well as afford- able tacos, tostadas, tortas and burritos. It's not a fancy place and the tables are covered in plastic tablecloths, but you'll feel like you're in Mexico. **A-**

Barry's Spot

If you're looking for a real mom & pop pizzeria, you've found it at Barry's.

5759 N Broadway St
773.769.2900
RED LINE to THORNDALE

The restaurant has been serving fresh slices for more than 30 years. Although Barry himself is long-gone, he sold the recipes for his thin and thick pan pizzas with the business. Loyal custom- ers say nothing else can match it. **A**

Broadway Cellars

If you want to feel sophis- ticated without changing out of your blue jeans,

5900 N Broadway St
773.944.1208
RED LINE to THORNDALE

this might be a good place to start. A 'globally inspired, but Italian influenced' menu makes your taste buds feel like they're in downtown while the rest of you remains in comfortable, no-at- titude Edgewater. It's probably the only place in Chicago that offers both 20 varieties of wine and a 'fat Wednesday' burger night. **A**

Indie Café

Even without the framed, adoring reviews that deco- rate the entrance walls, it

5951 N Broadway St
773.561.5577
RED LINE to THORNDALE

won't take long to realize that eating here will be a treat. The crisp, modern decoration is inviting. The fresh Thai and Japanese dishes are widely

TOP The Neo-Futurist Theater, 5153 N. Ashland Ave. LINDSEY MINEFF • **MIDDLE** Wild Pansy, 5739 N. Clark St. LINDSEY MINEFF • **BOTTOM** Gethsemane, 5739 N. Clark St. LINDSEY MINEFF

praised. And the prices are low enough to be printed on the menu. **A**

Little Corner Restaurant

There will be no 'yes sir' here. And that's exactly how they like it. The staff

5939 N Broadway St
773.878.1834
RED LINE to THORNDALE

of this neighborhood diner don t-shirts and call their customers by first name. The owner describes the place as a diner form of the television show Cheers. It's low key, it's grounded and it's cheap. **B**

Peacock Café and Restaurant

You'd almost miss this little brick storefront if it weren't painted bright red.

6014 N Broadway St
773.262.2005
RED LINE to THORNDALE

The Ethiopian restaurant claims that it tastes just a bit different from the rest due to gentle tweaking of standard Ethiopian recipes. Although you'll want to dig in with both hands, it's custom to use only the right. **B**

TO PLAY

Las Manos Gallery

According to owner Michelle Peterson-Albandoz, Las Manos

5220 N Clark St
773.728.8910
RED LINE to BERWYN

Gallery prides itself on offering 'River North quality without the attitude.' In addition to owning the gallery, Michelle's work is on display with a variety of other artists. The gallery shows a multitude of art work, ranging from paintings to video to sculpture. Stop in and spend a day looking at some truly unique pieces that range in price. **A**

Swedish American Museum Center

Located in Andersonville, this museum celebrates and preserves the

5211 N Clark St
773.728.8111
RED LINE to BERWYN

Swedish-American heritage in Chicago. The museum includes a permanent exhibit, gallery space, a children's section focusing on immigration and traveling exhibits throughout the year. You're sure to learn something about this lesser known subject without getting bored. If this place is good enough for the King of Sweden – who visited the museum several years ago – then it's good enough for you. **B+**

Pressure Billiards & Café

Pressure Billiards & Café pairs billiards with coffee instead of booze, which

6318 N Clark St
773.743.7665
RED LINE to LOYOLA

makes it less sleazy and more inviting than most pool halls. Open until 2 a.m. daily, Pressure Billiards & Café sells delicious caffeinated beverages and the café hosts stand-up comedy, improv, or open mic comedy Wednesday thru Saturday. It's a cool place to hang out and would make a great date. **A**

Woman & Children First

5233 N. Clark St.
773.769.9299
RED LINE to BERWYN

This independent bookstore is a favorite in Andersonville. With a wide selection of books ranging from gender/sexuality materials to art books to graphic novels, Women & Children First is a quirky shop that stands out among the corporate book chains. A knowledgeable staff not only helps you find what you're looking for, but often supplies personal book reviews. Membership gets you discounts every time you shop, as well as access to a yearly 40%-off sale. Customers rave about the unique selection and insist that they find something cool every time. Whatever is not carried in the store can be ordered, so there's really no reason not to check out Women & Children First.

Edgewater Antique Mall

6314 N. Broadway St.
773.262.2525
RED LINE to GRANVILLE

Every one of the 45 vendors whose collections are housed in this building has a piece of floor to maintain and arrange however he or she sees fit. This fosters astounding variety. A section made entirely of tin watering cans is squeezed between a section of mostly antique books and a section of vintage clothing. The variety in vendors also gives the store a great variety in price. Some of the items are expensive, sought-after antiques. Others are just old and affordable. No matter who you are or what your price range, if you rummage around long enough, you're bound to find something to love.

TO SHOP

Hip Fit

Denim is king at this trendy, unisex boutique where you are sure to find a pair of jeans that fits any hips. Hip Fit features a wide selection of new and used clothing, but, unlike many boutiques, Hip Fit has a lot to offer male shoppers. The owners are constantly bringing in new stuff, so keep coming back to

1513 W Foster Ave
773.878.4447
RED LINE to BERWYN

find a hot new pair of pants or a comfy, worn-in t shirt. **A-**

Kopi & Jalan-Jalan Boutique

Bright colors, eclectic decorations and clocks displaying times in differ-

5317 N Clark St
773.989.5674
RED LINE to BERWYN

ent countries make Kopi Café a relaxing, but still interesting place to grab some coffee or a light meal. Jalan-Jalan in the back of the café carries a little bit of everything, from travel books to

Heart of Chicago Motel, 5590 N. Ridge Blvd. NICK SCHWEIGER

soaps, from Indonesian clothing to jewelry. Enjoy a croissant, then purchase a cool new hand bag. Be sure to stop in and browse. **B+**

Marrakech Treasures

Walk into this funky boutique and you'll feel like you've entered a

| 5416 N Clark St |
| 773.271.2930 |
| **RED LINE to BERWYN** |

Moroccan bazaar. The owner Nadia travels to Morocco several times a year to hand-pick all the furniture, handicrafts and accessories. From beautiful jewelry to quirkier items like a goat-skinned lamp, you're sure to find something unique at Marrakech Treasures. **A-**

Paper Trail

As the name suggests, Paper Trail specializes in stationery. This funky

| 5309 N Clark St |
| 773.275.2191 |
| **RED LINE to BERWYN** |

shop, however, is more than just your typical station store. Selling small, quirky gifts, wrapping paper, cards, books and collectible trinkets, Paper Trail is a great place to wander around and kill some time. Perfect for last minute, one-stop shopping, Paper Trail allows you to buy the gift, wrapping paper and card all in the same place. **A**

Studio 90

Carrying fashionable but still professional-looking clothes, Studio 90 is the

| 5239 N Clark St |
| 773.878.0097 |
| **RED LINE to BERWYN** |

perfect place to take your mom. The store carries trendy, age-appropriate clothes and accessories for women. While some of the clothes, scarves and jewelry would appeal to a younger shopper, the store is definitely geared towards an older but not matronly crowd that has a funky, artsy flare. **B+**

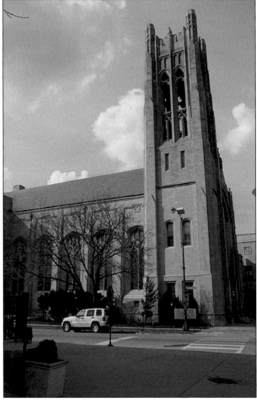

ABOVE Northside Catholic Academy. NICK SCHWEIGER
• **RIGHT** Edgewater. NICK SCHWEIGER

Johnny Sprocket's

The incredibly friendly and knowledgeable staff at Johnny Sprocket's makes buying a bike a fairly easy process. Customers are very satisfied with the bikes they've purchased and rave about how helpful the staff is. The store also does bike tune-ups and repairs and sells helmets, locks and other biking accessories as well. **A**

1052 W Bryn Mawr Ave
773.293.1697
RED LINE to BRYN MAWR

Kate the Great's Book Emporium

With categories of books like 'architecture' and 'fantasy,' Kate the Great's Book Emporium caters to the artistic community. Employees say that some of the regular customers come in and stay to read for hours. Providing a warm and comfortable environment, the bookstore holds special events during the month, including seasonal holiday readings. **B**

5550 N Broadway St
773.561.1932
RED LINE to BRYN MAWR

Granville Gallery

The Granville Gallery has been framing for 75 years. With over 4,000 samples, it's one of the largest custom framers in the city. But what's fun about its store isn't the custom or ready-made frames, it's the artwork. A modest-sized collection covers subjects and styles from every corner of the world. Although there are some museum copies, a good-sized amount are originals. **A**

6200 N Broadway St
773.764.1919
RED LINE to GRANVILLE

Lisa's Loot & Antiques

Lisa has loot as diverse as the neighborhood her store is settled in. Everything from $48 used furniture to $1200 true antique dressers pack the small floor space. The store doesn't aim for a specific decade or genre, but has most variety in lamps and dressers. It's hard to resist the suspicion that a floozy of an upscale rummage sale has mated with a furniture store from every decade and deserted its children here. **B**

6056 N Broadway St
773.338.1940
RED LINE to GRANVILLE

Patio Apartment Complex, 1602 W. Granville Ave. NICK SCHWEIGER

Harmony Art Glass Company

A business set up for stained glass custom design and restoration, Harmony Art Glass also displays a good size collection of lamps and windows in its Clark St. office. The pieces are beautiful glass created by obvious experts who will also make anything you come up with. The quality and nature of their projects make them a bit pricy, but if you're looking for something special, it's worth it. **A**

6323 N Clark St
773.743.2004
RED LINE to LOYOLA

Mustard Seed Christian Bookstore

Some things you expect to find in a Christian bookstore: wedding gifts, first communion gifts, an impressive collection of Christian literature and religious items. Mustard Seed has an ample supply of all these. Why you want to come to this Christian bookstore: a t-shirt collection, including such phrases as 'Satan is a stinkin' liar' and 'It's good to know the king.' **B+**

1143 W Sheridan Rd
773.973.7055
RED LINE to LOYOLA

UPTOWN

BLOCKS UPON BLOCKS OF UNIQUE ETHNIC SHOPS

From its beginnings as a summer resort in the late 1800s to a stomping ground for mobsters like Al Capone and John Dillinger to a rundown, dirty has-been neighborhood, Uptown has seen a lot changes over the years. Now, with national stores coming in and the Entertainment District stages drawing big names, its one area that's definitely on the upswing. The Aragon Ballroom has seen everyone from Frank Sinatra to Duke Ellington to Nirvana grace it's stage. The Green Mill Jazz Club and Uptown Theater blend good times with history. Along Argyle St. is Little Saigon or New Chinatown, depending on who you ask. Either way, you'll find blocks upon blocks of unique ethnic shops selling everything from candy to clothes. The area also abounds with authentic Asian food of all sorts. The Roots of Argyle mural celebrates the day to day life of the vibrant area. In the west is the Sheridan Park Historical District where a blend of historical styles lines the streets. To the south is Graceland Cemetery where Victorian architecture signals the final resting place of former mayors, prominent businessmen and even a former Chief Justice.

TO EAT

San Miguel Bakery

San Miguel Bakery sells traditional Mexican breads and pastries for mere pennies. Come practice your Spanish and try delicious new foods at the same time. Customers rave about piernas de pollo con fresa – strawberry filled pastries shaped like chicken legs. At 40 cents a piece, you can afford to try almost everything here until you figure out which is your favorite. **B+**

1607 W Montrose Ave
773.404.2241
BROWN LINE to MONTROSE

Chiu Quon Bakery

This Chinese bakery is a well-lit, quaint little escape from the bustle of Argyle St. The owners offer baked goods at a shockingly low price – huge almond and coconut cookies are only fifty cents each. The glowing display is packed with glazed, golden, pan-Asian pastries. Chiu Quon prides itself particularly in its moon cakes, a dense Chinese sweet bun typically filled with red bean paste. **B**

1127 W Argyle St
773.907.8888
RED LINE to ARGYLE

UPTOWN

Pho Xe Tang-Tank Restaurant

4953 N. Broadway St.
773.878.2253
RED LINE to ARGYLE

This roomy Vietnamese noodle joint earns points for cleanliness, speed and quality. Standouts on the large menu include the pho or beef noodle soup served with your choice of brisket, meatballs or thin, raw slices of steak. Each bowl of noodles is served with a plate of fresh greens that lightens up the meal. Standout appetizers include the perfectly-executed, lettuce-wrapped egg rolls with fish sauce. For the on-the-go customer, Tank Restaurant offers cheap Vietnamese sub sandwiches priced at only three dollars. Though the eatery offers much of the same cuisine as its surrounding restaurants, its large menu, knowledgeable staff and incredible prices set it above the rest. Great for old fans of Vietnamese food and adventurous newcomers, it is hard to go wrong when ordering from this menu.

Hai Yen

Hai Yen proudly sports its glowing reviews from the Chicago Tribune and

1055 W Argyle St
773.561.4077
RED LINE to ARGYLE

Chicago Magazine. This Zagat-rated Chinese and Vietnamese restaurant is tastefully decorated with live plants and abstract artwork. Probably the cleanest restaurant on the street, its cuisine differs little from the surrounding joint, but the friendly staff and do-it-yourself tabletop grill meals are a fun escape from the typical. Hai Yen is pricier than most places in the neighborhood, but worth it for a date. **A**

La Patisserie P

Don't be fooled by the French moniker of this corner bakery. The shop

1052 W Argyle St
773.878.3226
RED LINE to ARGYLE

resembles the pan-Asian patisseries in the area far more, and it specializes in everything from fresh fruit tarts and cream-filled éclairs to red bean cakes and barbecued pork buns. The famed bakery is famous for its Chinese, Vietnamese and Filipino specialty breads. No trip to Argyle's 'Little Vietnam' would be complete without a pastry and espresso from La Patisserie P. **A**

ABOVE: Balle Bakery, 5018 N. Broadway St. NICK INFUSINO • **LEFT:** Foursided Custom Framing, 5061 N. Clark St. NICK INFUSINO

UPTOWN

Lucks Food

Lucks Food is a jewel in what is becoming known as Chicago's 'Little Vietnam.' The unassuming storefront is dimly lit and often empty. But what the bakery lacks in grace it makes up for in value. Customers can order traditional Chinese and Vietnamese pastries for pennies. The sweet top and barbecue

1109 W Argyle St
773.878.7778
RED LINE to ARGYLE

pork buns are a steal at less than 50 cents each. Customers can stock up on a week's worth of baked goods for less than the 'El' ride over. **B+**

Pho 888

This Vietnamese noodle shop is one of at least a dozen off the Argyle 'El' stop. It's smaller than most, with crowded

1137 W Argyle St
773.907.8838
RED LINE to ARGYLE

THE ONLY LONG-RUNNING PLAY THAT IS NEVER THE SAME
BY NINA YUN

'Curtain!' a male performer yells and is met with frenzied response. '1!' '13!' '26!' audience members shout from their seats. A performer takes down a sheet with '26' scrawled on it and the other performers gather on stage to perform play number 26.

It's just another night at The Neo Futurarium, home to the longest running show in Chicago, Too Much Light Makes The Baby Go Blind. Going into its 20th year, the show still keeps its original format from its inception in 1988, featuring 30 two-minute plays in random order called by the audience until the alarm clock sounds the end of the show. The short plays constantly change but maintain the avant-garde edge that the show was founded on.

Keeping tradition has never been so exciting. Founder and owner, Greg Allen talks about his life as a Neo-Futurist. **What is your background in theatre?** I got into theatre late. I started off with photography and film while studying at Oberlin, but I was drawn to theatre because it's the greatest art form for self expression and the greatest form of com-

munication between people. And that's what art is for.

Where did you get your inspiration for TML? I felt theatre was not being used for what it could and should be used for. Theatres would try to create another world and suspend belief from the audience, which movies are better at. I'm a realist and I wanted to recreate that connection and communication between people and make an impact in their world. Older theatre folks didn't have much to say for younger folks and I was in my mid-20s. I wanted something that would speak to young people like myself, and now, we have an audience that everyone would kill for.

How did you come up with the format and philosophy? In college, I studied a lot of theatre history and connected with the Italian futurist movement. I was heavily influenced by post-modernism, Italian futurism, Dada and surrealism, so the show has components of live, real persons standing on stage and conception art. I fused those concepts together so people would have to think faster and respond quicker to adapt to changes of the future.

How did you come up with the name TML? I was researching this case study of an autistic child who was non-responsive except to light. And after smashing light bulbs the child would say 'Too much light makes the baby go blind'

seating, fluorescent lighting and tile floors. Pho 888 is typical of the restaurants in the area, but somewhat shabbier than others. The eatery is not a good bet for newcomers to this Asian enclave in North Chicago, but a safe choice for someone looking for a quick, cheap meal. Try the sugar cane juice for a nice change. **C+**

Sun Wah Barbecue Restaurant

Sun Wah's window display may be a little shocking for the less adventurous diner. Hanging from hooks near the entrance are whole roasted ducks and chickens, Chinese link sausages and entire slabs of short ribs. Popular with the locals, the Chinese butcher/barbecue has a booming take-out business. A safe

1134 W Argyle St
773.769.1251
RED LINE to ARGYLE

over and over.

What was the response when TML first began? Critics didn't know what to make of it. Audiences would be offended and confused. It was a very aggressive, in-your-face show.

How do you feel about the Chicago theatre scene? Chicago is very accessible in terms of theatre, a huge difference between New York and Chicago is finance. Chicago theatre is an open society, there's a show for everyone and most shows are extremely accessible. Chicago is amazing; the best theatre scene in the country – it's extremely diverse and there are some 200 shows on any given weekend night. The heart and soul of Chicago theatre are the companies that create their own work, like 500 Clown, Red Moon and Curious Theatre Branch.

Most memorable story during a TML performance? Where you can imagine things to go off in a show that is in random order, it's happened. There is vast number of stories, but one night we were doing a play called 'You're in Charge.' We would turn off the lights and then give a flash light to someone in the audience and then take them on the stage. Everyone had to do what the person says and usually it's a song or they dance around, it's always fascinating to see what happens, but one night this was our last play and the person turned on the flash light and then said, 'Alright let's

go,' and led the entire audience out of the theatre. I went around trying to stop people from stopping the audience and then someone asked about the flash light and I was like who cares about the fucking flash light? It was so beautiful. It was really gorgeous and quite moving, and very much of what we work and inspire to.

Has TML changed since it first started? The first year was truly experimental, it was very who knows what the hell will happen, but it has shifted in to more a skillful ensemble and the audience knows what to expect versus the first to second years, the show comes with a certain expectation but I think everything else has remained. I would rather play to a house with no expectations, but it's harder and more challenging to perform to an audience that has expectation. It forces us to try to take things further and throw the audience off balance.

Do you think you'll expand or change from the Futurist philosophy? Neo futurist is an endless expression and I don't feel like I've done all that I can do with it. It will always be dynamic and challenging, and what's the point of doing anything unless it's impossible?

TML is performed at The Neo-Futurarium, 5153 N. Ashland St., 50 weeks a year. Tickets are $7 plus [$1 times the roll of a single six-sided die], or $8 - $13 at the door, cash only.

UPTOWN

House of Ribs

1265 W. Wilson Ave.
773.878.9655
RED LINE to WILSON

This restaurant has everything, and it's cheap. The seafood selection is overwhelming, and I've never seen chicken offered in so many different ways. A variety of side orders can complement every meal except for the pizzas, which come thin, stuffed or in the pan, with an exhaustive list of toppings to choose from. International dishes such as Hawaiian, Mexican and Italian are served upon request. It's easy to go crazy with ordering at this restaurant due to the great selection and low prices, but save room for dessert; there are several different kinds of cakes and other desserts to satisfy your sweet tooth.

bet will be the perfectly roasted duck or barbecue pork fried rice. Ask for the duck pre-chopped if you're not up to the task. **B**

TOP: Green Mill Lounge, 4802 N. Broadway St. NICK INFUSINO • **BOTTOM:** Agami Sushi, 4712 N. Broadway St.
NICK INFUSINO

Taqueria Guerrero

This Mexican-American eatery is located just under the Argyle 'El'

1116 W Argyle St
773.769.1232
RED LINE to ARGYLE

tracks. In fact, one entrance to the small corner diner is attached to the station. Though a quick stop for the on-the-move traveler, the taqueria has an unwelcoming exterior and cramped indoor setup with one narrow row of booths. The unfocused menu is a confused mixture of Mexican-American cuisine and traditional diner fare. Its location under the 'El' tracks, which promises loud, frequent interruptions to your meal. **C**

Thai Binh Restaurant

Thai Binh Restaurant's baby blue and pink painted sign proclaims a world

1113 W Argyle St
773.728.0283
RED LINE to ARGYLE

of exotic Vietnamese flavors. The eatery, located steps off the Argyle 'El' stop, serves traditional Southeast Asian fare. Thai Binh's menu offers a variety of fried foods and grilled meats, with egg rolls and fresh veggies standing out. The interior is clean and well decorated, but gated windows give an ominous sense to passers-by. Decent food, but an unwelcoming exterior. **B‑**

Konak Pizza & Grill

Konak Pizza & Grill is a laid back, casual place. You can sit at the bar

5150 N Clark St
773.271.6688
RED LINE to BERWYN

and watch a game or play some pool with your friends while you wait for the pretty typical grill/bar dishes to be served. If you're bored of just burgers or some sort of chicken dish, try the vegetarian pizza, which comes highly recommended by the staff. The prices are reasonable, but Konak only takes cash. **B**

Agami

Agami is a swanky sushi restaurant and bar with over-the-top décor and classy seating. The restaurant itself is huge, and the floor-to-ceiling windows in the front show off the full bar [which includes more than 40 sakes]. Fancy cuisine such as the 'Inside-out Marinated Salmon Maki with Cucumber Dressing' or the 'Green Turtle' prove the menu to be unique and innovative. Bright red leather seats and booths mixed with the dark wooden tables create a modern and trendy look. **A**

4712 N Broadway St
773.506.1854
RED LINE to LAWRENCE

Broadway Grill & Pizza

This restaurant is for the fast food eaters in each of us. This red-and-white-schemed restaurant on the corner of Lawrence and N. Broadway serves basic diner food. The décor is kitschy [perhaps unintentionally], such as album covers from old Broadway shows covering the walls and bright blue pleather stools. The eatery offers carry out and delivery, though, so customers can enjoy eating the greasy cuisine in their own setting if they so wish. **C**

4800 N Broadway St
773.334.5650
RED LINE to LAWRENCE

A-Z Wallis Army Navy Depot, 4647 N. Broadway St. NICK INFUSINO

Crew Bar & Grill

This place is everything a macho man could desire. The gay sports bar and grill offers menu items like the 'Kickin' Chicken Salad' for those craving a spicy kick, the 'Pulled Pork Minis' as an appetizer and the 'Durango Steak Sandwich' served on a hoagie roll. Customers are also allowed to 'build your own

4804 N Broadway St
773.784.2739
RED LINE to LAWRENCE

The Neo-Futurists

5153 N. Ashland Ave.
773.878.4557
RED LINE to BERWYN

Best known for its 30-plays-in-60-minutes show Too Much Light Makes the Baby Go Blind, The Neo-Futurists makes seeing a show a must. Its unique, avant-garde shows entertain about 150 audience members. Sold-out shows mean the theater orders pizza for the crowd, so bring your friends along to ensure free grub. Audience participation is essential. Don't expect just to sit and watch. Randomness within shows, mixed with serious political awareness and sharp views on pop culture, makes coming here on weekend nights an unforgettable experience. With constantly new plays for $7, you can repeat that awesome experience over and over again.

Historic Uptown Bank Building, 4753 N. Broadway St. NICK INFUSINO

feel. The diner doesn't just offer pancakes; it has sandwiches, hamburgers and the essential diner accoutrements. The back side of the menu, however, is devoted to pancakes and waffles. The prices are a little strange in that items are $5.55 or $4.05, but it's still cheap. The 'Waffle a la Mode' sounds decadent, as do the 'Cinnamon Pancakes.' **B⁻**

Green Mill Cocktail Lounge

The Green Mill will have you wishing you were sharing a light with Fred Astaire. If you're into those swanky, smoky, 1920's-esque cocktail lounges, this is the place to go. A wide, dark wooded bar takes up most of the narrow venue, so either take a seat in a cushy green booth or at the bar of this legendary jazz venue. **B**

4802 N Broadway St
773.878.5552
RED LINE to LAWRENCE

sandwich' for $9. Sit back and watch the game on the 92-inch satellite HDTV screen. **B⁺**

Golden House Restaurant & Pancake House

Think IHOP in an even greater time warp. The red vinyl booths and marble countertop help give off the Pleasantville

4744 N Broadway St
773.334.0406
RED LINE to LAWRENCE

Marigold

Marigold fuses modern and traditional cuisine and décor. The walls are painted a yellow buttercream and brick red, and the long and narrow layout makes for a cozy, intimate atmosphere. The prices are reasonable as well, with the main dishes averaging about $16. Try the samosas [$5.25] or the South Indian Spicy Coconut Soup [$7.95]. **B⁺**

4832 N Broadway St
773.293.4653
RED LINE to LAWRENCE

Riviera Theater

4746 N. Racine Ave.
773.275.6800
RED LINE to LAWRENCE

A line-up of eager fans curls around the corner of Racine and Lawrence, awaiting entrance into the Riviera Theatre, huddled beneath scaffolding surrounding a building that appears as if it will never be worked on. The inside is not far removed from the outside, as the décor lies somewhere between rustic and dirty, with purple paint and blank space splashed across walls and the ceilings looming above. There is something undeniable about the Riviera: it has flavor. The Riviera's musical orientation leans toward the alternative and the more popular of the obscure acts that are too big to perform at smaller clubs like the Metro. Qualms are few, but one may be not getting a good spot for the show. If you don't arrive early enough, prepare to be standing tiptoe by the back bar because this place gets packed quickly.

Andies Restaurant

This Greek Mediterranean restaurant offers a huge selection of savory

1467 W Montrose Ave
773.348.0654
RED LINE to WILSON

appetizers that come in small or large portions and make great main courses for a group setting where everyone can have a sample of everything. There's a wide variety of vegetarian selections as well as lamb, beef, seafood and poultry for meat-lovers. Services include delivery and takeout and a buffet in addition to sit-down dining. **A-**

Anna Maria Pasteria

This quaint Italian restaurant has an authentic setting and a relaxed,

4400 N Clark St
773.506.2662
RED LINE to WILSON

soothing atmosphere. The lights are dim, the music is low, and the mood is lovely. Meals are delicious, but hefty, so be careful if you're planning on an appetizer, soup and salad, entrée and dessert. You get what you pay for here, so prices aren't cheap, but they're decent. **A**

Driftwood

This sports bar right off Wilson seems to be the kind of place where

1021 W Montrose Ave
773.975.3900
RED LINE to WILSON

everybody knows your name. The one pool table and long bar take up most of the small spot. The bar is more of a hangout place than a venue for events, though it does promote a Thursday night open mic. **B**

Fishpond

This Filipino restaurant offers ethnic dishes for a fair price as well as a

4416 N Clark St
773.271.1119
RED LINE to WILSON

12-course buffet option available on Wednesdays and Fridays from 5 p.m. to 9 p.m. and Saturdays and Sundays from noon to 3 p.m. for $7.95. This is a fun place to go to try new things and experience a casual and friendly atmosphere. **A-**

Frankie J's on Broadway

This restaurant offers American versions of a variety of foods, from

4437 N Broadway St
773.769.2959
RED LINE to WILSON

Italian to Mediterranean to Thai. Here you'll find juicy hand-cut steaks, grilled appetizers, meaty sandwiches and salads, large portions of pastas with creamy white or rich tomato sauces and an entire menu selection dedicated to a variety of chicken platters, all in an energetic and amiable setting. **A-**

TOP: Riviera Theater, 4746 N. Racine Ave. NICK INFUSINO • **MIDDLE:** Dogwalker, Foster St. & Ashland Ave. NICK INFUSINO • **BOTTOM:** Wilson Skate Park, Wilson Ave. & Lake Shore Dr. NICK INFUSINO

The Aragon Ballroom

1106 W. Lawrence Ave.
773.561.9500
RED LINE to LAWRENCE

▮ The Aragon Ballroom has been a music hot spot since it was built in the 1920s. Starting off as the 'it' place for the jazz scene, the Aragon has since shifted to a rock and hip hop venue. Legends from Duke Ellington to the Rolling Stones have taken the stage here, and, today, the venue continues to draw big-name acts. From The Strokes to Pitbull, the Aragon entertains crowds with the hottest music. The spacious venue is general admission, so line up early if you want to be up front. Take some time to look up at the ceiling and beautifully decorated interior – it's a lot nicer than some of the other venues in the area.

Grace African Restaurant

If you're up for undertaking different types of food, this is the place. Try interesting menu items such as 'Emo Tuo' [rice dough served with palm nut soup or peanut butter], 'Waakye' [rice with beans and a choice

4409 N Broadway St
773.271.6000
RED LINE to WILSON

of meat] and 'Kenkey' [corn dough with fish]. The place itself doesn't appear very appetizing – plastic tables, chairs and tablecloths make up the furniture – but trying new foods is always fun. **C+**

Jake's

Greasy goodness just oozes from this restaurant. The windows are painted

4401 N Sheridan Rd
773.728.1188
RED LINE to WILSON

with colorful, eye-catching advertisements for Jake's Breasted Chicken and wing specials. The menu items are inexpensive [a four-piece dinner special is $5.99]. This isn't really a sit-down restaurant, though, so most customers tend to use the 'super fast carry out service' printed on the menu. **B+**

Little Quiapo

Don't base your view of Filipino food on this restaurant if it's your first

4423 N Clark St
773.271.5441
RED LINE to WILSON

time trying Filipino cuisine. The food is cheap, but the prices should still be even lower, and while the waiters are nice enough, the setting and atmosphere are uncomfortable and slightly obnoxious. One of the amenities is carry-out, so if you do decide to give this restaurant a try, carry it out. **C**

Argyle 'El' Stop. NICK INFUSINO

Magnolia Café

This romantic restaurant has a reputation for being one of finest in uptown.

1224 W Wilson Ave
773.728.8785
RED LINE to WILSON

UPTOWN

LEFT: St. Mary of the Lake Parich, 4200 N. Sheridan Rd. NICK INFUSINO • **BELOW:** Uptown Baptist Church, 1011 W. Wilson Ave. NICK INFUSINO

The setting and atmosphere are conducive to intimate conversations, the décor is beautiful, and the service and food tie everything together. Prices for entrees range from $30 to $60, but you get your money's worth. The wine list is delightfully long, and so is the dessert menu, so save room as sharing a slice or bowl of dessert will only add to the romantic mood. **A**

Nigerian Kitchen

This small restaurant is casual and very open. The large dining area is

1363 W Wilson Ave
773.271.4010
RED LINE to WILSON

sparsely populated with tables covered in plastic tablecloth, and the décor is a bit random, but not obnoxious, though the small TV near the entrance becomes distracting after a while. The owner and the rest of the workers are very polite, and the food is tasty but not expensive. **A⁻**

Pizza Factory

This Italian and American cuisine restaurant only offers takeout and delivery

4443 N Sheridan Rd
773.769.1011
RED LINE to WILSON

services, but what the Pizza Factory lacks in dining options it makes up for in reliable, efficient service and delicious food for a fair price. Great for picking something up on the way home or for a late-night hunger attack. **B⁺**

Thai Uptown Rice and Noodles

Quaint and colorful best describe this Thai restaurant. Lime green seems

4621 N Broadway St
773.561.9999
RED LINE to WILSON

The Kinetic Playground

1113 W. Lawrence Ave.
773.769.5483
RED LINE to LAWRENCE

The windows of The Kinetic Playground are covered in graffiti-like designs and colorful, psychedelic patterns. This entertainment venue is 21+, and it hosts artists who play bluegrass, soul, blues, rock, jazz and more. The venue boasts – structurally – one of the best buildings to play in – the acoustics are sharp and clear, but the sound isn't so overpowering that you can't have a conversation with the person next to you. The place prides itself on encouraging and bringing in undiscovered artists to show off their talents. As if the music wasn't reason enough to come, cheap booze and friendly staff make the experience better – find Steve for a good story, he loves to talk. Stop by to check out the lesser known, underground Chicago music scene.

RIGHT: 'El' Stop. KAITLYN ELLISON • **BELOW:** N. Broadway St. KAITLYN ELLISON

to be the color scheme here, with painted walls and cushions dedicated to the shade. Despite the almost too-bright décor, the menu is extensive and the prices are reasonable. All appetizers are under $5, and there's a wide range of items for whatever mood you're in. **B-**

The Godfather's Famous Pizza

This restaurant's menu goes above and beyond pizza pies, but it would be a sin to not order at least one thin crust from the Godfather's. The dough is delicious, which almost makes the stuffed and pan pizzas better. Calling

1265 W Wilson Ave
773.878.8600
RED LINE to WILSON

for delivery works best with this restaurant, otherwise you may get frustrated with the cooking time for larger dishes such as the stuffed pizzas or steaks. **B+**

Three Harmony Restaurant

This is a wonderful Chinese restaurant with a great menu. There's a wide variety of vegetarian options, and every order is decently priced. Services include carry-out and delivery, but the atmosphere is quite nice, so dining in the restaurant is yet another

4546 N Magnolia Ave
773.728.6376
RED LINE to WILSON

Angel Food Bakery

1636 W. Montrose Ave.
773.728.1512
RED LINE to MONTROSE

The bright pink, blue and green colors on the sign outside remind you of cupcake icing, which is pretty appropriate for this bakery in Uptown. Angel Food can satisfy any sweet tooth with freshly toasted s'mores and the highly recommended 'Barthelona,' a Spanish-style hot chocolate with homemade whipped cream. Angel Food also serves delicious sandwiches on freshly baked rolls, as well as a homemade soup, which changes a couple times a week. Nothing here is too expensive, but if you're really low on cash, you can always buy a day-old muffin for 75 cents. Kids on their way home from school are often seen staring wide-eyed in the window – oh yeah, it's that good.

Shake Rattle & Read

4812 N. Broadway St.
773.334.5311
RED LINE to LAWRENCE

With the tagline, 'Chicago's Only Rock & Roll Book Store,' Shake Rattle & Read sells cassettes, albums, decade-old magazines, used books and more. Stop by and you can buy a Van Morrison album or an old Playboy for only $1 or just browse for hours among the old collectibles – 60,000 used books focusing heavily on the entertainment industry should keep you busy for a while. If you can get a hold of him, owner Ric Addy is one of this stores best gems; he has great stories to tell. Classic rock hits playing over the speakers adds the final touch to this Uptown gem.

option to consider. Good service, plus this place smells wonderful. **A**

Urban Tea Lounge

Visit this amazing place. The setting is quaint, comfortable and cozy,

838 W Montrose Ave
773.907.8726
RED LINE to WILSON

not to mention it smells exotic and sweet. Urban Tea Lounge is an ideal place to relax, read or chat while indulging in small treats, savory teas or coffee, or a light meal of soup, salad or a sandwich. You'll be getting your money's worth and then some. **A**

TO PLAY

The Annoyance

This theatre, bar and venue for classes is owned by Annoyance

4830 N Broadway St
773.561.4665
RED LINE to LAWRENCE

Productions, a local theater and comedy group. Past shows include 'Arm Soup,' a play about a group of people who traveled West and ate each other, and 'The Invention Show,' a musical about inventions and inventors in history. Not only is this the showing place for productions, but people can come in and take classes as well. **B**

Uptown Lounge

Uptown Lounge has everything a late-night bar should have: flat screen

1136 W Lawrence Ave
773.878.1136
RED LINE to LAWRENCE

satellite televisions, DJs, karaoke and a private party room. It gives off a laidback, casual vibe, so

TOP: Palmer Tomb, Graceland Cemetery, 4001 N. Clark St. NICK INFUSINO • **MIDDLE:** Chicago Tattoo Factory, N. Broadway St. KAITLYN ELLISON • **BOTTOM:** Hoa Nam Grocery, 1101 W. Argyle St. KAITLYN ELLISON

UPTOWN

if you're looking just to hang out and have a few drinks with some friends, this is the place. Just don't expect anything wild or unusual to go on [unless you start something]. **B⁻**

At Ease Wellness Center

Have a sore shoulder? Need an afternoon away from stress? 'Relax, Restore, Rejuvenate' is the slogan here. The establishment offers massage, chiropractic and physical therapy. The irony? The location is on the corner of Wilson and North Sheridan, which is probably one of the busiest intersections in the area. Not so relaxing. **B⁻**

4403 N Broadway St
773.561.7966
RED LINE to WILSON

Black Ensemble Theater

Black Ensemble Theater produces plays and musicals reflecting the importance of African American culture and celebrates the lives of famous Black performers. From Stax Records in Memphis to the Nat King Cole Story, the plays could appeal to anyone – theater lovers and soul lovers would equally enjoy a show. The group is currently based in the Uptown Center

4520 N Beacon St
773.769.5516
RED LINE to WILSON

Hull House, but hopes to move to a larger venue in the future. **A**

Tattoo Factory

This studio is neat, organized and very professional, and looks about as terrifying as a hair salon. The artists here take their work seriously, and prices aren't exactly cheap, with tattoos starting no lower than $30 and body piercing ranging between $60 and $70. But Tattoo Factory justifies its costliness with its high-quality work and exceptional sanitary conditions. **A**

4441 N Broadway St
773.989.4077
RED LINE to WILSON

Uptown Recording

Uptown Recording is a full service recording studio with top of the line digital equipment. The knowledgeable staff will help you put together the best album possible. The studio requires appointments, and studio time does not come cheap. A full day in the studio [12 hours] will set you back $650. A few clients have gone on to major record labels, so who knows, you could be next. **B⁺**

4656 N Clifton Ave
773.271.5119
RED LINE to WILSON

Montrose Harbor,
W. Montrose Ave.
NICK INFUSINO

TO SHOP

Fuss Salon

Customers rave about the shampoo and wash at Fuss – and the hair cut

1528 W Montrose Ave
773.293.4640
BROWN LINE to MONTROSE

hasn't even happened yet. With each hair experience off to such a good start, it's no wonder why Fuss is such a popular salon. Fuss offers moderately-priced services, but customers are very happy with the quality of service and the end results. **B**

The Comic Vault

The plain storefront with a simple green sign makes this place look really

1530 W Montrose Ave
773.728.2001
BROWN LINE to MONTROSE

boring. But once you get inside, bright colors, t-shirts, action figures and floor-to-ceiling shelves full of comics catch your eye. The Comic Vault has hundreds of comics to choose from, and the friendly staff can help you find anything from back issues of Super Man to the newest issue of Stephen King's Dark Tower, The Gunslinger Born. Oh, and ladies, you get 15% off every Thursday. **A-**

Borderline Music

Whoever said orange was the new pink has never been to Borderline

5111 N Clark St
773.784.0503
RED LINE to ARGYLE

Music. The bright, happy décor matches the upbeat dance music that the store specializes in. Borderline Music also carries a wide selection of imports difficult to find in many mainstream music stores. Other sections carry what one customer called 'gay staples,' such as Madonna or the Pet Shop Boys. Come on in, have a ball and dance your pants off. **B+**

Trung Tin

The eclectic window display of this Vietnamese CD and souvenir store

1057 W Argyle St
773.334.9299
RED LINE to ARGYLE

hints at a bit of funkiness. Golden good luck Bhuddas, Chinese New Year decorations and a manger scene are a bit incongruous with the

Foursided Custom Framing, 5061 N. Clark St. NICK INFUSINO

store's stacked interior. English-language music fans will find it difficult to navigate the neon and pastel rows of Vietnamese pop tracks, but it's fun to try. Tourists have a good shot at scoring some original knick knacks. **B**

Uptown Blues

This bike shop handles sales, service and parts. Come in with questions,

4653 N Broadway St
773.728.5212
RED LINE to WILSON

a need for repair or just a desire to peruse the items. Pimp out your bike [and yourself] with a selection of trendy and colorful helmets and other accessories. Take a look outside, where a rack of cool bikes for sale sits, including a rickshaw and tandem bikes. **A-**

Uptown Sweets

This shop generates great gift ideas with its stocked shelves of cute toys, el-

1218 W Wilson Ave
773.989.0200
RED LINE to WILSON

egant baskets and decorations, and tiny, wrapped treats. All candies and sweets are beautifully presented and available for purchase, and an array of favorites offers enough variety to satisfy anyone's sweet tooth. A few small tables inside the building, as well as a couple of benches outside, offer quiet, enjoyable places to savor the sweet delicacies. **A**

LINCOLN SQUARE

QUIRKY WITHOUT TOO MUCH EDGE

One of the fastest developing areas of Chicago, this neighborhood is quirky without too much edge. Shopping and dining is centered at the six-way intersection of Lawrence, Western and Lincoln Avenues. There's a strong German influence offering delicious food. Those looking for something more Asian- or Eastern-inspired will also find plenty of Middle Eastern and Thai establishments. Murals can be found scattered in the area. Lincoln Ave. offers fine dining, old-time delis and many boutique shops. Unique and less pricy than other up and coming neighborhoods, the European style buildings and bustling outdoor cafes of Lincoln Square invite you to slow down. The Old Town School of Folk Music brings in national acts but never forgets its roots. The Davis Theater and a summer concert series in Giddings Plaza also draw visitors. Ravenswood, the predominant community in the area, has turned old homes into tourist destinations. Small boutiques and cafes make it the perfect location for an afternoon. When you're done shopping take a stroll among the brick row homes with a few Victorians thrown in for variety.

TO EAT

Aroy Thai

This casual, cheerful restaurant serves typical Thai dishes, as the name hints. The Pad Thai is especially tasty, as is the basil duck, served with stir fry, basil leaves and chili peppers for a little kick. With dishes topping off around $8 you won't break the bank trying to get a decent meal. **B+**

4654 N Damen Ave
773.275.8360
BROWN LINE to DAMEN

Sweet Occasions

This newly-renovated café is perfect for anyone with a sweet tooth. Have a hearty sandwich or salad and top off your meal with their award-winning ice cream and an oversized cupcake. Since the new décor boasts large front windows and light, pastel-colored walls, skip the usual coffee shop to spend a few hours in this warm café next time winter has you feeling down. **B+**

4639 N Damen Ave
773.293.3080
BROWN LINE to DAMEN

Daily Bar & Grill

4560 N. Lincoln Ave.
773.561.6198
BROWN LINE to WESTERN

This homey, modern American eatery on the corner of Lincoln and Wilson in the Lincoln Square neighborhood offers a social atmosphere and a large wet bar. Daily Bar & Grill is low-lit with ample booth and bar seating making it a great spot for parties and large groups. The menu includes American classics like patty melts and cheese steaks, but those watching their health can dig into a decent vegetarian selection. Eaters should come hungry – almost everything on the menu comes with a colossal serving of fries. Order chili cheese fries off the menu if you're looking for a meal fit to feed a giant.

The Perfect Cup

4700 N Damen Ave
773.989.4177
BROWN LINE to DAMEN

With several Starbucks in the area, it's tough for a coffee shop to stand out, but The Perfect Cup does just that. Butterscotch and chocolate chip scones go well with any of the coffee drinks served. Anne's Special – espresso, chocolate and steamed milk – comes recommended by the extremely friendly staff, all of whom are cousins. Tea lovers should try any of the Oolongs. The cafe also sells soups and sandwiches. So order some food, grab a couch and relax. **A**

Bloom Yoga Studio

4663 N Rockwell St
773.463.9642
BROWN LINE to ROCKWELL

The brightly-colored, large studios hold a variety of classes for people of all skill levels. The friendly staff offers beginner/basic and more advanced classes, as well as a prenatal yoga class – very popular among to-be moms to be in the area. Classes are a bit pricey [about $15 per class or $50 for four weeks], but clients insist they're worth every penny. **B**

Rockwell's Neighborhood Grill

4632 N Rockwell St
773.509.1871
BROWN LINE to ROCKWELL

Rockwell's is your typical, friendly neighborhood place. The staff is welcoming, and the crowd is casual. Rockwell's serves classic American dishes, with the Southwest chicken sandwich a standout, but what sets this restaurant apart is the healthier atmosphere. The place went smoke-free before

TOP: Meyer Delicatessen, 4750 Herman Kranz Way. HEATHER OLKER • **MIDDLE:** Descartes Coffee, 4771 N. Lincoln Ave. HEATHER OLKER • **BOTTOM:** Posters, Melrose Ave. & Lincoln Ave. HEATHER OLKER

the ban in Chicago and proudly fries food in trans-fat free oil. Before you mistake this place with Whole Foods, though, note that Rockwell's often has some kind of drink special. **B+**

42 Degrees N. Latitude

This casual, friendly restaurant is a great place to come with friends. The drink specials, great food [entrees will set you back between $8 and $15] and relaxed atmosphere make hanging out at this bar/restaurant a fun experience. TVs broadcast games, but Latitude is cleaner and less rowdy than a smoky sports bar. **B+**

4500 N Lincoln Ave
773.907.2226
BROWN LINE to WESTERN

Bad Dog Tavern

Compared to some restaurants that have been in the area for decades, Bad Dog is the new kid in town and trying hard to stand out. The delicious blackened tuna with wasabi or any of the killer appetizers should certainly help it do so. But just to be safe, Bad Dog entices customers with half-priced, late night meals and a menu that changes seasonally – making it perfect for any time of day, or year. **A-**

4535 N Lincoln Ave
773.334.4040
BROWN LINE to WESTERN

Barba Yianni Grecian Taverna

The stone walkway and street lanterns make you feel like you're in Greece.

4761 N Lincoln Ave
773.878.6400
BROWN LINE to WESTERN

VINTAGE ON A BUDGET
BY RYAN KING

Unzipped visited five vintage stores within walking distance of the Belmont stop on the Red Line of the 'El' and assembled a complete outfit at each for trendy shoppers on a budget.
Brown Elephant, 3651 N. Halsted St., 773.549.5943 • Complete Outfit: $27. Shirt: Givenchy Paris, $5. Pants: Gap, $6. Shoes: J Crew, $5.

Brown Elephant, 3651 N. Halsted St.

Hat: Adam, $7. Belt: $3. Book: $1.
Brown Elephant is a staple in the Chicago thrift-store scene, and its proceeds benefit Howard Brown, which provides health services to those in need. With four locations throughout the city, each with its own unique style, it's hard not to stop in and peruse their wide assortment of items. The location we visited – in Lakeview's Boystown community – is by far the cheapest and most crowded of the stores to make our list. This particular Brown Elephant is not really so much a vintage store as a thrift store, but we love it all the same. Packed inside of a huge warehouse, this location is more or less run like an enormous garage sale with books, house-goods, and practically anything else you can imagine. On the downside, however, there are only three crowded fitting rooms that you have to fight over and they only have a small curtain to cover each room, making changing a bit awkward. Clothing donations are accepted and students receive 10 percent off with identification. You can find other Brown Elephants in the Andersonville, Wicker Park, and Oak Park neighborhoods.

Just in case the stucco walls didn't take you all the way though, the food will certainly make you feel like it. The incredibly friendly staff will make you feel at home in this casual restaurant that serves everything from saganaki to kabobs. Fairly large portions of this traditional Greek cuisine run around $10-$15. By the end of the meal, you'll be yelling 'Opa.' **A**

Bistro Champagne

This Zagat-rated French bistro offers an eclectic menu, from French classics to Asian fusion cuisine. Standouts include traditional favorites like onion soup and steak frites and the more adventurous ahi tuna and yel-

4518 N Lincoln Ave
773.271.6100
BROWN LINE to WESTERN

lowtail sashimi with grapefruit. The rustic eatery is a fine date location, with entrée prices running in the $20s. **A**

Bourbon Café

Bourbon Café is sort of this weird bar, café, restaurant hybrid, but it works. Enjoy a $3 omelet any time of day or a plate full of its delicious french fries. Live music can be heard on weekends – well, a synthesizer can be heard on weekends – and on occasional nights during the week. The crowd here is mostly local, so don't be surprised if you get a few stares when you walk in the door. **B**

4768 N Lincoln Ave
773.769.3543
BROWN LINE to WESTERN

Land of The Lost, 614 W. Belmont Ave., 773.529.4966 • Complete Outfit: $95. Sweater: $25. Pants: $20. Glasses: $10. Boots: Wrangler, $40.

Whereas you have to spend all day wading through tons of crap at the Brown Elephant to find a few gems, you have to spend all day at the Land of The Lost narrowing down your choices among all the amazing stuff you'll find there. This shop is the most vintage of the five we visited. Land of The Lost is a little on the pricey side, but has some pretty rare and

one-of-a-kind items to justify it. Vintage board games and Cubs merchandise can be found throughout the store, as can a rather extensive vinyl collection in the back corner. Also, if you are in need of cowboy boots, they have a massive collection. The fitting room is spacious – but there is only one.

Hollywood Mirror, 812 W. Belmont Ave., 773.404.2044 • Complete Outfit: $39. Dress: S.C. Vizcarra, $20. Scarf/Headband: $4. Shoes: J. Renee, $15.

ABOVE: Hollywood Mirror, 812 W. Belmont Ave. • **LEFT:** Land of The Lost, 614 W. Belmont Ave.

RIGHT: Kitsch'n Retro Lounge, 2005 W. Roscoe St. HEATHER OLKER • **BELOW:** Chicago Photography Center, 3301 N. Lincoln Ave. HEATHER OLKER

Brioso

'Modern Mexican' is the name of the game at this sleek Lincoln Square taqueria. Updated Tex-Mex specialties range from pan-seared steak to enchiladas, but newcomers should dive into Brioso's modern take on the taco. With offerings from shrimp with mango to vegetarian-friendly butternut squash, these tacos are a great deal for any adventure-loving foodie. The price is even better: get three very original tacos for just under $12. **A**

4605 N Lincoln Ave
773.989.9000
BROWN LINE to WESTERN

Hollywood Mirror is a fun little place reminiscent of an indie version of Spencer's Gifts. They sell all kinds of toys, gag gifts, costumes, and, of course, clothes. The guys' selection is better than the gals', but both have fun options to choose from. They have three spacious fitting rooms [with doors] that are brightly colored. This store is full of character, including sassy signing informing you to pick up after yourself and put your clothes back [your mother doesn't live there]. You can also purchase their items online.

Clothes Optional, 2918 N. Clark St., 773.296.6630 • Complete Outfit: $83. Dress: Made by Kate, $45. Red Handbag: $12. Shoes: Joseph, $26.

An all-time favorite, Clothes Optional is a super-cute store with a spunky staff. They have tons of vintage pieces that are nicely organized and reasonably priced. There is a local designers rack including several 'Made by Kate' originals, that are perfect for an original gift. She brings in 10-15 new pieces every week, so there's always a fresh supply. The store itself is a work of art, with a quirky owl collection in one corner and local art works displayed and available for sale throughout, or in the case of the

Clothes Optional, 2918 N. Clark St.

Chicago Brauhaus

This large German-American eatery is located in the heart of Lincoln Square, surrounded by blocks of little coffee shops and antique stores. Servers in traditional dress serve hearty schnitzel and soups year-round. The festival atmosphere and massive tables are great for large groups. Expect live music and dancing every night of the week. **A**

4732 N Lincoln Ave
773.784.4444
BROWN LINE to WESTERN

Costello Sandwich & Sides

Costello's colorful red, green and yellow awning proclaims it has the 'best baked sandwich in Chicago.' With a casual food court vibe, this sandwich shop is a laid-back stop for a quick, cheap eat. And the sandwiches? Customers can build subs themselves with very few limitations. Costello also offers a great

4647 N Lincoln Ave
773.989.7788
BROWN LINE to WESTERN

coffee deal – a cup for a buck for eating in or to go. **B**

Fiddlehead Café

This fairly casual restaurant offers a variety of contemporary American cuisine with some foreign flair thrown in. With over 350 bottles to choose from, Fiddlehead clearly focuses mainly on wine. The menu features symbols that describe the wine, so part of your time is spent deciphering the wine key. Once you figure out your wine of choice, pair it with a cheese – there are over 20 to choose from. **B**

4600 N Lincoln Ave
773.751.1500
BROWN LINE to WESTERN

Pizza D.O.C.

Meals start out with warm, fresh bread and olive oil and only get better from there. Though the restaurant serves

2251 W Lawrence Ave
773.784.8777
BROWN LINE to WESTERN

---

piece title 'His Suitcase,' available by trade only for a station wagon or van. They have art shows once every two months. Plus, for your non-clothing needs, you can find artfully decorated luggage and retro housewares. Don't pass this one up.

Yellow Jacket, 2959 N. Lincoln Ave., 773.248.1996 • Complete Outfit: $94. Jean Vest: Big Smith, $19. Shoes: Linds Bowling, $22. Jeans: Levi's, $22. Aviator Glasses: $11. Chicago T-shirt: $20.

Finally we get to Yellow Jacket, the most expensive, but most upscale vintage shop with a very 'boutique-y' feel. Friendly staff help you find that perfect piece, although as nicely organized as they have things, not much help is needed. This is one of the few vintage shops that actually have all their clothes sorted by size, saving you lots of time and disappointment when you find that one great item that is two sizes too small. They have

lots of fun accessories and four comfy fitting rooms to try them on. This store has been open since 2003, after several years of success for its sister store in Milwaukee.

Yellow Jacket, 2959 N. Lincoln Ave.

Bell Rd. HEATHER OLKER

Tank

Lincoln Square's sleek sushi bar ranks high both in style and flavor. Tank's

4514 N Lincoln Ave
773.769.2600
BROWN LINE to WESTERN

menu includes raw food and cooked offerings for the slightly less adventurous diner. The restaurant's blue and stainless steel interior evokes a modern, youthful mood. Try any combination of Tank's specialty maki rolls for a memorable dining experience. **A**

The Cheese Stands Alone

This cheese shop carries a variety of cheeses from around the world. In ad-

4547 N Western Ave
773.293.3870
BROWN LINE to WESTERN

dition to cheese from France, Holland, England, Spain, Australia and several other countries, the store sells an array of crackers, spreads, sauces and pasta. The store might be a bit pricy for college students, but for a special, slightly elegant party, definitely stop by and pick something up. The smells are a bit strong, but only a small price to pay for the tasty samples. **A-**

The Grind Café

Serving delicious breakfast sandwiches with even tastier coffee, The Grind

4613 N Lincoln Ave
773.271.4482
BROWN LINE to WESTERN

a variety of Italian dishes, the pizza is the main event. With 15 thin crust pizzas to choose from, there is something for everyone. Portions are large – individual pizzas are 12 inches – so don't be stingy if you come with friends. The well-stocked bar provides plenty of wine and beer options to wash down your dinner. **A-**

Café proves to be a great place for breakfast. What are even better are the café's great veggie-friendly dishes that make an excellent light lunch or snack. The hipster staff looks like a pretentiously cool bunch, but are actually some of the nicest and friendliest people to talk to. Bring your

Essence of India

4601 N. Lincoln Ave.
773.506.0002
BROWN LINE to WESTERN

Essence of India may be a small restaurant seating only 14, but its stellar food keeps it packed. A great lunch buffet deal is available on weekends. On weekdays, anything out of the clay and charcoal oven is a standout on the regular menu. Newcomers should try the tandoori chicken for a spicy, melt-in-your-mouth meal. This small Indian eatery offers vegetarian and meat options as well as a delectable selection of soft, fluffy Naan bread. Its menu announces a 'culinary and cultural passage to India,' and, from the eccentric dining room décor to the mouth-watering menu, Essence of India does not disappoint.

Los Nopales Restaurant

4544 N. Western Ave.
773.334.3149
BROWN LINE to WESTERN

Los Nopales is one many Mexican restaurants in the city, but none have guacamole like this place. Guac aside, the food at this BYOB restaurant is fantastic and reasonably priced. Top notch dishes like the skirt steak or the chipotle chicken make this Lincoln Square establishment stand out above others in the area. Ask any customer or waiter here what to order and everyone will tell you something different – but everyone agrees that the guacamole is a must. With plenty of choices, all of which are delicious, Los Nopales pleases anyone in the mood for good, affordable Mexican food.

laptop and spend an afternoon relaxing or studying at this great alternative to Starbucks. **A-**

TO PLAY

House Theatre of Chicago

Producing heavily pop-culture inspired shows, House Theatre blends
4700 N Ravenswood Ave
773.769.3832
BROWN LINE to DAMEN

music, magic, dance and theater to put on innovative, creative shows. The shows at House Theatre are fun and contemporary and aim to break down the barriers between the audience and the actors to build a community with the audience. Entry to most shows costs less than $20, but Saturday night is usually a few dollars more. **A-**

David Theatre

This small theater is pretty old and run down, and not in an endearing kind
4614 N Lincoln Ave
773.784.0893
BROWN LINE to WESTERN

of way. The theaters are tiny, and you can often hear the movie playing next door – so if that doesn't bother you, you get to see two movies. The only good thing is that the Davis sometimes shows movies that aren't playing elsewhere, plus it's local instead of a large chain theater. **C-**

Lincoln Square Arts Center

From concerts to plays to staged readings, the Lincoln Square Arts Center
4754 N Leavitt St
773.275.7930
BROWN LINE to WESTERN

has a little bit of everything. Aiming to address social, political and spiritual issues through the fine arts, the Arts Center puts on many unique performances throughout the year. The Arts Center also offers workshops from memoir writing to stage combat. Nothing about this venue says ordinary – it's definitely a fun place to check out. **A**

TO SHOP

Griffins & Gargoyles Antiques

The two floors in this shop are full – but not cluttered – of antique
2140 W Lawrence Ave
773.769.1255
BROWN LINE to DAMEN

furniture imported from Europe. Tables, armoires, mirrors, trunks and dressers from the turn of the century – the 20th Century that is – hail from Germany, Scandinavia and all over the continent. This father-daughter-owned store has some great finds, many of which are reasonably priced. Everything is in great condition and definitely worth a look. **A-**

Lather Chicago

The stylists at this funky salon are super friendly and always have great
4831 N Damen Ave
773.878.5600
BROWN LINE to DAMEN

ideas about what to do with your hair. High quality, personal service and killer hair cuts keep customers coming back. Each customer seems to have a favorite stylist, so no matter who you see, someone has something positive to say about

RIGHT: Paulina 'El' Stop. HEATHER OLKER
• **BELOW:** Waterhouse, Roscoe Ave. HEATHER OLKER

him or her. Men's haircuts are pretty reasonably priced, but, like most salons, women's services can be a bit pricy. **B⁺**

Glass Art Designs

Glass Art Designs makes beautiful pieces that would complement any home. The gallery uses a unique combination of glass staining and glass fusing to create its colorful works. The pieces probably wouldn't go well in a college dorm, but you should still come and look around. If you're really intrigued, Glass Art Designs offers glass fusing classes of all levels where you can produce your own simple piece to take home. **A**

1807 W Sunnyside Ave
773.297.5975
BROWN LINE to MONTROSE

Hazel

Unassuming from the outside, this Ravenswood treasure is the perfect place for anyone looking to find that special gift for someone. The jewelry and accessories counter offers a selection of unique items with an array of designs and price ranges for all customers. Also, half the store is dedicated to custom greeting cards and stationary sets. **A**

1902 W Montrose Ave
773.769.2227
BROWN LINE to MONTROSE

Scents and Sensibility

Scents and Sensibility is a local shop located in an area that reminds me of a small town – very cute. The store sells freshly cut flowers, candles, soaps [things with nice scents, get it?], as well as cards and stationery. Stop in if you're in the neighborhood. The staff is friendly, and the store carries some cute stuff. **B**

4654 N Rockwell St
773.267.3838
BROWN LINE to MONTROSE

Chakra Shoppe

Need to recharge your physical batteries, or are you low on Aura spray? Then Chakra Shoppe is perfect for you. Specializing in the health and energy of your mind and body, Chakra Shoppe offers everything from body oils to free meditation once a month. Be sure to talk to Blanche, the incredibly friendly owner who truly believes in mind and body connection, when you stop in. **B⁺**

5034 N Lincoln Ave
773.271.3054
BROWN LINE to WESTERN

City Mouse

Even if you don't have kids, you can't help but notice the adorable clothing City Mouse sells. The store carries Small Paul [Paul Frank's baby line] and the animals are

4657 N Lincoln Ave
773.878.7400
BROWN LINE to WESTERN

incredibly cute. Trendy baby wear does come at a price, and the slightly high prices do not match the small sizes. **B+**

Eclecticity

Eclecticity is very appro-priately named. The store sells a mix of vintage

4718 N Lincoln Ave
773.275.3080
BROWN LINE to WESTERN

collectibles and new, contemporary stuff – and the most Danish mobiles I've ever seen in a store, or ever for that matter. The store also hosts free concerts and other artsy events. From vintage ads to decorate your place to sarongs made in Thailand, you'll find a little bit of everything at this [I had to say it] eclectic store. **A**

Enjoy, An Urban General Store

Enjoy is a great place to find unique or wacky gifts. The store sells everything

4727 N Lincoln Ave
773.334.8626
BROWN LINE to WESTERN

from hand bags to baby clothes, from office sup-plies to quirky gag gifts. Everything in the store is reasonably priced, so that silly mug you bought for mom as a joke won't set you back much. The staff is super friendly and gift wraps. **B**

Hanger 18

This super cute, trendy shop sells toys and clothes for kids, as well as

4726 N Lincoln Ave
773.275.3349
BROWN LINE to WESTERN

house ware, kitchen ware, cards and stationery, handbags and very funky jewelry for adults. From leather purses to The Clash onesies, everything in Hanger 18 is contemporary and cool. The only downside is that the boutique is a bit pricy – the

adorable baby rock attire costs $40-$50. If noth-ing else the store is fun to look around in. **B+**

International Fashions by Ingrid

This store specializes in women's clothing from around the world, but

4710 N Lincoln Ave
773.878.8382
BROWN LINE to WESTERN

mostly from Europe. The clothes range from contemporary sweaters to traditional dresses and loden overcoats. The store also sells belts and jewelry to complete any outfit purchased here. The styles are different than what is seen in most American stores and may not appeal to everyone, but it is still interesting to see styles from other countries, especially the traditional outfits. **B-**

Laurie's Planet of Sound

This hip little corner of Lincoln Square announces itself to passersby with

4639 N Lincoln Ave
773.271.3569
BROWN LINE to WESTERN

an eclectic selection of old books and movies and the strong perfume of an incense rack in the back corner. Laurie's sells new and used CDs and DVDs at extremely discounted prices – some CDs are 10 for $10. Though the selection is off-beat, true musical jewels are to be found among the used CD and vinyl racks. New indie releases are also easy finds. **A**

Rock N Roll Vintage

While Rock N Roll Vintage sounds like some overpriced boutique that

4740 N Lincoln Ave
773.878.8616
BROWN LINE to WESTERN

sells leather and ripped up jeans, it actually sells vintage guitars and amps, as well as some new

Bouffe

2312 W. Leland Ave.
773.784.2314
BROWN LINE to WESTERN

From Italian pumpkin pesto to Indian red lentils, this gourmet cheese and bread grocery store carries food from every corner of the earth. In addition to ceiling-high shelves full of international foods, Bouffe, which means 'grub' in French, carries a wide variety of fresh pastries and cheeses as well as cured meats, all of which customers are free to sample. The brownies are some of the best I've ever tasted. The food is a bit pricy, but since it's such great quality, it's worth every penny. The store also carries kitchenware so you can spice up the rest of your room and not just the refrigerator.

Merz Apothecary

4716 N. Lincoln Ave.
773.989.0900
BROWN LINE to WESTERN

Has the brutal Chicago winter left you with a sore throat? How about some licorice tea or horehound lozenges to sooth you? This natural health and beauty store offers everything from rose lip salve to grass scented dryer sheets. The old apothecary jars and vintage interior take you back to your grandparents' days, which reflects the age of the store. Merz is great to walk around in because you never know what you will find. Just be careful, because what starts as a quick stop in for an avocado face mask can turn into a huge shopping spree on bath and body products – everything is just so cool.

guitars and effect pedals. The friendly staff really knows guitars and is happy to help any future rock stars in the market for a new guitar save a few bucks by buying vintage. **B+**

String A Strand

4632 N Lincoln Ave
773.275.1233
BROWN LINE to WESTERN

Why go searching shop-to-shop for the right piece of jewelry when you can make it yourself? This quaint store has just the right amount of materials to get you started without overwhelming you with decisions. Tables of colorful beads and charms, complemented with a selection of wire and string you'll need to put it together, allow for all the freedom you need to personalize your accessories [or really impress your girlfriend]. **B+**

The Book Cellar, Inc.

4736 N Lincoln Ave
773.293.2665
BROWN LINE to WESTERN

This quirky neighborhood book store offers a fun alternative to giant book chains like Borders. The Book Cellar features a great mix of local and national writers and often brings in the local writers they carry for book signings. The friendly and very knowledgeable staff is extremely helpful. The store also features a café that serves a mean cup of coffee and food to munch on. **A-**

ABOVE: La Mora, 2132 W. Roscoe St.
HEATHER OLKER • **RIGHT:** Flyers, W. Roscoe St.
HEATHER OLKER

LINCOLN SQUARE

Intersection, Roscoe
St. & Damen Ave.
HEATHER OLKER

The Chopping Block

Future Food Network stars, this is the place for you. The Chopping Block sells kitchen tools and house wares, as well as gourmet, ethnic ingredients. The biggest seller at this store is cooking classes. From hands-on cooking classes to wine tutorials, you can learn to sip and sauté with the best of them. **B**

4747 N Lincoln Ave
773.472.6700
BROWN LINE to WESTERN

The Dressing Room

The clothes here are very cute and definitely unique, but apparently unique comes at a price. Shirts, one of the store's least expensive items, run in the $40 range. The Dressing room is perfect for when you want to splurge on something special, or if you don't mind dropping some serious cash on your clothes. There are seasonal sales, so you never know when that sweater you've been eyeing will fall into your price range. **B**

4635 N Lincoln Ave
773.728.0088
BROWN LINE to WESTERN

Tigerlilie Salon

This funky salon has a vintage look to it, but the staff is nothing but hip, fresh and modern. Customers rave about the colorists here. From bright orange highlights to just adding some punch to your natural color, the stylists can do it all. For a hot new hair cut or a wild new color, come to Tigerlilie for a funky new do. **A**

4755 N Lincoln Ave
773.506.7870
BROWN LINE to WESTERN

Timeless Toys, Ltd.

Walk around Timeless Toys and you'll smile and think, 'I had one of those.' This toy store sells a combination of classic and modern toys, including lesser-known games, coloring books and dress up supplies. The stuff sold here is pretty unique, and you probably couldn't find it at Target. Great for finding a gift for a kid or browsing around and reliving your childhood. **A-**

4749 N Lincoln Ave
773.334.4445
BROWN LINE to WESTERN

Traipse

This spacious boutique has a carefully chosen collection of designer shoes with a unique down-to-earth flair. It's the perfect place to find a great shoe for your night downtown that won't leave you bed-ridden the next day, so skip the mall and allow yourself individualized service and room to make your decision. But be warned, the limited collection could make your shopping here a hit-or-miss experience. **B**

4724 N Lincoln Ave
773.275.5511
BROWN LINE to WESTERN

KELLY'S PUB

Kelly's Pub [949 W. Webster Ave.] has been in business since 1933, opening one day after the National Prohibition Act was repealed. This family-owned tavern has been serving up beer in true Irish fashion ever since to sports fans leaving the nearby Wrigley Field and college students from DePaul. In the summer, enjoy your drink outside underneath the 'El' tracks in the beer garden, which was constructed in 1986 for the Demi Moore and Rob Lowe film 'About Last Night.'

Photograph by Lydia Merrill

NORTH

LAKEVIEW

THE ECLECTIC POPULATION PRESERVES A KICK

Whether its sports, shopping or entertainment, anything you want can be found in Lakeview, with a twist. For nightlife, few areas beat this neighborhood that offers some of the city's premier music venues and crowded bars and clubs. The daytime is pretty fun too. Though young professionals have moved in swarms, the eclectic population preserves a kick. In the north is Wrigleyville, home of the Chicago Cubs and countless sports bars and late night eateries. In the summer, it can get a little rowdy with drunk [and sometimes unhappy] Cubs fans trolling the streets. Great stores line Clark St. and Belmont Ave. but beware, these are not your Grandmother's clothing stores. Vintage and thrift shops are abundant and cater to the younger, punkier demographic of the city. Head shops, trendy accessory boutiques and even the occasional sex shop find their homes in the area too. Toward Lake Michigan is Boystown, the largest gay community in Chicago. A raving night life, especially dense with gay bars and Irish pubs, make this a nightlife destination. It's also host to Chicago's annual Gay Pride Parade as well as Halsted St. Market Days, a flamboyant local tradition.

TO EAT

Aladdin's Eatery

With its bold, striped walls that resemble alternating colors of hummus, the interior of this Middle Eastern restaurant is as pleasing to the eye as it's fare is to the stomach. Aladdin's Eatery is worth checking out because it offers healthy fare at cheap prices with tons of vegetarian options. **A**

614 W Diversey Pkwy
773.327.6300
BROWN LINE to DIVERSEY

Barberry Asian Kitchen

Not only does this Thai restaurant have a huge carryout business on the first floor, but it also has a large in-house dining room on the second floor with a laidback and comfortable feel. Come here to nosh on some relatively cheap traditional Thai food with friends and family or to bring some food back home. **A-**

2819 N Southport Ave
773.525.6695
BROWN LINE to DIVERSEY

Café Furaibo

This BYOB Japanese restaurant guarantees a night filled with delicious

2907 N Lincoln Ave
773.472.7017
BROWN LINE to DIVERSEY

food, fun music and pretty surroundings. With two floors of dining, loud music and a huge water fountain, this place can seem more like a club than a restaurant. If you want to drag out the evening, order the tempura fried ice cream for dessert. **A**

Fit 'n' Fresh Café

With seating available outdoors as well as inside, this little café is especially

565 W Diversey Pkwy
773.325.9664
BROWN LINE to DIVERSEY

popular during the warm summer months. Enjoy a delicious fruit smoothie or a made-to-order vegetable juice along with your salad or wrap. After such a healthy lunch, go ahead and splurge on one or more of their delicious desserts. **A**

Penny's Noodle Shop

There are plenty of bowls and plates of noodles on the menu at this Thai

950 W Diversey Pkwy
773.281.8448
BROWN LINE to DIVERSEY

restaurant. Make a dish extra spicy or sweet, depending on your sauce selection. Choose among meat, vegetable and spice options and you can easily customize your own unique noodle dining experience. Come for an early dinner on the weekends because this place fills up quickly. **B**

Satay

Satay's fun bright green and magenta color scheme complements

936 W Diversey Pkwy
773.477.0100
BROWN LINE to DIVERSEY

its eclectic pan-Asian menu. Be sure to try the pad Thai – the peanut sauce and heap-load of veggies make it a must-have. Also, check out the Thai red curry and chive dumplings. The cute little dig is located just a few feet from the Diversey 'El' Stop, making it highly accessible. **B⁺**

House of Sushi & Noodles

By far one of the best all-you-can-eat-sushi establishments in

1610 W Belmont Ave
773.935.9110
BROWN LINE to PAULINA

Chicago. For only about $10, you can eat all of your favorite rolls with very few restrictions. The food comes out fast and fresh. But picky eaters beware – you can't change to a different type of roll once you've ordered it. **A⁻**

Kite Mandarin & Sushi

Kite Mandarin and Sushi offers delicious Japanese and Chinese cuisine. The

3341 N Lincoln Ave
773.472.2100
BROWN LINE to PAULINA

modern and spacious beige and cherry wood interior is aesthetically pleasing, and diet-conscious diners will be satisfied with the low-carb options, such as the chicken lettuce wraps and the stir-fry vegetarian plate. The menu boasts over 30 maki rolls, including the classic Dragon, Rainbow, and Spider rolls. **A⁻**

ABOVE: New Modern Grill, Belmont Ave. & Clark St. DAN BRANCA • **LEFT:** Rare Books, Clark St. DAN BRANCA

RIGHT: The Alley, 3222 N. Clark St. DAN BRANCA • BELOW: Kurt Cobain Mural, Belmont Ave. DAN BRANCA

Coobah

Coobah is a great place for innovative foods combining culinary influences from Spain, Cuba, Mexico, Brazil and the Philippines. Here, you can dine on carefully-prepared steak, lamb or chicken for only $15-20. But vegetarians should stay away – there aren't too many non-meat options available in this original Lakeview eatery. **B+**

3423 N Southport Ave
773.528.2220
BROWN LINE to SOUTHPORT

Ethel's Chocolate Lounge

Eating should be fun. With its colorful and delicious variation of chocolate treats, Ethel's makes it nearly impossible not to enjoy what you're noshing on. The Ethel's experi-

3404 N Southport Ave
773.525.1568
BROWN LINE to SOUTHPORT

ence starts with a plush couch in the cozy lounge atmosphere. Spoil yourself with either chocolate or caramel fondue, served with assorted fruit, graham crackers and marshmallows. Be sure not to stab your friends with the fondue stick when everyone is fighting for the last dip. **A**

Andalous

This small Moroccan restaurant is ideal for a romantic, cozy dinner date. But make sure you really have feelings for the person you bring along – dinner for two averages around $50. However, the service and food are both wonderful, creating a very pleasant dining experience and validating the monetary splurge. **B+**

3307 N Clark St
773.281.6885
RED LINE to ADDISON

Chen's

3506 N. Clark St.
773.549.9100
RED LINE to ADDISON

This restaurant's bay windows that open up onto Clark St. let the wafting food smells escape the intimate interior and lure in diners from outside. Serving a wide selection of authentic cuisine, ranging from lemon chicken and crispy duck to lo mein and udon, Chen's has what it takes to please almost anyone looking to satisfy an East Asian food craving. The multitude of sushi options offers added variety. The menu here is very vegetarian-friendly and the atmosphere is delightful. With plush inner booths for a bit more privacy and large storefront windows, Chen's makes for a pleasing dining experience.

Bar Louie Wrigley

Located just two blocks from their stadium, Bar Louie attracts numerous

3545 N Clark St
773.296.2500
RED LINE to ADDISON

Cubs fans during the season with its intimate, neighborhood feel. Black-and-white photographs of local Chicagoans line the walls while a huge mural of Wrigley Field hangs directly in front of the bar. The food is reasonably priced and has a Cajun flare. **B**

Cozy Noodles and Rice

Cozy Noodles and Rice offers an extensive selection of Thai cuisine including

3465 N Sheffield Ave
773.327.0100
RED LINE to ADDISON

noodles, curry dishes and delicious baby egg rolls with pineapple in them. Eat at Cozy for lunch and enjoy an entrée and a choice of spring rolls or cucumber salad, all for under $6. The walls of this restaurant are unusually and whimsically-decorated with shelves of small toys and trinkets. Adults can BYOB, and parking is available. **A-**

El Jardin Café

This diner serves affordable, authentic Mexican and Tex-Mex

3401 N Clark St
773.935.8133
RED LINE to ADDISON

food in a casual environment. Watch the cooks prepare your food in the open kitchen from your seats. Favorites include burritos, fajitas and the especially-strong margaritas. Chefs are flexible with how they prepare the food and will readily accommodate customers' needs. **B+**

Fernando's

This brightly-colored Mexican restaurant, with its distinctive green

3450 N Lincoln Ave
773.477.6930
RED LINE to ADDISON

awning, stands out due to both its appearance and its great food, not to mention its long lines. The homemade salsa, mole sauce, and rack of ribs are favorites, coming in second only to the tequila bar. The restaurant is known among regulars for its strong drinks and back patio which offers a great environment for kicking back and sipping fruity concoctions. **B+**

Jai Yen

This restaurant offers a variety of Asian menu items, from its famous pad

3736 N Broadway St
773.404.0555
RED LINE to ADDISON

Thai served over an omelet to traditional appetizers like seaweed salad and boiled spinach, with an emphasis on sushi. Following a low-carb diet? Try the Jai Yen Signature Roll, which replaces the outer layer of rice with a thin cucumber slice. The atmosphere here is nothing special, but there's a party room and sushi bar in the back. **B+**

TOP: Belmont Ave. DAN BRANCA • **MIDDLE:** Lakeview. LYDIA MERRILL • **BOTTOM:** Clark St. DAN BRANCA

RIGHT: Lakeview. LYDIA MERRILL • **BELOW:** Lakeview. LYDIA MERRILL

Lucky's Sandwich Company

If you're looking to avoid pricey dishes in the stands of Wrigley Field, this cozy diner is the perfect place for a pre-game dinner or post-game snack. Lucky's offers $5 meaty sandwiches on plates overflowing with French fries. Not headed to the field? Take in the action on one of the three big-screen TVs showing round-the-clock ESPN. **A-**

3472 N Clark St
773.549.0665
RED LINE to ADDISON

Matsuya Restaurant

This Japanese restaurant offers many teriyaki dishes, but also has a sushi bar and a number of vegetarian items on the menu. The sushi is reasonably-priced and there are inexpensive dinner combos, which include sushi or sashimi, a salad, Miso soup, teriyaki chicken or grilled fish, and ice cream. It may be best to use the 'El' for transportation, as parking can be hard to find. **A**

3469 N Clark St
773.248.2677
RED LINE to ADDISON

Pick Me Up

This fun, casual café located in Wrigleyville has long, brightly colored booths and is perfect for students looking for a place to study or locals looking for reason-ably-priced fare. The menu features a range of salads, soups, omelets, and sandwiches with

3408 N Clark St
773.248.6613
RED LINE to ADDISON

a wide variety of vegetarian and vegan options available. **A-**

Raw Bar & Grill

Raw Bar & Grill is an American seafood restau-rant that has an exotic, market-priced menu of fresh fish and adventurous dishes, including alligator. Dine at Raw Bar on the weekends when jazz artists perform in the adjacent lounge, giving the restaurant a romantic atmosphere. Dinner entrees run up to around $20. **A-**

3720 N Clark St
773.348.7291
RED LINE to ADDISON

Red Ivy

This upscale sports lounge is known for its sporty yet chic ambience. The restaurant features four 128-inch high-definition televisions and a 50-foot bar that curves around one side of the restaurant. The extensive menu of authentic Italian food features pizza as the signature dish. When sports games end around 10:00 p.m., the place transforms into a nightclub. With a live DJ and fun themes like Retro Night on Thursdays, it's no wonder this place is usually packed. **B**

3525 N Clark St
773.472.0900
RED LINE to ADDISON

Salt N' Pepper Diner

Come to this diner to get an all-American meal and top it all off with some

3537 N Clark St
773.883.9800
RED LINE to ADDISON

La Creperie

2845 N. Clark St.
773.528.9050
RED LINE to BELMONT

La Creperie, a historic neighborhood hotspot, has been serving some of the best crepes in Chicago since the 1970s. Many of their crepes, like their flavorful mushroom and chicken creation, are as filling as a standard meal. Their dessert crepes, filled with different varieties of fruit and covered in dollops of whipped cream, are a delectable treat for anyone with a sweet tooth. If you're a chocolate lover, try the Nutella creation. Not hungry? Come here simply for the unmatched French coffee. The reasonable prices, quaint atmosphere and friendly service make La Creperie a treat for both you and your tastebuds.

delicious apple pie. Specializing in chicken pot pie, burgers and meatloaf, this diner also offers low-fat options like veggie burgers, salads and skinless chicken breasts. Don't forget to put a few coins in the jukebox and live out the good old days of rock n' roll. **B+**

Tryst

3485 N Clark St
773.755.3890
RED LINE to ADDISON

This trendy lounge stands out among others lining the street because it's far more upscale and caters to an older, more sophisticated crowd. The brick walls and large mirrors give the restaurant a modern, hip feel, and its small entrees are perfect for sharing. Try the Southern-style shrimp and delicious slider sandwiches with one of the many alcoholic beverages they offer. **A-**

Vines on Clark

3554 N Clark St
773.327.8572
RED LINE to ADDISON

Want to dine in style? This classy Italian restaurant is moderately priced [entrees begin at $10 and libations around $8] and offers great views of the city on the rooftop patio. Enjoy your meal in their classy dining room or at a rooftop table for an intimate atmosphere on a sunny day. Combine all this with their flat-screen TVs, and you get a recipe for relaxation. **A-**

Adesso

3332 N Broadway St
773.868.1516
RED LINE to BELMONT

Make sure to save room for dessert at Adesso – the Limoncello gelato, which tastes like lemon meringue pie without the crust, melts deliciously in your mouth. Stop by this South Beach-style quaint café, complete

Clark St. Dog, 3040 N. Clark St. DANIEL HONIGMAN

Lakeview. LYDIA MERRILL

with steel furniture and Art Deco interior, for a weekend brunch of caramel apple pancakes. Don't miss their unforgettable rosemary sea salt fries with basil aioli. **A**

Azha

This Thai restaurant is a college student's dream, as it is both BYOB and has a full takeout menu. Though the atmosphere misses the mark – it's dark and creepy rather than the intended dim and sensual – the quality of the food and low prices make up for it. Though this isn't a romantic date spot, it's a good place to go for some cheap authentic Thai food. **B**

960 W Belmont Ave
773.525.0555
RED LINE to BELMONT

Bamboo Garden

The menu at Bamboo Garden is the same as any other run-of-the-mill Chinese restaurant's. The décor is nothing

3203 N Clark St
773.525.7600
RED LINE to BELMONT

extraordinary, nor is the food. You can BYOB, but the atmosphere is not lively and exciting, so unless you plan to create your own party, do not come here expecting anything lively. Despite this, their Egg Foo Young is surprisingly delicious, as is the Mongolian beef. Friendly, quick service and reasonably-priced dishes. **B⁻**

Bittersweet

Your sweet tooth will be satisfied after eating at this little pastry shop. The desserts, which include pies, tarts, cakes, brownies, cookies and more, are both visually pleasing and appetizing. Eat in the actual shop or pick up a treat to bring home. You can also grab lunch from the limited menu of sandwiches, salads, soups and other café basics. **A**

1114 W Belmont Ave
773.929.1100
RED LINE to BELMONT

Calliope Café

This bright and colorful Lakeview café offers foods with a unique flair. If you're seeking a dining experience far from ordinary, this place will satisfy your desire. The café serves strange food concoctions like salmon with orange marmalade and whips up hilariously-named foods like the 'Fat Bastard' steak sandwich. **A**

2826 N Lincoln Ave
773.528.8055
RED LINE to BELMONT

Cesar's Restaurant

Downing at least one margarita is a must at this Mexican restaurant. Drink at the bar with some chips and salsa or sit down at a table for a full meal. Much of the food on the menu is traditional Mexican, but if that's not your thing there are also Tex-Mex options available. **B⁺**

3166 N Clark St
773.248.2835
RED LINE to BELMONT

Chicago Nut Co.

This candy shop offers every kind of nut you could think of, prepared in various ways – roasted, salted and chocolate-covered, among others. They also sell many other confections like chocolate toffee, licorice

843 W Belmont Ave
773.871.4994
RED LINE to BELMONT

and gummy candies. This wholesaler even sells items by the pound, making them perfect for gift baskets or large occasions. **B**

Duck Walk

This small neighborhood Thai restaurant was featured in Chicago

919 W Belmont Ave
773.665.0455
RED LINE to BELMONT

Magazine's 2004 'Best of Chicago' issue but it hasn't retained that title over the years. The BYOB restaurant offers a simple, low-key atmosphere with tables focused around groups of two and a menu with traditional entrees, noodles and curries all at reasonable prices. **B**

Eat-A-Pita

Make fast food healthy at this joint. Select meats and vegetables to wrap

3155 N Halsted St
773.929.6727
RED LINE to BELMONT

in a pita and you'll have a quick, cheap and easy meal that isn't bad for you. Though hot dogs and burgers are also available and can be quite enticing, try to stick to the custom pitas. **B**

Fiorentino's Cucina Italiana

Fiorentino's Cucina Italiana has large front windows and understated

2901 N Ashland Ave
773.244.3026
RED LINE to BELMONT

beige and burnt red walls. It also features an outdoor patio for warm weather. Highlights of the menu include chicken vesuvio and eggplant parmesan. But the most delectable dish is their stuffed gnocchi – a lighter, fluffier version of the traditional dish. The portions are quite large, so come hungry or share a platter with friends. **B+**

Firefly

This small French bistro has red walls, black lacquered tables and

3335 N Halsted St
773.525.2505
RED LINE to BELMONT

intimate booths, but is a little too small for comfort and has limited seating. Though the menu has a French flair, it also features comfort food. Highlights include chicken crepes, charcuterie and cheese and the steak-frite. However, this restaurant is not recommended for college students as the staff is standoffish to those under 21. **B**

Golden Apple

This restaurant can fix any food craving at any time of the day or night.

2971 N Lincoln Ave
773.528.1413
RED LINE to BELMONT

Open 24 hours, seven days a week, Golden Apple has a menu so extensive that it's overwhelming. Breakfast fare is always offered – fitting, since omelets and pancakes are their specialties. The wait for seating can take some time so plan accordingly. **A-**

TOP: Lakeview. LYDIA MERRILL • **MIDDLE:** Lakeview. LYDIA MERRILL • **BOTTOM:** Lakeview. LYDIA MERRILL

LAKEVIEW

Pizza Capri

962 W. Belmont Ave.
773.296.6000
RED LINE to BELMONT

▌This casual eatery, which claims to 'transport you to a simpler time and place where the sun is always shining and the plate is always full,' was rated one of the top two pizzerias in the city by the Chicago Tribune and has been serving residents since 1987. What makes their pizza unique is the abundance of fresh ingredients they pile on. Some of their more creative creations are the 'Thai Pie Chicken' – a pizza dressed with spicy peanut ginger and sesame sauce, mozzarella, a variety of vegetables and roasted peanuts – and their 'Zorba the Greek' – topped with pesto, tomatoes, roasted red peppers, goat cheese, kalamata olives and basil. Salads, pasta, sandwiches and wraps are also offered, along with their award-winning desserts. Carrying out and dining in are both available options, and be aware: The friendly atmosphere, though pleasant, can hardly be equated to a romantic or warm ambiance.

Modern Grill

3171 N Halsted St
773.528.0705
RED LINE to BELMONT

Contrary to its name, there is definitely nothing modern about this grill: This old-school diner is outdated and lacks ambiance. Definitely think twice about eating here, despite the cheap prices of its generic breakfast items and sandwiches. The crowd also tends to be a bit sketchy, making it a far cry from a hot destination spot. **C−**

My Place for Tea

3210 N Sheffield Ave
773.525.8320
RED LINE to BELMONT

At first glance, this tea shop may seem a little homely, but once you're inside and settled its sterility becomes obvious. The bubble tea is just as deceiving, as it is definitely not made from real fruit. Yet the countless variety of tea flavors makes this place worth checking out – as long as you stay away from their 'boba.' **B−**

P.S. Bangkok

3345 N Clark St
773.871.9997
RED LINE to BELMONT

P.S. Bangkok is a traditional Thai restaurant furnished with ornate décor and extravagant art. The handmade menus include innovative dishes like Banana Blossom Salad and Sweet Corn Cake. The daintiness of this place is not for steak-and-potatoes fans, but if you're in the mood for something exotic and adventurous, you'll be impressed by the delicious food and the cheap prices. **B+**

Que Rico!

2814 N Southport Ave
773.975.7436
RED LINE to BELMONT

This brilliantly-decorated Mexican eatery cannot brag about its service, but it can take pride in its delicious edible offerings – all authentic, savory Mexican favorites. A

Lakeview. LYDIA MERRILL

LAKEVIEW

LEFT: Lakeview. LYDIA MERRILL • **BELOW:** Lakeview. LYDIA MERRILL

good atmosphere for a rowdy bunch of college students, come here to eat [enchiladas, onion-loaded guacamole], drink [frozen margaritas] and be merry [listen to the authentic Mexican music and samba]. If you come during nice weather, request a seat on the outdoor patio. **B**

Sinbad's

This 'delicious Mediterranean' restaurant and juice bar offers a wide

921 W Belmont Ave
773.477.6020
RED LINE to BELMONT

array of inexpensive fare. Whether you're looking for a good falafel or kabob, order at the counter and take a seat at this little restaurant. The décor is fairly traditional of a standard deli or fast food restaurant, though the Samurai swords on the walls provide a quirky, albeit misguided attempt, at reminding you of the restaurant's theme. **B**

The Great American Bagel

New York delis may find some competition from this Chicago joint.

1248 W Belmont Ave
773.325.0606
RED LINE to BELMONT

Choose from 28 different varieties of bagels and 18 unique kinds of cream cheese for the perfect breakfast, or try one of the many sandwiches available. If you're in the mood to sit down, this eatery offers a large, comfortable dining area. **A**

Tradicion

This hole-in-the-wall venue is located right by the Belmont 'L' stop and

958 W Belmont Ave
773.388.1574
RED LINE to BELMONT

offers a short list of traditional Mexican items such as tortas, tacos, burritos and chimichangas. This quick, cheap stop is open until 4 a.m. on most days, serving as the perfect remedy for a fit of drunken munchies. **C**

Wakamono

If you like the funky atmosphere and eclectic menu options available at

3317 N Broadway St
773.296.6800
RED LINE to BELMONT

the nearby Ping-Pong, you'll love the fine sushi selection at Wakamono, owned by the same person. The Dragon and Godzilla rolls are both works of art, and the quality and freshness of the fish are unbelievable. Boasting great ambiance, affordable food, friendly service, hip atmosphere, BYOB and a live DJ, Wakomono is a sushi lover's heaven. **A-**

Yen's

If you're craving a vast selection of Chinese food, Yen's is the perfect place

2856 N Clark St
773.549.0707
RED LINE to BELMONT

to go to satisfy your desires. Seafood, noodles,

beef, pork and a variety of vegetarian dishes are all available here. Take-out is strongly recommended on busier nights like weekends since the seating room is very small. **B**

Yoshi's Café

What do you get when you fuse Japanese, Italian, French and American cuisines? Entrées like barracuda and roasted pumpkin. At Yoshi's, you can enjoy the most eclectic, elegant dishes without having to dress to the nines. For 25 years, owners Yoshi and Nobuko Katsumura have put a delectable, slightly pricey spin on traditional dishes while providing a comfortable dining atmosphere. You can't go wrong with the 10-ounce Wagyu beef burger served with tomato, mizuna and brie cheese on homemade brioche. **B**

3257 N Halsted St
773.248.6160
RED LINE to BELMONT

Zad

Nothing special aesthetically, Zad's offers delectable Middle Eastern fare.
As the name implies [zad means 'food' in Arabic], Zad is serious about food. The sampler plate allows you to try a wide variety of traditional favorites, and the shawarma and falafel mimic the taste of authentic cuisine from the Middle East. The delicious dishes, authentic sounds and eye-catching décor guarantee a real bang for your buck at this Lakeview gem. **B+**

3112 N Broadway St
773.404.3473
RED LINE to BELMONT

Fly Me To The Moon

This corner restaurant is the definition of relaxation and intimacy. Italian dishes like farfalle al pollo, fettuccini alfredo and filet mignon are accented with nightly performances from musicians. Tables are moved at night to create a dance floor where patrons can sway to Sinatra's 'Fly Me to the Moon', or watch

3400 N Clark St
773.528.4033
RED LINE to BELMONT

Cherry Red

2833 N. Sheffield Ave.
773.477.3661
BROWN LINE to DIVERSEY

Head over to Cherry Red, this dance club in Lakeview if you're looking to paint the town red. Everything that you will see on the inside, from the lights to the walls, is awash in the color and after dancing to the music – which is usually house and hip-hop – blaring through the speakers, you'll be flushed as well. The club can fill almost 600 people and, as such, the dance floor is enormous. There are also plenty of couches and banquettes if you're in the mood to just lounge about and a private party room in the back.

from their seats while enjoying a cocktail. This is a great place for a first date or cozy night out. **B+**

Uncommon Ground

Uncommon Ground gives off a cozy and natural vibe with its fireplaces, leather

3800 N Clark St
773.929.3680
RED LINE to SHERIDAN

couches and windowsill pillow seats. Modern paintings adorn the brown and brick walls. The clientele served in this café ranges from college students to those in their mid-30s. Come here for their creative hot drinks that come in small bowls and yummy food selections. The service is friendly and fast. Uncommon Ground even features live music on most nights of the week. **A**

Chicago's Pizza

Chicago's Pizza is perhaps the only venue of its kind that serves the exquisite

3006 N Sheffield Ave
773.755.4030
RED LINE to WASHINGTON

queso de cabra pizza [warm goat cheese served with tomato sauce and toasted bread]. For those seeking authentic, piping-hot pies, Chicago's boasts a selection of gourmet pizza, thin crust pizza, and of course, the traditional stuffed pizza until 5 a.m. daily. It's also the perfect place to end a night of barhopping. **A–**

TO PLAY

Olé Lounge

When owner Gino opened Olé, he said he wanted to add some European flair

2812 N Lincoln Ave
773.388.3500
BROWN LINE to DIVERSEY

to Chicago nightlife. Housed in an old church, with its talented DJ, delicious mojitos and beautiful people, Olé Lounge makes clubbers feel as if they were in a club on the Mediterranean coast. The extensive tapas menu adds to the urbane feeling. Try the Solmillo al Cabrales [grilled beef tenderloin] and, if you're feeling brave, the tiny purple octopus perched atop the scrumptious seafood salad. **A–**

The Long Room

This tavern really does live up to its name – the room is noticeably long. With

1612 W Irving Park Rd
773.665.4500
BROWN LINE to IRVING PARK

a vast amount of seating at the bar as well as booths in the back, young adults can come here to get a casual drink with friends and enjoy frequent live musical performances. But even with the vast space, this place can get crowded. **A–**

404 Wine Bar

With three fireplaces – two on the inside and one on the patio – this bar

2852 N Southport Ave
773.404.5886
BROWN LINE to WELLINGTON

is cozy and relaxing. Soft leather sofas surround the fireplaces inside and bartenders are cheerful and welcoming. The wine itself, whether in bottle or glass comes from all over the world, though the bar grub is just simple American fare. **A**

Lakeview. LYDIA MERRILL

AK Salon

This small salon offers all the basics in hair care, nail care, waxing and

3452 N Clark St
773.248.7004
RED LINE to ADDISON

massages at reasonable prices. However, the staff is unfriendly and might not even acknowledge you when you walk in, so don't go here unless you already know a stylist. The average prices are worth neither the bland interior nor the uninviting employees. **C**

Bar Celona

Even if Bar Celona's shabby exterior seems off-putting, the lively

3474 N Clark St
773.244.8000
RED LINE to ADDISON

atmosphere and Spanish flair inside are not to be missed. This tapas-style restaurant offers unique food choices such as chipotle and orange barbeque fajitas and Sangria chicken, while still serving burgers for those craving standard bar grub. Parties are also very affordable here if you're looking to entertain: Three-hour open bar runs for only $25 and there are different drink specials each night. **A-**

Belly's

Craving more than your typical ratty, beer-drenched sports bar? Try

3210 N Lincoln Ave
773.525.3632
RED LINE to ADDISON

Belly's for a more upscale alternative. This venue offers large plasma screen TVs, a great beer selection, a menu that includes paninis, Pottery Barn-esque furniture, and live DJs, which all add to a more sophisticated feel. A great place to watch the game without having to worry about getting beer spilled all over you. **A-**

Bernie's

If you like baseball, you'll love Bernie's. This bar attracts rowdy sports fans

3664 N Clark St
773.525.1898
RED LINE to ADDISON

and many regulars who've probably attended every Cubs game in Wrigleyville. Though the bar is primarily dominated by males, girls can kick back and relax on the outdoor patio on a nice day. The food is typical ball game fare of hot dogs and burgers, and be prepared for long lines on game days. **B**

Exedus II

Deviate from your usual activities and check out Exedus II, a reggae

3477 N Clark St
773.348.3998
RED LINE to ADDISON

hotspot in Chicago. A block south of Wrigley Field, this dance club/bar has live reggae music four nights a week and a cover charge of only $5 Sunday through Friday [except Tuesdays, when it's closed]. Favorites include $3 Jamaican Rum Punch and $3 Red Stripe Wednesdays. Note: There is no cover charge after Cubs games. **A**

Gingerman Tavern

The Gingerman Tavern, one of the only bars close to Wrigley Field that isn't

3740 N Clark St
773.549.2050
RED LINE to ADDISON

a sports bar, has a hip atmosphere with a jukebox that plays a range of rock music. There's also a pinball machine. The restaurant serves 15 beers on tap and many bottled beers, but no food. **B**

Gordon in Lakeview Salon and Spa

Pottery and wooden sculptures ornamenting the walls give this small

3336 N Clark St
773.388.9999
RED LINE to ADDISON

salon an earthy feel. Gordon in Lakeview Salon and Spa offers a variety of services from facials to massages to manicures and waxing services. Prices are a bit steep with a simple pedicure sitting pretty at a minimum of $40. **B**

iO Chicago

This hip comedy club features seven shows a week and is the premier spot for

3541 N Clark St
773.880.0199
RED LINE to ADDISON

improvisational comedy. The theatre has brightly-colored walls and neon orange lights to spice up the atmosphere. The circular downstairs stage, with room for an audience of up to 125 people, is surrounded by tables, stools and a bar. Tickets range from $12 to $14 and can be purchased at the door. The most popular show, 'TJ & Dave,' is performed on Wednesday nights. **A**

LAKEVIEW

Working Professionals, Lakeview. DANIEL HONIGMAN

L&B Nail Salon

This salon is small, quiet and rarely busy. This is a great place to go if you

3456 N Clark St
773.880.0345
RED LINE to ADDISON

are looking for a quick and inexpensive manicure. The interior is clean and basic and the manicurists are always welcoming. Stop by if you are in a rush and want cheap nail service. **B+**

Live Bait Theater

Live Bait Theater houses 70 seats, hosts performances Thursdays through

3914 N Clark St
773.871.1212
RED LINE to ADDISON

Sundays, and produces new work by emerging Chicago playwrights. The theatre offers discounted student tickets for between $10 and $20. This summer, take a trip to the Live Bait Theater for the 12th Annual Fillet of Solo Festival, which runs from June through September and hosts notable solo performance artists in Chicago. **B**

Orbit Salon

This trendy salon offers a handful of services including waxing, manicures

3581 N Clark St
773.883.1166
RED LINE to ADDISON

and pedicures, haircuts, and Japanese thermal straightening, along with a variety of designer hair products by Kiwi, Redken and Aveda. Wiry, metallic blue lights hanging from the ceiling work to channel the salon's hip vibe down into the storefront. **B**

Sluggers World Class Sports Bar

Sluggers – located just around the corner from Wrigley Field – may seem

3540 N Clark St
773.248.0055
RED LINE to ADDISON

to have a split personality. The first floor, with its centrally-located bar, big-screen televisions and photo-lined walls, is reminiscent of your everyday sports bar and provides the perfect place to catch a game. The second floor, however, has a middle-school arcade feel with its run-down batting cages and random assortment of Skee Ball and air hockey. This blast from the past can be fun on a lazy afternoon. **A**

The Cubby Bear

This massive venue just across the street from Wrigley Field is the place

1059 W Addison St
773.327.1662
RED LINE to ADDISON

to congregate and top off those two Bud Lights you downed at the game. An extensive bar lines the far wall and serves the laid-back crowd that pours in to mingle and munch after a long day of baseball. **A-**

The Dark Horse

The Dark Horse is a sports bar with class. Black-and-white framed photographs

3443 N Sheffield Rd
773.248.4400
RED LINE to ADDISON

line the dark wooden walls making for a nice change from the dirty, beer-cap adorned walls of the other Wrigleyville sports bars. This one-room establishment serves appetizers late into the night and carries eight drafts and a wide assortment of cocktails. A great pre- or post-game pit stop if you're looking for a good place to enjoy a beer. **B**

The Wild Hare

The Wild Hare, a famous yet low-key reggae joint, is packed with dread-locked men who grope the bodies of voluptuous

3530 N Clark St
773.327.4273
RED LINE to ADDISON

women as live bands beat on steel drums. Authentic? Yes. Sketchy? You bet. It is strongly suggested that anyone under the age of 50 only attend on the monthly college nights and travel in packs. **B-**

Dennis' Place for Games

If you're looking for a retro, noisy game arcade, this is where you want

957 W Belmont Ave
773.528.8616
RED LINE to BELMONT

to be. Though the games here are good, the atmosphere is not: Dangling microphones hanging from the ceiling create a creepy vibe. But the mirrored back room serves as a great lounge area for customers on a break. **C+**

House of Hookah

Come to House of Hookah for both a caffeine and hookah buzz. Regular

607 W Belmont Ave
773.348.1550
RED LINE to BELMONT

coffee, mochas and lattes are available as well as plenty of hookah tobacco or shisha. Come to drink, smoke and relax with friends on a chill Friday night. This joint also sells hookah pipes and accessories, and the free Wi-Fi adds to its coffeehouse feel. **A**

Samah Lounge

Samah is not just a restaurant that happens to have hookah. Here,

3330-A N Clark St
773.248.4606
RED LINE to BELMONT

the wide variety of tobacco flavors, including melon and an exquisite house specialty, prove that Samah is foremost about hookah. Enjoy the Moroccan motif and nestle among the plush pillows while listening to Middle Eastern music for a truly authentic experience. Samah is open late, but be sure to make a reservation to secure a room. **A**

Spin

Down a few drinks, play some pool and dance at this gay, lesbian and bi-

800 W Belmont Ave
773.327.7711
RED LINE to BELMONT

sexual club. Though the bar is big, the dance floor certainly isn't, so don't spend the whole night shaking and grinding. Take time to relax and sit in

TOP: Lakeview. LYDIA MERRILL • **MIDDLE:** Lakeview. LYDIA MERRILL • **BOTTOM:** Lakeview. LYDIA MERRILL

one of the red vinyl booths in the back. There is another smaller bar back there as well. **B**

Spot 6

This club is trendy and affordable. The lighting may be dim, but it's impossible not to be blinded by the bright orange splashed everywhere. But upstairs, the décor is much more subtle and intimate. With a huge dance floor and a bar serving cheap alcohol, Spot 6 is the perfect place to jumpstart a Friday night. **A**

3343 N Clark St
773.388.0185
RED LINE to BELMONT

TO SHOP

A Little Bit of This

Just moved into a new apartment? This charming embroidery boutique is the perfect place for branding your favorite towel or bathrobe. It's also great for gifts, as well as club or Greek association gear. A Little Bit of This offers embroidered sweatshirts, bags, stationary and more, all at reasonable prices. **A-**

3515 N Lincoln Ave
773.935.3917
BROWN LINE to ADDISON

Love Is - Flowers and Gifts

Love Is boasts an extremely large selection of flowers ideal for gift giving or decorating your home. This quaint store delivers everything from roses to lilies right to your doorstep, and knowledgeable employees are happy to help you pick out your arrange-

3953 N Ashland Ave
773.281.3621
BROWN LINE to IRVING PARK

ment. Gifts like candles and other small trinkets abound. **A-**

Eye Spy Optical

This delightful eyewear shop is just about as far as you can get from a generic chain like Lenscrafters. Eye Spy sells handmade frames for all ages in all styles, from designers such as Frances Klein, Lafont, and Face a Face. The shop also has an optometrist on hand for eye exams. If you're allergic to dogs however, be careful. The owner's small pup keeps watch over shoppers. **A**

3350 N Lincoln Ave
773.477.2670
BROWN LINE to PAULINA

Glazed Expressions

This self-titled 'paint-it-yourself pottery place' is an awesome spot for flexing your creative muscle. Visitors to Glazed Expressions can choose a piece of unfinished pottery and paint it with available supplies. Employees will then glaze and fire the piece, which can be picked up after a week. The price is $8, in addition to the cost of the pottery purchased. **A**

3339 N Lincoln Ave
773.665.4072
BROWN LINE to PAULINA

Bourdage Pearls

Who said pearls have to be white and expensive? For $42 at Bourdage Pearls, you can buy a beautiful pearl bracelet ranging in colors from aqua green to burnt orange. And if you had something else in mind,

3530 N Southport Ave
773.244.1126
BROWN LINE to SOUTHPORT

Moxie

3517 N. Clark St.
773.935.6694
RED LINE to ADDISON

Don't be fooled by the sporty surroundings of this Lakeview bar. Although it definitely attracts a rowdy crowd, Moxie is anything but a 'beer bar.' With an award-winning chef, Moxie offers exotic prepared dishes like fresh-seared Ahi tuna, Szechuan peppercorn filet, Kahlua mashed sweet potatoes, and unique salad creations, but the sangria and white cosmopolitans are the bar's specialty. The crowd and staff are fun and provide a great party atmosphere for your night out. Moxie is a sure [and affordable] bet whether you're looking to celebrate post-Cubs game with some friends or just want to have a good time.

in-house designers Karma and Kathryn can create whatever your imagination conjures up. Bourdage only carries Chinese freshwater pearls, which are more affordable, more colorful, and last longer than your traditional pearls. **B+**

Flirt

Owner Channing Hesse wasn't just trying to be cute when she came up

3449 N Southport Ave
773.935.4789
BROWN LINE to SOUTHPORT

with the name for this ultra-girly boutique. The newsboy hats and peep-toe flats found here really do compose the perfect flirting gear. The accommodating and trend-conscious staff will help you find a fun and feminine dress for warm summer days. Don't be surprised if you attract catcalls while donning buys from Flirt. **A**

Krista K

If you don't mind spending the same amount of money on a basic cotton

3458 N Southport Ave
773.248.1967
BROWN LINE to SOUTHPORT

shirt as you would on a pair of designer jeans, then Krista K is the place for you. This upscale boutique is aesthetically pleasing and money-draining. With a sale section the size of a Tic-Tac, you won't find any bargains here, though the adorable designer cocktail dresses may be worth the splurge. **C+**

M2 Boutique

Sometimes accessories do make an outfit. At M2, you will find that perfect

3527 N Southport Ave
773.248.9866
BROWN LINE to SOUTHPORT

purse, belt, necklace or bracelet to top off any ensemble. The store is organized by color, which allows you to find just what you're looking for. But be sure to keep track of time because you can easily get lost in the adorable finds for hours. Don't forget to snag a gift for a girlfriend while you're at it. **A-**

Red Head Boutique

Finally, a place where you and your friends, despite your different body types,

3450 N Southport Ave
773.325.9898
BROWN LINE to SOUTHPORT

can all find flattering clothes. When owner Kerry Judy, a redhead herself, opened this boutique, she made sure that there was something for everyone, not to mention every price range. During one of the bi-annual sales you might be able to snag your favorite brand-name jeans for half price. Don't forget to check out the jewelry from local Chicago designers. **A-**

Trousseau

Parlez-vous sexy? Trousseau proves that everyone has the right to be

3543 N Southport Ave
773.472.2727
BROWN LINE to SOUTHPORT

sexy and that lingerie should not be reserved for

Lakeview. DANIEL HONIGMAN

your wedding night. Here, pretty undergarments come in all sizes and designs, with ranging price tags. So whether you like lace, mesh, or silk, take a gamble and treat yourself or that special someone to a new bustier and girdle. Throw in some sexy dice while you're at it. **A**

Wacky Cats

Shopping in this store is like browsing through many different people's old attic collections. If you shuffle through their collection of vintage clothing, you can find some truly wacky costumes and hats from the 1940s to the 1970s. Do a little dusting and take home some great and unique finds. **B+**

| 3012 N Lincoln Ave |
| 773.929.6701 |
| **BROWN LINE to WELLINGTON** |

Waxman Candles

Upon entering Waxman Candles, shoppers smell the powerful aroma of thousands of fragrances mingling together. The shop offers different varieties of homemade candles in hundreds of shapes, sizes and scents. Waxman may be a bit too serious for the college student just looking for something to mask the inevitable dorm room stench, but it's a pleasant experience for the nose. **B+**

| 3044 N Lincoln Ave |
| 773.929.3000 |
| **BROWN LINE to WELLINGTON** |

Yellow Jacket

This small and well-orga- nized consignment shop makes it easy for you to find the best vintage pieces. The bright yellow walls, friendly staff and large selection of tees, jeans and accessories that you'll find inside make Yellow Jacket a worthwhile shopping experience despite slightly higher prices than the nearest Goodwill. **A**

| 2959 N Lincoln Ave |
| 773.248.1996 |
| **BROWN LINE to WELLINGTON** |

Bookworks

This charming little shop is the perfect place to buy and sell any old books, re- cords or CDs. They also sell vintage screenplays and old-fashioned postcards. Organized by item and subject, the store is easy to navigate despite

| 3444 N Clark St |
| 773.871.5318 |
| **RED LINE to ADDISON** |

Lakeview. LYDIA MERRILL

its attic-like smell and feel. Prices are low [CDs cost an average of $8] and the employees seem prepared to help you find your way around. This is a gem for bookworms and music lovers alike. **A**

Brown Elephant Resale Shop

Everything in this store is a resold item, so you'll find lots of vintage goods ranging from appliances to apparel. This store is fun to browse in if you arrive with an open mind. What's more, all proceeds go to the Howard Brown Health Center, a facility that specializes in AIDS medicine and research. **A-**

| 3651 N Halsted St |
| 773.549.5943 |
| **RED LINE to ADDISON** |

Disgraceland

An ideal shopping experi- ence for vintage junkies, Disgraceland carries all things recycled. Tops, bottoms, shoes and other accessories for both men and women are fairly priced, with all sunglasses priced at less than $10. Unlike other vintage stores, this shop is well organized and designed. Definitely look out for the distinctive coat selection; every item is unique. Make sure you check out the basement for another floor of secondhand delight. **A**

| 3338 N Clark St |
| 773.281.5875 |
| **RED LINE to ADDISON** |

Evil Clown Compact Disc

For those of you who still purchase CDs, this is the store for you. There's a wide selection and you'll find most genres across a wide spectrum of music. You're also allowed to sample any album before you buy it, so you may find this place useful if you don't know exactly quite what you're looking for. **B+**

3418 N Halsted St
773.472.4761
RED LINE to ADDISON

Medusa's Circle

Located between Aldine Ave. and Belmont Ave., Medusa's Circle sells make-up and edgy, outlandish women's clothing. The boutique is small, but there's a wide range of eccentric clothing that shoppers can purchase to tailor to their own unique clothing styles. You can even order their clothing online. However, prices are steep. **B**

3268 N Clark St
773.935.5950
RED LINE to ADDISON

Strange Cargo

Friendly staff and a Beatles soundtrack give this Lakeview gem an alternative vibe without the intimidation. Geared primarily toward the production of custom-printed tees, Strange Cargo also offers an assortment of vintage pieces at cheap prices, including accessories, shoes and wigs. The trinkets are

3448 N Clark St
773.327.8090
RED LINE to ADDISON

reminiscent of Urban Outfitters – except they are more original and less expensive. **A**

Wrigleyville Sports

This sports apparel shop, just off the Addison stop of the 'L,' is the perfect place to grab a Cubs cap or jersey before heading off to the game. The store services all Chicago sports teams, though it's probably not a good idea to be caught buying a White Sox hat in the heart of Wrigleyville. Prices are reasonable, with the average T-shirt costing about $15. **B+**

959 W Addison St
630.694.8566
RED LINE to ADDISON

African Safari Imports

If you've always wanted to take an African safari, head over to this store to play some make-believe. The store sells clothing, jewelry, hand-carved masks and other art objects from all over Africa and the Caribbean. The native music played in the store is loud and the smell of leather and incense is strong. **A-**

3705 N Broadway St
773.549.2744
RED LINE to BELMONT

Amigos & Us

This place advertises itself as a 'hippy boutique, gift and smoke shop.' The claim rings true. Here, at Amigos & Us in Lakeview, you can shop for Chicago Bears

3223 N Clark St
773.281.1812
RED LINE to BELMONT

ABOVE: Lakeview. LYDIA MERRILL • **RIGHT:** Lakeview. LYDIA MERRILL

tie-dyed clothing, rock 'n' roll T-shirts, hemp necklaces and more. The burning incense in the shop gives it a fitting groovy ambiance. **B**

Beyond The Wall

This store is a treasure trove of eclectic items.

935 W Belmont Ave
773.871.5827
RED LINE to BELMONT

Selling everything from posters to bags to vintage prints, it offers a mix of trinkets both large and small and is a great place to sift for gift items or something to decorate your room. Spend time browsing through their extensive poster collection: They boast over thousands of images so there's sure to be something to suit your taste. **B+**

Caravan Beads

If you're in a creative mood, head over to Caravan Beads and get

3361 N Lincoln Ave
773.248.9555
RED LINE to BELMONT

in touch with your artsy side. You can purchase colorful beads from around the world and make a bracelet right in the store. If you're creatively-challenged, pick up one of their 'how-to' books on craft-making. Classes on such endeavors such as glass bead making and mask making are also offered here. **A**

Fashion Tomato

If you're searching for trendy apparel, Fashion Tomato is the place to go

937 W Belmont Ave
773.281.2921
RED LINE to BELMONT

– the store is rife with sparkly and glitzy clothes. But though the price tags aren't ridiculously steep, they certainly aren't reasonable, considering the cheap quality of the merchandise. Bottom line: Buyers beware – the clothes you purchase here will probably last only a few wears. **C+**

Guava

Ever wonder where to find those stones with tranquil words and Chinese

3327 N Broadway St
773.348.2432
RED LINE to BELMONT

symbols on them? If so, Guava has the answer to your questions. The Botanicus candles sold here are the perfect gifts for anyone into aromatherapy. Try the 'Fig' or 'A Day at the Beach' scents. If you aren't really into spending $20 on a candle, Guava sells mini versions for just $5.50. Though slightly overpriced, this boutique sells everything you need in order to de-stress. **B+**

He Who Eats Mud

He Who Eats Mud boasts 'cards and gifts of distinction.' In reality, this place

3247 N Broadway St
773.525.0616
RED LINE to BELMONT

has cards and gifts of excess. Along each wall, you'll find not only handmade cards, but also the humorous, inappropriate cards you won't find at your local gift shop. So make sure to stop by this store if you're looking for a unique gift card. But be forewarned – unless your friend is into peculiar figurines, don't expect to find the perfect gift in this place. **B-**

Hollywood Mirror

You never know what you'll find in this vintage boutique with a punk-rock

812 W Belmont Ave
773.404.2044
RED LINE to BELMONT

vibe. It's great if you're looking for a costume for a themed party or a Halloween ensemble, offering a range of new and old items from the 1950s to the 1980s. You'll find everything from bags, shoes, and accessories to gowns and pantsuits. **B**

Hubba Hubba

Hubba Hubba is a jewel amidst the numerous vintage stores that sur-

3309 N Clark St
773.477.1414
RED LINE to BELMONT

round it. In this chic boutique, nothing besides the fabulous costume jewelry is used, renewed or worn. The surplus of independent designers, trendy T-shirt brands and attentive salespeople reminds you what boutique shopping is all about. It's the perfect shopping destination whether you're looking for a unique party dress or an embroidered hoodie. **A-**

J. Toguri Mercantile Co.

This store is the Japanese version of Target. Merchandise overflows

851 W Belmont Ave
773.929.0779
RED LINE to BELMONT

and there is an odd assortment of various things for people of all ages. The giant room itself is ugly with plain walls, dirty floors and oddly-placed rugs, but the incense in the air and huge lanterns hanging from the ceiling add a nicer touch. **B**

Jive Monkey

Shopping here is the classic vintage hit-or-miss experience. Jive Monkey

3222 N Clark St
773.404.8000
RED LINE to BELMONT

offers a variety of items, but only one of each. Also, their clothes are a tad overpriced. But a few cool things to note that might bring you here: You can resell your old items and make customized T-shirts. **B-**

Never Mind Details

This trendy boutique is the sister store of Never Mind. While Never

953 W Belmont Ave
773.472.4922
RED LINE to BELMONT

Mind's collection focuses on apparel, Never Mind Details features trendy accessories, bags and jewelry. Their pieces are hip, young and cool – perfect for young fashionistas on a budget. This store also carries a lot of pieces that are knock-offs of current trends. Make sure to complement your clothing purchases at Never Mind, only a few doors down, with your finds here. **B**

Pink Frog [Main Store]

Like the rainbow-colored assortment of wigs on display in the back, this

3201 N Clark St
773.525.2680
RED LINE to BELMONT

store has a lot of variety, but not necessarily in a positive way. Though the clothes in the front of the store are trendy, as you walk further into the store, the clothes become absurdly outrageous [think Las Vegas-style costume shop]. But if you ever need that occasional showgirl ensemble, at least you'll know where to go. **C**

Pink Frog [Shoe Store Branch]

Down the street from the main store, this sister boutique sells only

905 W Belmont Ave
773.404.4350
RED LINE to BELMONT

shoes and accessories. This Pink Frog is badly organized and looks like a place to cram left-over merchandise with shoes lined up along the wall in battered-looking boxes. You can also find tacky jewelry and sunglasses behind the glass counters up front. Still, if you rifle around enough, you may find a cute pair for $15. **C-**

Reckless Records

Taking a trip back in time is inevitable when going into this store. Whether

3157 N Broadway St
773.404.5080
RED LINE to BELMONT

purchasing compact discs, cassettes, videos, or vinyl or selling music antiques to the store, this place is all about the love of music through the generations. But don't worry if you're into current music: There is a vast assortment of new releases along with posters, T-shirts and video games sold here. **B+**

Lakeview. DANIEL HONIGMAN

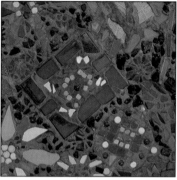

LEFT: Lakeview. LYDIA MERRILL • **BELOW:** Lakeview. LYDIA MERRILL

Shanghai Gallery

This Lakeview store prides itself on carrying tons of small trinkets and souvenirs from Asian countries, with all sorts of cliché Japanese items lining its walls. So whether you're looking for a traditional silk kimono or the Japanese Pocky snack, stop by Shanghai Gallery and you'll be sure to find it. **B**

931 W Belmont Ave
773.281.6288
RED LINE to BELMONT

Slaymaker

This upscale gallery sells fine decorative abstract and contemporary art. However, all works sold here are originals, making their prices hefty. Yet, the personable staff is willing to walk you through the three stories of the building while explaining every piece, so even if you're not planning to buy a painting, check out the gallery to learn something about the place and its merchandise. **A-**

934-936 W Roscoe St
773.935.2785
RED LINE to BELMONT

The Alley

This is a store for hardcore rockers only. Here, you can find underground T-shirts and clothes bearing skulls and crossbones. It's a great shop for those who enjoy motorcycle jackets and Grateful Dead T-shirts, but may be quite intimidating for shoppers adverse to this particular scene. While you're here, check out one of the most recommended piercing booths in town: it's sterile, friendly and carries a wide selection. **B+**

858 W Belmont Ave
773.525.3180
RED LINE to BELMONT

The Gallery Bookstore Ltd.

This tiny store contains a random assortment of books for both adults and children alike. But think twice before coming here rather than your local Border's — the shop has a creepy ambiance and is difficult to search through. If you're looking to resell some of your old books though, negotiations with the owner can be made. **C-**

923 W Belmont Ave
773.975.8200
RED LINE to BELMONT

Tragically Hip

This little shop is definitely hip. Party music blares in the store and rows of trendy dresses, jackets and shirts cram the shop along with stylish purses, belts and jewelry. This store is perfect for teenage girls looking to outfit themselves inexpensively from head-to-toe. Prices are extremely affordable — mostly everything in the store is under $100. **A**

852 W Belmont Ave
773.549.1500
RED LINE to BELMONT

LINCOLN PARK

THE PERFECT PLACE TO SPEND A QUIET DAY

Lincoln Park is an upscale neighborhood with a little bit of everything. The massive park of its namesake makes it the perfect place to spend a quiet day. Just north of the ruckus of the Magnificent Mile enjoy the tranquility of the lakefront or watch some penguins at Lincoln Park Zoo, the largest free zoo in the nation. Boats have been for rent since 1910 at the Boat Club with the Hancock Tower in the distance. Stroll down Clark St. and Lincoln St. for boutique shopping and have lunch in one of its many restaurants. The areas many cafes are prime locations for spotting Trixies or Chads, the area's notoriously rich and insipid residents. The Old Town Triangle Historical District is host to the Midwest Buddhist Temple [and its haiku contest], an annual summer art fair and Second City, Chicago's premier improv-comedy club. Mix it up on Halsted St. around the campus of DePaul. Frat boys abound in the areas plentiful bars and cheap eat joints, usually open late. Or class it up at the Steppenwolf Theater, where world class actors and prize-winning playwrights have collaborated for 30 years.

TO EAT

Ambrosia Café

1963 N Sheffield Ave
773.404.4450
BROWN LINE to ARMITAGE

If you're looking to enjoy the feeling of summer all year, immerse yourself in this café's bright ambiance. Fresh-squeezed juices and affordable scrumptious sandwiches are sold along with other Mediterranean-inspired dishes here. Ambrosia brings out hookah pipes after 7 p.m. and stays open late, so stick around after dusk for an enjoyable evening spent lounging with friends. **A**

Annette's Homemade Italian Ice

2009 N Bissell St
773.858.9000
BROWN LINE to ARMITAGE

This small, quaint dessert shop is a jewel. Renowned for its quality, homemade Italian ice as well as its sundaes and smoothies, everything here is fresh and reasonably-priced. On sunny days, Annette's sidewalk seating allows you to sit back and enjoy the weather. What better way to ease your stress than to lounge about eating sweet delicacies? **B**

Red Rooster Café and Wine Bar

2100 N. Halsted St.
773.929.7660
BROWN LINE to ARMITAGE

Tucked away in the backroom of its larger sister restaurant, Café Bernard, the Red Rooster Café and Wine Bar is accessed only by a narrow corridor leading to a small but quaint dark wood-paneled seating area. The quiet, candlelit tables inside provide this warm French restaurant with an intimate setting that is perfect for a romantic night out with a special someone. The friendly wait staff offer assistance in selecting le meilleur vin from the extensive wine list and patrons can choose from a wide variety of French appetizers, entrees and desserts all offered to you at reasonable prices.

Chicago Bagel Authority

953 W Armitage Ave
773.243.9606
BROWN LINE to ARMITAGE

Only steps away from the 'El' stop, this establishment is especially popular among neighborhood residents. The open bay windows offer an inviting yet casual setting. The fun and creative menu is posted on large chalkboards and it's almost impossible to choose from the huge variety of sandwiches offered. All come steamed unless otherwise noted. CBA stands by their mission to 'change the world one bagel at a time.' **B**

Dee's

1114 W Armitage Ave
773.477.1500
BROWN LINE to ARMITAGE

Dee's serves Mandarin and Schezuan cuisine to loyal neighborhood diners. The restaurant has a simple, clean décor with glossy wooden tables and floors, beige walls, and dim lighting. Specialties include Szechwan chicken, crab rangoon, Mongolian beef, and mooshu pork. The food tastes very fresh, and the menu offers a wide variety of options. **B+**

Doggie Diner

723 W Armitage Ave
312.266.2925
BROWN LINE to ARMITAGE

This shabby, paint-chipped hot dog stand is a neighborhood institution with quick service, no tables, and Chicago-style, genuine hot dogs. It's also right across the street from a high school, so you'll run into many students getting their fix here. If you crave a quickie, Doggie Diner provides a decent wiener. **B+**

LEFT: Halligan, 2274 N. Lincoln Ave. AMANDA ADLESICK • **ABOVE:** Twisted Lizard, 1964 N. Sheffield Ave. AMANDA ADLESICK

RIGHT: Lincoln Park Conservatory, 2391 N. Stockton Dr. AMANDA ADLESICK • **BELOW:** Alfred Caldwell Lily Pool, Lincoln Park Zoo. AMANDA ADLESICK

Ethel's Chocolate Lounge

819 W Armitage Ave
773.281.0029
BROWN LINE to ARMITAGE

The color explosion of pink and brown sets the tasty mood within the walls of this location in the Ethel's chain. Scrumptious treats of all sorts satisfy all sweet tooth cravings. Whether you're refueling in the afternoon or snacking late at night, this chocolate lounge is heaven for anyone with an appetite. **A**

John's Place

1202 W Webster Ave
773.525.6670
BROWN LINE to ARMITAGE

With both sidewalk and indoor seating, this homey restaurant is perhaps best-known for their Sunday brunch. Cheesy egg chilaquiles and pumpkin pie pancakes are just a few specialty breakfasts, made from recipes unique to John's. To accommodate both noisy families and quite couples throughout the week, one room is designated as the kids' room to keep the noise level down during breakfast, lunch and dinner. **B**

Karyn's

1901 N Halsted St
312.255.1590
BROWN LINE to ARMITAGE

This establishment aims to be a place to 'facilitate your individual path towards well-being.' They offer a raw vegan gourmet restaurant, fresh café and market, and a number of classes including detox classes, ballet and yoga. It was founded by Karyn Calabrese, and is the longest-standing raw food restaurant

The Twisted Lizard

1964 N. Sheffield Ave.
773.929.1414
BROWN LINE to ARMITAGE

This lively, fiesta-like Southwestern restaurant caters to the young and energetic Lincoln Park crowd. Though the menu is fairly traditional, the drinks list certainly isn't. With an extensive array of Mexican beers, tequila [over 20 brands], and flavorful, unique margaritas [which you can order by the pitcher], you're guaranteed to find a suitable libation to complement your meal. The baked cheese, queso fundido, is a must-order appetizer and the sincronizadas [layered flour tortillas stuffed with refried black beans and choice of meat or vegetables] are sure to delight your taste buds. They also offer outdoor patio seating in the summer.

in the Midwest, highly-acclaimed for its unique, flavorful dishes. The Karyn Center provides a sacred space for balancing the mind, body, and spirit. **B**

Merlo Ristorante

The homely décor of this restaurant makes you feel as if you've been invited over for a traditional Italian family dinner, as long as you're not sitting in the back room, which feels segregated from the rest of the restaurant. The food is just as authentic, but is too pricy for its small portions. While the restaurant smells deliciously of garlic and other spices, your fervor for the flavorful dishes dies as soon as the hefty bill is brought out. **C**

2638 N Lincoln Ave
773.529.0747
BROWN LINE to ARMITAGE

Minnies

This 'chic-eatery' may be small in size, but that doesn't mean they're lacking in taste. Walk onto the black-and-white checkered flooring and sit at the long counter on red leatherette stools to step back into an old 50's diner. Famous for their 'Minnies' and 'infamous fries,' this restaurant features a bit

1969 N Halsted St
312.943.9000
BROWN LINE to ARMITAGE

of retro with a mix of glamour and fun. A great place to come with your family or with friends to have a cocktail. **B+**

Mon Ami Gabi

Say bonjour to this quaint French restaurant. With its charming outdoor patio and tasteful décor, this restaurant oozes the ambiance expected of the Francais. But don't get too cozy if you're a college student on a budget – this place is a tad too expensive [entrees average $18-20], considering the small portions. This restaurant also tends to attract an older crowd. **B-**

2300 N Lincoln Park W.
773.348.8886
BROWN LINE to ARMITAGE

Nookies Too

With its classic diner ambiance, this local establishment prides itself on having 'three of the favorite B-words any restaurant should have - Breakfast, Brunch, and Burgers.' With its 24-hour service on Fridays and Saturdays, this joint is perfect for late-night munchies or an early brunch. Great for large groups, and you can expect a range of ages gathered here to dine on greasy, satisfying food. **B+**

2112 N Halsted St
773.327.1400
BROWN LINE to ARMITAGE

Blick Art Materials, 1574 N. Kingsbury St. AMANDA ADLESICK

R.J. Grunts

This laidback eatery boasts a salad bar unmatched by most. R.J. Grunts is a fun place to go when you're not quite sure what you're in the mood for. The juicy hamburgers on warm buns make for a delicious and affordable meal. The entrees are big enough for two, and the homemade potato chips are great.

2056 N Lincoln Park W.
773.929.5363
BROWN LINE to ARMITAGE

Ask for a seat by the window for a great view of the neighborhood. **B**

Stanley's Kitchen and Tap

On your next spin through town, check out Stanley's Kitchen and Tap if you're craving huge portions of good ol' Southern comfort food. Chow down on mashed potatoes and barbequed pork and, if you can't stand to wait for

1970 N Lincoln Ave
312.642.0007
BROWN LINE to ARMITAGE

DRINKS ABOUT TOWN: RECOMMENDATIONS FROM CHICAGO'S BEST BARTENDERS
BY JESSICA KELMON

The second city's reputation as a drinking town is well established. Whether you're enjoying a beer-filled summer day at Wrigley Field or a cocktail-infused night on the town, Chicago is the place to have a good time. For anyone who wants to push their experience a little further, Unzipped asked the city's resident experts – bartenders in some of the city's best neighborhoods – what drinks they recommend.

Adobo Grill • 1610 N. Wells St., 312.266.7999

Adjacent to the main stage of the Second City in Old Town is the Mexican restaurant and bar Adobo Grill. Good, reasonably priced food and great drinks before a late show next door is a Chicago must-do. May I suggest a flight of sipping tequilas? Veteran bartender Tino Diaz says the best choice is a Cocotazo. It's coconut sorbet mixed with Ron Botran Añejo and a splash of Malibu rum, served in a fresh coconut shell – perfect for those sweltering Chicago summers.

Blue Line Club Car • 1548 N. Damen Ave., 773.395.3700

Wicker Park is like Disneyland for adults – full of great music venues, restaurants, coffee houses and bars. One night in this neighborhood is simply not enough. Just outside the Damen 'El' stop, cruise inside this sleek Edward Hopper-esque dining car-come-bar and ask for Kimmy Spapperi. After almost three years bartending, she's ventured past the regular menu and created drinks of her own. Kimmy's mojito is by far the best iteration ever of this chic drink. She won't divulge the secret other than to say there are three flavors of Bacardi as well as strawberries, lemonade and soda. Her other concoction, as yet unnamed, is 'refreshing for summer.' It's Finlandia Wild Berries mixed with lemonade, with an orange slice, a cherry, a packet of sugar and a splash of 7Up.

Bella Lounge • 1212 N. State Pkwy., 312.787.9405

Suffering from an identity crisis, Bella Lounge can't decide whether it's upscale and suave [back bar] or the Mexican fiesta beach party section of Crate & Barrel [front bar]. Pass the first bar and relax in the comfy chairs in the second with new bartender Joe Quade's recommended Soco lime – that's Southern Comfort with a splash of lime. It's simple, but it gets the job done. Sip slowly and see if you agree that the back half of this

LINCOLN PARK

your meal, get up and join the crowd for some square dancing. **B**

Tarantino's

1112 W Armitage Ave
773.871.2929
BROWN LINE to ARMITAGE

Though the Italian food at this Armitage spot is savory and fresh, its atmosphere is what sets it apart from the countless other restaurants in Lincoln Park. You can feel the romance the moment you walk through its door

and sashay your way past the velvet curtain. The dim lighting and high ceilings are complimented by the dark wood walls and paneled floor. Their wine glasses are small, so trade it in for one of their signature martinis. **A-**

Tilli's

1952 N Halsted St
773.325.0044
BROWN LINE to ARMITAGE

What do you do when each party in your group is craving something differ-

place lives up to the beauty and class that its name promises.

Swirl Wine Bar • 111 W. Hubbard St., 312.828.9000

Try not to be put off by the adult bookstore two doors down, because this wine bar is anything but seedy. A long and lean bar lined with intimate seating, Swirl opens up in the back with low-rise chairs and an easily accessible bar. Tuesdays and Fridays are the nights to go: Tuesdays for the $3 tastes and $10 flights and Fridays for the TGIF crowd. Bartender Aneta Kowal, who has been pouring at Swirl's for six months, recommends a glass of the 2005 Domaine Robert Perroud Brouilly, calling it 'very light and tasty.' A bright wine with notes of cranberry and cherry, it's simple and straightforward, just as you should be when trying to get a date.

Rodan • 1530 N. Milwaukee St., 773.276.7036

On the north side of Bucktown, adjacent to Wicker Park, is Rodan, a loungy and upscale joint, which still manages to be very relaxed – open the door and the aroma of shrimp tempura reminds you quickly that you're still in the heart of bar-food city. Reluctant to push his own taste on anyone else, bartender Derek Payne first suggests the house drink: the Lychee Martini. True to his bartending roots, he suggests two others that pair

well with one another: a Tequila Gimlet and a Bloody Maria. Derek says he makes his own Bloody Mary mix on the premises and uses tequila rather than vodka for Mary's Latin cousin. Olé!

Tilli's • 1952 N. Halsted St., 773.325.0044

In Lincoln Park, where Patrick Clancy has been behind the bar for three years, there's a fun, young mid-20s to mid-30s crowd gathered pretty much every night at Tilli's. Clancy says he has to be honest: His favorite drink is Guinness. With a working fireplace in the wintertime, Tilli's might be the perfect destination one cold February night when you need the dual warming power of the Irish classic and hearth heat.

Schubas Tavern • 3159 N. Southport Ave., 773.525.2508

A classic all-wood dive bar downstairs, and a renowned small music venue upstairs, Schubas is a place you will want to return to many times. A clean, chill atmosphere in Lakeview makes you want to stay, and a surprisingly great menu makes you want to eat. Bartender Hanna Mutsch who is originally from the west coast, says she's particularly fond of micro-brews. Her favorite ale of all time is Full Sail Amber – but it's not distributed this far east. Her Chicago pick is Sierra Nevada Pale Ale or 'anything from Deschutes brewery.'

ent for dinner? Head to Tilli's. If you're looking for diversity, Tilli's won't disappoint. Offering everything from pad Thai to hamburgers to Caribbean

TOP Lelia Jane's, 1008 W. Armitage Ave. LYDIA MERRILL • MIDDLE Sweet Mandy B's, 1208 W. Webster Ave. LYDIA MERRILL • BOTTOM Webster Fitness Center, Sheffield & Webster Ave. LYDIA MERRILL

steak, everyone is bound to find something they like. You can even pick your atmosphere to fully personalize your night by choosing to dine fireside or on the patio. This restaurant caters to a young crowd and satisfies any mood. **A-**

Toast

Despite long lines and mediocre service, Toast is a great little brunch spot, channeling both creativity and comfort. Even their tables, covered by brown paper cloths, look like little pieces of toasts. Try their Orgasmic Stuffed French Toast covered in yogurt, fruit, and granola, which lives up to its name. **B+**

746 W Webster Ave
773.935.5600
BROWN LINE to ARMITAGE

Zella

This upscale restaurant/ bar is the perfect location for dancing or lounging. There's a bar at the entrance as well as another at the rear, and on a warm day the patio doubles as a beer garden. If it's too cold to go outside, you can warm up on the cozy couches and armchairs by the fireplace. **A**

1983 N Clybourn Ave
773.549.2910
BROWN LINE to ARMITAGE

Itto Sushi

Located along the theatrical stretch of Halsted, Itto Sushi is the perfect restaurant to stop by before or after a show. Though there's nothing fancy about the place itself, the sushi is fresh and of high quality. What's more, you can watch the chefs prepare it in front of you. **A-**

2616 N Halsted St
773.871.1800
BROWN LINE to DIVERSEY

Maza

If you're interested in trying something new, Maza is a great bet. This Lebanese restaurant, true to its name [maza means appetizer], serves a wide selection of nominally-priced, savory small dishes. Though the service here is slow, the staff is very friendly, so if you're willing to enjoy a meal at a leisurely place, a great new experience awaits you. **B-**

2748 N Lincoln Ave
773.929.9600
BROWN LINE to DIVERSEY

Bourgeois Pig

738 W. Fullerton Ave.
773.883.5282
RED LINE to FULLERTON

The Bourgeois Pig's book-lined brick walls and antique wooden tables do more than provide diners with an appealing, intellectual setting. They also make the perfect place for enjoying the mouth watering, cheaply-priced [all under $8] sandwiches bearing the names of famous tomes. Customer favorites include 'The Garden Eden,' a vegetarian delight, and 'The Sun Also Rises,' smoked turkey grilled on sun-dried tomato bread with hummus, Swiss cheese, tomato, bean sprouts and onion. There is no need for you to bring a novel or a chessboard to fit in – your mouth will be glad to do all the thinking [and eating] necessary.

LINCOLN PARK

Athenian Room

807 W Webster Ave
773.348.5155
BROWN LINE to FULLERTON

This authentic Greek restaurant provides excellent food at extremely reasonable prices. Greek salad, chicken, gyros, and kebabs are favorites to customers, but if you don't order early, your favorite dish could be sold out by dinnertime. Paintings of Greece line the walls, while the no-cell-phone and no-smoking policies create serenity within this Lincoln Park favorite. **A**

Sweet Mandy B's

1208 W Webster Ave
773.244.1174
BROWN LINE to FULLERTON

At Sweet Mandy B's, the delicious aroma that seeps through the windows doesn't hold a candle to the delightful tastes found inside. Packed with customers, the shop sells freshly baked cakes, muffins, and other desserts that melt in your mouth. Within the pastel-colored walls, you can find customers sitting at the bar, wrists deep in frosting, washing down their treats with the milk and water found in pitchers atop the tables. **A**

Via Carducci

1419 W Fullerton Ave
773.665.1981
BROWN LINE to FULLERTON

Small, intimate and constantly busy, this Italian restaurant provides monstrous portions for hungry customers. Via Carducci is famous for their spicy arrabiata sauce and thin-crust pizza, but all dishes can be special-ordered to cater to personal tastes. To top it off, thematic paintings cover the walls and ceiling, creating a fully Italian experience. **A-**

Weiner's Circle

2622 N Clark St
773.477.7444
BROWN LINE to FULLERTON

This hotdog stand, serving the 'Chicago Dog' and other ultra-greasy American delights, is an absolute must. For those

Chicago Historical Society, 1601 N. Clark St. AMANDA ADLESICK

craving a bite after a long night out, Weiner's Circle is open 24 hours. Crass employees, who constantly shout at customers, make the trip especially entertaining, but not for those with a sensitive side. **A**

Chi-Town Tap

This neighborhood pub serves some of the best homemade tortilla chips and salsa in town, along with genuine Mexican burritos, tacos and enchiladas. With high-definition plasma TVs all around, this is a great place to catch a game or simply kick back and relax on a Friday night with the $1 domestic beer specials. Note: Tap is small and tends to get crowded quickly. **A-**

2642 N Lincoln Ave
773.871.4832
RED LINE to BELMONT

The Pasta Bowl

Pasta lover? Check out this Italian pasta paradise. The Pasta Bowl offers anything from a simple bowl of your classic spaghetti and meatballs to an exquisite pasta

2434 N Clark St
773.525.2695
RED LINE to BELMONT

dish complemented with your choice of seafood. Their gnocchi is reputed to be one of the best in Chicago. The small and cozy interior is warm and inviting, and casual dress is the norm. Though the fare at The Pasta Bowl is simple, it's extremely satisfying. **A**

Hey Sushi

This modern sushi bar is down-to-earth and fun. With fresh fish flown in daily, its fare is guaranteed to be delicious. Take your pick from the chefs' creations that rotate on a circular conveyor belt at the sushi bar. Another bar in the corner offers specialty creations like a 'Saketini.' This is a great place to go with friends for a low-key, chill time, or for some fun sake-bombing. **B**

2630 N Clark St
773.248.3900
RED LINE to CLARK/DIVISION

Bird's Nest

Bird's Nest is the perfect hangout spot if you're in the mood for $1 burgers, hot chicken wings and cool pitchers of beer

2500 N Southport Ave
773.472.1502
RED LINE to FULLERTON

ABOVE: Scarecrow, Oz Park, 2021 N. Burling St. LYDIA MERRILL • **RIGHT:** Sweet Mandy B's, 1208 W. Webster Ave. LYDIA MERRILL

LEFT: St. Vincent, DePaul University, Webster & Sheffield. LYDIA MERRILL • **BELOW**: St. Vincent, DePaul University, Webster & Sheffield. LYDIA MERRILL

in a collegiate atmosphere. The scene is very laidback, though Tuesday night performances liven up the crowd. The beer signs decorating the walls give the bar an authentic vibe. **B-**

Bordo's Eatery Sauce

Bordo's, a popular restaurant and bar in Lincoln Park, offers a fusion of American and Italian cuisine. The menu features burgers, wraps, sandwiches and pastas. The inviting atmosphere makes the restaurant an

2476 N Lincoln Ave
773.529.5900
RED LINE to FULLERTON

ideal place to dine or order cocktails with a few friends. Outdoor seating is available when it is warm enough. **A**

Buffalo Wild Wings Bar & Grill

Boasting an impressive 43 TVs, including seven big screens, four flat-screens and two plasmas, this restaurant has a sporty, casual atmosphere. The menu includes sauce-spun wings, half-pound burgers, ribs and sandwiches. Most of the TVs are tuned in to sports channels.

2464 N Lincoln Ave
773.858.9453
RED LINE to FULLERTON

Boka

1729 N. Halsted St.
312.337.6070
RED LINE to NORTH/CLYBOURN

Though you may be quick to dismiss Boka as overpriced, if you have the cash to drop on a night out on the town then give this place a chance; the quality of the food, service and atmosphere make it a near-perfect dining experience worth every pretty penny. The luscious spinach-stuffed baby squid with black tapioca and spicy pineapple, as well as the whole-roasted quail with wild rice and organic apricot, are delectably-unique dishes you won't find anywhere but here. The striking presentation of the food is also delightful: Everything about Boka is first-class. Try the banana bread pudding for dessert.

Trattoria Gianni

1711 N. Halsted St.
312.266.1976
RED LINE to NORTH/CLYBOURN

Trattoria Gianni sports an informal interior you would expect to find in an Italian eatery: mahogany floors and chairs, brick walls, and black-and-white framed photographs. The restaurant offers a wide selection of regional Italian dishes. Highlights include Linguine Portofino, a savory combination of scallops, shrimp scampi, tomatoes and garlic, and Petto d'Anatra alla Julia, a juicy, grilled duck breast with mushrooms, onions and tomatoes. A prime spot to eat before or after seeing a show at any of the nearby theaters, Trattoria Gianni caters to an older crowd ready for a hearty Italian meal and the high bill that accompanies it.

This is a perfect restaurant to catch up with friends in a laid-back environment. **B**

Fiesta Mexicana Restaurant

An ideal restaurant for a casual afternoon meal, Fiesta Mexicana has an extensive menu of reasonably-priced lunch spe-

2423 N Lincoln Ave
773.769.4244
RED LINE to FULLERTON

cials. The restaurant is festooned with colorful piñatas hanging from the ceiling that complement the bright red tablecloths. Upbeat Mexican music blares loudly in the background. The most popular dishes are the fajitas and the enchiladas. **A-**

Frances' Restaurant and Delicatessen

Who knew there were seven different kinds of root beer? Before visiting Frances', probably no one. This Lincoln Park joint also specializes in milkshakes, enormous sandwiches, soups and omelets. But be prepared to wait for this food on the weekends – the place is usually packed with people of all ages. **A-**

2552 N Clark St
773.248.4580
RED LINE to FULLERTON

Hanabi Japanese Restaurant

Hanabi Japanese Restaurant offers standard Japanese fare such as shrimp tempura and teriyaki chicken, bee, and salmon. The service is friendly, but the food is mediocre. A highlight is the Hurricane Maki, a spicy, deep-fried tempura roll. Come if you're hungry and in the area, but this joint is nothing special. **B-**

806 W Webster Ave
773.935.3474
RED LINE to FULLERTON

Jade East Chinese Cuisine

There's a visible refrigerator on one side of Jade East, which gives the atmosphere a low-key feel, perhaps one that is

2511 N Lincoln Ave
773.883.9797
RED LINE to FULLERTON

Cycle Smithy, 2468 1/2 N. Clark St. AMANDA ADLESICK

LEFT: Coffee and the City, 2201 N. Sheffield Ave. LYDIA MERRILL • **BELOW:** Graffiti, N. Sheffield Ave. LYDIA MERRILL

LINCOLN PARK

even too low-key. One unusual aspect of this otherwise typical Chinese food joint is that it serves fresh fruit smoothies, which come in rare flavors such as avocado and papaya. **C–**

Lincoln Station

This fun bar and grill serves a variety of American cuisine ranging from burgers to their most popular dish, the California chicken sandwich. Perfect for a private event or a casual night at the bar, Lincoln Station has 13 TVs, with two big screens and a satellite dish. Specials include $2.50 beer pints and 25 cent jumbo wings on Mondays. **A**

2432 N Lincoln Ave
773.472.8100
RED LINE to FULLERTON

Lincoln Town Gyros

After a night of bar and club hopping in Lincoln Park, college students can stumble into this restaurant to satisfy their late-night munchies. Open until 2 a.m. during the week and 4 a.m. on the weekend, Lincoln Town Gyros specializes in cheese steaks, hamburgers,

2500 N Halsted St
773.929.9411
RED LINE to FULLERTON

Greek salads and, of course, gyros. All the eats are cheap but make sure to bring cash because credit cards are not accepted. **B**

Luna Caprese

If you crave home-style Southern Italian cooking, visit Luna Caprese. The chef/owner, a native of Capri, makes all 14 of his fresh, flavorful pastas from scratch. The restaurant is romantic and cozy with its brick and dark wood walls. Because most of the waiters know the customers by name, you're bound to feel right at home. **A–**

2239 N Clybourn Ave
773.281.4825
RED LINE to FULLERTON

O'Famé

O'Famé has the looks and portions of a family-style Italian eatery, but not the flavor. The restaurant's specialty, aglio e olio [olive oil and garlic] sauce goes great on penne noodles or pizza. However, the pies and pasta aren't the best in town and the wait for a table can be painstakingly long. **C+**

750 W Webster Ave
773.929.5111
RED LINE to FULLERTON

Ringo Japanese Restaurant

Ringo Japanese Restaurant features a unique 'kushi' bar, which

2507 N Lincoln Ave
773.248.5788
RED LINE to FULLERTON

is a sushi bar that offers skewered foods instead of raw fish. The restaurant has an all-you-can-eat special on Mondays, which allows customers the option of an unlimited buffet for $19.50 per person. The room is decorated in a contemporary style, with bare yellow walls. **B+**

Rose Angelis

Perfect for a romantic date, Rose Angelis has an intimate, cozy vibe.

1314 W Wrightwood Ave
773.296.0081
RED LINE to FULLERTON

Smaller rooms lead up to the larger dining area. The moderately-priced menu offers scant options and doesn't serve any red meat, but the quality of the rest of the items makes up for the lack of protein. Highlights include the duck-filled tortellini and the ricotta-stuffed ravioli. **A-**

Savor the Flavor Coffee House

Just blocks away from DePaul University, this unique ice cream and

2574 N Lincoln Ave
773.883.5287
RED LINE to FULLERTON

smoothie shop is an ideal stop for students looking for a quiet place to study or people craving a cup of coffee. This bright Lincoln Park shop offers free wireless internet to customers. Their menu includes teas, muffins, milkshakes and cookies. **A**

Simply It

Simply don't come here! This Vietnamese restaurant is less than pleasing

2269 N Lincoln Ave
773.248.0884
RED LINE to FULLERTON

with its dirty glasses and dishes. To top it off, the food is over-fried and over-spiced. Surprisingly, the tables are filled by a middle-aged crowd. The only upside that we can see at this restaurant is the BYOB policy. **C-**

Sweet Basil

Sweet Basil, closed on Wednesdays, is a low-key Thai restaurant

2410 N Lincoln Ave
773.929.9996
RED LINE to FULLERTON

with reasonable prices. A talk show plays in the background, giving the restaurant a laid-back atmosphere. There are a few plants in the front by the windows, and there's a flat screen TV on one wall. The menu has a choice of 76 dishes, the most popular of which are the Pad Thai, Pad Khee Mao and Panang Curry. **C**

TOP Chicago Historical Society, 1601 N. Clark St. AMANDA ADLESICK • **MIDDLE** The Left Bank, 1155 W. Webster Ave. AMANDA ADLESICK • **BOTTOM** North Beach Club, 1551 N. Sheffield Ave. AMANDA ADLESICK

Sweets & Savories

Decorated in pinks and browns with chandeliers and artwork on the walls, this café is a charming little place to stop by for afternoon tea. Served during the week by reservation only, the tasty tea is complimented by sweet breads and finger sandwiches. Dinner here is fancier, and pricier, though there is a fixed-price menu option for the seven-course meal. **A-**

1534 W Fullerton Ave
773.281.6778
RED LINE to FULLERTON

Swirlz Cupcakes

The motto for this pastel-painted shop is 'cupcakes make people happy,' and the space, though small, certainly conveys that very message. Swirlz offers the five same flavors every day, in addition to five rotating flavors, some of which are gluten-free or low in sugar, though the bestselling one is bittersweet chocolate. Seating is limited, but you shouldn't have a problem, even on a warm spring afternoon. **A**

705 W Belden Ave
773.404.2253
RED LINE to FULLERTON

The Gramercy

Enjoy a cocktail in this classy all-white lounge. This chic hotspot has a contemporary style and is perfect for a romantic dinner for two or a large party looking for a night of dancing. The menu includes American cuisine

2438 N Lincoln Ave
773.477.8880
RED LINE to FULLERTON

Akira, 2357 N. Clark St. LYDIA MERRILL

LINCOLN PARK

such as portabella ravioli and grilled salmon served on a bed of basmati rice. **A**

Lincoln Park Zoo

2200 N. Cannon Dr.
312.742.2000
BROWN LINE to ARMITAGE

Established in 1868, this Lincoln Park gem is one of the oldest zoos in the country, as well as one of the most popular. With its exotic exhibits featuring everything from penguins and polar bears to cheetahs and lions and even yellow-spotted Amazon River turtles, the zoo's diversity of animals attracts nearly three million visitors a year. A perfect diversion for a warm summer day, stroll through the zebra area to embark on an African trek without straying a centimeter from Chicago. Lincoln Park Zoo's intimate setting, expertly-planned layout and plethora of amusement offerings – including a 4-D Virtual Safari simulator and swan boat and paddle boat rides – provide fun for all visitors, regardless of age. Open 365 days a year with free admission, this cultural venue makes for a great date location.

RIGHT: Alfred Caldwell Lily Pool, Lincoln Park Zoo. LYDIA MERRILL • **BELOW:** DePaul University. LYDIA MERRILL

The Hoagie Hut

The Hoagie Hut, a low-key, fast food restaurant just around the corner from DePaul University, sells grilled-to-order subs; one of the favorite dishes is the chicken finger sandwich. The Hoagie Hut is ideal for a late night snack, open until 3 a.m. on Fridays and 4 a.m. on Saturdays. There are also vegetarian options on the menu. **B-**

2580 N Lincoln Ave
773.248.0900
RED LINE to FULLERTON

The Pita Pit

Grab lunch or a snack at this pita restaurant. Its bright green and red walls

2404 N Lincoln Ave
773.935.7842
RED LINE to FULLERTON

provide a fun, casual atmosphere for students looking for a quick bite to eat. The restaurant serves made-to-order pita sandwiches, with a wide range of toppings including baby spinach, jalapeños and banana peppers. Sauces range from ranch to tzatziki. You can place a delivery order in advance online at pitapitusa.com **A-**

The Red Lion Pub

This old-fashioned English-style pub, adorned with paintings of English rulers, is a perfect getaway from the fast-paced streets of Chicago. It has a comfortable, homey feel, with papers lying around the bar and an old

2442 N Lincoln Ave
773.348.2695
RED LINE to FULLERTON

The Second City

1616 N. Wells St.
312.337.3992
BROWN LINE to SEDGWICK

Come to this comedy club and in no time, you'll be laughing so hard you'll have to pee. Known for its witty sketch comedy and improv, this venue has been in operation since 1959 and is now a Chicago landmark. Boasting two resident stages, The Second City Mainstage and The Second City, this venue offers superb performances: past actors have included talented comic greats like Bill Murray and Gilda Radner. With its nightly comedy shows, this place is especially popular among the adult crowd, specifically those in their 20s and 30s. While the drinks and food are expensive, the overall experience is worth every penny. Seats are assigned on a first-come, first-serve basis.

bookcase in the back of the room. Their most popular dishes are fish and chips and shepherd's pie. **A⁻**

Wokki Asian Eatery

Located just off the corner of Alley and W. Fullerton Ave., this casual restaurant offers a broad selection of typical Asian cuisine to its customers, who are primarily students and staff from the nearby hospital. The most popular dish, the 'Wokki Specialty' – orange chicken – is priced at $7.99. Too busy for a sit-down meal? The restaurant delivers and has a coupon for free delivery printed on their menu. **C**

818 W Fullerton Ave
773.327.6701
RED LINE to FULLERTON

Filippo's

Filippo's simple yet aesthetically-pleasing interior features yellow walls, wooden floors and a large jade-green curtain draped over the front door and windows. The menu offers original Italian options such as risotto with fresh crabmeat and crab legs smothered in tomato sauce and Ravioli Neri [ravioli

2211 N Clybourn Ave
773.528.2211
RED LINE to NORTH/CLYBOURN

stuffed with salmon and ricotta cheese served in a light pink sauce]. **B⁺**

Pequod's Pizza

This pizza joint is a guaranteed good time. The atmosphere can be a little loud on hot nights, but it's much more fun that way. The pizza is absolutely incredible, with a sweet crust, and the walls are covered with graffiti art, giving the whole restaurant an edgy, alternative vibe. **A**

2207 N Clybourn Ave
773.327.1512
RED LINE to NORTH/CLYBOURN

TO PLAY

Cleise Brazilian Day Spa

Craving chocolate? Get your fill without breaking your diet when you indulge in Cleise's unique Body Chocolate Glow treatment. This day spa is known for providing unique Brazilian procedures to the women of Lincoln Park. Though it specializes in Brazilian bikini waxes and eyebrow waxing, this salon also

1841 N Sheffield Ave
312.440.1060
BROWN LINE to ARMITAGE

LINCOLN PARK

LEFT: Chicago Green City Market. LYDIA MERRILL • **ABOVE:** Lincoln Ave. LYDIA MERRILL

does bust care and facial treatments. The owner, Cleise, is very sweet and takes pride in her practice. So treat yourself to all the chocolate you want — guilt-free. **B**

Clybar

Somehow, even from the outside, this lounge stands out among the slew of sports bars lining the same street. Its interior upholds this claim: The red décor, working fireplace and candles all channel a romantic mood. But this joint is definitely not ideal for a large gathering as the long, narrow shape can be difficult to maneuver through when crowded. **B-**

2417 N Clybourn Ave
773.388.1877
BROWN LINE to ARMITAGE

Kincades Bar and Grill

Just off the Armitage 'El' stop, this feel-good bar is constantly bustling with a vibrant young crowd ready to drink and socialize. For those looking to mingle, Kincades offers an extensive bar and standing tables on the first floor. A smoky downstairs provides a grittier feel

950 W Armitage Ave
773.348.0010
BROWN LINE to ARMITAGE

while larger tables on the second floor are perfect for those patrons looking to chat with friends and chow down on classic bar food. **B**

Steppenwolf Theatre

The Steppenwolf Theatre, an internationally-renowned company of 41 artists was founded in 1976 and has grown tremendously since that year. The Chicago-based, Tony-Award-winning garage theatre offers many unique ensemble collaborations and has won worldwide recognition for its creative and innovative productions. With tickets priced at an affordable $20 each, a show here is not to be missed. Gather your artsy friends together for a cultural alternative to a night of heavy-drinking and bar-hopping. **A-**

1650 N Halsted St
312.335.1650
BROWN LINE to ARMITAGE

Delilah's

This is the ultimate eclectic hang-out spot. The bar is long and has plenty of tables for seating as well as an upstairs

2771 N Lincoln Ave
773.472.2771
BROWN LINE to DIVERSEY

ABOVE: Lincoln Ave. LYDIA MERRILL • **RIGHT:** Clark St. LYDIA MERRILL

1154 Lill Studio

904 W. Armitage Ave.
773.477.5455
BROWN LINE to ARMITAGE

Pick your style. Pick your fabrics. Love your LILL. These are the directions you are given when entering this spacious, one-of-a-kind boutique. In the age of the designer handbag, a girl's purse often defines her. However, owner Jennifer Velarde gives you the chance to decide what you would like your handbag to say about you by allowing you to custom-make your own clutch, shoulder bag or large tote. Choose from hundreds of rich fabrics, from silk to cotton, and a variety of hues and patterns that line the store's wall and dictate everything from the shape to the color of your bag. Then all you have to do is pick it up when it's ready, usually two weeks after your visit.

LINCOLN PARK

area with a pinball machine. Every night boasts a different theme, so you'll always be experiencing something fresh. Weekdays are the most crowded but a free movie is screened every Saturday. Come to Delilah's to enjoy a friendly staff, $2 beer/whiskey specials, unique music and an artsy crowd. **A-**

Kingston Mines

For those in the mood for all-night blues music, and good blues music at

2548 N Halsted St
773.477.4646
BROWN LINE to DIVERSEY

that, Kingston Mines is definitely the place to go. Open until 5 a.m. on Saturdays and 4 a.m. the rest of the week, this huge venue boasts two music stages, a bustling bar and a kitchen serving barbecued food. College nights are frequent, so bring a school ID and bypass the usual cover charges. **A**

Bacchus

This three-story venue feels like three different clubs. Downstairs, you'll

2242 N Lincoln Ave
773.477.5238
RED LINE to FULLERTON

find a small, smoky bar area. On the second level, neon lights, a blue mosaic-tiled bar and lush couches convey a club-scene vibe. On the top floor, a smaller balcony and bar give weary club-goers a respite from the heavier crowds on lower levels. The DJs spin a variety of music, from low-key acid jazz in the early evenings to hip hop and dance music in the later hours. **A**

Frank's

A small lounge with just enough breathing room for a bar, a few tables, a pool table and a jukebox, Frank's isn't the place for

2503 N Clark St
773.549.2700
RED LINE to FULLERTON

Mural, N. Halsted St. LYDIA MERRILL

Old Town School of Folk Music, 4544 N. Lincoln Ave. LYDIA MERRILL

– it's open until 5 a.m. on Saturdays and 4 a.m. the rest of the week. **B**

Gramercy

	2438 N Lincoln Ave
	773.477.8880
	RED LINE to FULLERTON

This chic, trendy bar has the ambiance of an uptown bar without all the snobbery. The all-white interior gives it a cool and relaxing vibe and the cozy coves make great nooks and crannies. With two bars and a DJ booth pumping out tunes, this bar has a little bit of everything to give you a good time. **A-**

Kendall's Pub

	2263 N Lincoln Ave
	773.348.7200
	RED LINE to FULLERTON

This bar is a haven for sports fans. With seven huge projection screens, tons of other smaller televisions and access to 16 satellite and cable providers, almost any athletic game can be watched. With so many screens around, you may forget you're at a bar and feel like you're actually at a game. But don't expect the typical grub served in the stands – the menu offers nicer fare with its pasta and sandwich selections. **A**

Lasky Martial Arts

	2442 N Lincoln Ave
	773.549.5425
	RED LINE to FULLERTON

Take a break from the monotony of your daily schedule and sign up for a martial arts class with Lasky Martial Arts. There is a high-energy teen class designed to teach students self-defense combinations and an adult class for total fitness training of the mind, body

a night of dancing. This demure venue, with its candlelight and lava lamps, is a place to unwind while sipping a few drinks. Just make sure to stay awake because this place gets started late

Cynthia Rowley

808 W. Armitage Ave.
773.528.6160
BROWN LINE to ARMITAGE

It's true, not all couture divas hail from the dark and musty sex-filled streets of Paris. Illinois native Cynthia Rowley designs some of the trendiest and most fashionable clothes available today. Walking into her Lincoln Park boutique is like frolicking at a carnival. The variety of shapes, colors and fabrics pulls your attention to all different corners of the store. Some pieces, like a stunning electric blue jumpsuit, are a bit too bold for the average girl to sport, but others, the classic black cocktail dress with built-in pockets, for example, have the ability to make the average girl feel undeniably unique.

and spirit. For more advanced participants, Lasky Martial Arts offers a weekly class called the Black Belt Club. **B+**

Neo

Not quite your standard college fraternity boy hangout, Neo aims for

2305 N Clark St
773.528.2622
RED LINE to FULLERTON

the industrial Goth crew. But don't worry about accidentally wandering in; if you make it up the dimly-lit alley to the door, the lack of lighting and surplus of eyeliner will definitely clue you in as to what awaits you inside. **B+**

Notabaert Nature Museum

The Notabaert is a great museum for discovering how fascinating science

2430 N Cannon Dr
773.755.5100
RED LINE to FULLERTON

can be and enjoying a seamless blend of science and nature. Don't just come once – stop by often to check out the constantly changing exhibits and bring along a younger sibling for an enjoyable [and educational] day in the city. **A-**

Trim

This unique body shop is one of Chicago's only salons that specializes

2503 N Lincoln Ave
773.525.8746
RED LINE to FULLERTON

in custom-tailored waxing. The salon provides a range of waxing services, using the finest waxes and pre- and post-treatment oils and gels. The services range from eyebrow shaping to the 'boy-friend' packages – where you and your significant other both go for treatment. **B**

Victory Gardens Theater

Victory Gardens Theater is located at the site of the historical and suppos-

2257 N Lincoln Ave
773.549.5788
RED LINE to FULLERTON

edly haunted Biograph Theater, which includes a spacious lobby, comfortable seats and a 12-row theater – assuring that seats are a maximum of 45 feet away from the stage. The theater shows world-premiere performances, including the 'Snow Queen' and 'Denmark.' Though situated in the heart of Lincoln Park, it has easily-accessible parking. **A**

Krem

Krem is Lincoln Park's new 'dine and disco.' Inside you'll find white tables and ottomans, a 33-foot-long 'bed' and all-en-

1750 N Clark St
312.932.1750
RED LINE to NORTH/CLYBOURN

TOP The Victory Gardens Biograph Theater, 2433 N. Lincoln Ave. AMANDA ADLESICK • **MIDDLE** The Tin Lizzie, 2483 N. Clark St. AMANDA ADLESICK • **BOTTOM** The Basil Leaf Cafe, 2460 N. Clark St. AMANDA ADLESICK

LINCOLN PARK

RIGHT: William Shakespeare, Lincoln Park. AMANDA ADLESICK • **BELOW:** Alfred Caldwell Lily Pool, Lincoln Park Zoo. AMANDA ADLESICK

compassing blue lighting. Krem has a champagne and martini bar as well as a main bar, but drink prices run steep [anywhere from $10-15]. Small plates like ceviche and pork empanadas are perfect to nibble on while drinking. Though Krem tries hard to be chic, it's still far from rivaling a New York City or Miami hotspot. **B**

TO SHOP

Active Endeavors

Active Endeavors provides adorable clothing for young women craving
853 W Armitage Ave
773.281.0957
BROWN LINE to ARMITAGE

high fashion who don't mind paying steep prices. Home to a multitude of top-of-the-line brands, the store is designed well for browsing. Unique yet highly-trendy clothing covers the walls of this modern apparel store, and it's guaranteed to rob your wallet. **B⁻**

All She Wrote

All She Wrote sells tons of cute invitation cards, stationary and other small
825 W Armitage Ave
773.529.0100
BROWN LINE to ARMITAGE

gifts. The paper styles here are unique and girly,

perfect for writing that letter to your best friend from home. Make sure to come here and pick up an adorable picture frame if you're searching for a birthday gift for your girlfriend. The staff is friendly and eager to help customers looking to design invites. **A**

Aroma Workshop

Have you been endlessly searching in vain for that perfect new signature
2050 N Halsted St
773.871.1985
BROWN LINE to ARMITAGE

scent? Then come to Aroma Workshop and make your own. The employees will help you mix all the scents together to create your perfect fragrance. Once you've decided, you can pair your new scent with a shower gel or body lotion of the same note. This is a good place to buy a gift for your best girl friend or your sister. **A**

Barker & Meowsky

Attention all animal lov-ers: This cute store may be a new favorite of yours.
1003 W Armitage Ave
773.868.0200
BROWN LINE to ARMITAGE

Selling trendy items for your furry one, it offers a fun and inviting atmosphere. This 'paw firm' offers more than just gourmet dog biscuits and doggie couture; it's ready to primp and prime your loved one, making them ready for a walk out on the town. **B+**

Benefit

Decorated like a classic 70's salon, Benefit will transform you into a true

852 W Armitage Ave
773.880.9192
BROWN LINE to ARMITAGE

'Betty.' Nowadays, it's hard to find a beautician who won't smoke your eyes until you look like a raccoon. However, Benefit's accommodating staff listens to all of your beauty concerns so that you will leave looking and feeling a bit more fabulous than when you first walked in. Not to mention, the make-up products are to die for. **A-**

Endo-Exo Apothecary Cosmetics

This store carries several lines of cosmetic necessi- ties. If you're in the area

2034 N Halsted St
773.525.0500
BROWN LINE to ARMITAGE

and need make-up, shampoo or a new fragrance, Endo-Exo has a large selection to choose from. The staff is helpful and knows their inventory well so they can help you quickly find whatever you're looking for. The prices are similar to those in chain cosmetic stores like Sephora, but this shop is a little more personal. **A**

Francesca's Collections

If you're trying to save your hard-earned cash but still want to find

2012 N Halsted St
773.244.4075
BROWN LINE to ARMITAGE

something cute, Francesca's is a great option. In the expensive realm of Lincoln Park shopping, this boutique provides shoppers with comfort- ing relief. They carry great dresses, shoes and jewelry but also have other trinkets. Perhaps the best part of this store is their huge selection of earrings, guaranteed to match that difficult hue of your formal dress. **A-**

Guise

Guise is the perfect pit- stop for guys shopping in the Lincoln Park area. The

2217 N Halsted St
773.929.6101
BROWN LINE to ARMITAGE

creators of this store have ingeniously combined a hair salon with a men's clothing shop to boost its convenience. The stylists also offer customers beer in the barber's chair. Plus, they do nails for men. Though this venue is probably more appeal- ing to the appearance-conscious due to the steep price of the cuts, the concept of the store is too cool to ignore. **A**

Clarke's Diner, 2441 N. Lincoln Ave.
AMANDA ADLESICK

LINCOLN PARK

Keihl's

Kiehl's is a great option if you're searching for cosmetics in Lincoln Park.

907 W Armitage Ave
773.665.2515
BROWN LINE to ARMITAGE

They're most known for their extensive line of skincare products, especially their delightful lotions. Plus, you'll love shopping here because of the friendly staff that are happy to fill your bag with free samples on the way out. **A**

Lori's

From slingbacks to peep-toes, Lori's has every kind of shoe a woman could

824 W Armitage Ave
773.281.5655
BROWN LINE to ARMITAGE

want. Not to mention, every item in the store is sold at discounted retail prices. Lori's should be called the 'sole of Chicago' because it caters to any shoe lover's heart. The only downside is that the high stacks of Steve Maddens and Michael Kors boxes can cause a hectic rat race of shoe-hungry ladies. **A**

Lucy

Lucy carries great exercise gear that is trendy yet functional. The staff is

2122 N Halsted St
773.248.3605
BROWN LINE to ARMITAGE

happy to help you sort through all the active-girl basics from cute yoga apparel to sports bras, all reasonably priced. Even though most prices are low, make sure to scour the clearance and sale racks. You might find something you love. **A-**

Margaret O'Leary

This clean boutique takes the idea of spring fashions too seriously. The

857 W Armitage Ave
773.598.5625
BROWN LINE to ARMITAGE

overwhelming amount of powder pink and baby blue items make it seem as if Easter is eternally celebrated within the doors of this store. Aside from the typical cashmere sweaters, the $100+ prices don't seem to match the value of Margaret O'Leary's plain pieces. **C+**

Mint Boutique

Easily one of the best boutiques in Lincoln Park, Mint carries great jeans,

2150 N Seminary Ave
773.322.2944
BROWN LINE to ARMITAGE

tops, jewelry, purses and other girly accessories. Most of the designs come from local designers and artists so you can be sure to find something unique. The price range is large so it's up to you if you want to buy something cheap or splurge on

ABOVE: Savor the Flavor, 2545 N. Sheffield Ave. LYDIA MERRILL • **RIGHT:** 3rd Annual Chalk Festival, 2021 N. Burling St. LYDIA MERRILL

LEFT: Advertisement, Clark St. AMANDA ADLESICK
• **BELOW:** Halligan's Bar, 2274 N. Lincoln Ave. AMANDA ADLESICK

something a little pricier. Either way, you won't regret browsing in this shop. **A**

Nau

The three design prin-
ciples behind this environ-
mentally-friendly outdoor

2118 N Halsted St
773.289.1363
BROWN LINE to ARMITAGE

apparel company are 'beauty, performance and sustainability.' They use simple earthy colors and designs in their clothing, and have been the innovative mind behind brands like Nike, Adidas and Patagonia. The store even features computer kiosks so that customers can order online, should their sizes be out of stock in-store. **B**

Out of the West

This little boutique,
resembling a ranch on
the inside, channels a

1000 W Armitage Ave
773.404.9378
BROWN LINE to ARMITAGE

Southwestern vibe. The selling of saddles and cowboys boots set the mood, while designer jeans and tops make a visit to Out of the West worthwhile. Although it can get a little pricy, the one-of-a-kind items for your household top off the shop. **A⁻**

Paper Source

As its name implies, the
Paper Source carries every
color, texture and style of

919 W Armitage Ave
773.525.7300
BROWN LINE to ARMITAGE

paper you could possibly imagine. This is good place to shop if you are into scrapbooking or simply need to make invitations. They carry tons of rubber stamps, binding supplies, ribbons and whimsical wrapping paper. The shop is large, the prices are reasonable, and the staff is helpful. **B+**

Coffee and the City, 2201 N. Sheffield Ave. LYDIA MERRILL

to shop

LINCOLN PARK

RIGHT: Lincoln Park Zoo, 2200 N. Cannon Ave. AMANDA ADLESICK • **BELOW:** DePaul University. AMANDA ADLESICK

Paul Frank

	851 W Armitage Ave
	773.388.3122
	BROWN LINE to ARMITAGE

Paul Frank was definitely more fun when you were in middle school. The cute little cartoon animals that decorate this store's T-shirts, pajamas and accessories are more nostalgic than anything else. This is a great store to buy a gift for a younger sibling if you think you're too old to plaster a cartoon monkey's face across your chest, although Paul Frank's style can still be fun. **B+**

Rachel Ashwell Shabby Chic

	2146 N Halsted St
	773.327.9372
	BROWN LINE to ARMITAGE

Contrary to the name, 'shabby chic' means elegant, comfortable, vintage-y, and eclectic. You may remember Ashwell from the E! Style Network, where her TV show premiered. In-store, you'll find a number of eccentric accessories to spruce up your home, from aromas to feathers and furs. Ashwell uses everything from shells to beads, creating a comforting ambiance for your home. **B+**

Rugby

	1000 W Armitage Ave
	773.525.4627
	BROWN LINE to ARMITAGE

This is Ralph Lauren's hip casual line, but don't worry, the classic preppy style remains intact. The store is divided into four separate rooms packed with colorful knits, Oxford shirts, blazers, skirts, accessories and more. The battered leather sofas and wood furniture displays create a rugged ambiance. Not satisfied with the Rugby shirt designs? Go ahead and design your own right in the store. **B+**

Studio 910

	910 W Armitage Ave
	773.929.2400
	BROWN LINE to ARMITAGE

The offerings of Studio 910 look like they were just dug out of the back of your closet. This dimly-lit store offers a meager display of last season's fashion. Though they carry designers such as Diane Von Furstenburg, Hudson jeans and Da-Nang, they don't do justice to these fabulous brands. They are in the process of re-vamping their store, so check back in the near future and hopefully it will be better than its present state. **C⁻**

Tabula Tua

This tableware store features a range of casual everyday pieces as well

1015 W Armitage Ave
773.525.3500
BROWN LINE to ARMITAGE

as unique accents and accessories for your home. The perfect place to find caprice shell plates for a classy dinner party or delicate trays to serve your home-cooked pies, Tabula Tua caters to homemakers. They've recently expanded their line to include home furnishings, including rugs, furniture, clocks, and pillows. **B**

Performance Bike Shop

If you're a cycling fanatic, this is definitely the store for you: It has everything a

2720 N Halsted St
773.248.0107
BROWN LINE to DIVERSEY

cyclist needs to boost performance. Selling everything from gear parts to accessories, Performance Bike Shop ensures that you won't have to look hard to find things to make your bike the hottest in town. The shop is located in a small strip mall, so may initially be hard to spot. **B⁺**

Betsy Johnson

Uniqueness is a notable trait of Betsy Johnson dresses, as a multitude

2120 N Halsted St
773.871.3961
BROWN LINE to FULLERTON

of vibrant colors and embellishments make each piece of merchandise that you'll find here one-of-a-kind. Patterns and prints bring life to the bold store. Fusing extravagance and elegance, these vintage yet trendy designs are definitely worth the price. **A⁻**

Barney's New York Co-Op

What do we all love about Barney's? The fabulous fashion. What do we all

2209 N Halsted St
773.248.0426
RED LINE to FULLERTON

hate about it? The painful prices. Unfortunately, Barney's Co-Op is no different from Barney's, the department store: The clothes are just as stunning and the prices are just as steep. However, Barney's Co-Op is preferred because everything

in the store is something you would actually wear on a regular basis. **A**

Bluemercury Apothecary Spa

With its pastel walls, fruity fragrance and rows of hair, makeup and skin-

2208 N Halsted St
773.327.6900
RED LINE to FULLERTON

care products displayed on light wooden shelves,

TOP Tomato Head Pizza, 1001 W. Webster Ave. LYDIA MERRILL • **MIDDLE** Ray Meyer Fitness Center, 2235 N. Sheffield Ave. LYDIA MERRILL • **BOTTOM** Corner of Dickens and Sheffield Ave. LYDIA MERRILL

DePaul University. LYDIA MERRILL

this store is inviting and charming. It also doubles as a spa. Many exclusive but expensive makeup lines are sold here, and the friendly, knowledge-able make-up artists are more than happy to pick out the perfect mauve lipstick for your skin tone. **A⁻**

Bunches

Step into this shop to find an unusual variety of flowers and combinations to choose from. Typically described as a garden shop, Bunches sells arrangements that are fresh and seasonal. Surprise a friend or loved one with a beautiful arrangement of flowers and choose from a range of vases, ribbons and cards to accompany the bouquet. **A⁻**

2456 N Lincoln Ave
773.975.2444
RED LINE to FULLERTON

Buy Popular Demand

In business for 17 years, this popular Lincoln Park women's consignment boutique has everything from business wear to

2629 N Halsted St
773.868.0404
RED LINE to FULLERTON

designer jeans. They even sell décor items like quirky china and mugs, all priced extremely low. Buy Popular Demand is a great place for the college student hunting for a good bargain – they sell Kate Spade purses for $30. Make sure you check out their backroom as well: though hidden from view, it's where all the sale items are. **B⁺**

Calvin Tran

In this small but personal boutique, you won't find your standard cookie-cutter women's fashion items. Calvin Tran uses beautiful, deep-hued silks to make asymmetrical, flowy and multi-functional skirts and shirts. He thinks of his products as original works of art, a thought that is reflected in the overwhelming price tags. **B**

2154 N Halsted St
773.529.4070
RED LINE to FULLERTON

Chicago Center for the Print

This Lincoln Park gallery houses many vintage European posters along

1509 W Fullerton Ave
773.477.1585
RED LINE to FULLERTON

with trendy contemporary prints. If you're looking for framing, the store provides the service on-site. The vast selection of art here allows you to find the perfect decorations for your apartment or dorm – it's time to break away from those black and white pictures of kissing couples and your 'Café Terrace At Night' print. **B+**

Contemporary Art Workshop

Renowned for being one of the oldest artist-run alternative spaces in the country, Contemporary Art Workshop features a wide range of exhibitions across media types. If you're an aspiring artist, you can bring in some of your creations, as the gallery frequently purchases pieces by new names. Or come simply to explore and enjoy the innovative art. **B+**

542 W Grant Place
773.472.4004
RED LINE to FULLERTON

Elliot Consignment

This easy-to-miss store is a hidden gem for unique designer clothes, shoes and handbags for nearly half the retail price. The catch? The items have been used, but for less than two years. You can find anything from

2465 N Lincoln Ave
773.404.6090
RED LINE to FULLERTON

Marc Jacobs wallets to True Religion jeans in this store, which has a basement full of sale merchandise priced as low as $4 per item. **A**

Fox's

Shopping should never have to feel like work. At Fox's, however, determination is key if you want to find what you're looking for. Be prepared to sift through tacky shirts with phrases like 'Hot Mama' printed across them and articles with unnecessary holes in them in your search for something worthy. However, it's worth the effort – you might be lucky enough to find an article of clothing from your favorite designer at half the normal price. **C+**

2150 N Halsted St
773.281.0700
RED LINE to FULLERTON

Londo Mondo

This trendy women's boutique, which carries stylish workout gear at reasonable prices, has a pop culture vibe, perhaps due to the hip-hop radio blaring through the speakers. While the motto at Londo Mondo is 'swim, skate, and fitness,' it really should be 'glamour sport,'

2148 N Halsted St
773.327.2218
RED LINE to FULLERTON

LEFT: Clark St. LYDIA MERRILL • **ABOVE:** Clark St. LYDIA MERRILL

since you can manage to find dresses among all the pink spandex. **B⁻**

TOP The Red Rooster, 2100 N. Halsted Ave. LYDIA
MERRILL • **MIDDLE** DePaul University. LYDIA MERRILL
• **BOTTOM** Glazed Expressions, 717 W. Armitage
Ave. LYDIA MERRILL

Lululemon

Lululemon, a yoga-inspired apparel line, aims to 'provide components

2104 N Halsted St
773.883.8860
RED LINE to FULLERTON

for people to live longer, healthier and more fun lives.' Their workout gear offers a great fit in a variety of trendy styles made from breathable materials. While some of their clothing can be expensive, the quality makes up for it. **A**

O & I Shoes

Shoes for kids, juniors, women and men are abound in this little shop.

2205 N Halsted St
773.281.5583
RED LINE to FULLERTON

Crazed shoe lovers should not get too excited though, because the sneakers, boots and sandals on display are more scattered about than organized. The mismatched Oriental carpets, techno music and unhelpful salespeople also add to the store's muddled feel. **C**

Spex

With its lime-green exterior and simple glass logo, this quirky spectacle store

2316 N Clark St
773.404.0777
RED LINE to FULLERTON

is sure to catch your attention as you walk past. Inside, you'll find a wide array of 'spex' to choose from. The helpful staff makes the experience of picking out just the right pair of trendy glasses painless and easy. **B**

The Blue Jeans Bar

Piles of neatly-folded brand-name jeans line dark wooden shelves

2210 N Halsted St
773.248.5326
RED LINE to FULLERTON

along the walls in this popular neighborhood store. Ranging from $150 to $250 a pair, they come in a wide assortment of rises and styles for a variety of customers: men, women and teenagers. While customers primarily come for the jeans, belts, jewelry and clothes are also available, from tiny printed cotton shirts to oversized True Religion vests. **A**

True Religion

True Religion's new Lincoln Park boutique has a rustic, country vibe and

| 2202 N Halsted St |
| 773.281.9590 |
| RED LINE to FULLERTON |

stocks various styles and cuts of True Religion jeans, hooded sweatshirts, tees, jackets and sweatpants for both men and women. But shoppers should be wary of the steep prices: Most items range from $150-400. If you're in the mood for a splurge, this fashionable boutique is the place to go. **B**

Underthings

Looking for lingerie? Come to this little tucked-away store, if you can fit inside.

| 804 W Webster St |
| 773.472.9291 |
| RED LINE to FULLERTON |

While the ceilings are high, making it a little less claustrophobic, the store is tiny and jam-packed with sleepwear, daywear and swimwear. Bouquets of red and pink roses, lacy underwear and pretty, blond employees all add to the store's cute and sexy feel. **B⁺**

White Elephant Resale Shop

You can find almost anything you want at White Elephant, whether

| 759 W Belden Ave |
| 773.883.6184 |
| RED LINE to FULLERTON |

it's a radio, a designer dress, or a novel – if you have the time to look for it, that is. Though this spacious store provides an array of new to slightly-used secondhand goods, everything is messily jumbled together. Bowls are hidden inside other bowls and furniture is scattered in the clothing section. With too many products and too expansive a space, shopping here can be overwhelming. **C⁺**

Xana Chambray Boutique

Step into the chandelier-lit Xana Chambray, and you might think you've

| 2154 N Halsted St |
| 773.404.2800 |
| RED LINE to FULLERTON |

walked into one of Lincoln Park's most expensive boutiques. But looks can be deceiving – though undeniably trendy and high-quality, the shop's inventory is reasonably-priced, partially because the owner, a DePaul graduate, had college students in mind when she opened it a year ago.

You'll find anything from linen pants to velvet blazers to locally-designed beaded jewelry here. **A**

TOP Lincoln Park Zoo, 2200 N. Cannon Ave. LYDIA MERRILL • **BOTTOM** Dickens Avenue Residences. LYDIA MERRILL

LINCOLN PARK

NORTH CENTER

**THE FEEL OF
A SECURITY
BLANKET**

Suburban bliss can be found in the city in the neighborhood of North Center, along with shops and restaurants that hark back to the good old days. Cute vintage and antique shops line Roscoe St. as well as a plethora of diners and cafes. There are also ritzier restaurants a plenty, catering to the wealthy yuppies that have recently populated the area. A weekly farmer's market runs every Sunday from June until October and there are enough bowling alleys to keep any kid – or kid at heart – entertained. Take a walk around the town square to enjoy the European-inspired architecture of the area. Along the tree-lined streets and in the three parks in this neighborhood, children run rampant but a few quality pubs provide fun of the grown-up variety. Though not the most happening area in Chicago [you won't find as many clubs or bars here as you will in the surrounding neighborhoods], it has the feel of a security blanket – warm, nostalgic and safe. The 19th district police headquarters is here too, so criminals on the north side beware.

TO EAT

Alps East

With its convenient hours [5:30 a.m. to 11 p.m., seven days a week], this joint is perfect if you're craving some quick sustenance. Though it may not be anything fancy, its fare is cheap and fairly good, especially its breakfast items and desserts. Make sure to bring cash though, because it's the only form of payment they accept. **B**

2012 W Irving Park Rd
773.975.0527
BROWN LINE to IRVING PARK

Always Thai

This local establishment serves all your Thai favorites. With entrees averaging about $8, this place is perfect for a quick, cheap bite with friends. The desired spiciness of dishes can also be customized to the customer's taste. Try their fried red snapper or their Thai pepper steak. However, the good food is detracted from by an obvious lack of ambiance. **B-**

1825 W Irving Park Rd
773.929.0100
BROWN LINE to IRVING PARK

Brownstone Tavern & Grill

This classy restaurant boasts a great atmosphere as well as great food. The interior is spacious and sophisticated. Serving American food along with a few foreign favorites like queso, chicken tortilla soup, and hummus, this tavern is known for its scrumptious salads, sandwiches and wraps. If the weather is nice, sit in their outdoor patio for the prefect backdrop to a laid-back meal. All carry-out orders are taken online. **B+**

3937 N Lincoln Ave
773.528.3700
BROWN LINE to IRVING PARK

Chicago Joe's

Joe's is a good restaurant to try if you crave the 'real Chicago' taste. Serving classic family entrees and appetizers, the menu includes raw oysters, barbeque chicken, and even 'Ma's Homemade Meatloaf.' Make sure you stop by when clam chowder is the soup of the day – it's worth the trip. Be warned however: The food can be a little pricy. **B+**

2256 W Irving Park Rd
773.478.7000
BROWN LINE to IRVING PARK

El Llano Restaurant

This restaurant is authentic all around. From the traditional Colombian cuisine to the cozy, ethnic atmosphere created by decorations and ornaments straight from Colombia, you feel transported to the land upon arrival. The food is great and the portions are enormous. Don't overlook the reasonable prices – especially for items on the lunch menu: A guaranteed bang for your buck. **B+**

3941 N Lincoln Ave
773.868.1708
BROWN LINE to IRVING PARK

Images Restaurant

If you're looking to spice up your night, this is just the place. Known for its authentic Cuban food, Images provides the recipe for a fabulous night out: food and fun. The restaurant offers free salsa classes on Mondays and free tango classes on Tuesdays. Top off a night of dancing on the spacious dance floor with a $5 margarita or mojito. Dancing, dining, and drinks all in one stop. **A-**

3908 N Lincoln Ave
773.348.7444
BROWN LINE to IRVING PARK

Katerina's

This swanky restaurant is a great place for a romantic evening. With its red walls, covered with pictures of blues singers, it boasts a classic and timeless atmosphere. The restaurant features live jazz and blues every night of the week along with some special ethnic performances. The food is reasonably priced, and its dim lighting and dreamy music make for a great first date location. **A-**

1920 W Irving Park Rd
773.348.7592
BROWN LINE to IRVING PARK

Laschet's Inn

Even from the outside of this split-level establishment, you'll feel as if you've suddenly stepped into the mountains of the German Alps. Inside, Laschet's Inn is decked out in German memorabilia, including ceramic mugs hanging from the wooden beams overhead. They offer a number of German delicacies such as goulash and Wiener schnitzel. Don't forget to order German beers to wash it all down with. **B-**

2119 W Irving Park Rd
773.478.7915
BROWN LINE to IRVING PARK

Snappy's Shrimp House

This takeout restaurant offers delicious entrees like fried jumbo shrimp, shrimp cocktail, fish and chips and chicken wings sold by the quarter pound. They claim to sell the best-tasting Gulf Shrimp around. Pair your meal with one of their numerous sides. Snappy's is the perfect place to pick up seafood hor'douvres for an upcoming party. **B**

1901 W Irving Park Rd
773.244.1008
BROWN LINE to IRVING PARK

Sola

At Sola, you'll find a seasonal menu with items boasting an 'American with California flair' as well as plenty of Asian and Hawaiian flavors. This place may be a little pricey, but your taste buds will love you for the splurge. Dishes like the trio of tuna tartares with Thai cucumber salsa, Dijon-encrusted rack of lamb stuffed with cambazola, and Hawaiian snapper are mouth-watering, while the classy décor is also very inviting. **A-**

3868 N Lincoln Ave
773.327.3868
BROWN LINE to IRVING PARK

Stella's Grill and Fast Foods

This corner fast food shop offers quick, quality food at reasonable prices. Specializing in gyros, burgers and soups, and using only Vienna beef, this restaurant has great food and an aroma that fills the area. Though you won't find a great atmosphere in the seating area, you can count on speed and taste satisfaction. **B**

| 2200 W Irving Park Rd |
| 773.588.2222 |
| BROWN LINE to IRVING PARK |

The Globe Pub

This typical bar, complete with a digital jukebox and drop-down TV screens,

| 1934 W Irving Park Rd |
| 773.871.3757 |
| BROWN LINE to IRVING PARK |

is mediocre at best, but if you can deal with an older crowd, the $3.50 pints of the featured beer of the month can add up to a good night. Though the weekends are usually the biggest nights, Wednesdays open mic nights draw a big crowd. **B-**

TO PLAY

Belle Plain Studio

This dance studio is unique in the city, offering both traditional jazz and ballet classes as well as yoga and music classes.

| 2014 W Bella Plain Rd |
| 773.935.1890 |
| BROWN LINE to IRVING PARK |

SPY STORE
BY BRAD FLORA

Do not be fooled. Wicker Park's the Boring Store is anything but.

Just a brisk walk from the Blue Line's Division station, The Boring Store is an after-school tutoring center disguised as an ultra-chic, secret agent supply shop that half-heartedly masquerades as a purveyor of drill-bits, holes and digging tools. It's an educational program hidden in a one-of-a-kind retail space, wrapped in a bad double-entendre.

Nothing ever happens at the Boring Store.

And they sell drill bits and holes.

Get it?

Despite its beautifully-designed, neon orange storefront's claims to the contrary, there's actually quite a bit going on inside. 826CHI, the writing center housed within, is one of several in a nation-wide chain of writing programs founded by novelist Dave Eggers, who also publishes the popular McSweeney's magazine and humor Web site. Eggers founded the first 826 center in Valencia,

California in the belief that 'great leaps in learning can happen with one-on-one attention and that strong writing skills are fundamental to crucial success,' according to the 826National Web site.

The program has been offering drop-in, field trip and bookmaking programs for local school kids for more than a year and has only this spring put the finishing touches on its storefront: a mysterious and often-times hilarious 'secret agent supply store' known as 'The Boring Store' that claims to be 'the nation's first exclusive supplier of holes.'

'All of our merchandise is specially labeled so that no one will ever know what you walk out of the store with,' said Leah Guenther, 826CHI's executive director, playing along while dutifully filling in behind the register on a cold and wet Monday afternoon.

She speaks truth. Every bit of spy gear sold at the Boring Store comes with a sticker saying what it does NOT contain, like the label on the grappling hook box, which proclaims: 'This is NOT a thirty-three foot nylon rope and collapsible hook for grappling.'

According to Guenther, the

Here adults and children are encouraged to fuse the learning of movement and music into one, creating an all-around performance experience. A great stop for aspiring Broadway stars. **B⁺**

Bodysense

This fitness facility specializes in personal fitness training and adheres to its appointment-only policy. The gym is small with only one of each machine, and the machines are geared more towards body sculpting and weight training than cardio. If you're looking for personalized attention without the crowds usually found

2110 W Irving Park Rd
773.583.8222
BROWN LINE to IRVING PARK

at large gyms, this clean and organized facility is perfect for you. **B**

Kenpo Karate Self-Defense Centers

Instead of preparing students for tournaments, this studio focuses primarily on street fighting. The most unique part of the training program is that they offer a combination of private and group lessons for every student at the same price most studios charge for group lessons alone. If you're looking for an inexpensive, flexible, and efficient way to learn how to

2151 W Irving Park Rd
773.539.2900
BROWN LINE to IRVING PARK

secret camera-glasses, mustache disguise kits and underwater voice amplifiers for sale in The Boring Store serve a triple purpose: funding new programs for the 826CHI kids, jolting them with quick doses of imagination every time they drop by for lessons and grabbing the attention of every adult [a.k.a. potential volunteer tutor] who secretly thinks he would have made one heck of a spy in another life.

Guenther says the Boring Store runs on foundation grants and private donations that come in through events like last spring's Mustache-a-thon, in

which volunteers competed to grow the best facial hair. Not surprisingly, Guenther says the storefront has fast-grown into an obsession for the 30 or so 6-to-18-year-old students who drop by every day for writing help.

That's all well and good, but what you really want to do is poke around the spy store, which features some grade-A comedy writing and clever design.

For starters, the store's awning consists of a devilishly clever piece of writing that claims the Boring Store is NO LONGER selling ANYTHING of utility. They

protect yourself on the street, Kenpo is the place for you. **B**

O'Donovan's

With an awesome atmosphere, outdoor seating and a cool backroom with an additional bar, this joint is a great place to hang out. Different specials run each night, from $2.00 burgers and fries on Mondays to 25-cent

2100 W Irving Park Rd
773.478.2100
BROWN LINE to IRVING PARK

wings on Tuesdays and Fridays. The food is offered all night long in huge portions and is very satisfying. **A**

Resi's Bierstube

If you're looking to celebrate Oktoberfest with an authentic German beer selection and German menu, this is the right place. This bar is known for its large selection

2034 W Irving Park Rd
773.472.1749
BROWN LINE to IRVING PARK

claim to sell only the most 'characterless and opiating stock of wearisome and lifeless items available in the United States.' The awning also claims the store hasn't had a customer in 28 years. The fine print even urges visitors to visit other 'stores' in the area, the name's of which all rhyme with 'boring.'

To screen visitors, an array of twenty-five surveillance cameras greets you at the door. Who knew such a boring store could be so paranoid? When the cameras sense movement they adjust positioning, creating an unnerving and somewhat sinister chorus of muted whirring noises. I imagine it does not feel so different than being sized up by a platoon

of hissing cobras.

The display closest to the front door hawks various concealment tools, like a rubber banana that doubles as a 'clever and unobtrusive cell phone hiding place.'

The labels on these boxes, like everything in the Boring Store, are written in the riotous, dry style common to McSweeney's, like this description of 'Watergate Fingers,' gloves that attach mini flashlights to each of your fingers for late-night snooping:

'The most influential legacy of the twentieth century boils down to one man, Bob Fosse. With his majesty in mind, we present you with these state of the art, jazz hand enhancers ... which should never be confused with WATERGATE FINGERS. You would never use something like this to rifle through file cabinets in the dead of night, cursing your poor alphabetization skills all the while. You have no time for such shenanigans. You are too busy reworking your bowler hat routine.'

One corner of the store is devoted to disguises, well mostly wigs and fake mustaches, actually.

When students hit a roadblock in their writing, they're sent to this corner to write about what they could get away with if they used a wig as a disguise. According to Guenther, one student charmingly wrote that he would use one

of beers as well as its beer garden. To complete a fun night, be sure to try the mystery beer – an anonymous beer hand-picked by the bartender. **B+**

Shirley John's Palm and Mind Reader

Though it's quite a hunt to find the location, whether you seek love or general life advice, make sure to visit this psychic. Be

3947 N Lincoln Ave
773.525.1753
BROWN LINE to IRVING PARK

immersed in a mystical setting after going up the stairs and learn a lot about yourself by getting a palm or mind reading. At only $10, readings are somewhat cheap. **B**

Penny Lane Lounge

The most popular time to visit this bar is from 2 a.m. to 4 a.m. It's almost always crowded during these hours, with patrons

4301 N Western Ave
773.539.1402
BROWN LINE to WESTERN

of the wigs to disguise himself as his own grandmother. Then he would head over to his school to explain to his teacher that his grandson was staying home sick.

My favorite item from this corner is the truly awesome mustache wallet, a $22 leather billfold with a mustache tacked to it, emblazoned with this blurb:

'The only reason wallets get stolen is because they look so much like wallets. This one, however, is carefully disguised.'

If that doesn't put a smile on your face, I don't know what will.

There isn't another store like The Boring Store in the city. The 826CHI team has put together an oddball, espionage fun-zone in the name of getting their kids psyched up for writing and it happens to be a fun place for adults to visit too, especially adults who appreciate

good writing. Guenther said she's received around 1000 applications from Chicagoans looking to tutor since the program started over a year ago.

If you live in Wicker Park, if you visit Wicker Park, or, heck, if you just live in Chicago. You probably owe it to your inner child to drop by The Boring Store and snoop around, even if it's just to chuckle at the spy gear and to try on a wig or two.

Who knows, maybe you'll find yourself cut out for life as a secret agent?

The Boring Store is located at 1331 N. Milwaukee Ave.

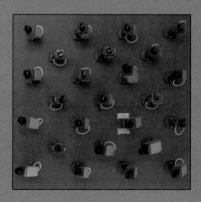

Café 28

1800 W. Irving Park Rd.
773.528.2883
BROWN LINE to IRVING PARK

This family-owned café prides itself on serving up dishes in a 'traditional Cuban and Mexican style with an eclectic Latin twist'. The Latin music and Mexican décor give this restaurant an authentic feel and the clean, modern furniture coupled with the sparse plant-life set visitors in an ambiance that looks more expensive than it is. Prices aren't the cheapest, but Café 28 is the perfect little North Center establishment to take a first date if you are willing to take the trip. Be sure to taste the quesadillas and check out the extensive drink list – they're known for their mojitos cocktails.

sitting amongst the Beatles décor awaiting their $3 beers and other inexpensive drinks. On the weekends, Penny Lane Lounge offers karaoke and trivia nights, while darts and video games are available all week. **C**

Crabby Kim's Bikini Bar

3655 N Western Ave
773.404.8156
RED LINE to ADDISON

True to the bar's name, bartenders really do wear bikinis all year-round. Don't show up wearing a bikini though – leave that to the professionals. But do dress casual – this place is anything but fancy. Besides the skin-baring bartenders, Crabbby Kim's is just like any other bar, though there is a beer garden outside. **B‒**

TO SHOP

Homey

3656 N Lincoln Ave
773.248.0050
BROWN LINE to ADDISON

Though you most likely won't be purchasing anything unless you're an avid art collector, Homey is a lovely gallery to walk through and enjoy. The art features a variety of mediums from photography to paint on canvas to sculpture, and the garden accessories are fun to look at as well. **B**

Blue Highway

3823 N Lincoln Ave
312.549.5640
BROWN LINE to IRVING PARK

If you're looking for something handmade to decorate your home with, Blue Highway is the place to find it. Because of their eclectic assortment, this is a great place to browse, even if you aren't interested in buying anything. If you like faux antiques, the shop remakes pieces from the 20th century. Beware the store's limited hours, however [12 p.m. – 5 p.m., closed Mondays]. **C**

Deadwax

3819 N Lincoln Ave
773.529.1932
BROWN LINE to IRVING PARK

This music store carries absolutely every kind of music imaginable, from pop to vintage records. Passionate music lovers will find it a great place to browse, even if they're not planning to buy anything. Don't be intimidated by the huge selection – the helpful staff make it easy to find what you're looking for. **A‒**

Dollar Discount

4024 N Lincoln Ave
773.477.5007
BROWN LINE to IRVING PARK

Looking for necessities on a budget? This is your number one stop for everything from groceries to purses to holiday accessories at the lowest prices. The clothes and other items may not be straight from the runways of Paris, but where else can you find belts for $1.99? This store is a must for back-to-school dorm or apartment shopping. **B+**

Extra Fancy

3827 N Lincoln Ave
312.665.2367
BROWN LINE to IRVING PARK

This shop's name may or may not be misleading depending upon your definition of fancy. It may not be elegant, but it certainly does offer objects that a select few would truly 'fancy' or enjoy. This is a very specialized market, so if you aren't looking for to explore a random collection of 20th century collectibles, stay away. **C⁺**

Hannoun Rugs from Morocco

The only reason you might want to go to Hannoun is if you are looking for a

3817 N Lincoln Ave
Phone
BROWN LINE to IRVING PARK

Moroccan rug or textile. Its selection, however, is truly beautiful if you are in the mood just to browse. The store carries many authentic and unique designs that would look perfect in a new or older home. Prices are appropriate, considering these rugs are hand-woven. **B**

Irving Food Mart

This corner shop resembles a convenience store you'd find in a gas

2125 W Irving Park Rd
773.267.7788
BROWN LINE to IRVING PARK

station. Don't count on much selection, but if a fast pre-packaged snack is on your mind, chances are you'll find it here. There aren't many hot or fresh foods in this store, and the interior is very basic and unfurnished, but it's the perfect quick food stop. **C⁻**

Marky Exclusive European Shoe Boutique

This petite boutique is lined with the most fashionable women's designer

3919 N Lincoln Ave
773.248.1500
BROWN LINE to IRVING PARK

shoes. Each pair of shoes is unique and can make an outfit by itself, so don't be alarmed if your bill goes well over $400. Ladies, if you're feeling indulgent or need special shoes for a special event, look no further. **B**

Play It Again Sports

Play It Again is great for college students looking for sporting goods. It sells

2101 W Irving Park Rd
773.463.9900
BROWN LINE to IRVING PARK

both used and new equipment for basketball players, baseball lovers, and any other type of sports fanatic. It also showcases a variety of bikes in a wide rage of prices, from as low as $50 to as high as $700. Play It Again is ideal for any guy trying to stock the garage at his new apartment. **A⁻**

Simmon's Pro Shop

Calling all bowling addicts, Simmon's Pro Shop provides all the

2147 W Irving Park Rd
773.267.0926
BROWN LINE to IRVING PARK

necessities you need for this popular pastime, from shoes to balls to bags. The store is not very big and the lighting can be harsh, but with so few stores selling solely bowling accessories, it remains a treasure chest for enthusiasts. **C⁺**

The Barking Lot

This establishment is a dog lover's haven, offering everything necessary to

2442 W Irving Park Rd
773.583.0065
BROWN LINE to IRVING PARK

primp and pamper your furry little friend. They are a dedicated company offering a mixture of

Beat Kitchen

2100 W. Belmont Ave.
773.281.4444
BROWN LINE to PAULINA

The Beat Kitchen is a great place to go for lunch, dinner, drinks or for viewing local shows – though locals will tell you the concerts are what make this venue stand out from surrounding establishments. The pizza here is delicious and interesting, with choices as varied and mouthwatering as Thai pizza and smoked chicken. The restaurant also serves brunch on Saturdays and Sundays, where it offers unique specialties such as smoked chicken and Andouille hash. A local band or minor touring act graces the stage on most nights, so check out their show schedule before making plans for a night out.

T-Spot Sushi and Tea Bar

3925 N. Lincoln Ave.
773.549.4500
BROWN LINE to IRVING PARK

This clean and modern one-of-a-kind restaurant in the North Center neighborhood that specializes in matching tea with sushi is a hidden gem for sushi lovers. With 30 to 50 different kinds of tea varying in intensity and flavor – you can find anything from Organic Darjeeling to Fruit De Bois and Ginger Jasmine – customers can match their mood with their meal. The signature makis, such as the 'Chicago Fire' and 'Lincoln Avenue,' are delicious. Vegetarians need not despair either: Veggie specials are available. Customer favorites include Tako [Octopus], Ika [Squid] and Saba [Mackerel]. Affordable and unique, this sushi bar is a must-try.

services 'all under one woof' from grooming to training classes to doggie daycare. There's even massage therapy for your pup. Spanning an extensive 10,000 square feet, this facility boasts more than enough room for your dog to feel right at home. **A-**

Toni's Hair Salon and Spa

2216 W Irving Park Rd
773.583.8664
BROWN LINE to IRVING PARK

The allure of this salon begins in the street as you notice the black leather chairs and trendy interior. The atmosphere inside is very posh, though prices surprisingly are not. Women's cuts start from $20 and men's from $15. The salon is very professional and has enough chairs to welcome walk-ins and a friendly enough staff to entertain you during your stay. **B+**

Andy's Music

2300 W Belmont Ave
773.868.1234
BROWN LINE to PAULINA

This small corner shop should come with a warning: Music experts only. Extremely knowledgeable employees are on hand to help local musicians repair and tune rare and exotic instruments, but the shop also houses a sizable collection of sitars, bongos and other musical devices. These instruments do not come cheap – many are priced at well over a few hundred dollars. **B**

Father Time

2108 W Belmont Ave
773.880.5599
BROWN LINE to PAULINA

Young shoppers may feel a bit out of place in this old-fashioned clock shop. Selling hundreds of vintage watches, clocks and other timepieces, Father Time is fascinating – for your grandfather. Employees will probably give you suspicious looks when you enter, especially when they know your bank account can barely afford one watch here. **C**

Good Old Days, Inc.

2138 W Belmont Ave
773.472.8837
BROWN LINE to PAULINA

This is the ultimate antique shop for guys. Packed with old working radios and vintage sports gear, Good Old Days is a great shop for those decorating a new apartment or an off-campus house. The store also carries a huge collection of antique metal signs perfect for wall-décor. One classic reads: 'Beauty is in the eye of the Beerholder.' Don't forget to look upstairs at the unique furniture collection. **B+**

Jeweled Souls

2257 W Belmont Ave
773.880.9093
BROWN LINE to PAULINA

The jewelry at Jeweled Souls is fun, funky, and totally fitting with the antique feel of West Belmont. All the jewelry is imported from European artists and the prices match their origin. Though the pieces are beautiful, don't expect to spend under $100, unless there is a sale. The store also carries a clothing line, but the styles are geared towards middle-aged women. **B+**

Leonie's

The perfect shop for party planning or gift giving, Leonie's carries gift cards, picture frames, sweet treats and wrapping supplies. You can design your own invitations and get decorations for your next get-together, and the staff is helpful and enthusiastic. Prices are affordable too, making Leonie's an ideal place to buy gifts for your mom or best friend. **A**

2129 W Belmont Ave
773.935.1076
BROWN LINE to PAULINA

Miscellania Antiques

Miscellania lives up to its name. The small antique shop is filled from floor to ceiling and from wall to wall with ancient furnishings. The cluttered atmosphere can be a bit overwhelming, but if you have the patience to sift through the seemingly huge mess, you can be sure to find a few treasures of considerable value. **B-**

2323 W Belmont Ave
773.348.9647
BROWN LINE to PAULINA

Night and Day Vintage

This musty vintage shop is a mish-mash of disco-era furniture, jazz-age get-ups, rusty cowboy boots, colorful scarves, umbrellas and old purses. Night and Day requires several trips, as there is always something new to be discovered. Prices are affordable, but the shop is fun to explore even if you're not buying anything. **A**

2228 W Belmont Ave
773.327.4045
BROWN LINE to PAULINA

Revolver

Boys feeling left out in the girl-powered world of fashion need look no further than Revolver, an upscale men's clothing store that offers cold beer and customized condoms to its shoppers. Friendly employees will help any guy find the perfect fit of jeans or shirts, but be willing to shell out some cash. Designer jeans range from $160 to $200 and tees range from $30 to $150. **A**

2135 W Belmont Ave
773.386.3663
BROWN LINE to PAULINA

Salon de Vive

Large windows give this upscale salon a bright and clean feeling that is especially pleasurable while receiving one of the shop's signature facials or hair treatments. Employees are friendly and helpful, but prices can be steep. Women's haircuts start at $55 and facials can run you anywhere from $65 to $120. **A-**

2137 W Belmont Ave
773.477.7535
BROWN LINE to PAULINA

Skyscraper Heels

If you aren't intimidated by the 5-inch heels tilting against the front window, step inside Skyscraper Heels and walk around. This shoe store carries shoes for both exotic dancers and transgender clients. If you ever need a hot pair of 8-inch light-up stilettos, size 17 metallic pumps, or patent leather boots that reach your mid-thigh, this is the spot. Skyscraper Heels is the perfect place to shop for costume parties. **B-**

2202 W Belmont Ave
773.477.8495
BROWN LINE to PAULINA

Four Moon Tavern

1847 W. Roscoe St.
773.929.6666
RED LINE to ADDISON

Do you consider yourself more artsy than sporty? Then Four Moon Tavern is your place. The adorable outdoor patio, decorated with Christmas lights that are lit at night, big plush couches, a jukebox and pool table give this restaurant a very relaxed, comfortable feel. The staff is friendly and the service is great. Though they serve the standard fare of chicken strips, meat loaf and sloppy joes, they're known for their delicious Southern-style breakfast and all-you-can-eat fish and chips special on Saturdays. Stop by Four Moon Tavern for one of the city's best places to relax without too much pretension.

PENELOPE'S

Located in the trendy Wicker Park village in the West Town neighborhood, Penelope's [1913 W. Division St.] features the latest designers and trends in clothing and accessories. This bright and funky vintage boutique is known around town for helping customers obtain a bit of hipster flare without the attitude: its impeccable service and friendly, helpful staff make this shop stand out. Owned by Joe Lauer and Jena Frey, this shopper's paradise also offers books and small gifts.

Photograph by Christopher Starbody

NORTHWEST

LOGAN SQUARE

HANDMADE CANDIES TO THE LATEST FASHIONS

Logan Square is a mix of working class, white-collar, ethnic and bohemian. A scattering of small, distinct communities surrounding Illinois Centennial Memorial Column, there's plenty to discover in this area. Many of Chicago's artists and musicians have made the area around Logan Square Park their home. With them come hip but affordable clothing stores and boutiques. The restaurant scene is also bustling which can be sampled at the yearly Taste of Logan Square. It isn't short of entertainment either, with the Fireside Bowl and Logan Square Auditorium bringing in lots of rock concerts. Palmer Square features gorgeous mansions along tree-lined streets. The park in this community is its main draw, especially the yearly Arts Festival with local artists, live music and activities for kids. Bucktown, located in the southeast corner of Logan Square, is another hip area. Find fashionable restaurants and loads of bars and clubs among the brownstones and cobblestone roads. The shopping isn't shabby either, with independent boutiques selling everything from handmade candies to the latest fashions. The yearly Bucktown Arts Fest displays the areas artistic spirit.

TO EAT

George's Hot Dogs

1876 N Damen Ave
773.227.4034
BLUE LINE to DAMEN

This hole-in-the-wall hot dog joint goes beyond the average ballpark dog and fries. The Ziampara family makes the food fresh, with a Grecian flair. Moderate prices and great cooking make choosing between a Polish and a gyro near impossible. However, one thing's for sure: the Greek fries are a must – you won't be sorry. If you've got a minute, hang out and check out the cartoon featuring Northwestern U. winning the Rose Bowl on the back wall. **A**

Li'l Guys

2010 N Damen Ave
773.394.6900
BLUE LINE to DAMEN

Li'l Guys brings the mini bun to traditional deli meats, but the novelty ends there. Li'l Guys is cramped in the same storefront as My Pie, a pizza place, and seating is limited to uncomfortable stools. The corned beef is cooked and cured onsite, but that doesn't save it from being overly dry. For a deal, get the spe-

Il Covo

2152 N. Damen Ave.
773.862.5555
BROWN LINE to DAMEN

Il Covo offers an upscale range and depth of Italian fare and wine for a leisurely evening of fine dining. With high-quality entrees ranging from $13 to $28, wine by the bottle is half price on Wednesday nights. Knowledgeable waiters help choose complementary dishes, wine and most importantly, dessert. Il Covo's chefs make fresh pasta daily and create innovative plates, like sea scallops with sweet corn topped with popcorn, and by fully utilizing spices and seasonal, fresh ingredients, the traditional becomes truly distinctive. Their lasagna includes veal and spinach noodles, and Executive Chef Luka Lukic develops items like tuna carpaccio, or 'Italian sushi,' and lemon tart with plum slices for the summer menu. The second floor lounge with full bar holds about 50, and seating 'coves' with plush red and gray décor are available gratis for private parties. Il Covo is the perfect hideaway to celebrate a special occasion.

cial: two mini sandwiches, a side and a fountain drink for $6.25. **C**

My Pie

2010 N Damen Ave
773.394.6904
BLUE LINE to DAMEN

My Pie offers only an ultra thin crust or deep dish pizza with no happy medium. The texture of the $2.50 thin crust slice is reminiscent of a soggy cracker, and the store is cramped in the same storefront as Li'l Guy's, a mini sandwich place. Seating is limited to uncomfortable stools. With pizza slices sitting in a carousel heater, you probably have to order a whole pie for $9.50 to get a fresh slice. **C**

Nick's Pit Stop

2011 N Damen Ave
773.342.9736
BLUE LINE to DAMEN

Nick's Pit Stop satisfies international comfort food cravings with both dark and white meat chicken grilled fresh behind the counter along with sides like mild and buttery macaroni and cheese, spicy chicken chili and warmed pitas available for takeout. Prices range from $1.99 for small sides to $8.99 for a whole roasted chicken. All food is steaming hot, so it's perfect to take home and snack on, but Nick's isn't a destination eatery. **B**

LEFT: Logan Square. LINDSEY MINEFF • **ABOVE:** Logan Square. LINDSEY MINEFF

Verona

Even though there's a pizza oven behind the counter, don't expect the

2009 N Damen Ave
773.227.9944
BLUE LINE to DAMEN

charm of an independently -owned pizza parlor or the quality of a family recipe. Good thing Verona serves snack food favorites like Philly cheesesteaks, wings and gyros, because the thin crust pizza came out with copious pools of oil on top. Make sure to try the refreshingly tart Limonata soda – it will wash just about anything down. **C**

Brown Sak

Do you miss your grandma's cooking? The Brown Sack could be what you

3706 W Armitage Ave
773.661.0675
BLUE LINE to LOGAN SQUARE

are looking for: old-fashioned soul food in a cozy atmosphere. Adam Lebin and Malaika Marion opened their 'soup, sandwich and shake shack' in 2007, using Lebin's grandmother's recipes. Sadly, the Brown Sack is rather far away from an 'El' stop, but its organic peanut butter banana sandwich, along with soup and a smoothie, make it well worth the bus ride. **B+**

Lulu Café

Tucked away next to Logan Square Auditorium, Lula's food is as eclectic

2537 N Kedzie Blvd
773.489.9554
BLUE LINE to LOGAN SQUARE

as the concertgoers. Prices range from more expensive seasonal dishes [Spanish mackerel – $24] to very reasonable Lula classics [Yiayia, a Greek version of macaroni and cheese – $7]. The ideal portions leave room for dessert, such as a date cake with homemade caramel sauce. They don't take reservations, but the food makes the long wait worth it. **A**

Café Laguardia

Leopard-print chairs and Cuban music set the mood at Café Laguardia. Amid

2111 W Armitage Ave
773.862.5996
BLUE LINE to N WESTERN

BIG MUSIC IN A SMALL PLACE: CHICAGO'S DOUBLE DOOR

BY JESSICA KELMON

When it comes to live music in Chicago, Double Door is one of the major players. The unassuming venue located at 1572 N. Milwaukee Ave. in Wicker Park is the kind of place where big acts begin, and where larger-than-life acts come to play a small venue. In 1997, before playing two nights at Soldier Field for their Bridges to Babylon tour, the Rolling Stones booked a small show at Double Door. Word got out, the streets had to be blocked off, and now, more than a decade later, the club is still famous for it.

On any given night at Double Door, more likely than a chance encounter with the Stones, is the chance to see a band on the rise. Swan, Billy Corrigan of Smashing Pumpkins, Bush, Foo Fighters, and Sonic Youth, to name a few, have all played this small Chicago venue. And just three and a half years ago Jack Black's band Tenacious D opened for Urge Overkill.

'They played two nights in a row, both sold out,' says bartender Mark De Rosa, who has been there for more than five of the club's 12-year existence. 'It was one of the best nights we've ever had here just in terms of energy. Everyone was really excited.'

The show was booked in advance, but the opening act was hush-hush. Again, rumors were flying. 'The Jack Black thing was kind of a secret, but it kind of got out, so most people were wondering if he was going to be here,' De Rosa says.

As you enter the club from the rear, you are greeted by a cavernous room with the stage up front and a bar lining

the exotic, yet slightly overdone atmosphere, this restaurant offers a large variety of Cuban dishes, with specialties including whole fried red snapper fillet and the Tropical Heatwave soup for spice lovers. Don't miss out on the delicious coconut and pineapple sorbets. **B+**

Margie's Candles

Since its opening in the 1920s, the store has served as part museum

| 1960 N Western Ave |
| 773.384.1035 |
| **BLUE LINE to N WESTERN** |

and part local hangout, making the old-fashioned ambiance a dining delight. Jukeboxes rest on each table and old photographs, trinkets and stuffed animals fill surrounding shelves. For the price of a sundae, you get an oversized dessert served in a seashell with a wafer on the side. Beware of Friday night crowds, with waiting lines wrapping around the store and little standing space. **B+**

Vella Café

When its farmer's market stand with coffees, 'sammies' and salads grew

| 1912 N Western Ave |
| 773.489.7777 |
| **BLUE LINE to N WESTERN** |

too big, this café tucked itself away under the 'El.' The homemade brisket panino is the perfect blend of sweet fruits and savory meat, complemented by crunchy homemade blue potato chips. They offer 'blunch' on weekends, highlighted by crepes and frittatas, and their well-known Vietnamese iced coffee, a creamy blend of sweet espresso, doesn't disappoint. Vella is a friendly dining experience for creative taste buds. **A**

TO PLAY

Stellaria Natural Health

Leave your shoes and inhibitions at the door: well-being in all its forms

| 2755 W Logan Blvd |
| 773.486.3797 |
| **BLUE LINE to CALIFORNIA** |

the left side. A small balcony in the back houses a cozy sofa with an unobstructed view of the stage if you are lucky enough – and early enough – to snag it. Downstairs is a revamped lounge with some seating, pool tables and a micro bar.

The 475-capacity venue generally sells out a couple times each month during its high seasons in the fall and spring, but as likely as not, there will still be tickets sold at the door. Currently, the club is only open on nights with live music. That may change in the near future, however, as management contemplates opening just the downstairs lounge on non-performance nights.

Whether you're following a specific band or walking in off the street in search of live music, on any given night there will be anywhere from two to five acts. De Rosa says there's usually at least three bands, 'unless there's a big headliner we know is going to sell out.

And sometimes we may have four bands, like four local bands. It depends on the night — sometimes we can have as many as five.'

The acts vary across genres. Tonight it's an all alt-country lineup. 'Every night's different, that's kind of what's cool

is the center of attention at Stellaria Natural Health. Whether you come for massages, acupuncture or herbal medicine, the intimate and cozy atmosphere is bound to leave you more relaxed. Yoga, Tai-chi and belly-dancing lessons are also available, making for a fun break from a hectic urban lifestyle. **A**

Tini Martini

Whether you want to kick back or shake it, Tini Martini satisfies either

| 2169 N Milwaukee Ave |
| 773.269.2900 |
| **BLUE LINE to CALIFORNIA** |

mood with two rooms offering both lounge and nightclub atmospheres. Priding itself in appealing to a diverse crowd, Tini features a different international DJ every Saturday. And there's nothing 'Tini' about the huge variety of delicious martinis to choose from. At Tini Martini it's all about options – but you can forget about wearing sneakers if you want to get through the velvet rope. **B**

Bucktown Pub

Bucktown Pub is one of the most down-to-earth bars you'll find, which is

| 1658 W Cortland St |
| 773.394.9898 |
| **BLUE LINE to DAMEN** |

why it's so popular with the locals – that and the ever-popular beer of the month and $3 pints. The beer garden is a treasure hidden away in back, and the open mic Sundays always draw a crowd. **B+**

Cortland's Garage

Don't be fooled by the name, this is a very classy place. It starts with the

| 1645 W Cortland St |
| 773.862.7877 |
| **BLUE LINE to DAMEN** |

drinks – sangria on tap and 24 beers. The dozen garage-themed martinis will make your mouth water. Try the Mud Flap – Stoli Vanil, white and dark Godiva liquor, Chambord and Oreo crumbs. The candles, dark wood furniture and black-and-white photos on the brick walls up the sophistication factor. Oh, and the live music too. **B+**

about working here,' De Rosa says. 'You know, you walk in and it could be a yuppie crowd or it could be a metal crowd or it could be a punk rock crowd, and you kind of have to adjust every night.'

What De Rosa likes best about the venue is that many of the employees are musicians, too. It gives the club credibility as a launching pad for local bands. Insiders at the club always stay positive. 'There's no bad-mouthing bands,' De Rosa says, but there is discussion at the end of the night about an act's sound and direction. 'You've got to give them credit for doing what they're doing,' he says, regardless of whether he's a fan of a particular act or not. 'There's something out there for everyone.'

De Rosa plays bass and is the vocalist for his post-punk band, Dummy, which often plays the Double Door itself. After playing many venues in Chicago and around the world, he says it's nice to play here, where it's familiar. 'Everyone knows us, the energy's really good. It's kind of a home crowd,' he says.

Asked whether there's a big local focus, De Rosa says, 'There's a lot of local acts, but there's also international acts, national acts, touring bands constantly ... different genres ... we accommodate pretty much anyone.'

Insider's tip: Note the ROCK PASS logo next to some of the show listings. This pass gets you discounted or free admission to select concerts throughout the year, as well as a limited hosted bar during a ROCK PASS show. To get one, just ask your bartender. They are free, but the bartender is the only one who can give it to you.

Double Door is owned by a mix of vocal and silent partners, most notably Sean Mulroney, bassist for Million Yen, and Joe Shanahan, who also owns powerhouse venue Metro in Wrigleyville.

LEFT: Logan Square. LINDSEY MINEFF • **BOTTOM:** Logan Square. LINDSEY MINEFF

LOGAN SQUARE

Marie's Rip Tide Lounge

Entering the bar before midnight, you won't understand why it's been on just about every 'best of' list in Chicago. Marie's is an after-hours joint, where you'll find a mixed group of people, including the bartender you were flirting with at another bar earlier that night. You won't get any food or be able to charge your drinks, but you can dance next to the juke box until the wee hours and have a great So-Co and Coke. Cheers. **A–**

1745 W Armitage Ave
773.278.7317
BLUE LINE to DAMEN

Visage

Visage is a day spa that offers a wide variety of the usual treatments, from facials and peels to waxing and hair. Most space is devoted to hair styling, cuts and color. The space is bright and contemporary with terracotta walls and black accents, more resort than spa, and customers are satisfied and relaxed – though with prices over $100 for most options, an entire day at the spa is extravagant. **B+**

2100 N Damen Ave
847.312.2317
BLUE LINE to DAMEN

Scylla

1952 N. Damen Ave.
773.227.2995
BROWN LINE to DAMEN

Find yourself surrounded by chic accents, like oriental cushions and art glass lighting, in this quaint bungalow restaurant that shields patrons from the hectic and noisy city streets. Expect interesting but delectable and truly imaginative combinations of ingredients that represent Scylla's culinary sophistication, such as the chicken with pistachios and blood oranges. The knowledgeable and friendly wait staff excels at pairing entrées with complementary wines. Hagen-Daäzs pales in comparison to the pastry chef's ingenious ice cream creations, such as the Black Olive Marshmallow, which you can sample by ordering the ice cream tasting option from the dessert menu. Main Chef Stephanie Izard does as much of the food preparation as she can herself. Save this place for special occasions, as entrées average $17 and a full meal for two including appetizer and dessert averages $80-90.

Gloss Salon

If you want to primp incognito, this is the place for you. Both ladies and

1945 N Damen Ave
773.227.8671
BLUE LINE to DIVISION

gentlemen are welcome at this small, cozy salon that offers special services for everyone. Women can get everything from haircuts and styling to makeup application and wardrobe consultations. Men can receive cuts, facial grooming and scalp treatments. Clients can even be models for a day with a custom photo session. Prices range from $15 to $350, depending on your special service. **B**

Logan Square Auditorium

Logan Square Auditorium has fast become a staple music venue, with past

2539 N Kedzie Ave
773.252.6179
BLUE LINE to LOGAN SQUARE

performances boasting Joanna Newsom, OK Go and DeVotchKa. The second floor auditorium can hold about 850 people but has been known to push 1,000. The stage is equipped with a full sound system specifically for live music, and there's a full bar. Also, it's easy to run into artists after the shows because there is no backstage. Come early for a good spot. **A**

Map Room

Pack your bags and head to the Map Room, because if you're a beer

1949 N Hoyne Ave
773.252.7636
BLUE LINE to N WESTERN

lover, there's a good chance you'll never want to leave this cozy, travel-themed bar. Over 200 brands of beer are available on any given day, so you won't need a compass to track down your favorite bottled, on-tap or hand-pumped drink.

Bring your favorite travel story and a sense of adventure. **A**

Diversey River Bowl

The most up-to-date bowling technology lets you see a photo of yourself

2211 W Diversey Ave
773.227.5800
BROWN LINE to DIVERSEY

and the speed of your roll when you bowl, but prices are a little steep: $19-32 an hour per lane depending on when you go. There's a quick-service restaurant, a fully-stocked bar and cosmic bowling at night with retro music and neon lights. Go later to avoid the swarm of kids, but watch out, as it gets packed on weekend nights. **B+**

Danny's Tavern

The first trouble is finding the tavern. Located blocks away from the well popu-

1951 W Dickens Ave
773.789.6457
BLUE LINE to DAMEN

lated North and Milwaukee intersection, it's easy to get discouraged, but don't. Some of the friendliest, least pretentious people in Wicker Park are at Danny's. Once you get past the crowded bar area, a spacious sitting area with enough room to dance awaits. With reasonably-priced drinks and late hours, this is a great bar to visit. **A-**

TO SHOP

La Casa Del Vaquero

This niche shop caters to the childhood dreams of urban cowboys by sending

2427 N Milwaukee Ave
773.862.0208
BLUE LINE to CALIFORNIA

shoppers back into the Wild West. With wall-

Radiance

2139 N. Damen Ave.
773.486.5710
BROWN LINE to DAMEN

You've heard it said that nothing says 'I love you' quite like jewelry. But this small Logan Square shop proves that jewelry doesn't have to be too expensive to be beautiful. The owner's own line of creation, named for herself, Rebecca Claire, features several simple yet gorgeous designs with exquisite details, such as heart-shaped fasteners. If you stop in, Rebecca will be more than happy to show you around her store, regardless of your poor student status. For only $40 you don't need to hesitate to treat your lady, or yourself, to a beautiful pair of amethyst earrings or a pearl necklace.

Kachi Bachi

2041 N. Damen Ave.
773.645.8640
BROWN LINE to DAMEN

I Though it started out by selling only home décor, this unique Lincoln Park shop has recently expanded to include fashion from Argentinean, Brazilian and Chilean designers. The clothing is hand-chosen by the shop owners, with only one or two items of each style available to emphasize their variety and originality. The tops, dresses and accessories that you'll find here are distinctive, yet fashionable. Home décor is still the specialty of this trendy establishment, though, and Kachi Bachi is one of the few places where you can work directly with a designer to create the bedding or lampshade of your dreams.

to-wall cowboy boots, Wrangler jeans, studded belt buckles, hats, jackets and plaid shirts, this is definitely a destination shopping experience if you want to ride off into the sunset. Make your way to the back corner to gaze upon the stuffed ostrich on the balcony and elk above the fireplace. Prices reflect quality craftsmanship. **B+**

Touch of Vintage

2506 N California Ave
773.384.8427
BLUE LINE to CALIFORNIA

Vintage is in. But sifting through thrift stores can be hit or miss. That's why Touch of Vintage is ideal. Owner Brigid Hernandez personally selects all the goods from estate sales. The small store even sells furniture, but the most popular items are dresses and jewelry – pins are $2 and earrings are $3. The store is open only 25 hours a week, so be sure to check the hours. The rest of the time Hernandez is out antiquing. **A⁻**

Asha Salon Spa

1806 N Damen Ave
773.292.1100
BLUE LINE to DAMEN

Aside from the noisy hair dryers, this salonspa offers a Zen-like environment that provides services including hair cuts, waxing, facials and massages. Asha is known for using Aveda products, and prices range from $25 for manicures to $230 for a deep tissue massage. Staff was a bit snooty, but they had almonds and cranberries to munch on while waiting. **B**

C'est Moi

2129 N Damen Ave
773.269.2116
BLUE LINE to DAMEN

When Anne Chalesle opened her petite furniture store two years ago, she was undoubtedly inspired by her husband's country of origin – France. The floral-printed lampshades, brightly-colored retro cutlery, and

TOP Logan Square. LINDSEY MINEFF • **BOTTOM** Logan Square. LINDSEY MINEFF

Rios D'Sudamerica

2010 W. Armitage Ave.
773.278.0170
BROWN LINE to WESTERN

The high ceilings, long, hanging red curtains and beautiful hand-painted wall murals of Rio de Janeiro make Rios D'Sudamerica's interior truly one-of-a-kind. The elegant white tablecloths and cushioned booths and seats, roses and high ceilings exude an open and impressive ambiance, yet the dim lighting, candles and warm colors give off a tranquil vibe. An eclectic fusion of Peruvian, Argentinean, and Brazilian, Rios' seafood selection is more impressive than its beef, though the Brochetas Rio D'Janeiro, tenderloin medallions with scallops, shrimp and roasted pepper, is a must. Steaks are a bit fatty, but the tasty chimichurri will hold you over. The upstairs mezzanine hosts private parties and special events for 30 to 35 people but opens to the masses on Fridays and Saturdays. Be impressed by the professional wait staff, the exquisite sink of rocks in the bathroom, and the BYOB – the bar will even mix drinks for you.

comfortable-looking fleece robes displayed exude an old-fashioned charm. Even if you just feel like looking, Anne is always ready to talk about anything French. From quilts to linden-scented hand lotions, C'est Moi is the place to go if you have a thing for the European feel. **B+**

Crosell & Co.

1922 N Damen Ave
773.252.9010
BLUE LINE to DAMEN

Find the final touch for any home decorating project in this cottage-like boutique. The scent of candles fills the room as you wander past furniture and trinkets that would make marvelous wedding or housewarming gifts. Owned by interior designers, Crosell & Co. give you plenty of good advice to complement your new purchase. It's a fabulous place to shop if you have eclectic taste and the means to feed it, but save up your money, because quality doesn't come cheap. **B+**

d. Marie Boutique

1867 N Damen Ave
773.489.3220
BLUE LINE to DAMEN

Cute bags are the d. Marie forte. A handful of tops and David Kahn jeans, along with some funky eyeglasses and jewelry, round off the selection in this quiet store, but it's the collection of purses and handbags that grabs your attention. The assortment of couture isn't

Logan Square.
LINDSEY MINEFF

LEFT Logan Square. LINDSEY MINEFF • **BOTTOM** Logan Square. LINDSEY MINEFF

particularly unique, but there are some cute totes that may make it worth the walk up Damen. **B+**

Eye Spy Optical

It's hard to believe when you first enter Eye Spy Optical that you entered
an eyeglass store. The place is set up like a European café, complete with bar and creaking wooden floor. With their extensive collection, Eye Spy proves that glasses don't have to be boring – funky, bright colors are more than encouraged. **B**

2130 N Damen Ave
773.252.8660
BLUE LINE to DAMEN

G Boutique

For those who don't go for whips and glow-in-the-dark dildos in flashy
window displays but still want to have a good time, G Boutique offers a more subtle shopping atmosphere. Created by women for women, the shop features everything from lingerie to toys to instructional videos, all without the flashing neon sign advertising SEX. **B**

2131 N Damen Ave
773.235.1234
BLUE LINE to DAMEN

Jean Alan Inc.

Though small, Jean Alan is a classy, stylish furniture store. The shop
displays mostly lamps and cushions, along with some leather armchairs. Designs are trendy with catchy colors, but the prices are clearly not suited

2134 N Damen Ave
773.278.2389
BLUE LINE to DAMEN

for students. Cushions cost more than $200 and lamps at least $500. Additionally, the employees look unenthusiastic and don't spontaneously help those who don't look like they can afford the items, making for a rather unpleasant shopping experience. **C**

Larkspur Flowers

The unique flower selection at Larkspur, handpicked by the owner,
changes daily and comes from around the world, including Holland, South America and New Zealand. Vintage meets modern in their flower displays, as they use many antique vases to show off their floral arrangements. They deliver to Chicago and the suburbs and customize designs for weddings and commercial accounts. **A-**

2123 N Damen Ave
773.489.2898
BLUE LINE to DAMEN

Malabar

Affordable couture fashion, shoes and acces-sories make Malabar a
stunning boutique that allows high style and your budget to coexist peacefully. While you browse, the knowledgeable and friendly sales staff will let you know what's 'haute' and what's not. Along with highlighting local Chicago designers, Malabar features runway-ready couture from South America and Europe. The store's owner also creates and sells her own gorgeous, flatter-

1880 N Damen Ave
773.321.6685
BLUE LINE to DAMEN

ing designs, making this store a destination for fashionistas seeking unique and edgy clothing. **A**

Mexus the T-Shirt Store

Mexus specializes in custom-made heat-transfer and screen-printed

2104 N Damen Ave
773.342.8245
BLUE LINE to DAMEN

apparel, and its distinctive Mexican flair gives it a trendy feel. The bright yellow walls of the family-owned store set it apart from the usual online custom wholesalers. T-shirts average $15 each, but prices decrease with larger orders, and the store can take orders as large as 1,000 custom garments. Graphic design artists are available to help with orders on site. **A-**

Michelle Tan

Michelle Tan looks like a warehouse; the minimalist look is complete with

1872 N Damen Ave
773.252.1888
BLUE LINE to DAMEN

concrete floors and bare walls. But the clothes on the dangling metal bars definitely speak for themselves. Lesser-known designers are featured in the assortment of gorgeous, trendy dresses, tops, skirts and beaded jewelry. Unique is the best word for both the chic duds and the atmosphere. The prices are high but totally justified – these clothes are worth it for a distinctive, yet fashionable look. **A**

Ms. Catwalk

Ms. Catwalk carries reasonably-priced fashion, offering a combination of

2042 N Damen Ave
773.235.2750
BLUE LINE to DAMEN

more expensive trends and cheaper items as well as abundant sales racks. Funky tops, trendy jeans and a slew of sassy T-shirts with local appeal fit in perfectly with the Destiny's Child mix playing in the background. With a wide variety of items, the selection is more reminiscent of a department store than a boutique. **B+**

Ooh La La!

The friendly staff at this boutique will help you find everything you need for

1872 N Damen Ave
773.789.5252
BLUE LINE to DAMEN

a night out on the town. Glitzy tops and dresses abound at Ooh La La!, and the store features lesser-known designers, meaning slightly lower prices for trendy items. It also offers scarves, jewelry, totes, belts and shoes at moderate prices, and the reggae music playing fits the style of the breezy knitwear duds. **A-**

TOP Logan Square. LINDSEY MINEFF • **MIDDLE** Logan Square. LINDSEY MINEFF • **BOTTOM** Logan Square. LINDSEY MINEFF

Paper and Print

Have a party coming up? Need to send a thank you card? This place offers custom printing for every occasion. You can design charming and elegant invitations, stationery, place cards and more. Choose from different colors, textures and embellishments to create the perfect fit for you. Fun extras are also available, like photo albums and journals, to keep memories of your event. **B+**

1940 N Damen Ave
773.384.1600
BLUE LINE to DAMEN

Pavilion

At Pavilion, European attention to design and sleek, modern sensibilities meld to create a stunning collection of chic, yet functional, furniture. Pristinely preserved, these antiques are regularly showcased across the country at modernist furniture shows. The brightly lit, highly stylized showroom is designed to help you imagine the furniture as it would actually look in your bedroom or living room. Pavilion also sells accessories, such as lamps and mirrors, to give your home a cohesive, retro feel that radiates sophistication. **A-**

2055 N Damen Ave
773.645.0924
BLUE LINE to DAMEN

Logan Square. LINDSEY MINEFF

LOGAN SQUARE

Raizy

A woman's dream come true: lacy lingerie paired with fresh bath and beauty products all in one chandelier-draped, pink and white room that resembles Paris Hilton's bathroom. Here you'll find hip-hugging Hanky Panky's

1944 N Damen Ave
773.227.2221
BLUE LINE to DAMEN

and barely-there Cosabella. Pamper yourself with a variety of different high-end crèmes, cosmetics and perfumes. This boutique also offers beauty services, including brow shaping and makeup application and lessons. A woman's nightmare: the huge credit card bill after shopping here. **B+**

Red 21

For those tired of scouring department store racks for stylish clothing for the adorable little boys in their lives, Red 21 is

1858 N Damen Ave
773.252.9570
BLUE LINE to DAMEN

Red Dog House

2031 N. Damen Ave.
773.227.7341
BROWN LINE to DAMEN

There's an old adage that says dogs resemble their owners, so why not make your pooch look and feel as good as you do? Allow your dog to sniff around at the trendy pet apparel and accessories in this doggie wonderland. The bright red floor complements the colorful clothing and leashes that will make the other neighborhood pets jealous. Pamper your pooch with a variety of grooming products and four-star treats. After all this shopping your dog will need some beauty sleep, so let your pup snooze in style with a lavish and comfy futon. Items are pricey, but wouldn't you give anything for your four-legged best friend?

entirely devoted to dressing tykes. A variety of reasonably-priced items are offered for everyday play, as well as nights on the town, and there are plenty of toys to keep the little ones busy while you shop. **A**

Roslyn

This rustic boutique's brick walls perfectly match the earth-toned, chic and comfortable clothing. The metal racks display basic colored essentials, including slip dresses by Fenzii and cotton camis by Clu. Each rack has a biography of the featured designers, so you can raise your fashion G.P.A. while shopping. Pick up some stylish pieces for your significant other from the 'boyfriend rack,' but of course, being this style savvy will cost you. **A**

2035 N Damen Ave
773.489.1311
BLUE LINE to DAMEN

Saffron

A subtle yet encompassing lavender fragrance greets guests just before friendly workers recommend the eclectic mix of books, small housewares and finely-tailored clothing. Saffron features laid back, yet feminine quality styles. The nine-year-old shop has offered clientele 'a respite from all things hurried' and encouraged care and relaxation since its opening. Its well-organized racks display designers such as Sweet Pea and Max Studio as well as specialty designers, such as Yoanna Baraschi. **A-**

2064 N Damen Ave
773.486.7753
BLUE LINE to DAMEN

Soutache

Soutache, meaning 'braid' in French, is a specialty boutique with an eye for embellishment. The owner collects handmade ribbons from New York, France, England, Italy, Switzerland and Japan. She stocks buttons, purse handles and other hand-crafted odds and ends to add flair to anything imaginable. A great source for costuming, wedding planning and designers, Soutache also offers craft classes to work with the raw materials. **A**

2125 N Damen Ave
773.282.9110
BLUE LINE to DAMEN

The Red Balloon Co.

While this one-stop-shop for kids lacks stuffed animals, the book section is extensive and the staff is extremely helpful. Don't hesitate to get Little Golden Books for $3 and wooden fruits and vegetables for $2 each. The clothes, for ages six and under, include adorable, yet somewhat formal and expensive, dresses and shirts – count $40 for a dress or shoes. **B+**

2060 N Damen Ave
773.489.9800
BLUE LINE to DAMEN

Vermillion

For some people, antiquing is a lifestyle – they spend years amassing a collection ranging from stunning pieces of hulking furniture to cheap trinkets that tell a priceless story. The carefully compiled collection at Vermillion has it all, whether you're

2062 N Damen Ave
773.384.8880
BLUE LINE to DAMEN

The Painted Lady

2128 N. Damen Ave.
773.489.9145
BROWN LINE to DAMEN

Specializing in vintage-looking furniture reminiscent of southern France, The Painted Lady features items that the owner, Beth Brace, paints herself, mostly in whites and a variety of pastels. The tables, lamps and other furniture items available have a very old-fashioned feel, sometimes bordering on kitsch, with frilly lampshades and seashell picture frames. Nevertheless, the prices are reasonable – around $45 for a lamp and shade – and the personnel are friendly and talkative. Depending on the ambiance you're hoping to create, this can be a hit or miss destination, but is nonetheless worth a try. If the items here aren't for you, the artistry involved in their creation can be appreciated by anybody.

Logan Square.
LINDSEY MINEFF

looking for Ming Dynasty pottery, hand-carved icons or delicate black and white photographs. Surprisingly affordable and knowledgably staffed, the store gives you a variety of options when it comes to adding an Asian sensibility to your living space. **B+**

Virtu

2034 N Damen Ave
773.235.3790
BLUE LINE to DAMEN

Pottery, glass, candles and jewelry are only a few of the unique items featured at this store. Each piece is individually handcrafted by a group of select artists, whose bios are conspicuously displayed. From $3 stationery to a $500 gold and diamond necklace, this boutique is 'a place to find something for someone who has everything.' **B+**

Vive La Femme

2048 N Damen Ave
773.772.7429
BLUE LINE to DAMEN

'Style beyond size' is the mantra at this boutique, which features high-fashion items for sizes 12-24, a rarity in a society where most couture is made for the underweight. The specialty here is weekend wear and clothes for more fashion-forward workplaces, and the flowy tops, stylish jeans and flirty dresses do the trick. The helpful and knowledgeable employees offer honest advice to clients based on their body types and are well-informed about where to find other plus-sized couture. **A**

Wow & Zen

1912 N Damen Ave
773.269.2600
BLUE LINE to DAMEN

Whether you're looking to add a sturdy piece of furniture to your apartment or just enjoy browsing beautifully hand-carved antiques, Wow & Zen has stunning pieces that make you feel like you've entered an interactive museum. Antiques spanning the 18th to early 20th century hail from regions such as China, Burma and Indonesia and range from large chests to small, handmade accessories, such as chairs and Buddha statues, that will add a tasteful Asian flair to your home. **A**

Disco City Records

2630 N Milwaukee Ave
773.486.1495
BLUE LINE to LOGAN SQUARE

A used-CD shop featuring an impressive collection of Latino music from Central and South America, Disco City boasts an extensive inventory of what has become a rare commodity these days – used cassettes. However, unlike the CDs', the cassette bins' poor organization randomly intersperses predominantly Hispanic titles with more mainstream artists, from The Beach Boys to Cake. Disco City also sells percussion instruments common to Latino recordings and offers an inventory of music-related movies. **B**

WEST TOWN

CHIC CLOTHES AND USED RECORDS

West Town is a soup of several communities. Though some flavors stand out more than others, each add a little something to the mix. The neighborhood's most famous area is Wicker Park, the setting for MTV's 'The Real World' when it was set in Chicago. Home to those who know they are cooler than you, it also hosts some of the best shopping and nightlife in the city. Damen St. and Division St. are lined with trendy boutiques selling lots of chic clothes and used records. Numerous cafés and restaurants offer tasty food and a great place to people watch during the day. But at night Wicker Park really comes out to play. Some of Chicago's best music venues are here alongside chill pubs and clubs to see and be seen at. The Eastern European legacy is strong in the Ukrainian Village. Have an authentic bowl of borscht in a neighborhood restaurant or visit the beautiful Holy Trinity Russian Orthodox Cathedral. Humboldt Park offers a taste of the Puerto Rican heritage that used to fill West Town. Paseo Boricua, the main commercial drag, proudly shows off its pride with flags, stores and restaurants.

TO EAT

Butterfly

This sushi restaurant features orange hues with black leather chairs. A very narrow space, one side has tables for four and the other side has tables for two that can be combined for larger groups. The BYOB policy helps attract a full house during dinner, and the menu boasts an extensive list of Asian staples such as teriyakis, curries and noodles. They don't

> 1156 W Grand Ave
> 312.563.5555
> BLUE LINE to CHICAGO

call the giant maki 'giant' for nothing – it's at least four inches in diameter. **B+**

Flo

The folk art, dim lighting and earth tones create an American Contemporary feel, but the seasonal menu gives away the Latin influence. Ideal for seafood lovers, try the shrimp nachos, tilapia tacos or the Flo Bowl, a jambalaya-like treat with chicken, shrimp, tequila sausage, vegetables and roasted publamo sauce. For the less daring, try the sandwiches, but don't

> 1434 W Chicago Ave
> 312.243.0477
> BLUE LINE to CHICAGO

miss their most popular meal: brunch. There's quick service and Spanish wines, so kick back, relax, and let it Flo. **A‑**

Muse Café

Enjoy poetry readings on Monday nights or live music two nights a week,

817 N Milwaukee Ave
312.850.2233
BLUE LINE to CHICAGO

ranging from electronica to experimental in the music corner partitioned by crimson curtains, or enjoy reading in the comfortable contemporary arm chairs by the front window. Wash down a delicious Pavo Avocado sandwich with drinks made with Ghirardelli chocolate. All coffee ingredients are one hundred percent fair trade certified. Cyclists enjoy a ten percent discount, while intellectuals take advantage of the free Wi-Fi. **A**

Sip Coffee House

Sage and mauve-colored walls, an exposed loft, large windows, and mod-

1223 W Grand Ave
312.563.1123
BLUE LINE to CHICAGO

ern-styled but soft seats make this an ideal place for an afternoon of reading or working on your laptop with free Wi-Fi. Paintings for sale line the walls while antique lamps illuminate the tables. Each day, lucky patrons with different selected

first names get free drinks. Treat your pooch to free dog biscuits placed by the door. **A**

Swim Café

Inspired by the indoor pool across the street, Swim Café's décor, food

1357 W Chicago Ave
312.492.8600
BLUE LINE to CHICAGO

and philosophy are as stimulating as its name. In keeping with the artwork that changes monthly on the mint-colored walls, it offers a rotating menu of baked goods. Coffees and teas are 100 percent fair trade, and the drinks' profoundly intense flavors, rare at other coffee shops, attest to their being freshly brewed instead of pre-mixed. Indulge yourself in the sumptuous truffles and bar cookies. **A**

Adobo Grill

Dusky jewel shades set the tone for this vibrant and spacious restaurant.

2005 W Division St
773.252.9990
BLUE LINE to DAMEN

Enjoy the theatrics of Adobo's tableside guacamole service while sipping tangy hand-shaken lime margaritas or sampling one of their eighty-plus tequilas. Try the impressively presented Monte Alban, a cilantro-marinated grilled skirt steak layered with tomatillo guacamole and grilled tomatoes, or the spicy Chile Relleno for a hearty dinner with Mexican flair. **A‑**

LEFT: Penelope's, 1913 W. Division St. CHRISTOPHER STARBODY • **ABOVE:** Penelope's, 1913 W. Division St. CHRISTOPHER STARBODY

Una Mae's Freak Boutique, 1422 N. Milwaukee Ave. CHRISTOPHER STARBODY

homage to Chef John Bubala's trip to Piedmont. Meals can be ordered in an appetizer size, allowing for a lighter meal and a lighter budget. Between the intimate ambiance and friendly service, you can't ask for a more delightful Friday evening dining experience. **A**

Barcello's

Serving classy Italian food in a warm, elegant setting, Barcello's mixes home-style favorites with gourmet cuisine, such as trattoria-style brick-oven personal pizzas. Choose from a range of pizza options like the Funghi [roasted wild mushrooms, Fontina cheese and basil] or the Anatra [duck, braised fennel and goat cheese]. The pizzas range in price from $8-14, except for the Caviale, a $100 delicacy featuring Russian caviar and crème fraiche. **A-**

1647 N Milwaukee Ave
773.486.8444
BLUE LINE to DAMEN

Blue Line Bar and Grill

This combination restaurant/bar/lounge is the perfect setting for dinner or pre/post-clubbing snacks. Open until 2 a.m. on weekends, it offers everything from a 'Hangover Brunch' on Saturday and Sunday mornings to a late night lounge atmosphere. From 'Bar Nosh,' [food that's easy to eat while drinking] to elegantly-flavored steak dinners, the menu

1548 N Damen Ave
773.395.3700
BLUE LINE to DAMEN

Baccala

With swanky décor and rustic cuisine, the restaurant serves authentic baccala, a salted cod dish, while also offering an array of seafood and beef dishes. Snapshots of rustic Italy blanket the restaurant walls and pay

1540 N Milwaukee Ave
773.227.1400
BLUE LINE to DAMEN

Green Zebra

1460 W. Chicago Ave.
312.243.7100
BLUE LINE to CHICAGO

Walking down Chicago Ave.'s conglomeration of shops and restaurants, you'd never expect to find a place like Green Zebra. The small restaurant's sleek décor and healthy menu attracts the city's hip vegetarian crowd – that is, the ones who can afford it. The small portions allow for a sampling of a variety of dishes, and the menu is specifically designed for the dinner to progress from lighter dishes, like the shaved artichoke salad, to heavier ones, like the chickpea pancake and turnip risotto cake. You might have to dig deep into the depths of your pockets but you're not going to want to skip out on dessert. Who can say no to chocolate coconut ice cream cake? Tasty food, friendly staff, mood lighting – vegetarians will think they're in heaven at Green Zebra, and even carnivores will have nothing to complain about.

is diverse. The venue is loud and social, but the energetic music and the intimately curved tables make it ideal for group outings. **A**

Caffe Gelato

A little trip to Rome might only be an 'El' ride away. At Caffé Gelato, indulge

| 2034 W Division St |
| 773.227.7333 |
| BLUE LINE to DAMEN |

in homemade Italian ice cream while sipping on your cappuccino and listening to Italian music. The staff is very friendly, and the prices are reasonable, so close your eyes for a moment and enjoy la dolce vita. **B**

Club Lucky

Take Johnny Rockets décor, add mediocre Italian food, subtract

| 1824 W Wabansia St |
| 773.227.2300 |
| BLUE LINE to DAMEN |

the children and voila, you've got Club Lucky. The funky red leather booths and dim lighting create a subdued atmosphere for a relaxing late night dinner. The moderately-priced food won't impress, but it's a comfortable spot if you're in the neighborhood. **C**

Coco Rouge

Coco Rouge's red and silver décor may seem more appropriate for a

| 1940 W Division St |
| 773.772.2626 |
| BLUE LINE to DAMEN |

science fiction movie than a high-end chocolate shop, but its strangely fabulous chocolates leave no question of quality. Expect original combinations of chocolate with single-origin ingredients including olives, honey and paprika. The prices are high, but regular customers call the store 'really addictive.' Perfect for special occasion dates and presents, be sure to check out the specialty hot chocolates: they bear a striking resemblance to melted truffles. **A**

Cooking Fools

Though it specializes in catering and private parties, Cooking Fools

| 1916 W North Ave |
| 773.276.5565 |
| BLUE LINE to DAMEN |

also sells eclectic kitchen essentials, such as Nutella and Sriracha hot chili sauce, and quality liquor, beer and wine. Made from scratch daily

with no trans fat and hardly any butter, feel free to indulge in their flavorful items, such as sliced paprika and roasted potato coconut rice. The upstairs provides room for wine/beer tastings, scheduled cooking classes and corporate events, where up to 300 people can learn to cook. **B**

TOP Bob San Sushi Bar, 2015 W. Division St. KAITLYN ELLISON • **MIDDLE** Mas, 1670 W. Division St. KAITLYN ELLISON • **BOTTOM** W. Chicago Ave. KAITLYN ELLISON

BELOW: Ukrainian Institute of Modern Art, 2318 W. Chicago St. CHRISTOPHER STARBODY • **RIGHT:** Ukrainian Institute of Modern Art, 2318 W. Chicago St. CHRISTOPHER STARBODY

Enoteca Roma Wine Bar

2144-46 W Division St
773.342.1011
BLUE LINE to DAMEN

Enoteca Roma does not serve the faint of heart. If you don't know much about wine, their ample wine list makes this a terrible place to fake it for a date. If you do, the service staff proves knowledgeable, making it a popular locale. Loud music keeps this potentially stuffy joint geared toward a young crowd. Try the food: sophisticated and subtle. The patio dining option and an attached natural bakery leave plenty of options for indulgence. Make reservations. **A-**

Feast

1616 N Damen Ave
773.772.7100
BLUE LINE to DAMEN

Featuring comfort food from around the globe, Feast's menu has Mexican, American, Italian, Greek and even Japanese influences. Try the made-to-order guacamole with huge chunks of avocado then the tender chicken breast stuffed with herbed goat cheese over potato gnocchi. There are wine tastings from 7 to 9 p.m. every third Wednesday and half-price wine bottles Mondays and Tuesdays. From the outside patio and large back 'happenin''

room to a cozy spot next to the front fireplace, seating is plentiful. **A**

Filter

1585 N Milwaukee Ave
773.227.4850
BLUE LINE to DAMEN

Students and older patrons gather to study, socialize, eat and drink in this eclectic coffeehouse that fuses both soulful and hip. Funky, vibrant art covers the 'Soul Lounge' while smooth Blues plays in the background. Filter serves a veggie-friendly salad and sandwich menu and a wide variety of caffeinated drinks, and has a bit of fun with breakfast all day that features the 'Hobo Breakfast' and 'Hipster Hash'. **B+**

Francesco's Forno

1576 N Milwaukee Ave
773.770.0184
BLUE LINE to DAMEN

The copper-tinted panel ceilings and antique mirrors on the walls bask in warm lighting as you survey the heart of Wicker Park through a wall of windows. Contemplate your savory meal as the candles on each table flicker and Depeche Mode plays in the background at this perfect 'first date' spot sure to charm any romantic's heart. The menu offers

Blue Fin Sushi Bar

1952 W. North Ave.
773.394.7373
BLUE LINE to DAMEN

Come to Blue Fin on Thursdays for the half-price drinks or the live DJs spinning trance, but come any night to try one of the exceptional Blue Fin maki rolls. Try one of five different dragon rolls, with white tuna in the White Dragon and spicy mayo and soft-shell crab in the Golden Dragon. The Hot Night maki is a must: a truly out-of-the-ordinary shrimp tempura roll with spicy tuna, masago, tempura crumbs and unagi sauce. With dim lighting, red crushed velvet seats, candles and tables for two along either wall, Blue Fin exudes an ideal first-date ambiance. There are also tables for four and room at the bar. The wooden bar, floors and wall decorations paired with the colorful rice-paper light hangings exhibit a heavy Asian influence, much like the drinks, where Asian grape juice, lychee and Asian pear juice serve as mixers. BYOB is also encouraged.

reasonably priced Italian fare with rare treats such as Pecorino Tartufato – aged sheep's milk cheese with truffles. **A**

Goddess and Grocer

1646 N Damen Ave
773.342.3200
BLUE LINE to DAMEN

A stop here will satisfy the munchies or a rumbling stomach with anything from their menu, which specializes in gourmet goodies and dishes. Pasta salads, wine and Ciao Bello ice cream are just some of the things you can pick up. The chalkboard menu, tables and benches create a relaxed and inviting

environment, and you can get a taste of the good life at a very practical price. **A**

Handlebar

2311 W North Ave
773.384.9546
BLUE LINE to DAMEN

Vegetarians and vegans rejoice: the bicycle-themed Handlebar Restaurant contains a staggering amount of creative options that will be sure to satisfy you and your carnivorous friends. The laid-back atmosphere masks the fact that this cozy joint is a passionately progressive pro-bicycle space. Try the fresh grilled tuna steak sandwich and pair

Alliance Bakery,
1736 W. Division St.
CHRISTOPHER STARBODY

Cafe Gelato, 2034 W. Division St. KAITLYN ELLISON

it with one of the cycling haven's many unique beers or liquors. Outdoor seating and free bicycle parking are available. **B+**

Las Palmas

Las Palmas gives Mexican classics a kick, surrounding dinners with colorful

1835 W North St
773.289.4991
BLUE LINE to DAMEN

Frida Kahlo paintings, crisp décor and sky-high ceilings filled with windows. Spanish-speaking waiters and barstaff add to the scene, serving 50 tequilas, mixed cocktails and wines from Latin America. The affordable Mexican fare doesn't disappoint either, with clever additions like seared salmon with orange salsa or spinach enchiladas. Live Mariachi music tops off the night. **A**

Lucia Gourmet Italian Cuisine

The deli section of Lucia is much more than just ham and cheese. Specialties

1825 W North Ave
773.292.9700
BLUE LINE to DAMEN

such as the Yale [prosciutto, buffalo mozzarella, tomato, basil, pesto mayonnaise] cost about $6 and come with so much meat, you actually feel full off of something other than bread. Lucia also

has a dining section with about ten tables and a different menu, but be prepared to pay a little extra [$15-20] for fish and meat dishes. **A**

Papajin Chinese and Sushi

Papajin has resolved the timeless problem of choosing between

1551 N Milwaukee Ave
773.384.9638
BLUE LINE to DAMEN

Chinese food and sushi by serving both in this swanky, romantic restaurant. Bold reds contrasted with angular white walls and large windows overlooking a bustling sidewalk lend an expansive feel to the space as you pore over the extensive menu. While the sushi is overly fishy, the Lemon Chicken is pleasantly tangy and aromatic, and the egg rolls are delectably light. Delivery and valet parking are available. **B**

Penny's Noodle Shop

The combination of the restaurant's red walls, abstract artwork and in-

1542 N Damen Ave
773.394.0100
BLUE LINE to DAMEN

dustrial pipes crossing overhead helps contribute to the restaurant's energetic environment, though the unfriendly staff hurts the atmosphere. The wide variety of noodles is excellent, the prices are reasonable, and the service is extremely fast. Dinner attracts a mix of trendy young couples, yuppies with their children, and aging hippies. **B−**

Picante

Picante offers a wide range of Mexican favorites – tacos, burritos,

2016 1/2 W Division St
773.328.8800
BLUE LINE to DAMEN

fajitas and enchiladas with the usual steak, chicken and pork options for take-out – but the sides and condiments outshine the entrees. Their hot salsa verde has a balance of flavor and heat, and without it, the burrito lacks a distinctive Mexican zest. Other restaurants are likely to offer better value and more fresh-grilled taste. **B**

Pot Pan Thai

The abundance of Thai restaurants in Chicago makes for a difficult

1750 W North Ave
773.862.6990
BLUE LINE to DAMEN

choice, but Pot Pan Thai's homeland-approved

cuisine makes the decision a little easier. The restaurant's interior is impeccably decorated with beautiful lamps throughout. You won't feel guilty about indulging in the tasty appetizers and desserts because most entrees cost less than $8. Before digging into your main dish, make sure you try the crab rangoon, and remember to leave room for the deliciously sweet Thai custard. **A**

Red Hen Bread

Red Hen Bread is so small it could be easy to miss. But if you ever come in, it would be hard not to come back. This European-style bakery offers delicious sandwiches and mouth-watering pastries. From the basic peanut butter and jelly sandwich to the tasty spinach feta croissant, Red Hen Bread knows the bread business like the back of its hand. Try the pumpkin-cranberry scone, and don't forget to bring home an authentic baguette. **B+**

1623 N Milwaukee Ave
773.342.6823
BLUE LINE to DAMEN

Rodan

It's fair to say that Rodan attracts a lot of attention purely based on hype. On any given night, a crowd of hipsters fills the space, desiring only to see and be seen.

1530 N Milwaukee Ave
773.276.7036
BLUE LINE to DAMEN

Nonetheless, this trendy restaurant earns its uber-chic rep with its funky East meets West fare [try the wasabi tempura fries] and its sublime setting [video art wall projections and electronic lounge music]. If nothing else, check out their daily drink specials, including lychee-flavored cocktails. **A-**

Santullo's Eatery

Pizza is the clear specialty at Santullo's – chewy yet flaky thin crust and fresh-to-the-taste toppings. Italian-themed salads, soups and pasta round out the menu, perfect for a quick bite. Go at happy hour, weekdays 4-6 p.m., for $2 slices – a steal, especially when each slice overwhelms a paper dinner plate. It feels like Potbelly's but with New-York-style pizza. You might be lucky enough to catch the chef twirling the disk of dough high above his head. **A-**

1943 W North Ave
773.227.7960
BLUE LINE to DAMEN

Silver Cloud Bar and Grill

Missing your mom's good ole home cooking? Pay a visit to Silver Cloud, a cozy, retro, 1940's-style dining room and bar. No offense to your mothers, but it dishes out better comfort food than your mom could ever make.

1700 N Damen Ave
773.489.6212
BLUE LINE to DAMEN

WEST TOWN

ABOVE: N. Damen Ave. KAITLYN ELLISON • **LEFT:** Wicker Park. KAITLYN ELLISON

Silver Cloud serves up classic American food, like mouthwatering mashed potatoes and meat loaf, and offers vegetarian options like veggie lasagna. And while you're there, top off your meal with a Smore'tini, another one of the restaurant's claims to fame. **A**

Swank Frank

Swank Frank fuses home-style, punk-rock edge with a 1950's

1589 N Damen Ave
773.862.4000
BLUE LINE to DAMEN

feel. With an easy-to-follow menu of classic American favorites plus some unique items, the food is worth every dollar. Famous for their fried Twinkies, topped with chocolate and powdered sugar, Swank Frank accepts cash only. Strike up a conversation with Big Al, a fry cook who'll make you feel like you're just sitting down for a home-cooked meal. Seating is sparse, but it's a spot you don't want to miss. **A-**

Thai Lagoon

Snag a coveted window seat at this casually inti-mate Thai restaurant and

2322 W North Ave
773.489.5747
BLUE LINE to DAMEN

order up some fresh, complexly-flavored Pad Thai for a meal that will fill you up without weighing you down. Vegetarian options abound throughout the menu and the staff, although slow on busy

nights, does its best to accommodate any dietary needs. BYOB or enjoy a fresh fruit smoothie with your meal and relish Thai Lagoon's bustling, youthful atmosphere. **B**

ZFK

BYOB and family-friendly – all diners can get their kicks at ZKF. Known for

1633 N Milwaukee Ave
773.278.9600
BLUE LINE to DAMEN

its weekend brunch, this sleek American eatery serves classed-up renditions of meatloaf and mashed potatoes along with healthier favorites, such as salad Niçoise and a vegan soup du jour. Try the hibiscus iced tea and cupcakes, dubbed Molly Cakes for their creator. With extensive barista offerings and flat screens playing sports, ZKF proves a safe choice for anyone, and all for $12 or less. **B+**

Alliance Bakery

Part Willy Wonka, part European coffee shop, the Alliance Bakery offers

1736 W Division St
773.278.0366
BLUE LINE to DIVISION

treats for all. Custom-made cakes are proudly displayed in the front window and make it dif-ficult for people to pass by. Inside, the antique woodwork from Poland and the golden tin ceiling make the bakery an experience. Although treats, such as the double-fudge brownie, come at a

ABOVE: Silver Room, 1442 N. Milwaukee Ave. CHRISTOPHER STARBODY • **RIGHT:** Silver Room, 1442 N. Milwaukee Ave. CHRISTOPHER STARBODY

WEST TOWN

higher-than-average $1.75, they quickly redeem themselves. The rich frosting compliments the airy brownie perfectly. **A**

Blu Coral

1265 N Milwaukee Ave
773.252.2020
BLUE LINE to DIVISION

The sleek wave-like steel walls and red leather stools mirror the rounded perfection of Blu Coral's delicious sushi. The huge menu boasts both classic and contemporary maki and naira. The rolls tend toward the exotic side, but if you aren't ready to dive into assorted fish eggs, you can always order a salad or steak. **A**

Buenos Aires Forever

939 N Ashland Ave
773.486.8081
BLUE LINE to DIVISION

Though the sparsely-decorated, modestly-furnished Buenos Aires Forever might look like a high school cafeteria, its Argentinean flavors are far from juvenile. Menu highlights include tira de asado [beef ribs] and bife de chorizo [boneless strip steak], and entrees sell for $10-15. But if you're looking for cheaper eats, just drop in for a BYOB lunch – the eatery's $5.95 special includes salad, soda and two piping hot empanadas [baked or fried]. Take that, Taco Bell. **B+**

Caffe de Luca

1721 N. Damen Ave.
773.342.6000
BLUE LINE to DAMEN

The epitome of a quaint Italian café, this hole-in-the-wall restaurant offers the freshest ingredients and friendliest service this side of the Atlantic. While the décor is made to look like an Italian street, with decorative balcony windows and bloomers hanging on a clothesline across the ceiling, it's the food that really takes diners to the heart of Italy. Fresh ingredients are delivered almost every day, and each dish, such as the incredible appetizers, salads, quiches, authentic paninis and mouth-watering desserts, takes your taste buds on a wild ride through the streets of Rome. Be sure to plan for a feast: The servings are big, the prices low, and the food so good you won't be able to resist another appetizer or slice of cake.

Bleeding Heart Bakery

2018 W. Chicago Ave.
773.278.3638
BLUE LINE to DIVISION

▌Calling all vegans, vegetarians, organic fanatics and pastry lovers – the first bakery in the country to be certified organic, Bleeding Heart Bakery offers a great selection of cookies, bagels, quiches and even creative creations like s'mores tarts. With the head chef recognized as the 2007 American Culinary Federation Pastry Chef of the Year, you can't go wrong. For the up and coming baker, the shop also offers organic baking supplies and mixes you can use at home. The brightly painted pink, green and blue walls welcome a diverse community of all ages, and a local artist is featured each month on one wall with no gallery charge for all to enjoy. This is the perfect place to study, hang out or just grab a quick bite while supporting the arts and loving the earth. Who knew you could do so many things at once.

Crust

Feel free to indulge without pangs of guilt from your waistline or your wal-

2056 W Division St
773.235.5511
BLUE LINE to DIVISION

let. The first certified organic restaurant in the Midwest, Crust offers affordable, healthy meals with ingenious combinations of ingredients, such as their Mexcali Blues wood-oven flatbread pizza with wood-fired shrimp, Chihuahua cheese, pico de gallo, heirloom peppers and cilantro. The drinks are just as original – the vodka infusion specialties are concocted by soaking ingredients such as strawberry and sweet woodruff in big glass barrels of vodka. **A**

Una Mae's Freak Boutique, 1422 N. Milwaukee Ave. KAITLYN ELLISON

Eat First

With all the other quality Chinese restaurants in Chicago, it's not worth the

1289 N Milwaukee Ave
773.227.8899
BLUE LINE to DIVISION

trek to Eat First for meals and service that rank below even most Chinese fast-food restaurants. If you want to give your wallet a break and have a cheap and hugely-portioned, but mediocre, meal, this is the place for you. There are lunch and dinner specials featuring many different meat, seafood and vegetable dishes, all without MSG. Delivery and take-out are available. **C-**

El Barco Mariscos

With flatscreen TVs lining ocean-blue walls and pop music blasting near

1035 N Ashland Ave
773.486.6850
BLUE LINE to DIVISION

anchor-shaped baubles, stepping inside El Barco Mariscos is like walking into an episode of Pimp

My Boat. But while giant silver sharks might hang from the rafters, it's the seafood on the menu that'll shiver your timbers. From the strange [octopus in white wine sauce] to the scrumptious [batter-fried red snapper], Barco boasts an ambrosial array of Mexican favorites – all for under $20. And there's nothing fishy about that. **A-**

Janik's Subs

Crabcakes and eggplant parmigiana are no longer just appetizers and entrées – Janik's transforms these delicious dishes into compact sandwiches among its variety of foot-long subs. A crossover of meaty deli meets comfy coffee shop, Janik's provides a relaxing environment and moderately-priced food including sandwiches, all-day breakfast food, exotically fruity smoothies, homemade ice cream or simply a hot cup of cappuccino. **A-**

2011 W Division St
773.276.7930
BLUE LINE to DIVISION

La Pasadita

Just in case one's closed, there are three La Pasaditas on the same block. The inexpensive meals cost $5-8, serving authentic and large-portioned Mexican dishes. The venue you choose will be based on how quickly you want your meal, but be careful – all three fill up quick at night. Like every other Mexican restaurant in Chicago, they claim their tacos are the 'best in town,' and three will leave you satisfied for the night. **B**

1141 N Ashland Ave
773.378.0384
BLUE LINE to DIVISION

Marrakech Cuisine

'Our menu is small because every dish is good, authentic and home-cooked', said the personable owner/waiter/chef at Marrakech. Well worth the wait, you can't go wrong with any of the traditional plates [$8-10] featuring different kinds of couscous, kabob or pastilles. Get the Baba Ganoush just so you can say the name. Take in the Moroccan ambience and music, and check out the tiny jewelry and clothing store right by the bar. **B+**

1413 N Ashland Ave
773.227.6451
BLUE LINE to DIVISION

Saint Nicholas Ukrainian Church, 2238 W. Rice St. KAITLYN ELLISON

Mas

This endearing European getaway that serves Spanish delicacies such as yellowfin tail tacos, ceviche [seafood salad] and conejo [braised rabbit and Spanish chorizo with saffron risotto] boasts pure authenticity. Exotic Spanish cheeses and tangy sauces complemented with a cocktail margarita will make your taste buds melt. Margaritas, mojitos and martinis are only $5 every Monday. **A**

1670 W Division St
773.276.8700
BLUE LINE to DIVISION

Milk and Honey Café

Milk and Honey Café is a sort of Promised Land to go to for a date or just a quick bite. The warm paint tones and sociable staff add to the already beautiful ambiance created by the fireplace. The café also offers a unique menu that you can't find elsewhere, featuring items such as ham and caraway havarti with cracked mustard on a pretzel roll. **A**

1920 W Division St
773.395.9434
BLUE LINE to DIVISION

Moonshine

The orange cream walls and red lighting at the bars make Moonshine a

1824 W Division St
773.862.8686
BLUE LINE to DIVISION

cool place for a Friday night drink with friends, as does the excellent wine selection. The food, however, proves to be unexceptional for its price level, and the background music plays too loudly for pleasant dinner conversation. Substitute a place at the dinner table with one on the couches at the fireplace and any entrée with a glass of spirits. **B**

TOP Coco Rouge, 1940 W. Division St. KAITLYN ELLISON • **MIDDLE** Residences, W. Division St. KAITLYN ELLISON • **BOTTOM** Residences, W. Division St. KAITLYN ELLISON

Pizza Metro

The health-conscious can now binge on pizza: Pizza Metro offers authentic

1707 W Division St
773.278.1753
BLUE LINE to DIVISION

Roman-style pizza in bite-sized portions served by the slice, half or whole. The perfect amounts of cheese, sauce and toppings on the pies, such as the Potato Rosemary Pizza, seem guilt-free, leaving you satisfied but not heavily full. For a mini romantic dinner, BYOB to its cozy surroundings. Chef Juan's spontaneous pasta creations and homemade desserts are simply too hard to resist. **A**

Podhalanka

Wouldn't it be great if you could walk into your grandparents' comfy living

1549 W Division St
773.486.6655
BLUE LINE to DIVISION

room for a hot meal? At Podhalanka, you can come close. Offering traditional Polish cuisine, Podhalanka serves breakfast, lunch and dinner. Patrons can enjoy 10 different homemade soups ranging from hearty vegetable to sour borscht. Prices are affordable – dinner, soup and salad costs $11.75. Although not an ideal date spot, Podhalanka serves filling portions of authentic fare at a reasonable price. **B**

Ritz Tango Café

Every day, Ritz Tango's amicable owners serve up $1-2 pastries, $5-6

933 N Ashland Ave
773.235.2233
BLUE LINE to DIVISION

sandwiches and $3-4 coffee drinks [including an exquisite raspberry-chocolate Tango Latte]. But on Tuesday and Thursday evenings, the dainty café takes a daring turn: Mahogany tables are pushed against cream-colored walls, and amateur dancers tango through midnight. With its lively atmosphere and luscious treats, Ritz Tango surges past most Chicago coffee shops. It's Starbucks with star quality. **A-**

Sak's Ukrainian Village Restaurant & Lounge

The delicious old world aromas emanating from Sak's lure in one's appetite for a hearty Ukrainian meal. Start with an appetizer of flavorful borscht, and the main courses, like latkes, varenyky, pyrohy, syrnyky or mlyntsi, will satisfy your largest cravings. The beautiful, dreamlike abstract art on the walls contrasts bizarrely with the typical warm restaurant decor, yet it adds a pleasant viewing experience to a traditional meal. **B**

2301 W Chicago Ave
773.278.4445
BLUE LINE to DIVISION

Steelo

When you need the right shoe, bag or accessory, Steelo is your one-stop shop. Shoe styles range from sleek to daring and prices range anywhere from $39 to $159. The purses hanging on the walls are calling your name, but if you want big-time fashion with small-time cost, check out the sunglasses — no one will know they cost only $15. **A⁻**

1850 W Division St
773.227.4590
BLUE LINE to DIVISION

Thai Village

Apart from one tilapia dish, the menu's most expensive entrée will only set you back $7.95. In spite of budget-friendly prices, Thai Village doesn't skimp on quality. Aged wood tables and walls give this joint an old library feel, and who wouldn't love a library that serves Thai food? Try the Tom Ka, a spicy coconut milk, chili, lime, lemongrass and veggie concoction, if you're looking for sharp flavors to satisfy bold palates. **A**

2053 W Division St
773.384.5352
BLUE LINE to DIVISION

Usagi Ya

Not only does Usagi Ya serve excellent sushi, but its artistic atmosphere transforms your meal into a stylish dining experience. The trendy ambiance features subtle lighting, chopstick lanterns along the sushi bar, and distinctive paintings. Its innovative pan-Asian cuisine includes a standard sushi menu and tasty,

1178 N Milwaukee Ave
773.292.5885
BLUE LINE to DIVISION

original chef creations. Expect to spend $12 to $20 for a great meal. There's a full bar and free parking. **A**

Amelia's Mexican Grill

One stop at this restaurant is enough to get you hooked on its authentic Mexican cuisine. Hanging sombreros and sprawled-out ponchos catch your eye as the friendly staff delivers a nonstop supply of crispy tortilla chips and spicy salsa. With reasonably-priced menu options ranging from burritos to sizzling steaks, you're bound to calm any south-of-the-border craving. Colorful walls and tablecloths create an overall ambiance that is fun and friendly, and be sure to sample some of their margaritas. **B⁺**

1235 W Grand Ave
312.421.2000
BLUE LINE to GRAND

WEST TOWN

Las Palmas, 1835 W. North Ave. KAITLYN ELLISON

WEST TOWN

D'Amato's Bakery

Old photographs and sea-sonal decorations adorn this small mom-and-pop-style shop. Specialties include pizza and bread, but all goods are baked in a coal oven. For those new to Italian-style baked goods, the friendly staff will explain away any questions and make helpful suggestions. The unique flavor explains why this small bakery has been successfully operating for over fifty years. **A-**

1124 W Grand Ave
312.733.5456
BLUE LINE to GRAND

Oggie's Trattoria E Café

While the food is good and the staff friendly, the restaurant itself is nothing special. Boasting plastic tablecloths, old wine bottles on the walls and fake vine trellises on the ceiling, it feels like a movie set of a bad mafia movie – twenty years ago. But the pasta dishes are reasonably priced, and the Rigatoni alla Vodka might be worth the trip. **B**

1378 W Grand Ave
312.733.0442
BLUE LINE to GRAND

TO PLAY

All Rise Gallery

The three flights of stairs and the blue paint chips showering down from the

1542 N Milwaukee Ave
773.292.9255
BLUE LINE to DAMEN

doors provide little welcome, while the exposed steel pipes, austere white walls, and industrial lighting suggest anything but artistic creativity. Though mediocre, the selection of undeniably original pieces should at least give guests something to think about as they try not to fall on their way out. **B-**

Beachwood Inn

Beachwood Inn is a small family-owned tavern that looks like it hasn't changed since the 80s. Campy movie posters and ancient beer signs adorn the walls, and you can entertain your friends with board games or pool. The crowd isn't overly hipster-y, so men without beards will still feel welcome. Drinks are always cheap, but catch the Bass Ale and Pilsner Urquell weekend specials. **A-**

1415 N Wood St
773.486.9806
BLUE LINE to DAMEN

Care D'Offay Gallery

Across from dilapidated buildings, beauty resides in a seemingly empty storefront. This small gallery houses contemporary pieces that rotate bi-monthly. No matter whose art is on display, you can always find a friendly face and survey the gallery's exhibit of their patented art process called Lumetype,

2204 W North Ave
773.325.7400
BLUE LINE to DAMEN

Blend

1725 W. Division St.
773.489.4494
BLUE LINE to DIVISION

This café was made for you, no matter who you are. People of all walks of life can be found in deep conversation on the couches, watching TV on one of three flat-screens, or studying in a booth. And this colorful, creative café has a menu to match. Wash down the Monty Carmen, a Monte Cristo but on French toast with maple syrup, with a 100% fruit smoothie, such as the Samurai. Stop by if you're in the mood for good food, good people and even a little philanthropy. A not-for-profit café, most of the workers are volunteers, and fundraising events are often held for causes such as Africa Revolution and even a soccer program for war-affected youth in Liberia. Watch a movie or catch some live music on the weekends. During the week, drop in for a crocheting class or poetry reading. Whatever you're into, Blend has it.

a technique that combines photography and screen-printing for a striking effect. **B+**

Cellar Rat Wine Shop

Don't let the name fool you: This is not your bottom basement wine store. They feature a wide variety of affordable bottles with a focus on naturally produced and organic vintages. Most of the staff are wine connoisseurs themselves and have tried every bottle in the store, so customers are bound to find something that pleases their palettes. A special table stands in back devoted to bottles under $10, perfect for the frugal or broke. **A**

1811 W North Ave
773.489.2728
BLUE LINE to DAMEN

Cheetah Gym

In a neighborhood packed with delicious restaurants, Cheetah offers guests an exciting, modern way to work off extra calories. Located in the former MTV Real World House, the gym is now filled with top-of-the-line cardio and strength training equipment. After a hard workout, stop by the juice bar for a refreshing protein shake or smoothie made to order with fresh fruit. The spa, massages and wellness

1934 W North Ave
773.394.5900
BLUE LINE to DAMEN

network also provide a great way to relax sore muscles. **A**

Davenport's Piano Bar and Cabaret

Warm wood and rich blue accents highlight the piano bar where you are encouraged to sing with the talented performers, while the cabaret room in back is theatrical, yet intimate. Reservations are suggested for the cabaret room, and the piano bar can get a bit crowded, so arrive early, grab yourself a drink from the musically-inclined wait staff and be prepared to sing your heart out. **A-**

1383 N Milwaukee Ave
773.278.1830
BLUE LINE to DAMEN

D'Vine

This luscious lounge thinks that the louder the hip hop and house music, the more people will be encouraged to dance. The champagne bottles on the candlelit tables and the leather seats up against the invigorating red walls compliment this trendy nightspot's sexy décor. Midnight munchies? Go upscale and try their French vanilla ice cream drenched in Grand Marnier – the definition of deliciously divine. **B+**

1950 W North Ave
773.235.5700
BLUE LINE to DAMEN

ABOVE: Aki Sushi, 2015 W. Division St. KAITLYN ELLISON • **LEFT:** Bob San Sushi Bar, 2015 W. Division St. KAITLYN ELLISON

'Slow Down, Life's Too Short,' 1177 N. Elston Ave. CHRISTOPHER STARBODY

Innjoy

This retro-chic upscale bar attracts a young and sophisticated crowd.

2051 W Division St
773.394.2066
BLUE LINE to DAMEN

There are plenty of tables, and the subtle green lighting is more delicate than the bass-heavy dance beats. If you're looking to have a more intimate conversation, head to the back, where curtains separate the booths from the rest of the bar. Perfect for a flirty night out; make sure to try the luscious layered martini. **A-**

Kichula Hair Salon

At Kichula Hair Salon, don't be surprised to find larger-than-life statues

2152 W Division St
773.292.9192
BLUE LINE to DAMEN

of dandelions. This start-up salon, with exotic photographs by local artists, turns hair styling into as much of an art as its hand-designed and handcrafted whitewashed brick walls. Besides offering basic cuts and coloring, facials and ethnic straightening are also offered by the three friendly stylists at reasonable prices. Grab a hand-made purse or necklace on your way out. **B+**

Lava Lounge

Designed to look like the hottest place on earth – its core – the Lava

1270 N Milwaukee Ave
773.342.5282
BLUE LINE to DAMEN

Lounge's décor is its most striking element, but the trendy theme has enough modern appeal to save the bar from looking completely over-the-top in decoration. Glowing spheres offer plenty of lighting and gray leather couches offer plenty of seating. The DJ intermingles just enough hip-hop hits to make the dance floor erupt with energy and just enough trance and house to cool off the atmosphere. **B+**

Louie's Pub

Karaoke starts at 9 and goes until close every night at Louie's, where

1659 W North Ave
773.227.7947
BLUE LINE to DAMEN

the songbook is huge and sure to have something for everyone. There's no stage, so you're free to roam the crowd, which could be all of your friends if you book a party. The drink specials and atmosphere are ordinary, so go for the karaoke or go elsewhere. **B-**

Nail Boutique

Middle-aged women sit at reclining chairs and soak their feet in water at the

2142 W Division St
773.227.3090
BLUE LINE to DAMEN

Nail Boutique. The walls are plain and white with couches and shelves of unique nail polishes lining the dark space, but the service is cheap and effective. On Tuesdays and Thursdays when the pedicure price dips to under $30, locals flock to the boutique. The Nail Boutique offers a bargain for the luxury of beautifully painted nails that young adults can't resist. **C⁺**

Nick's Beer Garden

Self-proclaimed Wicker Park's favorite neighborhood tavern, Nick's Beer

1516 N Milwaukee Ave
773.252.1155
BLUE LINE to DAMEN

Garden is a spacious, tropical-themed bar that hosts live music on Fridays and Saturdays. The musical genres, ranging from R&B to rock n' roll, are as diverse as the clientele who comes to Nick's for the friendly atmosphere and reasonably-priced drinks. The bar regulars will make sure that first-timers never feel like strangers, quickly helping them catch up on the bar's silly insider trivia: just ask about Peaches. **B**

Park Tavern/Ohm

Feels hot when you enter but rapidly begins to cool off, Wicker Park Tavern

1958 W North Ave
773.278.5138
BLUE LINE to DAMEN

is more refined than the bars that occupied its space prior. The amber back-lit panels reflect the ambiance: No heat, just glow. The place gets crowded, but never chaotic. Looking to raise up

the temperature [and have the cash to burn]? The upstairs club by the same owners, Ohm, offers more friction. But even there, don't expect to start a fire. **C⁺**

Pint

A red British telephone booth stands sentinel on the patio of this Irish

1547 N Milwaukee Ave
773.772.0990
BLUE LINE to DAMEN

pub/sports bar. Lounge under the umbrellas on the patio, or make your way into the dark interior to watch the game on large-screen TVs. Nosh on mediocre bar fare, such as burgers and Buffalo wings, and wash it down with something from Pint's selection of imports. Bring in your iPod on Wednesday iDJ nights and play your own 15-minute playlist. **B⁻**

Pontiac Café

Stepping into Pontiac Café is like living out your high school dream of forming

1531 N Damen Ave
773.252.7767
BLUE LINE to DAMEN

a rock band in your best friend's basement. From the gritty, yet eclectic décor to the sizzling burgers that sound like feedback from an amplifier, this renovated garage with spacious patio space is a hotspot for thumping music and people-

ABOVE: Asrai Garden, 1935 W. North Ave. KAITLYN ELLISON • **LEFT:** Zen Noodles and Sushi, 1852 W. North Ave. KAITLYN ELLISON

watching. Drinks are expensive, so bring enough money, and wear your favorite band's t-shirt to make a statement. **B**

Prink Salon

2130 W Division St	
773.342.0298	
BLUE LINE to DAMEN	

With white curtains, black-and-white posters hugging shocking red walls, and funky rock music blaring, you'll think you're in an ultra-trendy nightclub when you walk into Prink. Skilled stylists showcase the tight A-line bobs and base-breaking highlights that placed Prink on many best color salons in the country lists. The offerings, often topping $100, range from bold, low-maintenance colorings to organic conditioning treatments. When stepping out, don't be surprised if strangers stare as you turn the street into a runway. **A-**

Ruby Room

1743 W Division St	
773.235.2323	
BLUE LINE to DAMEN	

Friendly staff at the Ruby Room provide yoga, spa and salon treatments and alternative medicine options to promote 'soul-searching' and 'energetic well-being.' Everything you need to rejuvenate mind and body is for sale in one of three adjoining gift shops. An aura therapy viewing – 'a must' at the healing sanctuary – reveals internal energy fields. Services start at $100, but you can get serious R&R just by visiting. **A**

Salon Blue

1931 W North Ave	
773.342.2583	
BLUE LINE to DAMEN	

Don't be overwhelmed by the selection of products on the cabinet-lined wall, and resist that urge to splurge. The tranquility in the atmosphere, everywhere from the worn hardwood floors to the contemporary design of the sinks, transforms any haircut into a mini spa experience. Take advantage of other spa services if you feel the need for more pampering, and top off your experience with a truffle from the front desk on your way out. **A-**

Salud Tequila Lounge

1471 N Milwaukee Ave	
773.235.5577	
BLUE LINE to DAMEN	

Offering over 75 premium 100 percent agave tequilas, Salud Tequila Lounge prides itself in knowing all there is to know about the Mexican spirit, and the cheerful staff is more than willing to share. The picturesque paintings decorating the walls give the bar a colorful and authentic south-of-the-border look and the resident DJ spins beats with a Latin twist, drawing an urbane crowd of well-dressed

TOP Enoteca Roma, 2144 W. Division St. KAITLYN ELLISON • **MIDDLE** Letzia's Natural Bakery, 2145 W. Division St. KAITLYN ELLISON • **BOTTOM** Thai Village, 2053 W. Division St. KAITLYN ELLISON

The Smoke Daddy

1804 W. Division St.
773.772.6656
BLUE LINE to DIVISION

The South may claim to have the best barbecue, but The Smoke Daddy puts the Midwest on the map with its perfectly smoked meats and special recipe barbecue sauces. The casual atmosphere, complete with full bar, live music every night, and an accommodating staff, makes it a great place to unwind. Apart from the variety of side dishes, three tasty desserts are available for you if you have room for them [and you're going to want to make room for them]. Even if you can't handle the dessert, make sure you don't leave without trying the famous cornbread – it's heavenly. And don't be afraid of the mess, because it's not barbecue without one.

twenty-somethings who enjoy a bit of flavor on their night out. **A-**

Small Bar

Although popular for its homemade desserts, this rather roomy bar is

2049 W Division St
773.772.2727
BLUE LINE to DAMEN

all about the beer after midnight. The staff is known to make great recommendations for those who might be unsure of their preference. The soccer games on the TV bring in a large number of sports fans, and the pinball machine is sure to keep them occupied in between drinks and commercials. **B-**

Subterranean

This two-story establishment has bars on each floor, with the stage lo-

2011 W North Ave
773.278.8600
BLUE LINE to DAMEN

cated on the first. Because of the age limit [18+], the inexpensive shows attract an older audience, leaving the pre-pubescent at the door. It can be a tight squeeze when it's crowded and the sound system isn't the best, but for a drink with good live music and friends, it's perfect. **A-**

Swig

Swig offers your usual selection of tavern drinks and a cozy, cabin-like at-

1464 N Milwaukee Ave
773.384.1439
BLUE LINE to DAMEN

mosphere thanks to the exposed brick walls and the fireplace. The clientele is older but not at all intimidating or awkward. A place to stop by for a few drinks, but don't expect to be entertained all

night. Except for the cheap drinks, nothing here really encourages you to swig. **C**

Tatu Tattoo

The diverse clientele of Tatu Tattoo – grandmothers, bikers, hipsters and

1754 W North Ave
773.772.8288
BLUE LINE to DAMEN

even Michael Jordan – definitely suggests its

Mural, W. Division St. KAITLYN ELLISON

WEST TOWN

RIGHT: Home Made Pizza Company, 1953 W. Wabansia Dr. KAITLYN ELLISON • **BELOW:** Wicker Park Tavern, 1958 W. North Ave. KAITLYN ELLISON

distinctiveness and repute. With a wide variety of tattoos and body piercing available, the customer service is remarkable. You can bring in just about anything, and the tattoo artists can make a unique design for you. With its great kindness, care and personality, Tatu Tattoo is a one-stop shop for all of your body expression needs. **A-**

The Kid's Table

Teaching cooking classes to kids and parents with the aim of exposing kids

2237 W North Ave
773.235.2665
BLUE LINE to DAMEN

to healthy foods and eating at an early age, the themed four-week sessions for kids aged 2-10 include Dynamite Dips and Comfort Foods. Parents can register their kids for an entire session or just a class. Though a little pricy, the idea and facilities are cool enough that they get a mixed clientele. Check out the child-sized cooking area, complete with granite countertops and cooking utensils. **B+**

The Note

This undecorated, warehouse-like music venue tends to become more

1565 N Milwaukee Ave
773.489.0011
BLUE LINE to DAMEN

popular as the night goes on. The two bars and the live acts keep the trendy and eclectic crowd entertained and satisfied well past the rest of Chicago's bed time, adding to The Note's fame as a premier nightspot for those in tuned with the underground. **B+**

Black Walnut Gallery

Be greeted by Abbey, the store dog, and clink a champagne glass amidst

2135 W Division St
773.772.8870
BLUE LINE to DIVISION

stunning modern paintings, photographs, and wooden sculptures and custom-commissioned tables created by Chicago locals. The amber glow of the walnut floor reflects upon brick walls to draw partygoers and newlyweds alike to this New-York-Times-profiled art gallery. The new age music and monthly exhibitions, such as Peace in the Middle East, showcase a combination of beautiful woodwork and classical and modern art. **A**

Chopin Theatre

With its daring and breathtaking Victorian-style antiques and café on

1543 W Division St
773.278.1500
BLUE LINE to DIVISION

the main floor and its small theater in the basement that's reminiscent of a Moulin Rouge set, Chopin is visually a treat for the eyes. Besides the small theater, Chopin has a larger theater that houses not only Polish theater, but also other unique theater experiences, often for one-night engagements, and occasionally films and music as well. It's a perfect place to go for a scintillating, stimulating night of performance. **A**

Easy Bar

In this hipster-bar-laden neighborhood, Easy Bar is a bit more yuppie and up-scale while remaining very casual. You still have your pool table and jukebox, but unlike many area peers, Easy Bar cooks up burgers and fried delectables. On weekends the second bar and dance floor in back open up, and the weekday specials are great, with $2 drafts on Tuesdays. **A⁻**

| 1944 W Division St |
| 773.227.4644 |
| BLUE LINE to DIVISION |

Evil Olive

Evil Olive is the appropriate name for a bar themed around the unlikely concept of palindromes. These phrases are found everywhere, painted on the walls and listed on the menu. The interior has a luxurious lounge-feel with plenty of space in the back to meet and mingle with the other swanky customers. The vintage photo booth will help you capture your stylish night and the three bars make that wordplay all the more fun. **B**

| 1551 W Division St |
| 773.235.9100 |
| BLUE LINE to DIVISION |

Glow Tan Studio

The smell of coconut reminds you of vacations on the beach as you enter. Although rather unexceptional in its tanning lotion selection, Glow Tan Studio is famous for its cleanliness. Don't let the small, oppressive lobby fool you. The contemporary décor of each individual room makes them seem spacey, so it's easy to relax while you get the gorgeous tan that all the employees sport. For the more health-conscious, this studio offers a spray-on tan called 'Mystic Tan.' **B**

| 2046 W Division St |
| 773.252.7700 |
| BLUE LINE to DIVISION |

Gold Star

The bike messenger's bar of choice, Gold Star also brings in a lot of hipsters, musicians and even some yuppies from the neighborhood. Free pool and a jukebox with inexplicable variety are surely part of the draw. Stella on tap is nice, $2 Old Styles are sufficient, and you have to like any bar that used to be under a whorehouse. **B⁺**

| 1755 W Division St |
| 773.227.8700 |
| BLUE LINE to DIVISION |

Green Dog Inc.

Are you going to be gone for the weekend and don't know who should take care of your dog? At this innovative, earth-friend-

| 2231 W Chicago Ave |
| 773.772.4877 |
| BLUE LINE to DIVISION |

Cans Bar and Canteen

1640 N. Damen Ave.
773.227.2277
BLUE LINE to DAMEN

If 13-year-old boys had the entrepreneurial skills to open a bar in 1983, it would most closely resemble Cans. Playful and endearingly adolescent, Cans serves a wide variety of canned beers, over 25 different types mostly from Milwaukee but also imports from Germany and Japan. The jukebox has enough Cars, Journey and A Flock of Seagulls classics to reminisce about the time when video killed the radio star. Even their Web site pays homage to the Reagan years by operating like a Tetris game. The clientele is young, mostly 80's kids who really appreciate such campy delight. The only thing that brings you back to the 21st century is the Palm Pilots used by the staff to send your drink order directly to the bar. Just like drinking canned beer in your parents' basement, but juvenile delinquents never had this much fun.

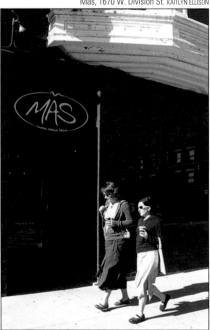

Mas, 1670 W. Division St. KAITLYN ELLISON

Jun Bar

The colorful art décor inside, with pastel colored shapes and lines,

2050 W Division St
773.486.6700
BLUE LINE to DIVISION

decorates the otherwise unadorned walls of Jun Bar. There are drink specials every weeknight [Tuesdays: $6 martinis, Wednesdays: $4 wine], and the food menu offers various sandwiches and salads that can be purchased at late hours of the night for a rather steep price. The clientele is older and looking for a calm night out, so don't expect debauchery even on fairly popular Friday nights. **C**

Nature Yoga

The hardwood floors, soft aroma of incense, driftwood bench and cool

2021 W Division St
773.227.5720
BLUE LINE to DIVISION

artwork in refreshing hues of blue-green give the studio a Zen-like atmosphere and put you in the mood before you step into the 'sanctuary,' the classroom that has an entire wall of thick, clear glass tiles. The quarterly-updated inclusive selection of classes caters to all skill levels and preferences. Regular classes cost $15 per 75-90-minute session, but donation classes are also offered. **B+**

ly dog care center, the owner of Green Dog Inc., Brenda, made sure that everything would be environmentally aware. From organic food to comfortable dog beds, there's even aromatherapy. **A-**

Debonair Social Club

1575 N. Milwaukee Ave.
773.227.7900
BLUE LINE to DAMEN

Debonair is more of a creative social space catering to artistic pretension and musical snobbery than a club. Urbane, chic and capitalizing on the revival of trashy-luxurious, you can find both bright red neon lights [think Vegas] and high-ceiling chandeliers [think Paris]. The electronic music and the egos are loud, the lighting and the socializing soft. The video projections add to the trance-like Twilight Zone feel, featuring slow-motion images of slow-moving bodies. Amidst the minimalist modern décor, the spacey music, and the multimedia displays, Debonair even smells cool. The dance floor has several large pastel-colored, back-lit panels which offer the ideal backdrop to your own iPod commercial. Although it sounds like an exclusively underground club, it actually attracts a diverse clientele, but expect those hothead hipsters and faux-pas fashionistas that have come to represent the reputation of Wicker Park.

Phyllis' Musical Inn

Featuring mostly head-banging local rock bands, Phyllis' still rocks out as

1800 W Division St
773.486.9862
BLUE LINE to DIVISION

hard as the next live-music venue, with bands playing mostly original acts and jazz shows on Monday and Sunday nights. Drink prices are moderate and the atmosphere allows you to practically be on stage with the band. The acoustics make the music fuzzy at times, but that doesn't matter much when your ears are already being blasted off. **B**

The Sigara Lounge

Sigara is an intimate hookah bar where you can enjoy over 25 different

2013 W Division St
773.292.9190
BLUE LINE to DIVISION

tobacco flavors, along with a variety of drinks and appetizers. Fridays and Saturdays are usually packed and 21 and up, so be sure to make a reservation and bring an ID. Other days are better if you just want to unwind in one of the curtained rooms. The staff is extremely friendly and helpful, and although a bit pricy, this is definitely an enjoyable experience. **A-**

Zakopane

Zakopane will awaken the burly Polish man deep inside you. The minimal

1734 W Division St
773.486.1559
BLUE LINE to DIVISION

décor and $2 Michelob drafts remind you what you're really here for – to drink. No frills is probably an understatement, as there's little more than Christmas lights, a few neon signs and maybe the barmaid to keep your eyes busy. Still, not a bad spot to get a few cheap drinks before moving on to one of the more exciting bars down the street. **C**

Around the Coyote Gallery

This non-profit gallery immediately gives off an atypical vibe with

1935 1/2 W North Ave
773.342.6777
BLUE LINE to GRAND

the brightly-colored, Korean-style dead cartoon winged elephants that line the staircase. The wall of windows, the hum from the video fixtures, and the high-backed bench prompt thoughtful

contemplation of the paintings, photographs, videos, sculptures, furniture and other pieces that refuse to be categorized, such as the shelf of glass bottles containing water and human hair and the video of them above. Annual festivals also offer chances for artistic exploration. **A-**

TOP The Bongo Room, 1470 N. Milwaukee Ave. KAITLYN ELLISON • **MIDDLE** John Fleuvog Shoes, 1539 N. Milwaukee Ave. KAITLYN ELLISON • **BOTTOM** Earwax Cafe, 1561 N. Milwaukee Ave. KAITLYN ELLISON

WEST TOWN

BELOW: Las Palmas, 1835 W. North Ave.
KAITLYN ELLISON • **RIGHT:** Las Palmas, 1835 W.
North Ave. KAITLYN ELLISON

Five Star Bar & Grill

Hosting a more sophisti-
cated crowd of 30-some-
things, Five Star isn't a

1424 W Chicago Ave
312.850.2555
BLUE LINE to CHICAGO

happening place – it's a neighborhood bar. You
can choose to sit at the huge L-shaped bar, the
high tables next to the floor-to-ceiling windows,
or the booths along the blue-padded walls. For
a more momentous occasion, there's a room in
the back with booth-type seats around a stripper
pole. The bar offers 46 different bourbons and
38 types of beer while the grill serves standard
American fare. **B+**

Empire Liquors

Empire Liquors borrows
much of its décor from
the Gothic era, emulating

1566 N Milwaukee Ave
773.278.1600
BLUE LINE to DAMEN

a dark forest with tree trunk stools and metal
antlers sprawling from the brick-exposed walls.
The candles flicker rapidly and provide much of
the illumination, creating an eerie, heavily-shad-
owed, dungeon-like glow. However, industrialized
elements offer a subtle contrast and a more
contemporary look. The large concrete bar is
always busy, but never too crowded, and the
'gangster booth' in the back might be worth the
reservation. **B**

TO SHOP

Abbey Brown Soap Shop

The promising quick
glimpses from the street
are deceiving, as Abbey

1162 W Grand Ave
312.738.2290
BLUE LINE to CHICAGO

Brown lacks the primary ingredient in any good
soap shop: the fragrance. Most items only come
in two or three scents that are indistinguishable
from each other in their blandness, despite being
crafted by 'local artisans,' as one worker proudly
proclaimed. The selection of jewelry, artwork and
shirts for sale is just as mediocre as the soap, but
at least the purses have original designs. **C**

The Realm

Skip cheap reproductions
– authentic variety is
everything at The Realm,

1430 W Chicago Ave
312.491.0999
BLUE LINE to CHICAGO

where a Ganesha sculpture from India sits next to
an African fertility statue. All pieces are original,
acquired from tiny villages in Africa and Asia, but
the prices reflect the authenticity. A Ghanaian
mask used in tribal ceremony costs well more
than $1000, but whether you're buying or not,
check out the trilobite fossil: it's over a million
years old. **A**

Akira Footware

A soft, sweet and undeniably feminine shoe store, Akira sells more

1849 W North Ave
773.342.8684
BLUE LINE to DAMEN

cutting-edge shoes than one would guess. The flower designs that adorn the store, as well as the classic girlie soundtrack, give off a pleasant, happy vibe that is matched by helpful, upbeat employees. The downside is that if you're looking for an everyday shoe, Akira Footwear probably can't help you – most of their shoes are high-fashion and low-necessity, though they are reasonably priced. **B-**

Akira Men

Mainly high-quality denim and new-wave-inspired t-shirts, Akira's most re-

1922 W North Ave
773.276.5640
BLUE LINE to DAMEN

freshing clothing features vibrant graffiti designs on bright and metallic royal patterns: crowns and shields, lions and eagles. The store lets the clothing do all the loud talking, so the décor is simple and unassuming compared to the fashion and the racks are made of light-colored wood. The small location gets very crowded during peak hours, so be prepared to bump and fight for rock royalty trends. **B**

Another Level

Another Level offers hard-to-find premium denim lines, such as 1921, and

1420 N Milwaukee Ave
773.325.0465
BLUE LINE to DAMEN

an extensive collection of garment-dyed, screen-printed T-shirts. The repetition of intricate floral patterns printed overlaying skulls and thorny roses with birds give their pieces an edgy art-school feel. Essentially most of the merchandise feels like Urban Outfitters sans Zoloft. **B+**

Aspen Kitchen & Bath

Varnished electric blue and purple ceilings hang above Aspen Kitchen &

2133 W Division St
773.227.5932
BLUE LINE to DAMEN

Bath's state-of-the-art cabinets complete with shiny glass shelves. The small shop, with ethnic flare and customer-friendly service, boasts free estimates and graphing redesigns. It offers something for everybody, from stock bathtubs and ovens to Georgian marble-lacquered dressers. If spending a few thousand dollars isn't an issue, Aspen is quickly becoming the hotspot for apartment and home remodeling. **B+**

Avenue North Guitar

Avenue North is a relic of the past with vintage acoustic and electric

1823 W North Ave
773.252.5580
BLUE LINE to DAMEN

guitars and expert salespeople reminiscent of mom-and-pop retail stores of yesteryear. The community-based guitar shop prides itself on making customers feel comfortable and providing affordable music products for a wide variety of shoppers. You'll find a stage in back where local performers can debut their latest work. **A**

Baccala, 1540 N. Milwaukee Ave. KAITLYN ELLISON

WEST TOWN

TK Men

1909 W. North Ave.
773.342.9800
BLUE LINE to DAMEN

This relatively new store devotes a lot of space to displaying their large collection of blazers, coats and jackets. Therefore, every other item in the store is in some sense a blazer accessory – sweaters, belts, graphic tees. The store itself is small and open, featuring exposed brick with metal lamps and vintage Playboy covers decorating the light blue walls of the dressing room. The owner is helpful without being intrusive, pinpointing the latest arrivals and deals [and will even add discounts for the most charismatic customers]. And for the shop-phobic, the large flat screen TV in the back, connected to an Xbox, or the kegerator offering free drinks to customers will surely provide a distraction for the boyish shoppers the store aims to attract.

Batteries Not Included

Whether planning a bachelorette party or just looking to spice up your

1439 N Milwaukee Ave
773.489.2200
BLUE LINE to DAMEN

life, Batteries Not Included has an extensive range of both funny gag gifts and useful sex toys. Besides your average collection of sexy flicks, brightly-colored vibrators and lots of lube, this fun shop offers everything from penis cake pans to a boob water gun. The staff is helpful and knowledgeable, but also not above laughing when customers try on the 'penis head' hat. **A**

Brainstorm

Brainstorm shoppers know they're geeks, and they embrace it. Whether

1648 W North Ave
773.384.8721
BLUE LINE to DAMEN

you're looking for the latest installment of your favorite comic, the cult classic you haven't been able to find at any video store, or the trading card missing from your collection, the staff is more than willing to help you find what you seek and chat about everything that excites you. **A**

Broadway Home Furnishings

Either everything at Broadway Home Furnishings is perenni-

1520 N Milwaukee Ave
773.252.7705
BLUE LINE to DAMEN

ally on sale or this furniture store is going out of business. The rich leather chairs and custom bar stool covers give the store a very masculine feel,

and the higher price range seems to be geared towards yuppies that want to make their studio apartments feel classy with artificial suede sectionals lined with geometrically-printed pillows. **C**

Climate

People crowd into this tiny gift shop in search of the perfect gift. A variety of

1702 N Damen Ave
773.862.7075
BLUE LINE to DAMEN

books, scented candles and baseball paraphernalia fill the tables in the first room. Venture into the back and you'll find a room filled with greeting cards that are sure to bring smiles to your friends' faces. If you continue farther into the back you'll unexpectedly find a room filled with children's clothing, toys and board games. **B+**

Decibel

Providing a huge selection of new and used speaker and sound systems for

1429 N Milwaukee Ave
773.862.6700
BLUE LINE to DAMEN

every budget, Decibel is as good as local stereo stores get. According to the owner, people on a budget can put together a good stereo system for around $200 and up instead of paying $300 for the mediocre products sold at Best Buy. They also provide warranties on all their products, buy used products, trade and do repairs. Note the funny hours on weekdays: 2-7 p.m. **A-**

Embelezar

This shop proudly displays Indian-inspired decorative treasures. Vases, picture frames, armoires and pillows are just some items that sprinkle the shelves. Future interior designers that would like spice up their life with a little Indian flair would most enjoy the items found here, as prices are rather steep. Make sure you're willing to invest if you're going to make the trip. **B⁻**

1639 N Damen Ave
773.645.9705
BLUE LINE to DAMEN

Eye Want

This certainly isn't the average eyeglass store. Eye Want features standard to funky eyeglass and sunglass styles from companies around the world, placed amid kitschy, colorful décor complete with wild wall hangings and antique decorations. Optometric exams are also available by appointment. The staff was less than friendly and the frames pricy, but it may be worth a visit for someone trying to find a new look – or get some looks – with eye-catching glasses. **B**

1543 N Milwaukee Ave
773.782.1744
BLUE LINE to DAMEN

Futurgarb

For the rock star that dwells within us all, Futurgarb offers a wide variety of clothing and accessories for both men and women. The friendly staff and the cats you might find lounging around make for a relaxed shopping experience, and the shop is crammed with all kinds of great finds. **B**

1359 N Milwaukee Ave
773.276.1450
BLUE LINE to DAMEN

Gem

This tiny shop offers a small selection of unique jewelry. You'll find anything ornamental – necklaces, bracelets, rings and even fragrances. Each piece is elegantly displayed in glass cases, allowing customers to easily browse through the selection. Save your money for a special occasion, for most pieces range in the triple digits. **B⁻**

1710 N Damen Ave
773.384.7700
BLUE LINE to DAMEN

Giraudon New York

This small shop tucked into a nook on a busy street offers footwear for

1616 N Damen Ave
773.276.0524
BLUE LINE to DAMEN

ABOVE: Wicker Park. KAITLYN ELLISON • **LEFT:** Wicker Park. KAITLYN ELLISON

men and women who want to stand out in a city of black leather and Uggs. Walking by the window display, you might see a pair that you just have to have, but for the most part the selection is limited and the prices a bit high. **B–**

G-Star Raw

A trendy clothing shop specializing in men's wear, G-Star Raw is unique

1525 N Milwaukee Ave
773.342.2623
BLUE LINE to DAMEN

for their different designer lines and their many denim jeans and jackets. The manager described the store and clothing as revolving around each other with the clothes highlighting the architecture. Prices are steep with jeans around $150 and jackets in the $200s. They can fit all sizes, but you have to be a denim fan or love the designer's concept to invest in these clothes. **B**

Hejfina

Fusing a clothing boutique, art gallery, and furniture showroom, Hejfina

1529 N Milwaukee Ave
773.772.0002
BLUE LINE to DAMEN

reflects a sleek minimalist design sensibility and showcases the threads of designers Alexander Wang and Chloe, while featuring Chicago furniture makers Carson Maddox, Michael Kohler and Andrew Kephart. Brainchild of owner Heiji Choy, Hejfina emphasizes clean lines and modernist form throughout its selection of clothing, shoes and accessories, art books, and custom furniture. The store is also used as an interactive design lab, hosting installation pieces by rising Chicago artists. **A**

Helen Yi

Though the price tags might send you running for the nearest exit, if

1645 N Damen Ave
773.252.3838
BLUE LINE to DAMEN

your credit limit is high enough, you're sure to find some beautiful garments at this upscale boutique. Helen Yi carries new, hot designers, as well as established ones, and even if your bank account is a little drier than you'd like, you might be able to find some great deals on the sale racks. **B+**

ABOVE: Sign, Hoyne Ave. KAITLYN ELLISON
• **RIGHT:** Saints Voldymyr and Olha Ukrainian Catholic Church. KAITLYN ELLISON

Her

Trendily aimed at a young and preferably wealthy audience, Her tries to recreate the feeling of a personal walk-in closet, mixing expensive, adorable clothing with vintage props and furniture amidst pink walls and wooden statuettes of couples kissing. While the prices may be too high for the casual shopper [girls' T-shirts run around $50, dresses near $200], the clothes are young and fun enough that many may consider the experience worth the price tag. **B**

1653 N Damen Ave
773.235.9515
BLUE LINE to DAMEN

Him

With blue walls offset by masculine bookshelves, Him's appeal comes more from the boutique than from the actual clothing. If you get tired of browsing through the small selection – thrift-shop-like T-shirts and dark blazers – you can always play foosball, take one of their complimentary beers, or browse through their excellent collection of vintage Playboys. Too bad the fashion fails to reflect the shop's playful mentality and is rather either simply indistinctive or morbidly unattractive. **C+**

1653 N Damen Ave
773.235.3360
BLUE LINE to DAMEN

Imperial Menswear

A men's clothing store with hundreds of reasonably-priced suits, dress shirts, pants and shoes lining the walls of the store, Imperial is great for anything from funny-colored Dumb and Dumber suits to ones for formals and clubbing. Shirts and pants individually come in several different colors and types, while a full suit starts at $100. **B+**

1401 N Milwaukee Ave
773.486.0413
BLUE LINE to DAMEN

Jade

If you consider yourself fashion savvy, your jaw will drop at the sight of fun print dresses and sparkly tops from brands including T-bags, Missoni, Nieves Lavi and Joyann hanging across jade green walls and hardwood flooring. Jade offers apparel and accessories from high-end brands as well as up-and-com-

1557 N Milwaukee Ave
773.342.5233
BLUE LINE to DAMEN

ing designers. Owner and former stylist Laura Haberman offers personal attention to customers in need of fashion advice. **A**

John Fleuvog

Unique is the perfect adjective to describe the shoes that cover the tables at John Fleuvog. The theater-themed store carries hundreds of colorful and distinct shoes with styles created solely by Fleuvog himself. The designer's innovative creativity results in funky and flamboyant footwear for men and women that adds flair to your individual style. To truly deviate from the ordinary you can purchase leather-free shoes called 'Veggie Vogs.' Staff is very friendly and prices range from $100 to $400. **A**

1539 N Milwaukee Ave
773.772.1983
BLUE LINE to DAMEN

La Casa del Tobacco

Showcasing more than 200 different brands of cigars in tasteful, custom-made, grade-A cherry and cedar humidors, this family-owned cigar shop hosts cigar tasting events every month, offering food, drink and valet parking. With Cuban photos and paintings on sale for $300-400 and a cigar lounge with big leather chairs, make yourself right at home – a very classy home. Selling your standard flasks, rolling papers, tobacco and lighters, splurge on their crystal and marble ashtrays or $250 luxury humidors. **A-**

1937 W North Ave
773.384.5225
BLUE LINE to DAMEN

Language

Do you hate shopping to the tune of loud music? If so, Language is the boutique for you. Tranquil house music reverberates off the white walls, which are covered in neatly hung women's clothing. The friendly and knowledgeable staff will help you choose from different wardrobe genres including 'luxe-glam,' 'sexy-bohemian' and 'retro-punk.' Merchandise is pricy, but you might get lucky with the sale rack that cuts up to 70 percent. **A**

1537 N Milwaukee Ave
773.772.5747
BLUE LINE to DAMEN

WEST TOWN

Lenny and Me

'You get what you pay for' could be the logic behind Lenny and Me's unusually high-priced, mainly designer used and vintage

1463 N Milwaukee Ave
773.489.5576
BLUE LINE to DAMEN

clothes and accessories. Parse through the last season BCBG skirts, and you may find a gem, like a $40 men's vintage Christian Dior jacket. Various sized graphic T-shirts are lumped together under the heading 'Androgynous T's.' Lenny and Me is a solid find for the brand-conscious thrift shopper. **B**

Meble

This custom furniture and design store's interior is decked out with a mixture

1462 N Milwaukee Ave
773.772.8200
BLUE LINE to DAMEN

of the elegant antique and funky modern. Design a piece of furniture in your image with the owners, a mother-daughter pair. Beware of the hefty price tags, though: Tables, light fixtures and couches off the floor range from $300 to $3,000. This store's furniture isn't meant to be shoved into a dorm room, but the shop's worth checking out for its artistic creations. **B**

Myopic Books

Open 'til 1 a.m. every night but Sunday, Myopic Books provides ample

1564 N Milwaukee Ave
773.862.4882
BLUE LINE to DAMEN

browsing for bookworms. A bit musty and spotted with kitschy academic sculptures, Myopic plays an admirably obscure mix of tunes for its shoppers. Grab a bottomless coffee mug [$1.36] and wander the winding shelves, marked with helpful signs. With categories such as SEX [all bold caps], Drugs., Nostradamus, GEEK and General Occult, everyone who's not allergic to dust will surely find a good read. **A**

TOP John Fleuvog Shoes, 1539 N. Milwaukee Ave. KAITLYN ELLISON • **MIDDLE** Earwax Cafe, 1561 N. Milwaukee Ave. KAITLYN ELLISON • **BOTTOM** W. North Ave. KAITLYN ELLISON

Niche

Don't let the woodsy, natural vibe of Niche fool you: this airy shoe store

1566 N Damen Ave
773.489.2001
BLUE LINE to DAMEN

contains elegant, high-fashion shoes that are definitely not made for a hike. A knowledgeable, friendly sales staff will readily lead you to what you're looking for, whether it's knee-high boots, sleek work shoes, or delicate suede pumps. While the shoes can be pricy, they're top-of-the-line in terms of construction and design, and will make anyone's feet look good. **A**

Revolution Books

1103 N. Ashland Ave.
773.489.0930
BLUE LINE to DIVISION

▍Without a doubt one of the most provocative bookshops on the Northwest Side, Revolution Books features an impressive inventory of radically leftist literature. The store's Communism-focused collection ranges from classic works of V.I. Lenin to recent writings on the future of communism in today's capitalist society. Revolution also sells books that explore different avenues of liberal political thought, like religions and philosophy. Affable proprietor Lou Downey explains that his shop aims to 'bring people a radically different view of the world' through literature. So if that's your bag, definitely check out Revolution Books. But be warned: If you still think 'Marxism' should become the eighth word you're not allowed to say on TV, stay away from Revolution's doors. No word yet on how the store reconciles its Communist leanings with its policy of charging patrons for books.

p.45

1643 N Damen Ave
773.862.4523
BLUE LINE to DAMEN

The display of elegant jewelry made by local designers, the hardwood floors and the intimate setting give this women's clothing boutique a sense of class. Music plays softly as you tediously search through the selection of blouses, dresses and pants. Good luck finding something trendy or chic because the clothes are plain and dull, and don't expect much help from the employees unless you're ready to buy. With prices ranging mostly in the triple digits, you're better off shopping elsewhere. **C**

Pagoda Red

1714 N Damen Ave
773.235.1188
BLUE LINE to DAMEN

Walking in to Pagoda Red makes you feel like you're entering a top-secret building. The short walkway leads you to a door where you have to be buzzed in. It's fascinating to see the Chinese and Tibetan antiques dating back centuries, but walking around this two-story shop can make you nervous. These antiques range in the thousands, so watch your step. **C+**

Propaganda

1418 N Milwaukee Ave
773.395.8337
BLUE LINE to DAMEN

This is not your typical T-shirt printing shop. The shop windows are lined with funny shirts from 'CUBS: Chicago's Ultimate Bitch Squad' to 'Don't F$%k with Chuck.' Inside, you'll find sale racks of even more shirts and quality deals on custom screen printing, photo T-shirts, lettering, hoodies, hats and even DJ slip mats. They have good deals on shirts for groups, with 24 shirts available for around $10-12. **B+**

Quimby's Bookstore

1854 W North Ave
773.342.0910
BLUE LINE to DAMEN

Any place that vows to 'satisfy the soul beaten flat by our mainstream culture's relentless insistence on dumb pictures and insulting syntax' has got to back those words up. Quimby's independent bookstore does. Here, the politically-edged aisles stock Che's pieces on revolutionary warfare and the graffiti section offers coffee table books of the city's finest 'vandalism.' Just make sure to turn your cell phone off, the staff takes huge offense to blabbermouths. **A**

Ragstock

1433 N Milwaukee Ave
773.486.1783
BLUE LINE to DAMEN

The welcoming blue ceilings with clouds are deceiving, as the workers here couldn't care less about you while you're shopping. Clothes lines feature the latest items and sales, like $19.99 men's skinny jeans.

Upstairs, you'll find department store rejects, cheapie lounging clothes and a grab bag of accessories, like earrings, fake tattoos, sunglasses and holiday costumes and novelties. Downstairs, there's new and used vintage, mostly only appropriate for tacky 80's prom parties. **C+**

Rapid Transit Cycle Shop

The owners of Rapid Transit are committed to spreading the two-wheel phenomenon to all Chicagoans. As the only recumbent bicycle dealer in the city, Rapid Transit

	1900 W North Ave
	773.227.2228
	BLUE LINE to DAMEN

lets customers test out eight different brands to find the perfect fit. They also offer full-service maintenance and all supplies and accessories to make your cycling commute hassle-free. If leaning back isn't your thing, they carry a wide range of urban bike brands, made obvious when you're ducking to avoid racks of bikes overhead. **A**

Reckless Records

Featuring an extensive selection of rock, hip-hop, soul and jazz pressed on

	1532 N Milwaukee Ave
	773.235.3727
	BLUE LINE to DAMEN

twelve-inch vinyl, Reckless is the kind of record store your parents probably shopped at. Their used CDs sell at the same fair prices of their LPs, classic films on old-school VHS tapes are each less than six bucks, and the impressive DVD inventory is also fun to browse. So if you're looking for a retro-record shop complete with all of today's modern amenities, get down to Reckless. **A-**

Running Away

A great destination for seasoned athletes or basic jogging enthusiasts,

	1634 W North Ave
	773.395.2929
	BLUE LINE to DAMEN

Running Away is a multi-sport retail store specializing in triathlon and distance running shoes and apparel. The extremely knowledgeable salespeople use a treadmill to analyze your stride to ensure that your next running shoe fits properly. The array of multicolored spandex and adorable running ensembles are enough to motivate even the laziest of couch potatoes. **A**

Shebang

This boutique was founded so that up-and-coming designers could have an

	1616 N Damen Ave
	773.486.3800
	BLUE LINE to DAMEN

outlet to showcase their work. Sophisticated and trendy purses by designers like Matt and Nat and hayden-harnett are displayed against vibrantly-colored walls. Jewelry and accessories also have their place in wall-length display cases. Although items run a little on the pricy side, women with a classic style shouldn't pass up the opportunity to go inside. **A-**

Pint, 1547 N. Milwaukee Ave. KAITLYN ELLISON

Shorty's Children's Boutique

Shorty's proves that statement-making clothing items that reflect pop

| 1410 N Milwaukee Ave |
| 773.252.4012 |
| BLUE LINE to DAMEN |

culture shouldn't be limited to adults. The walls are lined with miniature onesies featuring snappy screen prints reminiscent of Andy Warhol. It's a great place for the expecting modern-art enthusiast or baby shower gifts that will blow those tired Baby Gap ensembles out of the water. **A**

Silver Moon

Silver Moon is not your typical vintage shop. The pristine antique pieces

| 1755 W North Ave |
| 773.235.5797 |
| BLUE LINE to DAMEN |

are treated with great importance and homage paid to their history. Yet Silver Moon also brings vintage to a new high-fashion level, presenting some pieces that are over a century old in an urban, vogue setting, with an industrial look to the store and some groovy tunes playing in the background. Everything is sorted properly, clearly labeled and easy to find, which also sets it apart. **B**

Spoil Me

Upon stepping into the brightly-colored room and hearing loud pop music

| 1533 N Milwaukee Ave |
| 773.772.6868 |
| BLUE LINE to DAMEN |

blasting over the stereo, the only word that comes to mind is 'fun.' What's even more fun is the fact that all of the cute dangly earrings, big beaded necklaces, and trendy-looking 'designer inspired' bags are amazingly low-priced. In fact, almost everything in the store is under $40. But these aren't your average cheap knockoffs – Spoil Me sells inexpensive trends without looking cheap. **A**

Stitch

Walking into Stitch, you won't know where to look. From the sleek furniture

| 1723 N Damen Ave |
| 773.782.1570 |
| BLUE LINE to DAMEN |

to the rock star sunglasses to the throw pillows and unique bags, this shop is retail's version of a variety show. It's the kind of place you may enter with one thing in mind and exit with another item

Beauty Skool Dropout, 2200 W. Chicago Ave. KAITLYN ELLISON

in hand. Tempting as it may seem, this pricy shop is not an ideal place for a shopping spree. **B+**

Store B

Store B is a conglomeration of vintage cocktail dresses, skin care

| 1472 N Milwaukee Ave |
| 773.772.4296 |
| BLUE LINE to DAMEN |

products, greeting cards and costume jewelry. The juxtaposition of Burt's Bees next to a 1940's fur stole may not make sense, but for some unknown reason, the store maintains a cohesive feel. Store B is a great place to stumble upon for statement-making evening wear and eclectic gifts, but doesn't seem like somewhere to shop on a regular basis. **B**

Sultan's Market

Selling spices, incense and Turkish coffee, this market doubles as an

| 2057 W North Ave |
| 773.235.3072 |
| BLUE LINE to DAMEN |

eatery, serving salads, rice and falafel by day, and a hookah bar by night. Get in the mood for

Arabian romance with the beaded hanging lamps, mosaic tiles and peacock feathers that adorn the room. The very limited selection of Middle Eastern merchandise detracts from its merits as a grocery store, but it's a great place for a simple lunch salad and rice. **B**

Tangerine

While a small assortment of jewelry and accessories lie on a table near the entrance, blouses, skirts and jackets line the walls of this small boutique. The clothes lack color, and the most interesting part of this place is the register, which sits in a brown stand with a roof, making you feel like you're about to buy a cup of lemonade on a hot summer day. **C+**

1719 N Damen Ave
773.772.0505
BLUE LINE to DAMEN

The Brown Elephant

Finally, there's a store for the artsy philanthropist. The Brown Elephant is a thrift store where all proceeds from donated home and apparel items benefit the Howard Brown Health Center. While the majority of the vintage clothing items are pretty run-of-the-mill, at least your money is going to a good cause. **C+**

1459 N Milwaukee Ave
773.252.8801
BLUE LINE to DAMEN

The Gallery Café

The imaginative artist and the café intellectual can both get their way by

1760 W North Ave
773.252.8228
BLUE LINE to DAMEN

visiting the Galley Café. Featuring local art on the walls, art buffs won't feel so bad about missing the Art Institute, especially after seeing that everything on the menu is named after an artist. For a classic breakfast taste, try the Da Vinci, an egg sandwich. Those more adventurous might prefer the Hopper – smoked turkey, avocado spread, cucumber, radish, tomato, lettuce and olive oil. **B**

The Naughty Puppy

Sick of that t-shirt with the name of a college you don't attend? Then head down to the new outlet of self-expression in Wicker Park, The Naughty Puppy. Contrary to its name, the boutique has nothing to do with animals or misbehavior. Owner Ralph Massey has recruited local talent to create designs that pull from all aspects of pop culture. Pick a design and a shirt style and The Naughty Puppy creates a one-of-a-kind tee for you. **A**

1719 W North Ave
773.572.2361
BLUE LINE to DAMEN

The Silver Room

Upon entering the store, customers are greeted by a beautiful silver fountain mirroring much of the Silver Room's metallic merchandise. The majority of the store is dedicated to, you guessed it, silver jewelry. However, they do have a wide range of sunglasses, hats, scarves and watches. The standout collection is locally designed 'Tivi,' where unfinished silver

1442 N Milwaukee Ave
773.278.7130
BLUE LINE to DAMEN

Darkroom, 2210 W. Chicago Ave.
KAITLYN ELLISON

WEST TOWN

mixed with ebony gives chunky bracelets a natural yet industrial feel. **B+**

T-Shirt Deli

At this deli you don't get bologna and cheese, instead you can buy inex- | 1739 N Damen Ave
773.276.6266
BLUE LINE to DAMEN

pensive personalized T-shirts. Glass cases display an array of different colored rolled-up t-shirts, allowing you to choose a 'flavor' and create a 'fresh' new shirt. Work up an appetite by browsing through different colors and sizes, followed by picking the slogan or picture you want printed on your shirt. Want any sides with that? The deli serves personalized underwear, sweaters, baby hats and dog tees too. **A**

U.S. #1 Vintage Clothing and Denim

Walk into this store and it's as if you're back in the Old West. Some of the | 1460 N Milwaukee Ave
773.489.9428
BLUE LINE to DAMEN

vintage clothing dates back as far as 1880, and there's no shortage of leather overcoats or cowboy boots lining the walls in the winter. Warm weather replaces them with T-shirts and classic tennis shoes. Shirts range from $10 Hawaiian shirts to $500 for '60s rock band T-shirts. Selection is limited to similar styles of clothing, but good rummaging can lead to great finds. **B-**

Una Mae's Freak Boutique

When you're bored with the mall, come here to get your hands on bargain | 1422 N Milwaukee Ave
773.276.7002
BLUE LINE to DAMEN

treasures and fresh additions to your wardrobe, whether you want the latest fashion or vintage items. This boutique embodies the Wicker Park scene with its funky, chic atmosphere and provides a wide selection of retro jewelry and accessories. **A**

Untitled

An intimate space and a smiling, helpful staff set Untitled apart from other | 1941 W North Ave
773.342.0500
BLUE LINE to DAMEN

stores that carry similar hipster duds. While it's

easy to blow an insane amount of money on their clever t-shirts, colorful sweaters, funky shoes and unique accessories, the ability to walk away from the store with a cohesive outfit makes it worth it. The selection can be limited and sizes tend to run small so be ready to try things on. **A-**

Zella Brown

Zella Brown isn't your average Crate and Barrel, but then again, neither are | 1444 N Milwaukee Ave
773.276.1746
BLUE LINE to DAMEN

their prices. The home furnishing and accessory store boasts punchy items, such as artificial flowers made out of folded periodical clippings or pillows made of mohair. The contemporary pieces are beautiful, but they aren't exactly dorm room appropriate. **B-**

An.je.nu

If Hallmark cards aren't cutting it anymore, come to An.je.nu for cute | 1747 W Division St
773.469.2212
BLUE LINE to DIVISION

stationary handmade by local artists. Owner Kristie Lee has experience – she's been making cards since third grade. As well as offering single cards, Lee designs custom wedding invitations and personal stationary. The prices for cards vary from $4-7 and cover a wide range of subjects. Local artists also contribute to the small jewelry section in the back. **A**

Andina Buenos Aires

Though their products have a modern-Euro feel, this store channels a | 1740 W Division St
773.227.6225
BLUE LINE to DIVISION

folksy vibe, with a cowhide draped along one wall. The result is Andina's eclectic sleekness. Their main attractions are their belts, which start at $60, and purses, all under $200. The owners import all their leather accessories from Argentina. **B+**

Cassona Home Furnishings and Accessories

Cassona's Home Furnishings offers a multicolored display of home | 2121 W Division St
773.486.5525
BLUE LINE to DIVISION

decorations and vivid paintings complete with cool mood lamps of every shape and kind. Even the walls differ in hues from red to beige. The cultural infusions and prints add to the artistic and creatively inspired store, where customers can pick out their own fabrics for custom-designed sofas. A sale, however, might be as high as $600 for a single dresser. **B+**

Cattails

You won't find cheesy carnations at Cattails, 'a unique flower market.'

1935 W Division St
773.486.1621
BLUE LINE to DIVISION

Specializing in beautiful floral arrangements made from exotic flowers, they also offer hand-blown glass vases to complement their eclectic bouquets. Treat your pooch to the extensive variety of vegetarian dog treats in back meant for the flower-loving pet owner. **A−**

Chemise on Division

Although this clothing is far from over the top, these conventional style

1939 W Division St
773.276.8020
BLUE LINE to DIVISION

shirts in basic colors have an element of funky design that distinguishes them from the rest: skulls on the back of simple black, Hawaiian flowers decorating soft crème. The most ap-

pealing shirts, however, are the ones that are more subtle than that. You'll grab attention without screaming for it with one of their many white dress shirts with simple, symmetrical embroidery. **C+**

Crazy Man Records

If you can't find that one album you must have on vinyl, seek the Crazy Man.

1657 W Division St
773.489.9840
BLUE LINE to DIVISION

The Crazy Man himself looms ominously behind the cash register in the tiny store [he's a nice guy, but intimidating nonetheless], making customers want to leave as quickly as possible. Crazy Man's is somewhat lacking in the rock staples, like Beatles, Dylan, Stones and Young, but boasts quite an inventory of reasonably−priced, hard-to-find LPs, such as excellent Van Morrison, CSNY, and Santana records. **B+**

D/Vision

Bad eyes? With glasses from D/Vision flattering your face, don't worry

1756 W Division St
773.489.4848
BLUE LINE to DIVISION

about the label 'four-eyes.' Just concentrate on refilling your wallet. This eyewear boutique is for those who insist on having things others won't have. Their collections include I.C. Berlin, Oliver

Terry's Toffee

1117 W. Grand Ave.
312.733.2700
BLUE LINE to GRAND

The clean kitchen sitting in plain sight at the rear of the store exudes a sweet and rich aroma of spices that tempts the visitor's sweet tooth. Terry's sends free samples to the stars through Academy Awards' gift baskets, and celebrities such as Pierce Brosnan and Penelope Cruz attest to the taste by sending in autographed portraits displayed on the walls. For first-time customers, the friendly and knowledgeable staff gives helpful hints on making the right selection and encourages trying the free samples placed near the door, of which even frequent shoppers can partake. The adventurous can try the Asian Accent, which includes wasabi and Australian ginger, while the conventional can try McCall's Classic, made with milk chocolate and Georgian pecans. Accent any gift packages with beautiful boxes, some hand-crafted by a San Francisco artist. The well-designed Web site facilitates convenient online shopping.

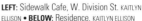

LEFT: Sidewalk Cafe, W. Division St. KAITLYN ELLISON • **BELOW:** Residence. KAITLYN ELLISON

Peoples and Lindberg. Frames start at $280 and sunglasses run from $250 and up, so bring in your insurance plan. Eye exams and frames customization are also available. **B+**

Diana Fashions

For a romantic night, lacy lingerie just doesn't cut it anymore. Try the padded butt for a quick boost at the back or sexy costumes such as French maid, sexy geek or Agent 0069. Diane Fashions doesn't just cater to the fun, curious lover, but attracts all age groups with their exotic designs. Check out their latest bridal wear, dance wear, girdles and corset shapers. **A-**

1251 N Milwaukee Ave
773.227.7010
BLUE LINE to DIVISION

Diana Shoes

You can walk in any style with this eclectic mix of flip-flops, flats, Nike Dunks, Timbs and even 7-inch platforms. Diana Shoes, located amidst many other shoe stores along Milwaukee Ave., serves the interested walk-in shopper, dancer, basketball player or drag queen looking for size 14 heels. With their wide array of designs, there's a shoe that'll fit any possible occasion. **A**

1272 N Milwaukee Ave
773.227.7743
BLUE LINE to DIVISION

Doggy Style

The doggie treats displayed at the front of this store look and smell good enough for any human, being made from organic, human-grade ingredients. Other interesting merchandise includes vintage clothing and giant, bed-sized cushions for your pets. The four staff members pride themselves on knowing all customers, human or animal, by name. **A**

2023 W Division St
773.235.9663
BLUE LINE to DIVISION

Dusty Groove America

Dusty Groove offers the northwest side's most extensive selection of jazz, hip-hop and soul recordings, both on vinyl and CD. If you dig those genres, Groove's incredible inventory – complemented by its bargain prices – will doubtlessly provide hours of entertainment. But if rock music is more your bag, Dusty Groove's more limited rock-and-roll selection boasts a few real gems as well. **A**

1120 N Ashland Ave
773.342.5800
BLUE LINE to DIVISION

Dynamic Hair Studio

Dynamic Hair Studio is a full service Aveda salon spa specializing in

1754 W Division St
773.772.2772
BLUE LINE to DIVISION

WEST TOWN

1952 N. Damen Ave.
KAITLYN ELLISON

treatments to help soothe the frazzled urbanite. Specialty treatments include the Foot Reflexology spa treatment or the head-to-toe Dynamic facial. The helpful receptionist can answer any questions about their many spa and salon services. Dynamic also has a nice selection of affordable freshwater pearl jewelry nestled by the bevy of Aveda hair and body products. **B+**

E Space

Girls all know this [and guys should]: shoes are more than utilitarian; they're a way to set yourself apart. Original footwear constitutes the centerpiece of E Space. You can find anything from All Star sneakers to flashy high-heeled sandals and dainty ballet flats. In addition to shoes, E Space sells brand clothing such as Lacoste. Although most of the merchandise is for those with well-endowed wallets [some shoes cost over $150], browsing through the sales can lead to pleasant surprises. **B**

1205 N Milwaukee Ave
773.252.6944
BLUE LINE to DIVISION

Elevenzees

Perfect for buying gifts, Elevenzees has a huge selection of French bath products ranging from bath bombs to scented candles, along with trendy pajamas, yoga mats and new-age-inspired books and CDs. For the

1901 W Division St
773.772.1150
BLUE LINE to DIVISION

more mainstream, the wide variety of kitchen accoutrements and epicurean delights are a surefire bet for a pleasing present. **B+**

Figaro European Shoes

Figaro claims they sell 'unique shoes to live in,' but their overpriced, gaudy men's and women's collections leave much to be desired. From tacky florescent orange walls to a fake animal skin rug, the boutique hardly connotes high-end European fashion. The overuse of pleather and cheesy patterns makes the shoes more appropriate for nightclubs than everyday wear. If the pseudo-trendy shoes don't deter customers, the snooty salespeople and strict return policy certainly will. **C-**

1238 N Milwaukee Ave
773.227.3502
BLUE LINE to DIVISION

Grow

Expecting hypochondriacs and granola parents-to-be rejoice: Grow is the one-stop shop for all of your high-maintenance baby needs. The walls of this chic baby store are lined with organic, non-toxic, pastel onesies. They also feature a wide selection of futuristic baby strollers, bassinette, cradles and high chairs that won't look out of place in contemporary lofts and urban homes. **B+**

1943 W Division St
773.489.0009
BLUE LINE to DIVISION

WEST TOWN

Habit

Don't you hate it when you see another girl rocking your outfit? Habit will help you avoid that problem by offering under-the-radar clothing and accessories from independent designers that will keep you ahead of the crowd. After the owner personally helps you choose exclusive items, you'll be able to brag to your friends about the cute bubble shorts or flowy dress you picked up. Or, on second thought, you may want to keep this fashion-forward gem all to yourself. **B+**

1951 W Division St
773.342.0093
BLUE LINE to DIVISION

Juliani

High-class stilettos line the multi-tiered wooden displays in this dimly lit boutique. Rock out to electronica as you check out Juliani's beautifully-designed heels and men's flats. In addition to offering high-quality service, Juliani's also features a price range reasonably under $100 for imported fashions from Italy, France and Brazil. Velvet displays of imported earrings and necklaces are reminiscent of designer boutiques in Milan. **A-**

2124 W Division St
773.486.8366
BLUE LINE to DIVISION

M.B. Sales

If you've ever felt there wasn't enough Texas flavor on Chicago's Northwest Side, you've clearly never visited M.B. Sales. A retail outfit that specializes in Country-Western-style clothing and accessories and has a deer head sits mounted on one of the walls, M.B. boasts two stories filled with enough hats, boots, shirts, jeans, belts and jewelry to make any cow-boy, -girl, or -tot [yes, they have a size-able children's section] happy. Even John Wayne would feel at home at M.B. **A**

918 N Ashland Ave
312.829.0045
BLUE LINE to DIVISION

Nina Knitting

This store dispels the notion that knitting is for little old ladies. Besides shelves of immaculate stacks of yarn, Nina also offers companion products, such as knitting hand balm and knitting bags, books, patterns and kits. From the classes offered to the sleek and simple contemporary interior design, Nina creates a welcome environment for young, hip knitters to channel their creative energy. The owner also converts knitting from hobby to social activism by offering products that support worthy causes. **A-**

1655 W Division St
773.486.8996
BLUE LINE to DIVISION

Noir

Techno music sets the mood as you enter this boutique. The trendy blouses, dresses and pants and the assortment of belts, purses and other accessories will keep you in front of the mirror torn over choosing the perfect outfit for your night out. There is a small selection of shoes and an even smaller selection of sexy, sequined bras. Take out your credit card and get ready to spend because it gets a bit pricey. **B**

1726 W Division St
773.489.1957
BLUE LINE to DIVISION

Paper Doll Inc.

Paper Doll explodes with creative giftware, includ-ing stationery, greeting cards, candles and artist-designed T-shirts. This cutesy store offers a gift-wrapping section and custom-designed invitations perfect for weddings or parties. It also houses a pug that roams freely around the spacious room, adding even more charm to the atmosphere. If you're looking to boost a gift's uniqueness by accessorizing, the options here are sure to satisfy. **B**

2048 W Division St
773.227.6950
BLUE LINE to DIVISION

Permanent Records

Permanent offers a superb collection of vinyl records amidst a super-cozy at-mosphere. Their very reasonably-priced inventory of LPs ranges from must-have Beatles albums to Neil Young's ultra-rare Time Fades Away and also includes jazz, soul and funk. Alongside all these great recordings is an impressive collection of used books – including a number of contempo-rary classics – that sells for bargain prices, used CDs and rock-themed films. What more could anyone ask of a record shop? **A**

1914 W Chicago Ave
773.278.1744
BLUE LINE to DIVISION

Porte Rouge

Imagine traveling the world on an unlimited budget and bringing home souvenirs for your friends. Porte Rouge is the portal to an international blend of old and new from antique dishware from Portugal, custom upholstered furniture and world-famous French tea that's imported four times a year. Items range from $3 to $6500 but prices depend on the Euro. The most popular-selling item on the Web site is the French Marriage tea. Porte Rouge also offers a wedding registry. **A**

> 1911 W Damen Ave
> 773.269.2800
> **BLUE LINE to DIVISION**

Public I

Public I lives up to its tagline: 'Urban Goods with a Passion for Style.' The boutique offers simple, sleek staples with clean lines for the urbane urban shopper. Though the goods are pricy, the atmosphere at Public I is friendly and laid back. The sales associates are friendly and have none of the pretentious attitudes of salespeople at similar boutiques. Public

> 1923 W Division St
> 773.772.9088
> **BLUE LINE to DIVISION**

I features independent designer fashions for men and women and a selection of accessories and travel goods. **A⁻**

Pump

Pump is the one-stop store for style-conscious urbanites looking for shoes that complement their outfit perfectly. Whether you're wearing a trendy one-piece dress or casual jeans, Pump's fantastic array of shoes is sure to provide what you'll need. Shoes range from spiky Miss Sixty heels to comfy Michelle K flats, and prices vary between $60 and $290. They also offer a varied mix of jewelry, belts, sunglasses and other fashion accessories. **A**

> 1659 W Division St
> 773.384.6750
> **BLUE LINE to DIVISION**

RotoFugi

At RotoFugi you're never too old to love toys. The small shop is geared towards adult collectors of various figurines, pictures, art and more. The subject matter ranges from the oddly adorable [small plush one-eyed

> 1953-55 W Chicago Ave
> 312.491.9501
> **BLUE LINE to DIVISION**

ABOVE: Pagoda Red, 1714 N. Damen Ave.
KAITLYN ELLISON • **RIGHT:** Pagoda Red, 1714 N. Damen Ave. KAITLYN ELLISON

'Uglydolls'] to the disturbing [figurines of a man vomiting]. Along with the art and collectibles, RotoFugi offers an art gallery in the space adjacent to their store, where they feature local work during the first Friday of each month. **B+**

RR#1 Chicago

Think of it – they've got it. Or at least a toy version or a book that mentions

| 814 N Ashland Ave |
| 312.421.9079 |
| BLUE LINE to DIVISION |

it. That's the impression RR#1 Chicago gives with the sheer number of gift items they offer. Lanterns, candles, handmade jewelry, wallets, stationery, incense, skin-care solutions, utensils and teas pack the place, and there's even a baby-goods corner. **B+**

Sunny Shoes

J-Lo enthusiasts and drag queens everywhere rejoice – Sunny Shoes

| 1282 N Milwaukee Ave |
| 773.252.8110 |
| BLUE LINE to DIVISION |

is the new Mecca for ghetto-fab foot apparel. Customers will be overwhelmed by the buzzing neon lights and floor-to-ceiling shoe displays. Although the multicolored seven-inch platform go-go boots may not be conducive to long walks, they certainly will enhance any Halloween costume. **C**

Tatine

If you're looking to buy candles, for yourself or for that friend with the 'man-

| 1742 W Division St |
| 773.342.1890 |
| BLUE LINE to DIVISION |

funk' apartment, come to Tatine. Owner Margo Breznik makes each candle by hand using pure soy wax in the attached workshop and keeps the store filled with the sweet scent of melting candles and tranquil music. In addition to more than 100 exotic scents, including Sake, Asian White Tea, and Bay Rum and Lime, much of its worldly décor of vases and dishes is purchasable. **B**

The Ark Thrift Shop

The Ark Thrift Shop offers a smattering of used clothing and household

| 1302 N Milwaukee Ave |
| 773.862.5011 |
| BLUE LINE to DIVISION |

items. Unfortunately, the disorganized display makes finding hidden treasures especially difficult and a funky, spicy nursing-home smell permeates the entire store and makes you want to get in and out as quickly as possible. Vintage lovers are better off heading down the street to any of Wicker Park's other thrift shops. **C-**

The Boring Store

If the irony of The Boring Store's name doesn't grab your attention, then

| 1331 N Milwaukee Ave |
| 773.772.8108 |
| BLUE LINE to DIVISION |

their witty merchandise individually packaged in cardboard boxes will. They certainly deserve the self-dubbed title, 'The Last Intriguing Retail Outlet of the Midwest.' Their serpentine shelving makes customers wind through the oddly laid-out store. Most of their products are quasi-spy inspired, such as a banana-shaped cell phone disguise or a cough disguiser. It's a great place to find irreverent and bizarre gifts. **A**

Bari Foods

Crowded aisles, crammed shelves, brisk employees and an unappetizing smell

| 1120 W Grand Ave |
| 312.666.0730 |
| BLUE LINE to GRAND |

give patrons a convenience-store feel, as do the limited selections of regular grocery items, such as produce and canned foods. At least you can find genuine Italian spices that actually have Italian on the labels and olive oil in rare and colorful three-liter cans. The deli in the back serves standard subs at reasonable prices good for a quick lunch. **B**

Lily's Record Shop

This shop has been described by Lily herself as specializing in salsa music

| 2733 W Division St |
| 773.252.7008 |
| BLUE LINE to S WESTERN |

and 'anything with the Puerto Rican flag on it.' And Lily, of course, is quite accurate in her depiction. Aside the extensive collection of salsa CDs and LPs are instruments, clothing and all kinds of other memorabilia originating from Puerto Rico. So if you're into salsa records and want to experience Puerto Rico without leaving Chicago, Lily's is a can't-miss. **B**

AVONDALE

KNOWN FOR ITS CLOSE-KNIT COMMUNITIES

Europeans, Hispanics and a bit of every other ethnic group have flocked to Avondale, making it just as colorful as the nickname of its most popular area, Jackowo. Known for its close-knit communities, Avondale is mostly residential – a holdover from the old blue-collar neighborhoods that sprung up in Chicago's industrial days – but there are treasures to be found for those looking off the beaten path. First populated by Germans, Scandinavians and Poles, the area's architecture reflects its heritage. Sausage makers still line the commercial streets of the area and you can smell it in the air. In the Polish Village, one of the city's largest and most vibrant, find Polish books, clothes and other goods. While the population today is dominated largely by Hispanics in Avondale, the polish culture still thrives. The large Roman Catholic churches that still stand are some of the area's hottest attractions. Other cultures are best understood through food and there's plenty to find along Milwaukee Ave. Locals flock to Abbey Pub for up and coming musical acts, traditional Irish breakfast or to watch rugby matches.

TO EAT

La Humita

Family-owned by the Correas, La Humita has an authentic Ecuadorian menu offering entrees featuring beef, chicken, pork and pasta. The name of the restaurant, humita, is the house specialty, a filling appetizer that looks like a tamale but is made mostly of cheese and corn and comes with a delicious homemade salsa. Every dish looks and tastes dif-

3466 N Pulaski Rd
773.794.9672
BLUE LINE to ADDISON

ferent and appeals to any appetite craving South American cuisine. **A-**

Hot Doug's

Fulfill any 'encased meat' cravings here, where owner Doug Sohn offers an affordable menu of eclectic hot dogs. Who knew a blue cheese pork sausage, topped with a green apple cream sauce and almonds, would taste so good? Enjoy the 50's-rock décor while trying the 'Game of the Week' sausage. Past meats include rabbit, elk, kangaroo, alligator,

3324 N California Ave
773.279.9550
BLUE LINE to BELMONT

rattlesnake and buffalo. For the less daring, have the classic Chicago-style hot dog for only $1.50. **A**

profit organization, all shows are technically free of charge, but if you like what you see, donations are happily accepted. **B**

TO PLAY

Elastic Arts Foundation

A hidden outlet at the top of a dimly-lit flight of stairs provides power for

2830 N Milwaukee Ave
773.772.3616
BLUE LINE to LOGAN SQUARE

local musicians and performers to light up this stage, while the vibrantly-colored walls, lined with a featured art exhibit, lure you to the center of this hole-in-the-wall gallery. You don't have to break the bank to make a visit either – as a non-

Gingarte Capoeira

For a completely different gym/dance/music experience, check out

2909 N Milwaukee Ave
773.924.3220
BLUE LINE to LOGAN SQUARE

capoeira – an Afro-Brazilian martial arts with dance, fighting, gymnastics and live music. As the largest capoeira organization in the Midwest, Gingarte not only has daily capoeira classes for only $10 [ask about student discounts], but also offers samba lessons, capoeira music classes and Portuguese language classes. **A-**

AVONDALE

FROM SLAVERY TO CELEBRITY: CAPOEIRA IN THE SPOTLIGHT
BY SETARREH MASSIHZADEGAN

Encircled by the delightful chaos of clapping, chanting and the drumming and plucking of anachronistic instruments, two players scuttle about like graceful spiders. In the true contradictory nature of the art of capoeira, they throw ominous kicks while weaving through one another's legs in an agile improvised dance. In the roda – pronounced 'hoda' – they are distrustful, watching one another with unwavering eyes as they contort into positions that rarely leave two legs on the ground. Bodies spin into pinwheels, become airborne, a web of legs whirl into kicks, and heads and torsos duck to avoid contact. They are capoeiristas, and this is their moment, the sweat-drenched, energy-infused grand finale that follows arduous training.

Capoeira is an Afro-Brazilian martial art whose hundreds of years of history incite as much debate as the mystery of its name. It marries art, music, dance, rituals and culture, says Marisa Cordeiro, founder of Chicago's Gingarte

Capoeira academy and the woman credited with bringing the phenomenon to the city. Cordeiro is director, teacher and a preacher of sorts, working to cart her craft to a burgeoning population of novices.

Those at Chicago's Gingarte Capoeira, founded in 1991 and now one of the Midwest's largest capoeira centers, do their best to preserve the details of their ancient art. Most attribute capoeira's birth to Portugal's colonization of Brazil and the subsequent enslaving of Africans, who were brought there after the country's native Indian population resisted slavery. In the past, capoeira was outlawed in Brazil due to its association with violence.

Class at the academy, a hole in the wall among Latino eateries and karaoke joints at 2909 N. Milwaukee Ave. in Avondale, is a sensory experience from the moment of entry. Without air conditioning, the vast, hardwood studio on a humid summer day has the feel of an equatorial country. But as class begins, usually 10 or 15 minutes past the appointed start time, capoeira music, Brazilian-accented commands and kicks cut through the heavy air. Sweat

pours from determined faces and the 30 or so students — standing in three lines — replicate Cordeiro's combinations. Most begin with the ginga [pronounced 'jinga'], which begins as a lunge to one side where one-foot then swings back and both feet rock in step with the music. The assignments increase in difficulty rapidly, from stretches and gingas into front kicks, to multi-step airborne turns and spinning kicks.

Cordeiro begins singing and her voice resonates from an unseen depth, unwavering and strident, even when joined by other voices and sounds. Two-by-two, the players enter the roda, cordially shaking hands before unleashing moves like those practiced in class, strung together in feigned effortlessness within the confined space of the circle. The students balance their weight on one arm, twist into head stands and end delicately as mirror images of one another. Then they exit, again taking one another's hands, and return to the circle where they continue clapping and singing.

Cordeiro claims to be of old age, but despite mothering two young children at home and teaching at summer camps nearly every day, her movements and physique suggest a woman of 25. She emerges fresh and alert after class, radiating a power that is both palpable and a bit intimidating. As a contra-mestre and one of the highest-ranked women capoeiristas in the world, Cordeiro welcomes about 100 students between her two academies [there is another located on the South Side], and between them an amalgam of ages and skill levels. 'You can play against anybody,' says four-year capoeirista Roger Simon. 'You can play a little kid who'll keep you on your toes, you can play an old person who will share their knowledge with you.' He says it's a way to converse on a deeper level without heeding conventional barriers, and it is a philosophy he applies in his everyday life.

Cordeiro's practice has multiplied nearly fivefold and she's getting plenty of attention around town. With an average of 100-150 shows annually at venues like Millennium Park and weekly performances by some capoeiristas, many are looking at full schedules. But the most cluttered of schedules is Cordeiro's, a reality that leaves her not the least bit frazzled.

Back in 1982, Sifu Bill Owens, secretary of the World Capoeira Organization, wrote, 'Ten years from now the word capoeira will become as popular as the words 'apple pie.' While the craze hasn't gone that far, capoeira has certainly infused itself into American culture. Hip-hop star Usher and Catwoman actress Halle Berry have infused capoeira moves into their mediums, while gyms like Bally Total Fitness boast aerobics classes they call capoeira. But for some, there is a fine line between sought-after recognition and unflattering imitation.

Cordeiro's confidence in her craft far outweighs any intimidation by move to the mainstream. In fact, she thinks the mounting attention is a good thing, provided that those truly interested in the game go the extra distance to learn its ins and outs. Whether in spite of or in defiance of the changing tides, Cordeiro is passionate about introducing more people to capoeira's doctrine. 'I think more people can benefit from it if they have the chance to be exposed to capoeira,' she says. She has faith in other academies, which she assumes convey the history as she does, 'teaching people not only to do the movements, which is the fun part, but to make sure that people understand exactly where it comes from and how and why it was created.'

Cordeiro's goals are larger than a mere title or competition win. She sees capoeira as a means for social change, even today. She hopes to further establish her academy and garner the funds to send money to Brazilian children in capoeira programs.

As the musicians pick up speed, the roda gains momentum with an impenetrable energy that signals the finale. Those playing capoeira in the center carry out their movements with increased urgency, their limbs whirling by, in hopes to execute the last au or handstand before time's up. When it is over, the circle unravels and two lines form, approaching one another, hands outstretched. As they meet, each capoeirista lightly taps fists with the other and then their fingers intertwine, in a secret handshake of sorts. 'Salve' they say, wishing one another salvation, as they sign out on another history lesson, conservational moment, social milieu, jogo de capoeira. While class should have ended at nine, it is past 10 and there are a few stragglers who can't seem to tear themselves away. 'We never go home,' one says.

WINDOW WASHER

Attached to a rope and harness that can support 6,300 pounds, this window washer is in the middle of one of many 'drops' required to clean the exterior of this downtown Chicago skyscraper. Most drops take less than an hour and, once completed, washers take a service elevator to the roof, move their ropes and rappel over the edge again. Washers typically cover one or two columns of windows on each drop, using suction cups to hold themselves in place. On average, they make about $15 per hour.

Photograph by Daniel Honigman

CENTRAL

NEAR NORTH SIDE

FOUR UNIQUE AREAS EACH WITH A FLAVOR ALL THEIR OWN

The near north side is Mecca for tourists and the wealthy of Chicago alike. It's made up of four unique areas each with a flavor all their own. Once a haven for the artier, edgier sets with art galleries galore, River North has since fallen into the mainstream. Hubbard St. has smoky bars and clubs at every turn while more traditional galleries still remain amongst the stunning architecture of the Marina Towers and Courthouse Place. Old Town deserves its name. Home of the Chicago Historical Society, walk down the cobblestone streets and look at the Victorian buildings -- some of the few that survived the great fire. Luxury hotels, condominiums and retailers make up Streeterville. For the young intellectuals, the Museum of Contemporary Art is one of the biggest draws. Just a few blocks west is the Magnificent Mile [actually only three fourths of a mile long] -- go for the shopping, stay for the street performers. The ritziest of the ritzy, the Gold Coast is where Chicago's Ritz-Carlton is located. Beautiful beaches line the coast while designers like Gucci and Prada line the sidewalks of Oak St. The Hancock Tower offers great views from above and delicious cheesecake below.

TO EAT

Japonais Restaurant

600 W Chicago Ave
312.822.9600
BROWN LINE to CHICAGO

If you're craving some sushi and have money to burn, stop by this 'see-and-be-seen' hot spot on the city's North Side. The sushi and sashimi is world class, and you'll feel like royalty while reclining in the expansive lounge area. Make sure to sample the crème brulee at the end of the night and to brace yourself when the bill arrives. **B+**

Brasserie Jo

59 W Hubbard St
312.595.0800
BROWN LINE to MERCH MART

If tasty French-inspired cuisine and inviting, stylish atmospheres appeal to your tastes, make a point to visit Brasserie Jo. This restaurant features a variety of succulent dishes, including the popular chicken coc au vine, the sweet alsacienne pork chops and the infamous 'shrimp-in-a-bag.' Service is not always speedy, but the atmosphere is such that you'll enjoy your time anyway. **B+**

Camille' Sidewalk Café

This small, north side café offers an extensive and diverse menu of wraps, gelato and beer. Sit inside for a more elegant dining experience or outside to enjoy the sun and listen to the nearby fountains. The reasonable prices and elegant décor make Camille's Sidewalk Café ideal for a romantic date. **B⁺**

400 N LaSalle St
312.329.9727
BROWN LINE to MERCH MART

Coco Pazzo

The popularity of this Italian restaurant can be credited to its classy twist on authentic Italian food. Each dish, from the bone-in rib eye to the array of pasta dishes, is made with exotic spices and hints of flavor that make the restaurant a first choice for many. Accents of blue, white and honey woods complete its atmosphere. Prepare to spend lavishly, however, with main course meals ranging from $18-35. **A**

300 W Hubbard St
312.836.0900
BROWN LINE to MERCH MART

Gene & Georgetti

Rumored to have been one of Frank Sinatra's favorite haunts, this steakhouse

500 N Franklin St
312.527.3718
BROWN LINE to MERCH MART

looks like something out of a black and white movie. The two story wooden building is nestled in the heart of the city and serves thick, scrumptious meat to politicians and tourists alike. It also offers a range of Italian favorites. Portions tend to be large, so make sure you're ready to eat. **B⁺**

Lou Malnati's Pizzeria

Whether you will like deep-dish pie is hit-or-miss; some love it, others hate it. It would be wasteful to order anything other than pizza, so here's what to expect: the cheese and toppings are the middle layer, covered by a slightly sweet tomato sauce. The crust is thick and buttery, and the cooking time is long [45 minutes is average]. The huge sodas will keep you hydrated while waiting, and, overall, it is worth it. **A**

439 N Wells St
312.828.9800
BROWN LINE to MERCH MART

1492 Tapas Bar

If moderately-priced flavorful food and colorful ambiance is what you're looking for, go no further than this restaurant. Customers are treated to Spanish music as they dine, and the wait and host staff are courteous

42 E Superior St
312.867.1492
RED LINE to CHICAGO

NEAR NORTH SIDE

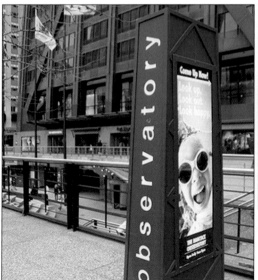

ABOVE: Michigan Ave. KATHERINE VILLAMIN
• **LEFT:** Michigan Ave. KATHERINE VILLAMIN

mk the Restaurant

868 N. Franklin St.
312.482.9179
BROWN LINE to CHICAGO

It's not cheap, and it's certainly not in the Loop, but executive chef Michael Kornick's mk is a gem for special occasions. Simple food is presented elegantly and efficiently, service is excellent and the split-level dining room's chic brick and wood combo makes this AmEuropean dinner spot a must-visit. Appetizers run in the $10-18 range and entrees range from $26-44. Whimsical desserts like The Peanut Gallery – peanut butter mousse served with a warm brownie, pretzels and peanuts on splotches of caramel and chocolate ganache – make young pastry chef Kate Neumann a rising star. Don't be surprised if the owner, general manager or a chef stop by to say hello; they mill around the dining room all night, creating a homey atmosphere.

and efficient. On the must-try list: The Sangria, rioja muscles and solomillo steak. Make sure to place reservations or you're likely to find a long wait ahead of you. **A**

CTA Bus, Michigan Ave. KATHERINE VILLAMIN

Argo Tea Café

819 N Rush St
312.951.5302
RED LINE to CHICAGO

Not in the mood for your average coffee? Visit Argo Tea Café, a unique alternative to shake up your usual routine. With its healthy signature drinks and selection of sandwiches, salads, baked goods and even quiche, this is a great place to meet for a quick breakfast or lunch date. Despite an unoriginal atmosphere [think Starbucks, but with tea], prices are reasonable and you can even buy a bag of loose tea to take home. **A-**

Café Spiaggia

980 N Michigan Ave
312.280.2755
RED LINE to CHICAGO

If you're looking for an upscale restaurant on a special occasion, look no further than Café Spiaggia. The gourmet entrées include various dishes of gnocchi, handmade pasta and truffle sauces prepared and served with an artist's touch. Finish off your satiating meal with an Italian favorite – gelato. If you're looking for a romantic atmosphere, be sure to ask for seating in the dining room. **A**

Corner Bakery

900 N Michigan Ave
312.573.9900
RED LINE to CHICAGO

Corner Bakery is a product of the latest boom of soup-and-sandwich cafes, with no argument that it's any better than the next little joint. Soups here aren't creative, salads

LEFT: Path Along The Chicago River. WENHONG NEOH • **BOTTOM:** Jean Baptiste du Sable Homesite, 400 N. Michigan Ave. WENHONG NEOH

are just greens and dressing and the sandwiches need work. Looking for a quick fix to silence your growling stomach without damaging your wallet? Stop on in. Otherwise, walk across the street to that 'next little joint.' **C-**

Devon Seafood Grill

Devon Seafood Grill features dishes inspired by the sea. The lobster and crab cakes are excellent options, and if you've never tried them, order the oysters Rockefeller. Because the chefs here are committed to serving only the finest foods, the menu changes seasonally and guarantees to offer guests new and exciting options at each visit. Although expensive, Devon promises to deliver delicious, high quality food. **A**

39 E Chicago Ave
312.440.8660
RED LINE to CHICAGO

Downtown Dogs

Downtown Dogs is a wonderful find in this typically commercialized neighborhood. Adjacent to the Park Hyatt Hotel, the little storefront is easy to pass by if you're not paying attention. Once inside, however, you'll be greeted by dog wallpaper and TV images that give the place the perfect amount of quirkiness. The hotdogs won't blow you away, but they're cheap, edible and slightly addicting. **B**

804 N Rush St
312.951.5141
RED LINE to CHICAGO

Ed Debevic's

This place is all-American from the greasy food to the purposefully ornery service and the retro jukebox. The dramatic waiters berate you if you only order water, take too long with the menu, or do anything for which they can make fun of you. If you have thick skin, a craving for a burger and fries, and the desire to see waiters dancing to 'Car Wash' on the bar, Ed Debevic's is an experience you can't miss. **A-**

640 N Wells St
312.664.1707
RED LINE to CHICAGO

Foodlife

When you get tired of walking Michigan Ave. and need a quick snack, check out Foodlife located on the Mezzanine floor of Water Tower Place. It has every variety of food imaginable ranging from Pad Thai to Cheddar Burgers to Chicken Tacos. Everything is made fresh and presented in an eye-appeasing display. While it is a little pricey, a midday snack here will leave you feeling full and, best of all, healthy. **A-**

845 N Michigan Ave
312.335.3663
RED LINE to CHICAGO

Garrett Popcorn

A Chicago favorite, Garrett Popcorn is Mecca for popcorn-lovers. It offers a variety of decadent, yummy flavors, and there is literally something for every taste bud. Favorites

670 N Michigan Ave
312.944.2630
RED LINE to CHICAGO

include the caramel corn and the macadamia-flavored batches, which can woo even the most skeptical patron. Interested? Just follow the sweet smell of buttery goodness or look for the line, which is usually out the door. **A**

Ghirardelli Ice Cream and Chocolate Shop

Step inside to take advantage of the free chocolate squares given to every

830 N Michigan Ave
312.337.9330
RED LINE to CHICAGO

entering customer, but hurry out before you're run

TOP Chicago Tribune Tower, 435 N. Michigan Ave. WENHONG NEOH • **MIDDLE** Jack Brickhouse Memorial. WENHONG NEOH • **BOTTOM** Rainforest Café, 605 N. Clark St. WENHONG NEOH

over by frazzled parents and their kids on sugar highs. You may be tempted to make a meal out of its $7 sundaes, but skip this tourist Mecca unless you're a chocoholic who doesn't mind being jostled by crowds of sticky-fingered shoppers. **B⁻**

Gino's East

While this traditional, Chicago deep-dish pizza place can be touristy, it

162 E Superior St
312.266.3337
RED LINE to CHICAGO

still emits a sense of local pride inside. A framed picture of Michael Jordan hangs on the wall, Cubs memorabilia is displayed with pride, and you're sure to see a bear snarling at you from the back of a local's jacket as he sips a beer at the bar. Once in, patiently wait for your pizza [try it with spinach] to arrive on your red-checkered tablecloth. **A⁻**

Hershey's Chicago

Hershey's Chicago is one part tourist trap, one part candy-lovers' dream. This

820 N Michigan Ave
312.337.7711
RED LINE to CHICAGO

store has every Hershey's product you could imagine, including a five-pound chocolate bar. With the song 'I Want Candy' playing overhead, it's difficult not to get excited by the myriad of sweets. Create your own cupcake, browse the merchandise or order a hot chocolate. The store is small and crowded with children, so if you're not a fan of kids, venture to a more grown up location. **B⁻**

L'Appetito

Not up for the Signature Room? L'Appetito, an authentic Italian deli in the

875 N Michigan Ave
312.337.0691
RED LINE to CHICAGO

John Hancock Center, is a perfect place to grab a quick bite to eat while you're exploring Chicago. You can find ready-made sandwiches, fresh pizza or even ingredients for a picnic at this tourist favorite. The staff is friendly but often busy, so be sure you've glanced over the menu before you go to place your order. **A**

Papa Milano

Don't be fooled by its un-friendly exterior, you will feel at home in this Italian kitchen with seating for no more than 50 people. The service is excellent, the prices are reasonable and the portions can feed a small army. However, since it costs three extra dollars to split a dish, just opt for taking home leftovers. The complimentary bread and freshly made cookies keep you satisfied throughout the whole meal. **A-**

951 N State St
312.787.3710
RED LINE to CHICAGO

Sarah's Pastries and Candies

Forget self-control at Sarah's Pastries and Candies. This tiny shop is filled with chocolates, cakes and other irresistible treats. Get sweets catered for your next event and your guests will love you for it. The Black and White Cupcake, a perfect balance between chocolate and vanilla, is a must-have. Although you may want to try a little of everything, the high prices put a damper on the feeding frenzy. **A-**

70 E Oak St
312.664.6223
RED LINE to CHICAGO

Michigan Ave. KATHERINE VILLAMIN

so be prepared to spend ample time choosing from dishes that range from curry rolls to stir-fry. Prices are extremely reasonable, but service is not always prompt. **B+**

Silver Spoon

This dimly-lit, quiet spot on Rush St. serves traditional Thai dishes in addition to the food found on its sushi bar. The menu is extensive and the portions are generous,

710 N Rush St
312.944.7100
RED LINE to CHICAGO

Soupbox

Freshness is the name of the game at Soupbox, a hole in the wall in the middle of downtown. The twelve soups change

50 E Chicago Ave
312.951.5900
RED LINE to CHICAGO

4 Taste off Rush

100 E. Walton St.
312.280.2400
RED LINE to CHICAGO

'You are about to experience an orgasm,' whispers a husky male voice over the techno beat followed by some rather suggestive female moaning. If this type of music doesn't put you in the mood for a night of drunken debauchery and passion, then the food at this appetizer lounge certainly will. Stop by 4 Taste before hitting up the nightclubs, and let yourself be seduced by the tender Australian beef tenderloin, sweet apple-stuffed raviolis and seared Ahi tuna. All appetizers are $10.95 each. Don't be afraid to try something exotic like escargot, Mississippi quail or grilled ostrich. Linger over each succulent bite while sipping a chocolate, mango, Rocketini or Malibu martini. Top off your evening by indulging in one of the six flavors of crème brulee and then force yourself to turn your attention away from the pleasures on your plate to your hot date.

daily with choices like cheese and bacon, tomato basil bisque, and even beer. Soups come in three different sizes, but the best deal is the 16-ounce bread bowl. Creative salads like Apple Berry – a mix of romaine lettuce, apples, dried cranberries, bleu cheese and raspberry vinaigrette – are made to order. **B+**

Su Casa

Su Casa offers a wide variety of Spanish dishes for hungry diners on a budget. Relatively proximate to Michigan Ave., it attracts a crowd with neon signs. While the cuisine is certain to fill your stomach, Su Casa lacks authenticity, and the quality of its food suffers as a result. If you're strapped for time and cash, Su Casa will ease your cravings, but consider looking elsewhere if you're seeking really great food. **B–**

> 49 E Ontario St
> 312.943.4041
> RED LINE to CHICAGO

Teavana

Its motto reads, 'Life's short. Relax. Drink some tea.' Teavana is located on the 3rd floor of Water Tower Place and holds over 100 kinds of teas that are bought by the ounce in loose leaf packages. You will find whatever you desire here, including fresh green, black, white, oolong, rooibos and chai teas. Free samples are hot and available. Check out the large assortment of tea ware, but don't get too attached since prices are steep. **A**

> 835 N Michigan Ave
> 312.335.9802
> RED LINE to CHICAGO

Tempo Café

With a diverse menu that offers breakfast, lunch and dinner 24/7, this quiet, out-of-the-way diner is a great place for a off-hour eating. Health-conscious customers can choose the Tempo DeLite, a half-cantaloupe filled with tuna, while the more adventurous can opt for the Jamaican omelet, a three egg concoction piled on hashbrowns and filled with bananas, walnuts and honey. The menu also boasts Greek toast, stir-fry, fresh fruit juice and a large seafood selection. **B+**

> 6 E Chicago Ave
> 312.943.4373
> RED LINE to CHICAGO

Tucci Benucch

Tucci Benucch's softly-lit atmosphere, reminiscent of an Italian villa, makes it the ideal eatery for a special occasion. Sinatra plays overhead as friendly, prompt servers offer up homemade pastas, fresh desserts and excellent wines at reasonable prices. Customer favorites include baked spaghetti, hand made gnocchi, chopped salad and fried calamari. End the meal with warm apple crostada and vanilla gelato, or try the tiramisu, which is perhaps the best in town. **A**

> 900 N Michigan Ave
> 312.266.2500
> RED LINE to CHICAGO

Wow Bao

This fast food stand at the base of Water Tower Place offers a refreshing, inexpensive alternative to the grease-soaked junk food upstairs. The 'Humble Bao,' a steamed bun filled with one of six different stuffings including Thai curry chicken and green vegetables, is the star of the show for only $1.29 a pop. Combos of two buns and soup or salad go for just $4.69, and the fresh ginger and pomegranate ginger ales are a new taste for soda. **B+**

> 835 N Michigan Ave
> 312.642.5888
> RED LINE to CHICAGO

3rd Coast Café

If you want your worries washed away, come relax with soft jazz music at the 3rd Coast Café. For breakfast you will find wonderful stuffed French toast and bacon along with many other tasty dishes. The kitchen will also sometimes serve the brunch menu late at night if you ask. If you appreciate art, you will enjoy the decorations that cover the walls – watercolors and acrylics from up-and-coming Chicago artists. **A–**

> 1260 N Dearborn St
> 312.649.0730
> RED LINE to CLARK/DIVISION

Bistrot Zinc

Bistrot Zinc serves delectable French food in a quaint dining room that screams, 'Bring someone here for an intimate date!' Unfortunately, expect steep prices, with appetizers starting around nine dollars. It's a

> 1131 N State St
> 312.337.1131
> RED LINE to CLARK/DIVISION

shame the unique flavors on the dessert menu don't match that of the entrées, but decently-sized portions won't leave you with a strong yearning for them anyway. The Sunday brunch is classy and perfect for entertaining visitors. **B**

Bombon Americano Bakeshop & Café

The inside of BomBon looks like a Dr. Seuss book come to life, complete

1000 N Sedgwick St
312.787.7717
RED LINE to CLARK/DIVISION

with pastel-colored walls decorated with colorful knickknacks. With such an interesting décor, it's no surprise that the menu includes such peculiar items as a 'Paris Hilton breakfast sandwich' prepared with Nutella and bananas. While the ambience is certainly interesting and the service is always pleasant, the shelves are usually not fully stocked, which makes shopping trips here a bit difficult. **B-**

Five Faces Ice Cream Shop

Avoid this dismal attempt at an eatery. Serving two flavors of ice cream

10 W Division St
312.642.7837
RED LINE to CLARK/DIVISION

shouldn't give any diner the right to call itself an ice cream shop. The meat served on every sandwich [save for one vegetarian option] is second-rate, tough and overcooked. Seating is limited, and unless you want a quick fountain drink to sip while exploring the Gold Coast, there isn't any reason to take time out of your day for a visit. **C-**

The Original Pancake House

You'll swear you're in a small town instead of the middle of the city

22 E Bellevue Pl
312.642.7917
RED LINE to CLARK/DIVISION

when you walk into The Original Pancake House. This tiny diner is filled with 50s furnishings and friendly wait staff in white paper hats. Service here is prompt, and there's plenty of food for the price. The pumpkin pancakes melt in your mouth, the turkey links are juicy, and the eggs are done however you please. **A**

Al's No. 1 Italian Beef

Al's is a strong competitor in the race to see who holds the crown of

169 W Ontario St
312.943.3222
RED LINE to GRAND

Chicago's best Italian beef. Done up with Au Jus and mozzarella cheese and paired with French fries [the kind that are fresh cut and tout a little potato skin], Al's signature sandwich will satisfy any craving for good ol' American grub. Expect other grill favorites to be on the menu as well, including some decently-sized burger creations. **B**

NEAR NORTH SIDE

Transfer Terminal, Jackson 'El' Stop. DANIEL HONIGMAN

Bake For Me

Whether you're planning for a wedding, organizing a birthday party, or looking

350 N Clark St
312.644.7750
RED LINE to GRAND

for a little self-indulgence, this Chicago bakery will satisfy your needs with its tempting baked goods and cakes. Choose from selections of fresh and ready-made donuts, cookies, tarts, cakes and brownies. Keep in mind that for cake orders the store requires 24 hours advance notice. **A**

Bandera

While this southwestern-inspired steakhouse is located on Chicago's main

535 N Michigan Ave
312.644.3524
RED LINE to GRAND

drag, the low lighting and posh décor, often accompanied by soft live music, make Bandera the perfect destination for those wishing to escape the bustling city. Upon walking in, guests pass fresh steaks roasting behind glass containers and behold the open-air kitchen where chefs furiously prepare delectable dishes. Bandera is on the pricier side, so save this restaurant for a special night out on the town. **A-**

Ben Pao

While most out-of-town-ers head to Chinatown for great Chinese cuisine

52 W Illinois St
312.222.1888
RED LINE to GRAND

in Chicago, why not go off the beaten path? Ben Pao serves superb versions of favorites like General Tso's chicken and Mongolian beef, but

its house specialties will really wow you. The Seven Flavor beef and Spicy Dragon noodles are particularly great items. Don't forget to leave room for dessert though. Treats like Banana Cheesecake and Mango Crème Brûlée are worth holding out for. **A**

Big Bowl Asian Kitchen

Who says only college students live off noodles? This cheap and delicious

60 E Ohio St
312.951.1888
RED LINE to GRAND

Asian restaurant offers huge bowls of great noodles complete with a variety of sauces and spices. There are 30 different types to choose from, but the prices are so low that you can order until your heart is content. Plus, the décor is kitschy and fun, so you will surely slurp away in style. **A**

Burrito Beach

This burrito restaurant is the gourmet version of Chipotle. With its

200 E Ohio St
312.335.0668
RED LINE to GRAND

breakfast burritos and specialty ingredients like chili-marinated salmon and jasmine rice, Burrito Beach proves itself a step above the average burrito shop. Come hungry, as the portions are huge and quite filling. As is the trend among fast food restaurants, Burrito Beach has started serving low-calorie alternatives on the menu – an appealing option for health-conscious customers. **A-**

Puck's at the Museum of Contemporary Art

220 E. Chicago Ave.
312.397.4034
RED LINE to CHICAGO

▌After taking a tour through the Museum of Contemporary Art, sit down to enjoy a light and masterful cuisine with dishes inspired by the renowned chef Wolfgang Puck. Customers can choose to either dine in or to order from the express café. Windows that stretch from ceiling to floor envelop the dining area, providing a beautiful view and an atmosphere ideal for a Sunday brunch. For those that choose to dine in, you will enjoy the delicious complementary bread served with an oil, cheese and eggplant dipping platter. The entrées are even more mouth-watering, featuring items such as the garden vegetable pizza or split pea soup with crab. Prices are more than reasonable, and the service is extremely friendly.

California Pizza Kitchen

It seems sacrilegious to have a pizza restaurant in Chicago that doesn't serve deep dish pizza. But if you're not a fan of the signature three-inch cheesy goo and crave something more gourmet instead, try out California Pizza Kitchen, or 'CPK.' Start with the tortilla soup, then go for the pear and gorgonzola pizza or the classic barbecue chicken pizza. **B+**

52 E Ohio St
312.787.6075
RED LINE to GRAND

Capi's Italian Kitchen

Whether you choose pasta, panini, or pizza, you cannot go wrong. You may as well order them all with the ultra-low prices and unbelievable taste at Capi's. Enjoy the favorite dish, a Penne Santarini, while sipping on Italian Sodas. When you're finished, put up your 'Attenzíone' sign, and the waiter will be right over to bring out gelato. Overall, this is a great spot for Chicago dining on a budget. **A**

600 E Grand Ave
312.276.0641
RED LINE to GRAND

Cyrano's Bistrot

If French food is to your taste, Cyrano's Bistrot is a great choice both for your taste buds and your wallet. Look forward to genuine cuisine – the owner is a native of France – and pay particular attention to the extensive list of roasted meats. In good weather, try to grab an outside table. Beware though – this Bistrot tends to attract a crowd. **A-**

546 N Wells St
312.467.0546
RED LINE to GRAND

David Burke's Primehouse

Located in the upscale James Chicago hotel, David Burke's Primehouse offers a unique and exciting take on the steakhouse. Dishes like tuna and salmon tartar and Kobe beef sashimi are sure to leave you wanting more. Finish off your meal with one of the decadent desserts; you won't regret it. Be prepared to shell out some serious cash though, it can be pricey. **A-**

616 N Rush St
312.660.6000
RED LINE to GRAND

Grand Lux Café

There's no better place to head out for an extravagant dinner for a less than extravagant cost. While the wait can rocket to two hours during evenings, the moderately-priced food and excellent view of Michigan Ave. inside warrant long lines. Lovers of The Cheesecake Factory will enjoy this sister company for anything from an intimate evening date to a large group party. Since the restaurant is so popular, visit during lunch to avoid a long wait. **A**

600 N Michigan Ave
312.276.2500
RED LINE to GRAND

ABOVE: Water Tower, 800 N. Michigan Ave. WENHONG NEOH • **LEFT:** Water Tower, 800 N. Michigan Ave. WENHONG NEOH

Harry Caray's Restaurant and Bar

This is not just another sports bar. The ambiance is sophisticated and fun, with walls decked with pictures of Caray and other celebrities. The food? Most Chicagoans consider these steaks the best in town, but considering that the restaurant is located in the heart of the steak-house district, they're debatable. High quality? Definitely. Pricey? Extremely. Though Caray's food is tasty enough to warrant a visit, one should visit just to get a taste of Chicago history. **C+**

33 W Kinzie St
312.828.0966
RED LINE to GRAND

Lalo's Mexican Restaurant

La Salle Dr. is home to one of the many Lalo's Restaurants scattered about Chicagoland. Lalo's has a comfortable south-of-the-border atmosphere, with a menu touting giant margaritas and burritos. Meals here are a change from the ordinary Mexican fare, as they're accompanied with soup as well as chips n' salsa and are apportioned generously. For Chicago dining, prices are reasonable, and the mariachi band, which performs tableside on selected nights, adds a unique touch of entertainment. **B+**

500 N LaSalle Dr
312.329.0030
RED LINE to GRAND

Maggiano's Little Italy

Few Italian restaurants can match Maggiano's combination of first-rate food and fair pricing. The menu is extensive and authentic. A signature element of the restaurant is the option of family-style serving, which, for about $25 a person, includes endless appetizers, entrees and deserts. Intimate enough for a date, yet suitable for larger parties [even banquets], Maggiano's deserves its reputation as a 'Little Italy.' Reservations are strongly recommended. **A**

516 N Clark St
312.644.7700
RED LINE to GRAND

Mezza Grilled Wraps and Pitas

Located in the food court of the Westfield Shopping Center on the Magnificent Mile, Mezza offers pitas, wraps and traditional Greek fare accompanied by the somewhat incongruous menu tack-on of curly fries. Pitas and wraps are made to order with your choice of toppings, but service doesn't always come with a smile. **C-**

520 N Michigan Ave
312.670.0200
RED LINE to GRAND

P.F. Chang's China Bistro

As the name indicates, this restaurant is equally part-Chinese cuisine and part-classy bistro. Brick fireplaces, high ceilings, candlelit tables and posh seating create a modish ambiance to accompany its dishes perfectly. Moderately priced, the cuisine features typical Chinese entrees that have been kicked up a few notches in both flavor and presentation. P.F. Chang's is perfect for rendezvousing as long as you make reservations because it is usually packed seven nights a week. **B**

530 N Wabash Ave
312.828.9977
RED LINE to GRAND

Phil Stefani's

Phil Stefani's has space for up to 400 diners to eat, drink and chat. Although the menu includes just standard Italian fare, chefs dress it up with unique sauces and spices. The crisp, white tablecloths, wall art and long, curving bar add a sophisticated and distinctive style to this huge Chicago restaurant. Grab the family and enjoy a light lunch or a relaxing dinner at Phil Stefani's. **B**

437 N Rush St
312.222.0101
RED LINE to GRAND

Pizzeria Due

This classic pizzeria set in a Victorian house among towering high rises offers some of the best Chicago-style deep dish around. Sister to Chicago's signature Pizzeria Uno, Due welcomes anyone seeking a quick salad and burger for lunch or a filling meal for dinner. To guarantee a good menu item, don't stray too far from the pizzas and beware that they take 45 minutes to bake. Prices are great, especially after a shopping spree on the Magnificent Mile. **B+**

619 N Wabash Ave
312.280.5110
RED LINE to GRAND

Gaylord India Restaurant

678 N. Clark St.
312.664.1700
RED LINE to CHICAGO

▮ Located just outside the chic Michigan Ave. area, Gaylord India is a pleasant find for upscale Indian cuisine. Gorgeous chandeliers and sconces decorate a warm and inviting dining room. Entrees range from $11-$19, and while the menu is physically huge, many choices are somewhat limited because so many dishes are similar. Regardless, do not miss the mango lassi, a smoothie-like drink blending fresh mango and yogurt into a creamy, cooling concoction that complements the spicy food perfectly. Korma naan, a flatbread stuffed with morsels of seasoned lamb, kicks off meals with a flair. The tandoori chicken, fish, lamb and breads are all roasted beautifully in the restaurant's wood-burning clay pot, and spice-lovers will go for the traditional vindaloos and Northern Indian curries. Service is quick and attentive without being obtrusive. Gaylord India may seem understated compared to its glitzy neighbors on Clark, but relax and unwind with a solid meal.

Portillo's Hot Dogs

100 W Ontario St
312.587.8910
RED LINE to GRAND

Deep-dish pizza is out-shone by another Chicago staple at Portillo's: the Italian beef sandwich. Onion rings, burgers, hot dogs and salads can be enjoyed in the retro-music blastin', West-side styled 'dining room,' or you can use the drive-thru window to pick up and run. Prices are comparable to other fast food joints. The difference here is quality. One recommendation: Order the Italian beef 'wet,' or soaked in Au Jus. **A**

Rock Bottom Restaurant and Brewery

1 W Grand Ave
312.755.9339
RED LINE to GRAND

It's all about the big American menu and beer-a-plenty at Rock Bottom. The on-site brewery is a big draw that is not to be missed. The food is typical American fare – large portions of pastas, burgers, sandwiches, steak and chicken. The servers are very friendly and create a mellow ambiance. Rock Bottom is a reasonable but ordinary place to dine before catching a concert or to take a nice lunch break during a day of shopping. **B+**

Ryba's Mackinas Island Fudge Shops

600 E Grand Ave
312.595.5515
RED LINE to GRAND

Ryba's Mackinas Island is the fudge shop you were hoping your hometown had. With five flavors of rich and creamy fudge, caramel apples of all variations and turtle every-thing, this shop will make you drool before you even step in the door. The sweets are expensive, but well worth the money. Make sure to buy a drink at another shop because only sweets are sold here and the fudge is too rich to eat alone. **A-**

State Street Bread Co.

30 E Hubbard St
312.595.0766
RED LINE to GRAND

In the restaurant-rich neighborhood just west of Michigan Ave., it's hard to come by a quick bite to eat. However, this soup and sandwich venue is a unique Chicago find that will have you in and out on your lunch break. For Chicagoans on the go, State St. Bread Co. surpasses its fellow vendors by providing an in-store Starbucks. **B+**

Volare

Although the wait can seem unbearable, the authentic Italian cuisine makes it all worthwhile. The variety of gourmet dishes and the Soprano's-esque atmosphere will make you feel like you're right back in Italy. Volare is the perfect place for an anniversary or special celebration, but a little too fancy for an every day dining experience. **A**

201 E Grand Ave
312.410.9900
RED LINE to GRAND

West Egg Café

Located just steps from the Magnificent Mile, the West Egg Cafe and Rotisserie is a viable option if you're looking to grab a quick bite in between shopping trips. This no-frills restaurant serves large portions of breakfast and lunch staples typical of your average American diner. The health conscious menu options are a perk, and don't forget to try a specialty omelet. **B⁻**

620 N Fairbanks Ct
312.280.8366
RED LINE to GRAND

Zest

Located in the Intercontinental Hotel, Zest serves cuisine that's as aesthetically pleasing as the views onto Michigan Ave. The restaurant boasts a full bar and extensive wine list and serves breakfast, lunch and dinner. The Zest Discovery dinner option offers a seven-course sampling of the menu, but it will set you back upwards of $50. **B**

505 N Michigan Ave
312.321.8766
RED LINE to GRAND

Klay Oven

Whether they stop in for the $10 buffet or for a sit-down dinner, customers leave satisfied after indulging in this Indian restaurant's up-scale dining experience. Great service accompanies the extensive menu, which boasts varieties of fish, lamb, poultry and breads. All dishes are cooked in the restaurant's clay ovens and prepared in different spices and curries that will make your mouth water for days. Main course meals range from $10-20. **A**

414 N Orleans St
312.527.3999
RED LINE to MONROE

TO PLAY

Chan's Nails

Looking for a quick, cheap polish? Chan's Nails will do the trick. The small parlor features $30 manicure/pedicures on Tuesdays and is more than welcoming to walk-ins. Keep in mind that you're getting what you pay for. If perfect nails are what you seek, you may want to consider looking elsewhere. **B⁻**

112 W Chicago Ave
312.280.8310
RED LINE to CHICAGO

Holy Name Catholic Cathedral

This massive cathedral is home to the Chicago Roman Catholic Archdiocese and went through major destruction and renovations before becoming the sanctuary it is today. After the Chicago fire, the church was rebuilt and now contains a detailed and intricate ceiling, columns and large, bright windows. The altar is minimalist, airy and peaceful. Holy Name makes a distinctive addition to a Chicago architecture tour. **B+**

735 N State St
312.787.8040
RED LINE to CHICAGO

Intuition Boutique

Astrology may not be for everyone, but if you're looking for an interesting experience, you'll want to consider this boutique. Its two floors offer a variety of services from 'the beyond' – including palm and tarot card readings – and the décor creates a Harry Potter-esque feel. Visit on a Tuesday to take advantage of the affordable $10 specials. While the readings themselves are dubious, the experience will leave you with a few good stories. **B**

224 E Ontario St
312.475.9295
RED LINE to CHICAGO

John Hancock Observatory

It may not get the tourist flocks like the Sears Tower, but the Hancock Observatory makes for just as scenic and romantic a view at a lower cost. With a 360-degree view that includes Lake Michigan, Navy Pier and downtown Chicago, the tower puts this massive city into a new perspective. Go at sunset for

875 N Michigan Ave
312.751.3681
RED LINE to CHICAGO

an awe-inspiring look westward and stay until dark with the cuddling couples and late-night visitors. **A**

LUMA

In the heart of Michigan Ave., the Loyola University Museum of Art [LUMA]	820 N Michigan Ave 312.915.7600 RED LINE to CHICAGO

features 'art that illuminates the spirit.' Not typical of that of most art galleries and museums, LUMA's goal is to showcase paintings and objects created for the purposes of answering the questions of spirituality. Stop by on Tuesdays to take advantage of free admission. Keep in mind the museum is new, so call before coming, as admittance fees and hours may change. **A**

The Museum of Contemporary Art

Stark rooms, muted light-ing and concrete floors fit the hipper-than-thou	220 E Chicago Ave 312.280.2660 RED LINE to CHICAGO

image of this modern museum. With current collections that focus on interactivity [including a huge entryway for do-it-yourself visitors] and pieces made from Styrofoam and carpet, you may need to stretch your definition of art to fit the works here. But for a change of pace, this mu-seum features current artists, obscure mediums and pleasantly shocking pieces. **B**

The Newberry Library

This quiet research library is located just a few blocks off Michigan Ave.	60 W Walton St 312.255.3520 RED LINE to CHICAGO

and provides a serene break from the downtown hustle. The exhibit gallery on the first floor is a quick diversion from the fast pace of the city, but unless you're looking for a specific historical document or reference text, the process of view-ing the collection is quite a hassle. **C**

Underground Wonder Bar

Looking for an authentic jazz club experience? This hole in the wall	10 E Walton St 312.266.7761 RED LINE to CHICAGO

probably won't catch your eye, but it's worth a

second look. The interior is dark, smoky and will make you feel like a hipster-in-the-making. The performers aren't necessarily the biggest names, but the music is always decent and the ambiance makes the trip enjoyable. **B**

TOP Michigan Ave. KATHERINE VILLAMIN • **MIDDLE** Michigan Ave. KATHERINE VILLAMIN • **BOTTOM** Bloomingdale's, Michigan Ave. KATHERINE VILLAMIN

Chicago Tribune Tower, 435 N. Michigan Ave.
WENHONG NEOH

Oak Street Beach

1000 N Lake Shore Dr
312.742.5121
RED LINE to CLARK/DIVISION

With all of the amazing sights Chicago has to offer, it's easy to forget the number one attraction: the lake. Lake Michigan single handedly gives Chicago the casual, airy appeal that brings thousands of visitors back each year. Oak St. Beach, the premier spot to enjoy the cool water, is just blocks from most of Chicago's major attractions and is complete with a full view of the beautiful north shore skyline – and it's all free. **A**

Ruth Page Center for the Arts

1016 N Dearborn Pkwy
312.337.6543
RED LINE to CLARK/DIVISION

Dedicated to hosting dance events for all ages, the Ruth Page Center for the Arts has a specialized culture. You can take lessons from the most basic form of ballet to professional workshops and can also attend local and traveling shows. The building, located right off the Magnificent Mile, holds practice studios and a main stage where you can see such prominent groups as the Civic Ballet and Luna Negra Dance Theater. **B**

Washington Square Park

901 N Clark St
312.742.7895
RED LINE to CLARK/DIVISION

Not far from Chicago's major shopping districts lies three acres of grass, walking paths and shaded hideaways at Washington Square Park. Grab a coffee or snack at a nearby restaurant and find a spot among the workers on lunch break. Historically, the park was a place of radical speeches and rallies, and you may still catch groups expressing their opinions in the park that has been designated 'Chicago's Premier Free Speech Forum.' **B+**

10pin Bowling Lounge

330 N State St
312.644.0300
RED LINE to GRAND

10pin is a bowling experience with a twist. In addition to 24 lanes of bowling and the wall of big screen TVs, 10pin has its own restaurant and bar that serve snack-sized items. Menu highlights include chocolate chip cookies with a shot of milk, mac 'n' cheese made with Wisconsin smoked cheddar and the venue's signature '10pintini,' a martini made with raspberry and pomegranate. **A**

ESPN Zone

43 E Ontario St
312.644.3776
RED LINE to GRAND

In this haven for ESPN lovers, every one of the 67 flat-screen, high-definition TVs is tuned to ESPN and ABC sports. The main attraction is the sports arena, an arcade overflowing with sports arcade games and simulators, including a 15-foot projection screen for Madden football. As great as the games are, the prices are rather expensive [$20 for approximately an hour's worth of play]. **B**

J Plus Bar

Slip on a sleek cocktail dress or suit up in style, grab some friends and

610 N Rush St
312.660.7200
RED LINE to GRAND

head down to J Bar. Chicago's hipsters flock to this sophisticated, yet young and modern lounge to chill after a long week or to spend a weekday night in the city. J Bar's inventive takes on the Martini make this club a standout, so be sure to try one of its signature drinks. **A**

Lucky Strike X Bowl

Old-fashioned fun can still be found in the windy city at this jazzy bowling

322 E Illinois St
312.245.8331
RED LINE to GRAND

alley, which, because of its better-than-average menu, also prides itself on being a 'lounge.' The environment is retro and somewhat mediocre. Friends will have a blast reminiscent of their teenage years without having to hang out with actual teenagers. [People under 21 must leave before 9 p.m.] Hourly rates are a little pricey, and on weekends the place gets packed. **B-**

McCormick Tribune Freedom Museum

Next door to the Chicago Tribune Tower, this museum is entirely devoted

445 N Michigan Ave
312.222.4860
RED LINE to GRAND

to explaining the First Amendment. How can one amendment make up an entire museum? Quite successfully, in fact. It is interactive, with computer activities, listening booths and the chance to videotape yourself talking about the meaning of freedom. Displays highlight the Bill of Rights, important court cases, censorship and the rights of minority groups through pictures, videos and graphics. Although the museum is relatively unknown, it is well-presented. **A-**

Navy Pier Imax Theater

If you're in the mood for complete immersion in a movie, a regular screen

600 E Grand Ave
312.595.5629
RED LINE to GRAND

just won't do. Instead, try Navy Pier's Imax Theater for extra-large sights, sounds, snacks and even ticket prices. With big box office flicks and 3D kids' shows, the theater usually appeals to younger audiences [especially those who don't get motion sick easily; beware of the sometimes overwhelming screen size]. **B+**

Wendella Boots

Looking for a one-of-a-kind way to spend a warm afternoon in Chicago? Try

400 N Michigan Ave
312.337.1446
RED LINE to GRAND

a Wendella Boat Tour. A $22 ticket will get you an architectural tour down the Chicago River. For the same price, you can take a longer tour that includes Lake Michigan. If you want something

The Goddess and Grocer

25 E. Delaware Pl.
312.896.2600
RED LINE to CHICAGO

I If you're tired of pounding the pavement on Michigan Ave. with all of the other shoppers and tourists, step inside The Goddess and Grocer for a truly heavenly respite. Just one block south of Chicago's main shopping artery, this tiny deli offers hungry shoppers an array of delectable snacks. The quiches and lasagna squares, each with little flagpoles of rosemary sticking out of the top, make for a great lunch. Or, buy a saucer-sized cookie and sip your latte in the back room. Better yet, skip the cramped seating area: select your favorite cheese, grab a baguette from the basket by the door and take your picnic across the street to Connors Park. If you're still hungry, look on the back wall for a variety of sweets [including to-die-for Michel Cluizel Chocolat]. With your appetite satiated, you will leave this gem of a deli ready to finish your shopping extravaganza.

RIGHT: Feinberg School of Medicine, 303 E. Chicago Ave. WENHONG NEOH • **BOTTOM:** Hershey's Store, 822 N. Michigan Ave. WENHONG NEOH

NEAR NORTH SIDE

romantic, Wendella also offers a Sunset Tour and a Wine Tasting Tour. Although it's not required, it's a good idea to call for reservations beforehand. **A⁻**

Andy's

Andy's is exactly what you'd expect from a jazz club: Small and hazy and constantly filled with talent. There's a $10 entrance fee and rather unfriendly staff, but if you can spare the cash and deal with the attitude, Andy's is a great location for jazz aficionados. Performers have included Chuck Hedges and Art Doyle, and the full service bar offers finger food to nosh on while you listen. **B**

11 E Hubbard St
312.642.6805
RED LINE to LAKE

House of Blues

The House of Blues attracts exclusive, genuine musicians isolated from mainstream hype. Indie rock, punk, blues, jazz and alternative music is usually what's being amplified in this intimate, highly-stylized venue. Whether seated in the lush balconies or on the ground floor, fans will feel a rare closeness to the musicians that other stadiums cannot match. The architecture is beautiful inside and out – truly a feast for both the eyes and ears. **A**

329 N Dearborn St
312.923.2000
RED LINE to LAKE

TO SHOP

Arrelle Fine Linens

If you're looking for high-end spa materials and linens, Arrelle Fine Linens is the place to go. While the layout of the store is nothing special, the items are well made and of high quality. Unfortunately, products this extravagant do not come cheaply. Check your wallets at the door if you are on a budget. **B⁺**

445 N Wells St
312.321.3696
BROWN LINE to MERCH MART

Merchandise Mart

The Merchandise Mart building, restored in the 1990s, merits a massive hats-off to Chicago's architectural accomplishments, but what's inside is just as interesting and unique. While there are a few food joints and clothing stores within, the Mart's greatest feature is its collection of luxury showrooms, housing home furnishings and interior decorating accessories. Technically, only retailers and professional buyers can shop these floors, but a walkthrough will still leave you with plenty of ideas. **B⁺**

222 Merch. Mart Pl
312.527.4141
BROWN LINE to MERCH MART

Eppy's Café and Deli

224 E. Ontario St.
312.943.7797
RED LINE to GRAND

Located near Michigan Ave. and Northwestern University's Chicago campus, Eppy's draws a diverse crowd of students and young professionals. With its well-priced menu and simple yet satisfying food, it's no wonder customers become regulars here. Owner Larry Epstein says, 'You never leave hungry.' And he's not lying. All sandwiches come with two sides and a beverage for around $7. If that's not enough to draw you in, Eppy's 'temperature soup' offers customers a unique deal. Just as the name suggests, the temperature outside dictates the price of the soup each day. If it's 20 degrees outside, you get your soup for only 20 cents! For even more of a steal, stop by on a notoriously cold Chicago day – if the weather's below zero, Eppy's will actually pay for your soup. If you're looking for a friendly, neighborhood deli with lots of personality and great prices, stop by Eppy's.

The Tile Gallery

225 W Illinois Ave
312.467.9590
BROWN LINE to MERCH MART

Most young people may not be able to afford expensive marble tiles in their bathroom. However, they can browse the selection of beautiful tiles in the gallery, dreaming of how they may one day deck out their dream house. The Tile Gallery offers very chic and elegant tile for the rich and comfortable and even for those who simply wish to dream. **A**

Biba Bis

744 N Clark St
312.988.9560
RED LINE to CHICAGO

Offering the wares of talented local designers, Biba Bis attracts the attention of both the sophisticated thirty-something and the fashion-forward teen. The chic window displays feature tapered, close-fitting designs. Within the store, rack after rack show off smart, tailored duds. Be warned: The clothes are expensive and salespeople are slightly smug, but if you've got the patience [and the cash], Biba Bis is a not-to-miss. **A−**

Borders

830 N Michigan Ave
312.573.0564
RED LINE to CHICAGO

For the bookworm in the family, it will be hard to pass by the largest bookstore on Michigan Ave. without stopping. Once inside the three-story store, you're sure to find what you want because the staff is friendly and the computer databases reliable. With all the travel guides, romance novels, CDs and more, however, this store spares little room for comfortable seating. **B+**

Chiaroscuro

700 N Michigan Ave
312.988.9253
RED LINE to CHICAGO

If you're looking for a gift for the artsy and unique or if you just want to see some incredible designs, Chiaroscuro's got it. The brightly colored, multi-textured inventory here is a plethora of delights for lovers of pop culture everywhere. While you'll pay somewhat high prices for items handcrafted by local artisans, any true Beatles fan will tell you that for a set of four chairs resembling the members of Sgt. Pepper's Lonely Hearts Club Band, prices are irrelevant. **A**

Crate and Barrel

646 N Michigan Ave
312.787.5900
RED LINE to CHICAGO

As Michigan Ave.'s home décor central, Crate and Barrel caters to both the modern, urban lifestyle as well as the suburban tourist crowd. Its four floors are stocked with everything from cheap kitchen gadgets to $2000 sofas. Large neutral furniture is accented with colored accessories in shades of green, blue

NEAR NORTH SIDE

and yellow. If you feel like braving the masses of out-of-towners that hit up this decorating hot spot, it's a reasonable and fresh way to style a new home. **A-**

Designer Resale East

Although it's always a treat to peek into the couture vendors that sparkle

658 N Dearborn St
312.587.3312
RED LINE to CHICAGO

along the Magnificent Mile, if you're looking for something more affordable, try Designer Resale East. This little shop is true to its name, with garments from Dolce and Gabbana and Chanel occupying the racks. Trendier shoppers steer clear, though; despite a good deal, clothes tend to be dated. **B-**

Diesel

Always on the cutting edge of urban fashion, Diesel is a must for

923 N Rush St
312.255.0157
RED LINE to CHICAGO

Chicago shoppers who exhibit a downtown taste.

Michigan Ave. DANIEL HONIGMAN

You can't help but admire its quality designer jeans, but Diesel also specializes in chic tops and trademark shoes to accessorize the famous denim. A word of warning, however: If you consider yourself more on the traditional side, you might want to skip this edgy emporium. **B+**

Europa Books

Take a vacation from Borders and go international to one of the

832 N State St
312.335.9677
RED LINE to CHICAGO

best-kept secrets on the Gold Coast. Immerse yourself in the wall-to-wall shelves of translated texts, from the popular ['The DaVinci Code'] to the praised ['100 Years of Solitude']. Learning a new language? Europa has a range of study aids. Though fluorescent lighting leaves it void of the coziness that defines most bookstores, the unique selection and devotion to foreign texts make it a worthwhile visit. **A-**

Filene's Basement

If you're shopping on a budget or just looking for a deal, visit Filene's

830 N Michigan Ave
312.482.8918
RED LINE to CHICAGO

Basement. Located on the Magnificent Mile, this department store offers brand name merchandise like Coach, Seven, Steve Madden, Ralph Lauren and Furla at generously-reduced prices. Filene's doesn't just sell clothing. Visit the top floor to find cozy comforters, room décor and even luggage. The fitting rooms are truly ancient, however, and don't expect the staff to go out of their way to assist you. **B+**

Glove Me Tender

If you're looking for a gift for the accessory-lover, Glove Me Tender features

900 N Michigan Ave
312.664.4022
RED LINE to CHICAGO

an array of hats, umbrellas, accessories and, of course, gloves to fit any taste. The small boutique has everything from stocking caps for men to formal gloves for women to animal-themed headwear for kids. Items are very pricey, but if you bring in a pair of old, usable gloves for the needy, you receive a 10% discount on gloves for yourself. **B-**

Jackson 'El' Stop.
DANIEL HONIGMAN

H&M

Shop along to the beat of funky club music in this multilevel Michigan Ave.

840 N Michigan Ave
312.640.0060
RED LINE to CHICAGO

staple. H&M offers trendy, reasonably-priced goods. It's like a bigger and higher quality version of Forever 21, complete with racks of color-coordinated clothing and jewelry. The only downsides are the large crowds in fitting rooms and long lines at the checkout. If waiting is a game you're not willing to play, think twice about how much you need those $8 camisoles in your hand. **B+**

J. Crew

This upscale retailer does not shy away from color. J. Crew bursts with bright

900 N Michigan Ave
312.751.2739
RED LINE to CHICAGO

yellows, reds and blues, and the selection isn't barred by seasons. Sandals in winter? You got it. Their classic design is a fusion of stylish and simple – aesthetically pleasing, yet comfortable. Though almost anyone can find something here, not everyone can afford it. Use J. Crew as a source to see what's trendy, then copy the styles by going somewhere cheaper and buying similar pieces. **C**

Lifeway Christian Store

One of the most well-known evangelical Christian colleges in

150 W Chicago Ave
312.664.0799
RED LINE to CHICAGO

the country, Moody Bible Institute, is home to LifeWay Christian Store, a resource for students and staff as well as the general public. With everything from Bibles and music to devotionals and church resources, this store attracts a specific audience and does so thoroughly. Though the store is not for everyone, the merchandise is reasonably priced and the staff is cheerful. **B**

Lucy

The fitness-oriented woman will be in heaven at this upscale active

835 N Michigan Ave
312.255.0257
RED LINE to CHICAGO

wear retailer. Located on the third floor of the downtown hotspot Water Tower Place, the store features upscale fitness apparel in a wide range of fits and styles. Check out the wall of workout bottoms for a comprehensive explanation of the activities suited to each pair, but be prepared to pay high-end prices for everything from socks to graphic tees. **B+**

Lush

In Macy's Water Tower, this cozy corner is devoted to sweet-smelling soaps,

835 N Michigan Ave
312.440.3166
RED LINE to CHICAGO

bath balls and various moderately-priced handmade cosmetics. The brightly-lit area is slightly crowded with customers passing through on their way to Macy's, and the staff can be slightly overzealous in its quest for customers due to the

Michigan Ave. DANIEL HONIGMAN

town or a company cocktail party, the fashion is never too bold or overdone. This store is aimed toward the petite, and prices are very fair considering everything is imported from Spain. **B+**

Niketown

Even the most cynical customer may not be able to resist the bright, colorful swooshes bedecking Niketown, the one-stop shop for all your active needs. Test out your purchases on the indoor basketball court or peruse the multi-room complex to find something to suit your sport. Items can be exorbitantly expensive and bargains are few and far between, but even if you're just browsing, Niketown is an experience in itself. **A-**

669 N Michigan Ave
312.642.6363
RED LINE to CHICAGO

Sur La Table

Even if your cooking skills are limited, you can look like a professional with gear from Sur La Table. This chain kitchen supply store has items that inspire any chef. From $3 chopsticks to $300 Cuisinart appliances, there's a variety of things you never knew you needed. [Think pickle slicers and tuna presses.] Prices are steep, so you're better off getting the basics elsewhere. If you want to add skills to your new image, try out one of their classes. **B+**

52 E Walton St
312.337.0600
RED LINE to CHICAGO

traffic. Nonetheless, Lush is a worthwhile stop to find some high-quality bath products. **B+**

MNG by Mango

Women looking for a little razzle, a little contempo and a little punk will find it at MNG by Mango. Jeans, where dresses and tops made for the twenty-something party girl feature a blend of upscale Hollywood and European flair. Whether it's for a night on the

835 N Michigan Ave
312.397.9800
RED LINE to CHICAGO

Heaven on Seven

600 N. Michigan Ave.
312.280.7774
RED LINE to GRAND

❙ Heaven on Seven transports customers to the festive world of New Orleans instantly. You can't help but get in the mood for Mardi Gras with the colorful green, yellow and purple décor. Here, customers enjoy traditional Cajun dining served with an abundance of hot sauces in the true fashion of New Orleans. The cuisine is faithful to its southern roots – while not all dishes are especially spicy, the menu consists primarily of large portions of hot Cajun. Unlike many of its competitors, Heaven on Seven serves all meals with complimentary bread and butter. While this Louisiana-inspired restaurant is known for its spicy dishes, you really will be in heaven after trying its delicious desserts. The service is excellent – don't be afraid to ask waiters for recommendations if you're new to southern cuisine.

NEAR NORTH SIDE

Tails in the City

Chicago's Paris Hilton wannabes and dog-loving glitterati shop at this fancy boutique for their pampered pooches. If you feel guilty about leaving little Tinkerbell home all day while you go to work or class, treat your pet to a glitzy collar or dog treats that look more delectable than the sweets you'll find in the fanciest bakeries. **B**

1 E Delaware Pl
312.649.0347
RED LINE to CHICAGO

The Apple Store

Feel like you're actually walking into a sleek Apple computer as you venture into this massive Apple Store. Whether you're looking to purchase the latest iPod or sample the newest Mac laptop, all the hottest products are on display with knowledgeable staff nearby to guide you. Although this Michigan Ave. favorite is usually bursting with tourists, the Apple Store also caters to serious Mac enthusiasts by offering periodic tutorials for the less technologically savvy in its chic upstairs forum. **A**

679 N Michigan Ave
312.981.4104
RED LINE to CHICAGO

The Disney Store

Walk in and you'll instantly return to your childhood as you reach for stuffed Disney characters and elegant Cinderella dresses and crowns. You can find the perfect gift for younger cousins and siblings here. Even if you don't plan to buy anything, the store is worth the stop to stroll down memory lane. **B+**

717 N Michigan Ave
312.654.9208
RED LINE to CHICAGO

Tiffany and Company

For any dreaming girl, blushing bride, or stylish diva, Tiffany and Company is a must-see. You can't buy anything with spare change here, but browsing the cases of shimmering gems in Audrey Hepburn style is almost as good as actually buying it. Timeless engagement rings, sterling silver necklaces and jewel-laden earrings mix with new designers' pieces. Don't worry too much about not fitting in with the upscale crowd; the shop is always bustling with tourists. **A**

730 N Michigan Ave
312.944.7500
RED LINE to CHICAGO

Westfield North Bridge

You won't get a taste of Chicago at Westfield North Bridge because, in essence, it is a mall. Nevertheless, this breezy, four-story shopping complex is a nice break from the chaos of Michigan Ave. The shops are conveniently organized by floor according to type, and the food court offers a surprising variety of tasty treats. Be prepared to bust out the plastic, as these stores can be pricey. **B+**

520 N Michigan Ave
312.327.2300
RED LINE to CHICAGO

NEAR NORTH SIDE

ABOVE: View Down Michigan Ave. WENHONG NEOH • **LEFT:** Newspaper Stands, Michigan Ave. WENHONG NEOH

American Apparel

The crisp white décor of this urban boutique is a perfect setting for its simple, yet vibrant clothing. Catering to men, women, and children, this socially-conscious outfitter offers simple, moderately-priced cotton products in every color you could think of. Whether it is legwarmers, headbands or polos,

> 46 E Walton St
> 312.255.8360
> RED LINE to CLARK/DIVISION

you'll find everything you need to complete the perfect outfit – as long as all you're looking for is solid colors. **A-**

Anthropologie

Step through the tall wood doors into an oasis of brightly colored clothes, artsy décor and beautiful house wares.

> 1120 N State St
> 312.255.1848
> RED LINE to CLARK/DIVISION

Don't expect to find the usual trendy items here. Anthropologie instead offers classic styles in wild patterns, often with fun button and ribbon details. The prices can run pretty high, but you're sure to find some gems on the sales rack. Before you leave, be sure to sample its exotic-smelling lotions like zucchini flower and truffles. **A**

Barneys New York

The pages of Vogue come to life in this legendary shopping oasis. With the

> 25 E Oak St
> 312.587.1700
> RED LINE to CLARK/DIVISION

absolute latest in fashion, who needs a magazine when you can witness all the fine garments first hand here? While the merchandise might seem to match your style, the prices also accent the fine real estate nearby. If you're on the search for a bargain, be prepared to just window shop here. **A**

Camelot Children's Kingdom

Camelot is a kingdom full of European-inspired clothing for kids,

> 1155 N State St
> 312.654.1672
> RED LINE to CLARK/DIVISION

appropriately located on the Gold Coast. Big spenders won't have an issue with the cost, and the fashion is quite remarkable. Imagining your seven-year-old in such sophisticated styles may be the biggest advertising ploy, but, then again, picturing them covered in dirt may be the biggest turn off. If you're shopping to dress him or her for a special engagement, Camelot works. Otherwise, spend wisely. **B**

Flight 001

This is a perfect place to find yourself when you are in need of cute accessories for your next aviation vacation. With ev-

> 1133 N State St
> 312.944.1001
> RED LINE to CLARK/DIVISION

TOP Chicago Fire Department. WENHONG NEOH • **MIDDLE** Museum of Contemporary Art, 22 E. Chicago Ave. WENHONG NEOH • **BOTTOM** Feinberg School of Medicine, 303 E. Chicago Ave. WENHONG NEOH

NEAR NORTH SIDE

erything from suitcases to first aid kits, this store is great for anything travel-oriented. However, the duffel bag you've had since you were nine will have to do if you do not have $300 to dish out on luggage. Luckily, smaller accessories like umbrellas are worth the splurge because of their great styles. **B**

Jake

Tucked between Le Colonial and Barneys, this trendy North Rush St.

939 N Rush St
312.664.5553
RED LINE to CLARK/DIVISION

boutique is an understated treasure for fashionistas. The designer duds double as conservative clubwear and classy street gear. The store is small, so selection is limited. Also, don't venture in unless three-digit prices don't scare you – few items cost less than $100. **B**

Londo Mondo

Whether it's a trip to the pool, lake or beach, Londo Mondo satisfies

1100 N Dearborn St
312.751.2794
RED LINE to CLARK/DIVISION

all of Chicago's nautical-bound shoppers. Stylish swimsuits decorate the walls with practical sporty pieces along with plenty of active wear for workouts on or off the beach. Londo Mondo is also a respected roller blade specialty shop for anyone looking to join the thousands of runners, walkers and bikers along Chicago's expansive recreational lakeshore. **B**

Mr. Kite's Confectionary

The good: Everything in this tiny mom-and-pop candy counter is fresh,

1153 N State St
312.664.7270
RED LINE to CLARK/DIVISION

homemade and visually stunning. The massive s'mores – some plain, others filled with caramel or peanut butter – are an irresistible specialty. The bad: Prices are high, chocolate truffles are a bit waxy and though the shop is relocating, no one seems to know the new address. **B-**

ps:accessories

Every fashionista knows that accessories can make or break an outfit,

1127 N State St
312.932.0077
RED LINE to CLARK/DIVISION

so after buying you're hot new top on Michigan Ave., make your way down to ps:accessories to complete your outfit. Here you'll find bright high heels, sparkly belts and hand-crafted jewelry. The clerks, however, seem more interested in talking to each other than in helping you find shoes in your size. **B**

Sabon

The body products here from the Dead Sea appeal to the all-natural girl.

1152 N State St
312.981.1234
RED LINE to CLARK/DIVISION

Each concoction comes in multiple flavors, but the products are a bit expensive for broke college students. The body butter, bubble bath, soap and all other products come with an added bonus: they claim to reduce migraines and other body aliments. Your friends will want to know where you got your impossibly trendy, spa-quality bath products. **B-**

TeaGschwender

Whether you are looking for black tea, white tea, or anything in between, this

1160 N State St
312.932.0639
RED LINE to CLARK/DIVISION

German teashop is a comfortable haven from the streets of Chicago. The small store is filled with teas of every variety, from affordable [$2.80 for 100 grams] to luxurious [$163.80 for 500 grams], from mundane [peppermint] to wild [Grandpa Harmsen, an herbal blend with coriander, fennel and licorice]. On Saturdays, TeaGschwender offers each customer free samples and a complimentary guide to the store's 300-plus teas. **A**

After-Words Books

This cozy shop with irresistible charm sells new and used books. Here,

23 E Illinois St
312.464.1110
RED LINE to GRAND

readers can find a plethora of quality texts at low prices within the kind of setting that keeps customers coming back for years. The top floor offers a selection of new books comparable to that of larger chain stores, and the basement has a wide range of well-organized used titles. Computers are available for use at an hourly fee. **A**

NEAR NORTH SIDE

RIGHT: Water Tower, 800 N. Michigan Ave.
WENHONG NEOH • **BOTTOM:** Water Tower, 800
N. Michigan Ave. WENHONG NEOH

Aldo

605 N Michigan Ave
312.664.6255
RED LINE to GRAND

Aldo is a shoe lover's paradise. The store is stocked with dozens of fashions for both men and women, not to mention an array of jewelry, accessories and handbags. At any given time, something in the store is on sale, so if you are anxious for some shopping but don't want to bust the bank, pick up a necklace or a belt. Shoes are reasonably priced, and accessories are guaranteed to add a little something extra to your outfit. **A⁻**

Armani Exchange

520 N Michigan Ave
312.467.5702
RED LINE to GRAND

Quality and fashion meet here to accommodate those looking for the runway look without runway prices. This store is teeming with racks of trendy tees, stylish trench coats, skinny jeans and more. Prices can be steep, but the quality and style of the clothing is worth the splurge. Beware that some items run small, so be sure to try clothing on before taking it home. **A⁻**

Bloomingdale's Home and Furnishings

600 N Wabash Ave
312.324.7500
RED LINE to GRAND

With beautiful mosaics and towering domes in full Islamic Revival style, the Medinah Temple is a breath-taking Chicago landmark ... and also the location of Bloomingdale's Home and Furnishings Store. Despite its exotic exterior, you will find mostly mundane [and overpriced] kitchenware here. Unless you desperately need to buy an expensive housewarming or wedding gift, visit this home décor store only for its dramatic architecture. **B**

Chicago Harley Division

66 E Ohio St
312.274.9666
RED LINE to GRAND

If only the walls were covered in denim and leather. Chicago Harley Davidson is a niche store, but worth a look for those who dream about the open road. The Harley insignia on the gear awakens the rider in everybody, with items such as riding boots [$78-$142 a pair], cycle jackets [a bargain at $195 or a splurge at $595], shot glasses and even teddy bears and dog toys. **B**

Coach

625 N Michigan Ave
312.587.3167
RED LINE to GRAND

There is no better place for bag lovers to stop and shop on the Magnificent Mile than here. The latest variety of Coach handbags, shoulder bags, travel bags and wallets occupy its white wall casings. Although prices can be high, friendly and helpful costumer service guarantees a pleasing experience as you shop for your next choice of arm candy. **A**

H2O+

As you're strolling down the Magnificent Mile, this small body shop is easy to pass by. Whether you're shopping for yourself or picking up a quick gift, however, the knowledgeable staff at H2O+ can quickly point you in the right direction. Because the vendor is situated in such a small building, be prepared to fight through tourists sifting through the all-organic products. Be sure to check out the signature Milk line though: It's a favorite for both men and women. **B**

600 N Michigan Ave
312.397.1243
RED LINE to GRAND

Hilligoss Galleries

Hilligoss Galleries houses a unique collection of paintings, drawings and sculptures. This two-story space is intimate, and the opera music in the background completes the sophisticated aura within. Pieces are expensive, but the employees are friendly and the art exquisite. If you're not in the market for art, stop by for a look anyway. You just may find yourself spending more time browsing than you expected. **B**

520 N Michigan Ave
312.755.0300
RED LINE to GRAND

Jazz Record Mart

From vintage LPs to the latest Norah Jones album, Jazz Record Mart is the place for any and all things jazz. In addition to jazz in CD and LP forms, customers can purchase cassettes, 45s, t-shirts, posters, and other jazz memorabilia. The employees are extremely helpful and knowledgeable – a characteristic that separates this store from its megastore competitors. Even those less familiar with the jazz scene will appreciate the store's authenticity and originality. **A**

444 N Wabash Ave
312.222.1467
RED LINE to GRAND

La Perla

This high-end lingerie store has the sex appeal of Victoria's Secret with the unique flare of Michigan Ave. shopping. The pieces are elegant and extravagant, though a little pricey, but well worth it for the glamour and

535 N Michigan Ave
312.494.0400
RED LINE to GRAND

pizzazz they will add to your wardrobe. For any special occasion, La Perla will give you a great excuse to indulge yourself. **A**

Levi's the Original Store

This well-organized jean emporium is a must-see during a jaunt down Michigan Ave. Levi's offers a plethora of quality basics that transfer easily from casual Fridays to weekend wear for both men and women. The styles are more professional than American Eagle, yet slightly more casual than the Gap. With the great service and easy-to-navigate displays of denim, the legendary vendor is an essential stop on your search for good jeans. **B+**

600 N Michigan Ave
312.642.9613
RED LINE to GRAND

Life's a Holiday

This shop hidden among the bright lights of Navy Pier is the kind of place you would take your grandparents if they were visiting. Inside it's Christmas all year-round, and you can purchase ornaments, snowmen, candles and wreaths. The inventory expands slightly to include Vera Bradley bags, Crocs, candles and jewelry as well. Whatever your shopping purposes, the cozy interior and the friendly service will make you feel instantly at home. **B**

700 E Grand Ave
312.595.5510
RED LINE to GRAND

Local Charm

This small jewelry shop features items handcrafted by jewelry designers from around the Chicago area. Prices are reasonable, and some unique items include apparel made from metals and precious stones. The style of jewelry ranges from the earthy to the ultra-glamorous, and extremely friendly salespeople are glad to help you choose the perfect piece. **B+**

502 N Michigan Ave
312.527.1643
RED LINE to GRAND

Nordstrom

For the high-end shopper, the racks at Nordstrom boast such designers as Donna Karan, Giorgio Armani and Michael Kors. The store is visually beautiful with three

55 E Grand Ave
312.464.1515
RED LINE to GRAND

floors of fodder for any fashionista. Because clothes are straight from the runway, it's easy to get wrapped up in a little self-indulgence, but beware the lofty prices. The clearance sections are always worth a peek, plus they promise huge savings. **B**

Oh Yes Chicago!

Navy Pier attracts millions of visitors every year. It's not surprising then that it is dotted with souvenir shops. Oh Yes Chicago! has Chicago apparel, mugs, socks, and even dog outfits. All items arc relatively cheap, which makes this little shop a great place to buy gifts for your family back home. The selection is small, so if you are a picky shopper, search elsewhere. **B+**

> 700 E Grand Ave
> 312.595.0020
> **RED LINE to GRAND**

Oilily

Oilily is a vibrant clothing boutique filled with eccentric and fun fashions. The small size allows customers to shop without being overwhelmed by racks of clothing. If you have any questions, the sales staff is engaging

> 520 N Michigan Ave
> 312.527.5747
> **RED LINE to GRAND**

and extremely helpful. Clothing is high quality, but the prices can be a shock. If you purchase anything, make sure it's something you can see lasting in your closet for the long run. **B**

P.O.S.H.

If you'd like to take a trip around the world while shopping for a unique place setting, look no further than the amazing products of P.O.S.H. With dinnerware to enhance any dish and souvenirs reminiscent of those you could find in Italy, Paris or Switzerland, P.O.S.H. has everything your heart desires. With reasonable prices and the chance to show off your rare find of a tulip-painted plate, you won't be disappointed. **A**

> 613 N State St
> 312.280.1602
> **RED LINE to GRAND**

Room and Board

Functional meets trendy at this three-story chain furniture store. Focusing on simple lines, Asian-inspired designs and neutral hues with bold accents, Room and Board attracts young urban dwellers. Prices can get a bit steep for large pieces, but an accessory or

> 55 E Ohio St
> 312.222.0970
> **RED LINE to GRAND**

Nicholas J. Melas Centennial Fountain, McClurg Court.
WENHONG NEOH

Mary Mary Gifts

706 N. Dearborn St.
312.654.8100
RED LINE to CHICAGO

Just a few blocks from the main drag of Michigan Ave., this quaint boutique is a gem for those shopping for eccentric, one-of-a-kind pieces. The owner personally purchases items from all over the world to decorate the shelves and walls of adobe. From handbags to picture frames and custom soaps to exquisite jeweled items, there is something for every taste within every price range. All ages are welcome – the children's section in the back of the store offers unique stuffed animals and other gifts for children that can't be found in any department store. While the treasures inside often lure customers, it's the diligent customer service that keeps them returning. The friendly staff will take the time to personally select a gift with you, giving you a thorough tour of the merchandise. Mary Mary is a quality find in the heart of the city that can't be missed.

two won't set you back too much. The store is customer-friendly, with helpful staff and a coffee bar to quench your thirst while you're browsing. The timeless designs and colors make this shop accessible for all ages. **B+**

The Body Shop

The aroma of the store itself is just as fresh and fruity as the aroma of

520 N Michigan Ave
312.645.0971
RED LINE to GRAND

the actual body products within. Shoppers can't pass up the signature body butter lotion or The Body Shop's extensive line of make-up and skin care. Not only are its products made with natural ingredients, but socially conscious customers can be satisfied because a portion of all purchases goes toward community trade efforts that promote struggling international economies. **B+**

The Funky Chameleon

Knock-off purses, tacky jewelry, and handmade soaps line the walls of

600 E Grand Ave
312.670.2606
RED LINE to GRAND

this Navy Pier shop. Its various headbands are exceptionally fashionable, but none of the buys are anything extraordinary. If nothing else, the purses and jewelry are good ideas for young teens that can't quite handle the responsibility of expensive accessories but still want to look fashionable. **B-**

TOP: Realtor Plaza. WENHONG NEOH • **BOTTOM:** Chicago 'El' Stop. KATHERINE VILLAMIN

NEAR NORTH SIDE

LOOP

WHERE ALL THINGS COME AND GO IN CHICAGO

Home of the tallest building in the U.S., one of the best collections of impressionist art and the largest mirrored bean known to man, the Loop is where all things come and go in Chicago. Named the Loop because the CTA tracks wrap around the area, it's undeniably the center of the city. Running between Lake Michigan and the Chicago River, the Loop covers the spectrum of entertainment – from high-brow to pop culture. Millennium and Grant Parks play host to several summer events: the Taste of Chicago, Chicago Blues Festival and Lollapalooza as well as free outdoor concerts by the Grant Park Orchestra. Hear the famous Chicago Symphony brass at Symphony Center while the Lyric Opera performs at the Civic Opera Theater along the river. The Chicago Cultural Center has world class performing, visual and literary arts year around, free of charge. The Loop is also the center of Chicago's thriving theater scene which premieres many productions before they reach New York. City hall, financial and business districts are all here. Shopping can be found at the massive Macy's or along area streets where flagship stores of almost every national retailer abound.

TO EAT

Intelligentsia Coffee

Intelligentsia serves as Chicago's savvy version of Starbucks, catered towards intellectuals, students and artists. The regular crowd includes students working quietly and young couples chatting over delicious cups of coffee and tea. Like any other coffee shop, it offers an array of coffee makers and baked goods to compliment your drink. The décor within is elegant and welcoming, with the smell of warm coffee permeating the air. **A⁻**

53 W Jackson Blvd
312.253.0594
BLUE LINE to JACKSON

Ohio House Coffee Shop Inc.

With a large variety of gourmet coffees [both whole bean and ground varieties], Ohio Coffee Shop is a viable, but not necessary, option for coffee lovers. It is more of a hang out for the Sunday morning hangover crowd, so try to get there early to avoid weekend rushes. After your coffee, make sure to order the delicious biscuits and gravy. **B⁻**

600 N LaSalle Dr
312.751.2038
BLUE LINE to LASALLE

Orange

75 W. Harrison St.
312.447.1000
BLUE LINE to LASALLE

Tastefully decorated with hints of orange, this charming brunch café offers a delicious assortment of eggs, french toast, pancakes and lunch sandwiches. The restaurant has a casual and up-beat feel that meshes well with the early morning buzz of its customers. Order a stack of delicious buttermilk pancakes topped with fresh fruit or an order of the restaurant's special Chai Tea french toast to put some spunk into your mornings. Wash everything down with a freshly-squeezed glass of juice made to order from a list of over a dozen fruits and vegetables. Prices are reasonable, with breakfast dishes running around $8 and all students raking in a 20% discount. Whether you are off to work or stopping in with the whole family, you are sure to enjoy every morsel.

Capra's Coffee and Sushi Express

East meets west at Capra's, a rare spot where you can order a latte with

46 S Clark St
312.422.0142
BLUE LINE to MONROE

Philadelphia rolls on the side. The décor mirrors the duality of the menu: an Italian sign reading 'Grazie' is positioned amidst colorful Chinese lanterns. The service is extremely friendly – if you sign up for a punch card, they'll keep it for you in a Rolodex on the counter. The only drawback at this unique place is the limited seating. **A-**

Marquette Inn Restaurant

Only three Marquette Inns exist in Chicago, and they're all within blocks

60 W Adams St
312.368.8704
BLUE LINE to MONROE

from each other. Using reputation more than sparkle to bring in the hungry, Marquette Inn is popular with the younger crowds for its cheap prices and hearty meals. Breakfast is best, since the lunch and dinner menu, consisting of Reuben sandwiches, melts and clubs, is pretty standard. Don't plan on making any of those late night pit stops – closing time is at eight. **B-**

Nick's Fish Market

If you're looking to impress, Nick's has the swanky feel and the high

51 S Clark St
312.621.0200
BLUE LINE to MONROE

prices to automatically filter potential customers into only those who are willing to empty their wallets. The ground floor features less expensive

LOOP

Anti-War Protest, Loop. DANIEL HONIGMAN

Carson, Pirie, Scott & Co. Building, 1 S. State St.

DANIEL HONIGMAN

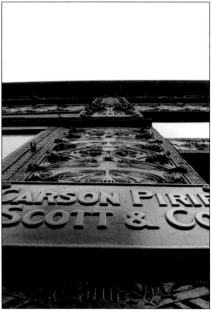

menu items, while the lower level offers a separate menu in which entrées range from $20 all the way to $50. The food is mediocre and there is a dress code: no shorts, and men are encouraged to wear jackets. **B-**

The Italian Village

If you're craving Italian food, look no further. The Italian Village is actually

71 W Monroe St
312.332.7005
BLUE LINE to MONROE

three restaurants in one, and together they serve every variety of Italy's finest cuisine. The Village offers mid-priced fare from Northern Italy, La Cantina serves steak and seafood and Vivere offers pricier, modern dishes. The atmosphere is warm and homey, the servers charming and efficient and the overall experience is one worth paying for. **A**

Lavazza

Take a break in this Italian-inspired contemporary café and sample

33 N Dearborn St
312.977.9971
BLUE LINE to WASHINGTON

the store's uniquely blended espressos. If the delicious coffee doesn't suit your fancy, perhaps you'll enjoy one of the savory gelato flavors like café espresso or one of the café's many croissants, baguette sandwiches and fresh salads. Decorated in the style of a genuine Italian café, the store offers customers a place to dine at one of the black and marble tables while they casually enjoy a taste of Italy. **A-**

Kramer's Health Food

To all of Chicago's health food nuts: Kramer's is the place for you. Although it

230 S Wabash Ave
312.922.0077
BROWN LINE to ADAMS

doesn't boast the selection of a larger counterpart such as Whole Foods, Kramer's is a great neighborhood stop for those looking to stock their cabinets or pick up a light meal or snack. Don't leave before visiting the most unique part of the store: the juice bar upstairs. **B**

Canady Le Chocolatier

824 S. Wabash Ave.
312.212.1270
RED LINE to JACKSON

❚ The simple storefront of Canady Le Chocolatier fails to reveal the wonders within. This South Loop treasure is an unassuming world of some of Chicago's best-made chocolates. The only thing sweeter than the treats inside is the amazing staff – always ready with a smile to serve you delectable indulgences. In the heart of several major Chicago college campuses, Canady knows the way to any student's heart is through rich, velvety chocolate or creamy gelato. The dessert shop offers tables and encourages students busy at work to stop in for a quick snack while they laboriously pour over pages of notes or click away on laptops.

Boni Vino Restaurant

Though it is usually crowded and noisy, if you don't mind the lack of

111 W Van Buren St
312.427.0231
BROWN LINE to LASALLE

ambiance, Boni Vino is a great place to duck into for cheap and yummy food. It's also open late, sometimes until 2 a.m., which means that a fun night out at the nearby Auditorium Theatre can end with a tasty thin crust pizza and eggplant parmesan. **B**

Oasis Café

With a variety of Middle Eastern dishes, the Oasis Café is a nice change

21 N Wabash Ave
312.558.1058
BROWN LINE to MADISON

from the normal sandwich and salad cafes of the area. Although seating can be hard to find during lunchtime, you can get your meal to go and enjoy the beautiful outdoors during a short walk in Millennium Park. Oasis Café is great for those with a taste for exotic dishes. **B**

Park Café

When the snow flurries give way to the warmth of spring, have a picnic in

11 N Michigan Ave
312.521.7275
BROWN LINE to MADISON

Millennium Park and expose your sun-deprived face to the rays. If you're too lazy to bring your own supplies, stop by the Park Café and have a picnic packed for you. The café can pack a multi-course gourmet meal for $15 a person or a made-to-order sandwich for $7. Don't forget dessert – after all, no afternoon in the sun is complete without ice cream. **A**

Taco Fresco

Is it really possible to have healthy Mexican fast food? Taco Fresco claims

218 S Clark St
312.641.9912
BROWN LINE to QUINCY

to have created a nutritious menu of delectable Mexican dishes that are prepared quickly. To help answer customers' questions about the healthiness of the cuisine, Taco Fresco provides nutritional information for each of its dishes. And don't worry – even though the calories are minimal, the taste certainly is not. **A-**

Australian Homemade Ice Cream and Chocolates

Before watching a show in Chicago's Theatre District, stop by this little

111 N State St
312.781.3004
BROWN LINE to RANDOLPH

sweet shop for some dessert. Considering it is inside Macy's Department store, the ambiance is neither particularly cozy nor inviting, but the over-priced offerings are quite tasty. The Belgian

ABOVE: Quincy St. 'El.' DANIEL HONIGMAN
• **LEFT:** Division St. DANIEL HONIGMAN

View of Millennium Park from Michigan Ave. COLETTE TAM

Cereality

The best thing about weekend mornings is that big bowl of cereal waiting for you when you wake up. At Cereality, you don't have to wait for the weekend or the morning. This unique chain gives customers the chance to combine their favorite brand name cereals to make totally new creations, morning, noon or night. The price might deter you from coming back for more, but it's definitely worth a try at least once. **B+**

100 S Wacker Dr
312.506.0010
BROWN LINE to WASHINGTON

Eleven City Diner

You won't miss the Big Apple one bit when you set foot inside Eleven City Diner, which takes Carnegie-deli-worthy fare up a notch by serving it amidst the welcoming attitude a diner should have. Comfy booths, dim lighting

1112 S Wabash Ave
312.212.1112
GREEN LINE to ROOSEVELT

chocolates are delicious, although you'd be better off going elsewhere if you want to sit at a nice table and savor your dessert. **B–**

ARCHITECTURE IN CHICAGO: LEADING THE WORLD SCENE
BY NATE BROWN

When any tourist comes to Chicago, it's all 'Architecture, architecture, architecture!' One of the unlikely upsides of the Great Chicago Fire of 1871 was a subsequent economic boom spurred by the redevelopment and rebuilding of the city's downtown. Not only is the manmade scenery incredibly fascinating, but it's one of the best things to visit to entertain your relatives and look smart at the same time.

The Chicago School and the Rise of the Skyscraper • Just a decade after the fire, Chicago was a hotbed of architectural activity and innovation. The Chicago School is the name that has been given to the group of architects who were working in the city around the turn of the century and included architects Daniel

Burnham, John Root and Louis Sullivan, all of whom designed impressive buildings in Chicago as well as several other American cities. While there was no single, driving aesthetic within the Chicago School, the movement is credited with a revived interest in neo-classical design and, most significantly, the use of steel frames and plate glass windows. Stronger and sturdier than iron framed buildings, these new steel constructions gave rise to the world's first skyscrapers and cemented Chicago's place in architectural history.

During the late 19th century and early 20th century, Chicago competed with other American cities like New York for the distinction of being home to the world's tallest building. Chicago still boasts some of the world's tallest skyscrapers, including Loebl, Schloss-man & Hackl's Two Prudential Plaza; Ken Pedersen Fox's 311 Wacker Drive, which is sometimes called the White Castle Building or the Wedding Cake Building

LOOP

and a vast selection of pies make it especially appealing to area students. If you're dining alone, camp out on a swivel barstool and partake in a frothy fountain soda. **A**

Fornetto's & Mei's Kitchen

This Italian restaurant offers reasonable prices and a quaint outdoor eat-

1109 S Michigan Ave
312.294.2488
GREEN LINE to ROOSEVELT

ing area. With such a close proximity to Museum Campus, Formetto and Mei's has a prime location for those on the way back from a cultured stroll through one of the museums. While the food is tasty and reasonably priced, the cheesy elevator music is a bit bothersome. **B**

The Bongo Room

There is no better place for a mid-day bite than in a restaurant solely

1152 S Wabash Ave
312.291.0100
GREEN LINE to ROOSEVELT

dedicated to breakfast, brunch and lunch. With an eclectic menu urging you to try the Key Lime Cheesecake Pancakes or the Smoked Chicken and Apple Club, The Bongo Room has enough choices for the brave and for those who prefer just a cheese omelet. But beware, this place draws a crowd and seating can be limited, so expect a wait. **A-**

Yang Chinese Restaurant

Tucked into the ground floor of the South Loop's historic Roosevelt Hotel,

28 E Roosevelt Rd
312.986.1688
GREEN LINE to ROOSEVELT

this is a popular place for takeout before hitting the nearby 'El' stop. In fact, the Chicago Tribune gave it three forks and called it one of the best restaurants in the area. Before dining here, go to its Web site and print out a few coupons for some cheap Chinese-American cuisine. Make sure to try the delectable crab wontons. **B+**

on account of it's illuminated crown; Skidmore, Owings and Merrill's [SOM] John Hancock Center; and, of course, the U.S.'s tallest building [when you include the antenna height] The Sears Tower, also designed by the famous Chicago-based architecture firm, SOM.

    Frank Lloyd Wright • One cannot talk about Chicago architecture without mentioning Frank Lloyd Wright and his now-famous architectural legacy, Prairie Style. Defined by clean, horizontal lines, the use of natural materials like wood and stone and the integration of architectural elements and practical items like chairs and tables, Wright's Prairie Style is perhaps the best-known, uniquely American architectural aesthetic.

    The greater Chicago area is home to several of Wright's most significant structures, including his own home and studio. Located in the western suburb of Oak Park, Wright lived in and ran his architectural firm out of the home from 1889

to 1909. Oak Park is also home to dozens of remaining Wright buildings, including his impressive 1905 Unity Temple and the Arthur B. Heurtley House, a striking brick home built in 1906. Now a museum, Wright's home and studio is open to the public. A resource for native Chicagoans and visitors alike, Oak Park is a great day-trip destination that also boasts the childhood home of American author Ernest Hemingway.

10 Spots All Residents and Any Visitor Should See:

10. John J. Glessner House, 1800 S. Prairie Ave. • Henry Hobson Richardson's John J. Glessner House is a Romanesque mansion and an historic landmark and museum.

9. Frederick C. Robie House, 5757 S. Woodlawn Ave. • Located on the University of Chicago's campus, the

LOOP

View of E. Monroe Ave. from Michigan Ave. COLETTE TAM

Patty Burger

Patty Burger is the Subway of burger restaurants. Go down the line

72 E Adams St
312.987.0900
PINK LINE to ADAMS

and do your damage: one patty or two? Ketchup or mayo? Your burger creation will cost a few dollars and more than satisfy your craving for something greasy. Overall, Patty Burger makes a respectable attempt to recreate the famed joints of the 50s, but, aesthetically, it's not quite there. Overall, the burgers – large and cheesy – are not a bad anchor for this establishment. **B**

Rhapsody

After a day of museum hopping around the city, relax and dine at this

65 E Adams St
312.786.9911
PINK LINE to ADAMS

swanky, reasonably-priced restaurant. Situated inside the Symphony Center, Rhapsody serves cuisine that is both tasty and unique [the onion-crusted sturgeon is a must], but make sure you

Frederick C. Robie House was designed by Frank Lloyd Wright in 1908 and survived many attempts by the Chicago Theological Seminary to raze it. The structure was the first building in the city to be designated a Chicago Landmark.

8. The University of Chicago, 5801 S. Ellis Ave. • It's somewhat ironic that Chicago is the birthplace of modern American architecture while its premier institution of higher education was designed in the English Gothic Style of Britain's renowned Oxford University. Still, its wide green quadrangles and cavernous stone, wood and slate buildings are as well worth a stroll around campus.

7. The John Hancock Center, 875 N. Michigan Ave. • It's the trademark of the Chicago skyline. Surrounded by great restaurants and shopping, and boasting an impressive observation deck, this is a must-see for visitors and natives alike.

6. Illinois Institute of Technology,

3300 S. Federal St. • The main campus includes significant buildings by Ludwig Mies van der Rohe, the German architect who is credited with the rise of the second Chicago school of architecture.

5. Chicago Water Tower, 800 N. Michigan Ave. • One of the sole survivors of the Great Chicago Fire, the city's famous Water Tower sits at the north end of the Magnificent Mile on the cusp of Chicago's Near North neighborhood. The structure's gothic design and warm yellowish limestone stands out among the surrounding buildings, reminding visitors that it is from another era of the city's history, one that was mostly lost to one of the most devastating urban fires in American history.

4. Shedd Aquarium, 1200 S. Lake Shore Dr. • In 1925, Chicago architecture firm Graham, Anderson, Probst & White was hired to build the aquarium that John G. Shedd had envisioned for the city. Shedd, a wealthy retired former executive

LOOP

don't fill up too much. The dessert menu features creative twists on old favorites, so save room. **B⁺**

Russian Tea Time

Steps from the Art Institute, this unique establishment is an alternative to the typical American café. Afternoon teas served with cookies make it an easy stop for a lunch date, while their extensive European dinner menu welcomes intimate dinners. [Warning: Be willing to try something new.] This tearoom doesn't cut corners in its authenticity: chandelier lighting, red chairs and decorated tea sets transport you to the real thing. And who doesn't like reasonable prices? **B**

77 E Adams St
312.360.0000
PINK LINE to ADAMS

Burrito Buggy

A favorite for Chicago business people on the go, this little shack serves up the strangest, largest burritos you'll ever see. The service is surprisingly zippy and polite, and the to-go food is perfect for the meandering tourist. If you dare, try the barbecue chicken burrito. Featuring zesty chicken, corn and mashed potatoes, it's an unusual dish that will surprise and delight. **B**

206 W Van Buren St
312.362.0199
PINK LINE to LASALLE

Dearborn Street Oyster Bar

With its blue paint and nautical accessories, this mid-priced seafood powerhouse almost feels like a trip to the seashore. The atmosphere is swanky and the food superb,

409 S Dearborn St
312.922.1217
PINK LINE to LIBRARY

of Marshall Field, had wanted to build the world's largest and best aquarium near the lakefront. The resulting Beaux Arts structure stands today as an excellent example of form following function. From the cool green marble details to the greenish bronze detail work, the Shedd is architectural eye candy.

3. Millennium Park, 201 E. Randolph St. • Perhaps the best known recent addition to Chicago's art and architecture scene is the 24.5 acre Millennium Park project which opened to the public in 2004. The Pavilion, which is billed as the most sophisticated outdoor musical venue in the country, and the BP Bridge are clad in stainless steel, bringing a bright, reflective and vaguely futuristic feel to this reinvigorated parkland. The site also includes large works of public art, the most famous of which is almost certainly Anish Kapoor's giant reflective sculpture 'Cloud Gate,' which has affectionately been dubbed 'The Bean.'

2. Marina City, 300 N. State St. • Bertrand Goldberg's vision for urban living came to life in Chicago when the construction of Marina City finished in 1964. A combination of commercial and residential space, the 'city within a city' was supposed to work as a fully functioning, microcosmic world wherein residents would have quick and easy access to many kinds of amenities. The two cylindrical towers, which have been likened to corn cobs, have become icons of sorts, and even graced the cover of the Chicago-based band Wilco's award-winning 2001 album Yankee Hotel Foxtrot.

1. The Sears Tower, 233 S. Wacker Dr. • Commissioned by Sears, Roebuck and Co. and designed by the landmark Chicago architecture firm Skidmore, Owings and Merrill, the Sears Tower held the record for the world's tallest building from its opening in 1973 until it was surpassed in 1998 by Malaysia's Petronas Towers. The Tower's famous Skydeck was featured in the hit 1986 film Ferris Bueller's Day Off.

LOOP

Java Java Coffee Café

2 N. State St.
312.759.2233
RED LINE to WASHINGTON

In Chicago's business district, there is no shortage of cafés to service the armies of suit-clad men and women that march the streets on their lunch hour. Java Java is a rare treasure amongst the many chains. Just blocks from the busy shopping district on Michigan Ave. and two of Chicago's train hubs, this is an ideal stop regardless of your destination. Obviously Java Java specializes in its caffeinated treats, but the pastries displayed at the counter and delicious smoothie menu will lure even the most adamant coffee addict. Also, if you aren't in a hurry, take a minute to enjoy its second floor lounge that offers a muted view of the business district with comfortable seating.

but the mid-range prices make it so that eating a lot won't empty your wallet. Try the mouth-watering soft-shell crab, or if seafood isn't your thing, you can choose from an ample selection of pasta dishes too. **A⁻**

Ada's Famous Deli

14 S Wabash Ave
312.214.4282
PINK LINE to MADISON

Ada's promises its food is 'as good as mother's and better than others.' If that's not enough to draw you in, then consider the huge selection of soups, salads and sandwiches at prices that won't break the bank. The Rueben Sandwich is a famous favorite among the regulars. Before you leave, don't forget to stop by the deli and pick up some edibles for later. **A**

Caffé Bacci

20 N Michigan Ave
312.214.2224
PINK LINE to MADISON

With a motto like 'Eat Italian, Dream Italian,' it's no wonder Caffé Baci is devoted to Italian-inspired dishes. Take your pick from their huge selection of soups, salads, Paninis, wraps, 'pizzettes,' desserts and drinks. This eatery is the perfect place to pick up breakfast on the go, a quick lunch or a coffee break. Look the restaurant up for your next company event as well; it is known in Chicago for its quality gourmet catering. **B**

ABOVE: Northern Skyline, Grant Park. COLETTE TAM • **RIGHT:** Skyline, Jackson Ave. & Columbus Dr. COLETTE TAM

Roosevelt 'El' Stop. DAVE SCHRIMPF

Pizano's Pizza and Pasta

61 E Madison St
312.236.1777
PINK LINE to MADISON

Pizano's has class without letting it reflect onto the menu prices. The restaurant is intimate with candlelit tables, yet not claustrophobic – the gaping dining area leaves room to breathe after stuffing yourself with some deep-dish pizza or quality pasta and sandwiches. If anything, Pizano's is comfortable, and the paper tablecloths save you from feeling embarrassed if you happen to drip a little red sauce from one of the many Americanized Italian dishes. **B⁻**

Haifa Café

19 N Wells St
312.214.1144
PINK LINE to WASHINGTON

This traditional Mediterranean café is a great alternative to the plethora of fast food establishments that clog the Loop. Prided by its fresh cuisine, Haifa Café is not only a healthier stop for your lunch break but is also extremely friendly on your wallet – items typically range between three and eight dollars. From now on, you'll find yourself asking for falafel – not fries. **B**

A.P. Deli

704 S Wabash Ave
312.697.0283
RED LINE to JACKSON

A dirty hidden hole in the side of the wall claims to offer the best corned beef sandwich in Chicago, but it really only offers a chewy substitute to that of an average sandwich place. A.P. Deli redeems itself slightly with a wide selection of somewhat appetizing desserts, including cheesecake, carrot cake and others. Its everyday special features two hotdogs and chips for only $2.50, but it's really not worth the money you're saving. **C**

Amarit

600 S Dearborn St
312.939.1179
RED LINE to JACKSON

Make your way down to a quiet little Thai place hiding on the Columbia College campus. Amarit offers a wide selection of scrumptious dishes from the classic Orange Chicken to the exotic Crying Dragon – a platter of spiced steak. A meal for two can cost less than thirty dollars, and you can also indulge in a Green Tea flavored bubble tea to go. This simple yet sophisticated restaurant will charm any visitor. **B⁺**

Artist's Snack Shop

This adorable snack shop is nestled right below the Fine Arts Building. It

410 S Michigan Ave
312.427.7602
RED LINE to JACKSON

is exactly what the name suggests: a place for artists working in the building to shop in between rehearsals and shows. It is bright and cheery with reasonably priced, generally tasty food. If you're in the neighborhood or thinking about a quick perusal in the Fine Arts Building, stop by for a quick bite. **A**

Bar Louie

On a warm day, there are always patrons dining at the sidewalk tables of

47 W Polk St
312.347.0000
RED LINE to JACKSON

Bar Louie. An oasis in the vast sea of industrial Chicago south of Congress, Bar Louie offers a mix of commercial familiarity and casual comfort. Despite the close proximity to four major Chicago college campuses, Bar Louie can be on the pricier side, so save an outing to this restaurant for a special occasion if you're trying to pinch pennies. **B+**

Blackie's

Hungry Chicagoans flock to Blackie's as early as 7:30 in the morning to

755 S Clark St
312.786.1161
RED LINE to JACKSON

fill up on their favorite breakfast foods when a quick latte just won't do. Breakfast isn't all that Blackie's is known for. Upon entering this classic burger restaurant, the friendly atmosphere is such that even tourists feel like patrons who have just walked into their favorite local neighborhood burger joint rather than a big city establishment. **B**

Caribou Coffee

Midwesterners will tell you that Caribou could take on Starbucks any day.

41 E 8th St
312.786.9205
RED LINE to JACKSON

With such classics as the sinful Caramel High Rise and the cool Mint Condition served amidst a north woods atmosphere, this claim has ample validity. Caribou Coolers give Frappuccinos a run for their money with sweet flavor shots and just the right amount of coffee. Service is quick and friendly, and you can't resist being whisked away into the rustic cabin décor. **A**

Charming Woks

Cozy and welcoming, this small Asian restaurant offers both standard favor-

601 S Wabash Ave
312.939.0966
RED LINE to JACKSON

ites and exotic fare. The traditional bubble tea is definitely worth tasting, especially if you've never had it before, and the sushi is varied, unusual and cheap. Service is a bit slow at times, but the food is worth the wait. **B+**

ABOVE: Polish Constitution Day Parade. COLETTE TAM • **RIGHT:** Polish Constitution Day Parade. COLETTE TAM

Chicago Carry Out

If you're in the mood for cheap, greasy and satisfy-ing grub, try Chicago Carry Out. Hungry Columbia College students on a budget make up much of its clientele. For under $5, you can get a giant sandwich with any type of meat, ranging from beef to gyros. It's open all hours of the day. An order of fries and soda will stifle even the most gnawing of hunger pains, but don't expect a taste-bud-blasting experience. **c**

63 E Harrison St
312.341.1270
RED LINE to JACKSON

Chicken Planet

The food at Chicken Planet is tasty, cheap and fast. The chicken is cooked on an open grill and prepared quickly. Unfortunately, the greasy floors in the dining area and the large dirty buckets behind the cluttered counter make the atmosphere far from appealing. Chicken Planet is really only meant for customers with low standards. **c**

21 W Jackson Blvd
312.360.1409
RED LINE to JACKSON

Gioia Candy & More

Step inside to get away from the cold and snow to have a sweet treat at Gioia chocolate. They offer homemade chocolate snacks, great gift baskets and – a delectable

333 S State St
312.663.9775
RED LINE to JACKSON

treat for any season – gelato. Gioia is located right on the DePaul campus and offers free special toppings on gelato for all students. While you're in the shop, indulge in a few flavors of Jelly Bellies or a Willy Wonka lollipop. **B+**

Harold's Chicken Shack

Harold's Chicken Shack is practically a legend. Both Chicago natives and nearby college students flock to this location to enjoy the ever-popular fried chicken dinner. Other favorites include wings, catfish and chicken ten-ders. Don't expect much in the ambiance depart-ment, though. While many customers complain of long waits, they also agree that the food is more than worth it. **A-**

636 S Wabash Ave
312.362.0442
RED LINE to JACKSON

La Cocina Mexican Grill

Imagine a place some-where between Taco Bell and upscale gourmet dining. This hole-in-the-wall Mexican restau-rant is just that: an upgrade from typical fast food Mexican cuisine. Though the décor is a bit rundown and the dining area a bit crowded, the low prices and tasty food keep customers coming back for quick meals. **B+**

11 W Jackson Blvd
312.427.2094
RED LINE to JACKSON

LOOP

Millennium Park

201 E. Randolph St.
312.742.1168
BROWN LINE to RANDOLPH

A once-unsightly bed of railroad ties now serves as one of Chicago's main attractions, thanks to its transformation into almost 25 acres of green grass, wide promenades, blooming flowers and architectural wonders. Crowds of adults and children marvel at their warped reflections in the immensely popular Cloud Gate [a.k.a. The Bean]. In winter, ice skaters brave the cold for old-fashioned fun. In summer, the lawns are packed with people watching their favorite bands in Frank Gehry's amphitheater or sampling the city's finest foods in the Taste of Chicago festival. On the other side of the amphitheater, Gehry's pedestrian bridge stretches out to the lakeshore like a silver snake undulating over traffic. If the weather is warm, kick off your shoes and play in the Crown Fountain, which contains two 50-foot glass blocks that flash faces of Chicago residents.

Pat's Pizzeria

With so many college campuses in Chicago's South Loop, Pat's Pizzeria is perfect for late night munchies during intense cramming sessions. The pizzeria opens promptly at 11 a.m. for the lunchtime rush, stays open until 11 p.m. for all the night owls and, of course, offers delivery. If you crave traditional Italian cuisine but want to steer clear from pizza, Pat's also offers several different sandwiches, pastas and salads to suit your fancy. **B‾**

638 S Clark St
312.427.2320
RED LINE to JACKSON

Pizza-Ria

This pizzeria will deliver a taco salad and a pizza right to your door with a call. Whether you want a traditional pepperoni pizza or a broccoli and chicken 'Manhattan,' you'll be satisfied with your order. Salads come in gigantic proportions and have more unhealthy ingredients than healthy ones, so don't expect to maintain your diet at Pizza-Ria. The meals run about $15 more than a regular chain, but it's worth the extra cash. **B**

719 S State St
312.957.1111
RED LINE to JACKSON

Standing Room Only

Standing Room Only is a heart-healthy choice for those seeking a good, quick meal. The hidden deli is home to Chicago's number one turkey burger and will also satisfy the vegetarians and health nuts of the city. The Cubs and Bears memorabilia dotting the walls set a fun tone, and the extremely low prices and abundance of seats keep customers coming back for more. **A‾**

610 S Dearborn St
312.360.1776
RED LINE to JACKSON

Tamarind

Tamarind adds a touch of sophistication to the South Loop neighborhood. The slick décor and tantalizing menu are reminiscent of Chicago's most upscale, urban restaurants. The menu boasts Chinese, Japanese and Vietnamese dishes, but if you're ordering sushi, sit at the sushi bar where you can watch the chefs prepare your food. Don't forget to try the sake or an original dessert. This place is great, both for intimate diners and for large groups. **A‾**

614 S Wabash Ave
312.379.0970
RED LINE to JACKSON

Thai Spoon

If you're in the mood for Southeast Asian food, avoid this restaurant and go across the street to Tamarind. Although you'll spend a few dollars more per person at Tamarind, it'll be worth it. Thai Spoon is frequented by hungry Columbia College students after class, but the food is mediocre, and the ambiance leaves much

601 S Wabash Ave
312.427.9470
RED LINE to JACKSON

TOP Eleven City Diner, 1112 S. Wabash Ave. COLETTE TAM
• **MIDDLE** Eleven City Diner, 1112 S. Wabash Ave. COLETTE TAM
• **BOTTOM** Eleven City Diner, 1112 S. Wabash Ave. COLETTE TAM

Chicago Symphony Center

220 S. Michigan Ave.
312.294.3000
PINK LINE to ADAMS

The first time you enter the Symphony Center, the spectacular sight will leave you in awe. From the main floor, the seats appear to stretch upwards without end, and the stage shines under huge chandeliers. The red carpets, the steep staircases and the shiny wooden stage give the venue a classic look. Even if you're not a classical music fan, the setting alone has the potential to evoke a love of Mozart and Bach. It's refined, but not snooty, so tourists and students can blend easily with seasoned listeners. Located directly across from the Art Institute of Chicago on Michigan Ave., the Center is in a prime location, so there is no excuse to pass it by while in the Loop.

to be desired. There are, however, two redeeming qualities: reasonable prices and large portions. **C+**

Argo Tea

This Starbucks alternative is a popular choice for tea drinkers throughout Chicago. The zen-like atmosphere blends well with the store's unique tea menu and its tempting array of pastries, quiches, sandwiches and, yes, coffee too. Order one of the store's flavorful teas, served hot or cold, relish in the store's free Wi-Fi and sip away. **A-**

16 W Randolph St
312.553.1551
RED LINE to LAKE

Au Bon Pain

Au Bon Pain is your 'everything' breakfast and lunch stop for a meal on the go. Frequented by businesspeople in the bustling downtown area, this bakery and café has enough salads, soups, sandwiches and baked goods to fill any empty stomach. The fare is not unusual or particularly distinctive, but it accomplishes its goal as a marketplace restaurant. The café is bright and airy, with a charm and efficiency fit for a downtown hotspot. **A-**

200 E Randolph St
312.616.9249
RED LINE to LAKE

Café Descartes

With a sea of chain coffee stores littering the city, this warm and welcoming café is an intellectual escape from the norm. Coffee lovers can enjoy their warm

327 N Michigan Ave
312.263.0583
RED LINE to LAKE

beverages among portraits of the likes of Sartre, Aristotle, and of course Descartes himself. Café Descartes is the perfect place to study, but if your sweet tooth dragged you there instead of your workload, be sure to try their famous ½ pound cookie. **A**

Caffecafe

State St. shoppers longing for a latte without the frenzy of a Starbucks-esque café will enjoy Caffecafe. Coffee drinks, pastries, sandwiches and salads are brought to the table with a smile, and patrons can enjoy the view of State St. from a quiet, brightly-lit window seat. The atmosphere is idyllic, but be warned: Coffee drinks are very strong and though pastries pack potential, they aren't quite up to par. **B**

1 E Wacker Dr
312.644.2233
RED LINE to LAKE

Elephant & Castle

Known to Americans as 'excellent' or 'right on,' the abundant use of 'bang on' is just part of what creates the atmosphere in this British pub. The menu combines American fare with British staples like fish 'n chips, bangers and beans 'n mash. And don't worry, beer is a priority here. Stop in during soccer – or shall we say football – season because the pub keeps its tube tuned to matches all season long. **B**

185 N Wabash Ave
312.345.1710
RED LINE to LAKE

Moonstruck Chocolate Café

A must-visit on a cold Chicago day, this swanky café offers a variety of hot

320 N Michigan Ave
312.696.1201
RED LINE to LAKE

chocolates, truffles, cakes and other chocolate delights. Each candy is flawless in design and taste. It's a joy to take a rest from shopping in one of the gigantic leather chairs and read a magazine as you sip your delicious drink. This is a perfect place to buy your chocolate-crazed sweetheart just what they desire, with a moon- or heart-shaped box of chocolatey goodness. **A**

Mrs. Field's Cookies

Looking for fresh baked goods on the go? Mrs. Field's Cookies is the best

100 W Randolph St
312.263.1636
RED LINE to LAKE

choice in the area. Cookies, brownies and other sweet treats are specialties at this delicious chain cookie shop. With a cozy décor and a con-sistently fragrant location, Mrs. Field's does not disappoint. The treats are always fresh, delicious and affordable. **A**

Potbelly Sandwich Works

This chain that originated on Chicago's north side represents a hometown

190 N State St
312.683.1234
RED LINE to LAKE

feel despite the big city location. Their cus-tom sandwiches, freshly baked cookies and tantalizing shakes keep Chicagoans filtering through every day. The ordering system can be complicated, so pay attention to the customers in front of you at your first visit. Don't forget: If you're looking for a healthy snack, be sure to take advantage of Potbelly's low-carb options. **A-**

Sixty-Five Chinese Restaurant

Sixty-Five, a Chinese restaurant and bakery, is the ideal stop for

336 N Michigan Ave
312.372.0306
RED LINE to LAKE

Michigan Ave. crowds with large appetites and tiny budgets. Diners can purchase a generous portion of traditional Chinese fare and a drink for around six dollars, but the selection can be a little sparse. This restaurant is perfect for people on the go as there is no dinnerware here – even the dine-in items are served in a Styrofoam box with plastic utensils. **B**

Big Downtown

Step out of the less-than classy 'El' and into Big Downtown, a restaurant

124 S Wabash Ave
312.917.7399
RED LINE to MONROE

made to look like the inside of a Chicago Transit Authority car, minus the grime and time delays. Big Downtown offers the diverse menu of a stan-dard bar and grill, all set within a 1940s art-deco themed train car. **A-**

Miller's Pub Restaurant

Open until 4 a.m., this restaurant is a great stop for college kids looking

134 S Wabash Ave
312.263.4988
RED LINE to MONROE

for a cocktail, a mug of cold beer or a nice meal. Miller's is famous for its Canadian Back Ribs and its service to stars like Hulk Hogan, Jay Leno and

Oriental Theater: Ford Century for the Performing Arts

24 W. Randolph St.
312.902.1400
RED LINE to LAKE

As one of the anchors of Chicago's theater district, the glitzy Oriental Theater has attracted some of the most famous shows in the world, including Wicked and Ragtime. The theater embodies the grandeur of New York City, but because it draws in only the most-hunted shows, tickets can be expensive and hard to come by. Often, shows will be completely sold-out several months before the actual curtain call, so don't plan to stop by and be able to get in – order your tickets online or through the box office instead. Nevertheless, you'll have to fight through a crowd of tourists and fur-clad old ladies to get to your seats.

LEFT: Artist's Café, 412 S. Michigan Ave. COLETTE TAM • **BELOW:** Artist's Café, 412 S. Michigan Ave. COLETTE TAM

Arnold Schwarzenegger. Make reservations for this popular and reasonably-priced bar and grill. **A**

Rosebud Theater District

This Italian restaurant has top-quality service, food, desserts, and ambiance.

70 W Madison St
312.332.9500
RED LINE to MONROE

If you need to go to a show after dinner, the waiters are particularly accommodating and will deliver your beautifully-presented food with promptness. Try their eggplant rotolo or the veal dishes. The low lighting is perfect for a romantic date, but the TV over the bar is a bit distracting, especially since its picture is reflected throughout the restaurant thanks to its mirrored walls. **A**

Hi Tea

It's hard to find quaint cafés in the South Loop, but Hi Tea offers just that,

14 E 11th St
312.880.0832
RED LINE to ROOSEVELT

tucked away amongst the high rise industrial scene south of Congress. Students are often found studying or clicking away on laptops as they enjoy a refreshing green tea or one of Hi Tea's unique gelato flavors. If Whole Foods and fair trade coffee is your scene, you will feel right at home at this healthy tea and coffee bar. **A**

Oysy Japanese Sushi Restaurant

Conveniently located on the less-crowded end of Michigan Ave., this

888 S Michigan Ave
312.922.1127
RED LINE to ROOSEVELT

inviting and upbeat Japanese sushi restaurant is decorated with wooden tables and colorful chrome settings. The sushi is fresh and delectable, with prices easy on any budget. It's a popular joint for many Chicago sushi lovers, so you can anticipate a crowd. **A**

Yolk

For all those morning people, Yolk's perkiness will surely match your

1120 S Michigan Ave
312.789.9655
RED LINE to ROOSEVELT

mood. Those nursing a hangover, however, will find its bright, yolk-yellow walls a bit too cute to handle. Open for breakfast and lunch only, Yolk's specialties are delicious pancakes, and, yes, you guessed it, eggs. It's very popular with South Loop locals, so be sure you have the time to wait. **B**

Atwood Café

Great service meets even better food at this upscale café with its lively

1 W Washington St
312.368.1900
RED LINE to WASHINGTON

atmosphere. The café's convenient location in

Chicago's theater district makes it a perfect stop for a meal before or after a show. The extensive, American-inspired menu tempts you with dishes like the Duck and Manchego Cheese Quesadilla for lunch or the Porcini Dusted Pan Seared Scallops for dinner. Main dishes can be pricey, but you will leave with a satiated appetite. **A**

Frango Café

In addition to soups, salads and sandwiches, this café on the seventh

111 N State St
312.781.2945
RED LINE to WASHINGTON

floor of Macy's on State St. features an irresistible dessert and ice cream menu. Frango appears to blend into the adjacent Seven on State food court, but friendly servers seat and serve patrons everything from flourless chocolate lollipops to 'Frangoreos' and milk. **A**

Wacker Dr. & Franklin St. Stop. COLETTE TAM

Hannah's Bretzel

Hannah's Breztel sells traditional pretzels in an untraditional way

180 W Washington St
312.621.1111
RED LINE to WASHINGTON

– Chicagoans can now order their favorite sandwich on something other than just plain bread. While it's a little pricey, this cute, European-inspired café is worth a try, if not for its unique pretzel creations, then for its traditional European chocolates, cheeses or crackers. **B+**

Seven on State

Located on the seventh floor of Macy's on State St., this is a food court

111 N State St
312.781.3693
RED LINE to WASHINGTON

without the atmosphere of one. Those shopping on an empty stomach can satisfy cravings for just about anything with Seven on State's diverse menu items. Gourmet food is served quickly in an open atmosphere brightly lit by windows stretching from the floor to the skylights. Seven on State is a classy way to do lunch on the go. **A**

The Walnut Room

Hungry shoppers looking for a more traditional option on the seventh floor

111 N State St
312.781.3125
RED LINE to WASHINGTON

of Macy's on State St. can turn to the elegant Walnut Room. The upscale eatery, with its vaulted ceiling, gaping views of the city and rich, luxurious décor, boasts fine cuisine at reasonable prices. The Walnut Room is an essential stop, especially during the holiday season when a grand Christmas tree shines in the center of the restaurant. **A**

TO PLAY

Sears Tower Skydeck

There's a lot to see when you're more than 1300 feet above the ground.

233 S Wacker Dr
312.875.9696
BROWN LINE to QUINCY

From the Skydeck at the Sears Tower, surrounding states and Chicago's landmarks are just a glance away. More than just a stunning view, the Skydeck is a museum itself, with Chicago's

Chicago Skyline.
DAVE SCHRIMPF

history on display while you wander the window-lined floor. The trip up the elevator will cost tourist trap prices, but seeing Chicago lit up at night makes it worthwhile. **A-**

Dahn Yoga Tai Chi Meditation

If your time in Chicago is looking stressful, why not take a break from shop-

332 N Michigan Ave
312.263.9642
BROWN LINE to RANDOLPH

ping and museum-hopping to get in touch with your chi? Dahn Yoga's central location makes it an easy stop any time of day. The soothing music pouring from the studio immediately transports any haggard travelers to tranquility. Dahn has classes for all levels of ability, so don't let inexperience keep you from being more 'healthy, happy and peaceful!' **B+**

Civic Opera House

If you like the opera, you can't leave Chicago without catching a per-

20 N Wacker Dr
312.419.0033
ORANGE LINE to WASHINGTON

formance at the famous Lyric Opera House. This opera house has attracted the likes of Placido Domingo with its mix of old classics and modern works. Some staunch enthusiasts find the combination unappealing, but, regardless of your

taste, the breathtaking beauty of the building is worth the visit. **A**

Cortiva Institute

As part of the Chicago School of Massage Therapy, the Cortiva

18 N Wabash Ave
312.753.7990
PINK LINE to MADISON

Institute specializes in both teaching and providing massage therapy. You would never guess from the sophisticated lobby, but because it is a teaching institute, services are available to clientele at a discounted price of $40 for an hour of treatment. If you don't mind dropping some extra cash, you can request therapeutic, herbal and botanical services by a professional masseuse. **B**

Chicago Cultural Center

The Cultural Center hosts Chicago history, art and musical events through-

78 E Washington St
312.744.6630
PINK LINE to RANDOLPH

out the year. It also serves as a popular stop for tourists planning a trip to the city. The Office of Tourism provides a plethora of maps and brochures, but don't rely on the exhibits for much entertainment, as they barely make a dent in the expansive space. If nothing else, the ritzy 1897 building, complete with Tiffany glass domes, is worth a look. **B**

Daley Plaza

50 W. Washington St.
312.744.3315
RED LINE to WASHINGTON

While the giant Picasso sculpture is a Chicago landmark in its own right, tourists and locals alike flock to Daley Plaza for its festivals. During Halloween, stop by to admire the orange-dyed fountain and the makeshift haunted village set in the shadow of the sculpture. Avoid the zoo-like daylight hours though, when you're likely to be run over by throngs of face-painted kids clamoring to decorate pumpkins. The German Christkindlmarket, running from late November through December, is a kitschy Chicago favorite worthy of a visit. Here you'll find real German merchants selling scarves, ornaments, baubles, ceramics and, best of all, delicious gingerbread. Buy some hot wine to stay warm and keep the boot-shaped mug as a souvenir. The giant Christmas tree may also inspire some warm and fuzzy holiday cheer. If you're still young at heart, visit Santa's House to make sure the right presents end up under the tree.

Harris Theater for Music and Dance

205 E Randolph St
312.334.7777
PINK LINE to RANDOLPH

With all the performance venues in Chicago, it's hard to find one that's distinctive enough to take note of. However, the Harris Theater, with its prime location in the midst of Millennium Park, is an example of modern architecture and quality art at its finest. The non-profit theater hosts a variety of local dance, opera and theater in its stark, underground home. Its philanthropic mission adds to the mix of cultures it presents. **A**

Auditorium Theatre

50 E Congress Pkwy
312.922.2110
RED LINE to JACKSON

This theater owned by Roosevelt U. makes a valiant effort to compete with the grandiosity of other nearby theaters. The auditorium, glowing in gold and bronze, is designed in a way that eliminates bad seating, and the lobby is spacious enough for congregating before shows and during intermissions. Famous for its ballets, the theater also chooses to showcase works exposing Chicago diversity and culture in lieu of the standard mainstream musical. **B**

Buddy Guy's Legends

754 S Wabash Ave
312.427.1190
RED LINE to JACKSON

This 21-plus blues bar is stuck between being a legitimate, soulful music pad and a victim of hype. The bar's fame manages to bring in big names like John Mayer, but the Creole menu pricing will leave you singing your own blues. Reservations aren't accepted, which makes it difficult to just drop on by, even if you're willing to stand. There's no harm in taking a peek, but there are more authentic Chicago blues bars to check out first. **C+**

Chicago Public Library, Harold Washington Branch

400 S State St
312.747.4396
RED LINE to JACKSON

Even if you don't need a new book, visiting the Chicago Public Library is an adventure in itself. The massive ten-floor building is a downtown landmark and looks ancient, despite the fact that it opened in 1991. The library has a vast mix of resources, including books, periodicals, audiovisual material, a children's library and artwork throughout. Don't miss the airy ninth floor Winter Garden and Chicago history displays. **A**

LEFT: The Field Museum. DAVE SCHRIMPF
• **BELOW:** The Field Museum. DAVE SCHRIMPF

LOOP

Hostelling International Chicago

It might seem odd to stay in a hostel in a city blanketed with first-class

24 E Congress Pkwy
312.360.0300
RED LINE to JACKSON

hotels, but when you're young and on a budget, it may be viewed more as an adventure. The rooms are similar to college dorm rooms, and rates are extremely cheap. Luxuries are, of course, nonexistent. But, if you're on a cross-country escapade with friends, this simple establishment can serve as an appropriate headquarters. Recommended only for younger crowds. **B**

HotHouse

Home to the Center for International Performance and Exhibition, HotHouse

31 E Balboa Dr
312.362.9707
RED LINE to JACKSON

prides itself on showcasing a variety of artists from around the world. Part gallery, part performance stage and part club, this center has established itself as a cultural staple in Chicago, hosting around 800 events yearly. With praise from publications like the New York Times and Chicago Magazine, HotHouse is a Mecca for both under-exposed artists and those looking to expand their artistic tastes. **A**

Museum of Contemporary Photography

Columbia College's museum-in-residence is conveniently located on

600 S Michigan Ave
312.344.7104
RED LINE to JACKSON

Michigan Ave. and is worth a jaunt on the grand tour of the Loop. The gallery is small and stark, with rotating exhibits of modern photography, lectures and educational events. The art is very specialized, so if you're looking for classic works, you're out of luck. But it's good at what it does – presenting a showcase of underrepresented photographers. **B+**

Gene Siskel Film Center

Gene Siskel of Siskel and Ebert gave the Film Center of the Art Institute

164 N State St
312.846.2600
RED LINE to LAKE

of Chicago 'two thumbs up.' After his death, the center took his name and continued to show an array of independent, foreign and classic films. The building houses a café perfect for pre-movie treats and a gallery of movie memorabilia. The summer's top releases aren't to be found here, but the artsy viewer will enjoy the obscure selections. **A-**

Illinois State Museum Chicago Gallery

It's relatively unknown and out of the way, but the Illinois State Museum

100 W Randolph St
312.814.5322
RED LINE to LAKE

is worth a quick browse if you're in the area. Located on the James R. Thompson Center's second floor, this gallery rotates Illinois-related exhibits that showcase the state's culture, history and artisans. Mediums range from paintings and photography to wildlife and textiles. The local gem is a great diversion, but don't make a special trip for the hole-in-the-wall gallery. **B**

The Goodman Theatre

Take advantage of Chicago's theater scene and go to a show at

170 N Dearborn St
312.443.3800
RED LINE to LAKE

the Goodman Theatre, the oldest not-for-profit theater in the city. Since the 1920s, Chicago audiences have frequented this establishment, taking in a variety of shows created by various artists throughout the world. Ticket prices vary depending on the performance, but anyone who enjoys theater should venture on over to the Goodman. **A**

The Art Institute

The Art Institute is famous for a reason, and every visitor to Chicago should

111 S Michigan Ave
312.443.3600
RED LINE to MONROE

experience it at least once. Art gurus can absorb the masterworks of Monet, Renoir and Cezanne among others, but even those who know nothing about art at all can enjoy the Institute's massive collection. The price of admission is reasonable, and the wait is usually less than a few minutes, so make sure to add this to your must-see list. **A**

Chicago School of Massage Therapy

Work out those knots without working out your wallet. Slip away for 55

17 N State St
312.753.7990
RED LINE to WASHINGTON

minutes for the low price of $40 or less through some of Chicago's best massage therapist students. Expertise varies, but the training is good, and the service is professional. Indulge yourself, because you have little to loose and much-needed relaxation to gain. **A-**

TOP Merchandise Mart, Wacker Dr. COLETTE TAM
• **MIDDLE** Wacker Dr. COLETTE TAM • **BOTTOM** Wacker Dr. & LaSalle St. COLETTE TAM

Florodora

This boutique is far from Chicago's main shopping artery on Michigan Ave.,

330 S Dearborn St
312.212.8860
BLUE LINE to JACKSON

but its beautiful, unique clothes make it worth a detour. The interesting fabrics, bright colors and stunning dresses are a refreshing break from the chain stores that have devoured Chicago's downtown. The boutique is the essence of all that is feminine and flirty without being too trashy. **A**

Akira Shoes

Located near the Chicago River and just outside the shopping district of State

131 S Dearborn St
312.346.3034
BLUE LINE to MONROE

St., this little shoe shop is a fabulous find. The shelves are lined with the hottest brands and styles including Akira's own signature collection. However, along with the brand names come the brand-name prices. If you are on a budget, don't forget to check out the many hats, purses and jewelry scattered amongst the shoes. **A⁻**

Fabrile Gallery

The Fabrile Gallery is home to unique art, featuring items that range

224 S Michigan Ave
312.427.1510
BROWN LINE to ADAMS

from glass ornaments to ornate jewelry. While the items are eclectic and intriguing, the prices are usually high, so patrons should expect to just browse unless they are not on a strict budget. If nothing else, the gallery is a satisfying break after strolling through nearby Millennium Park. **B**

Poster Plus

If an afternoon at the Art Institute inspires you to cover your drab walls

200 S Michigan Ave
312.461.9277
BROWN LINE to ADAMS

with something more interesting, skip the pricey museum gift shop and venture across the street to Poster Plus. Browse through posters of every size or shop for kitschy Chicago souvenirs. At the entrance, look up – a huge fiberglass cow hangs upside down from the ceiling. It's left over from the famous 1999 Cows on Parade public-art project. **B⁺**

Iwan Ries

Have a taste for fine cigars? Iwan Ries offers over 100 different types

19 S Wabash Ave
312.372.1306
BROWN LINE to MADISON

in addition to its wide selection of pipes and pipe tobacco. Though you can't smoke your purchases in public, you'll find a place to savor a souvenir from a shop that just celebrated its 150th an-

Macy's on State Street

111 N. State St.
312.781.1000
RED LINE to WASHINGTON

Macy's on State St. is equal parts shopping haven and must-see Chicago holiday attraction. Formerly the flagship location for Marshall Field's, the store packs more than 100 years of history. Visitors come to Macy's in droves from late November to early January to view some of the best holiday displays the city has to offer, including the 45-foot Great Tree in the Walnut Room on the seventh floor. The second largest department store in the world, Macy's has a selection of apparel, accessories, home furnishings and gourmet culinary items that won't disappoint. The 28 Shop offers couture fashions, and Macy's even does dining well. Seven on State, a sophisticated food court, offers quick bites without the shopping mall feel, and The Walnut Room is a fine dining experience that affords wonderful views of the city. Don't miss this one while you're in the Windy City.

niversary in 2007. Be prepared to pay big – the expert craftsmanship doesn't come cheap. **B**

Books A Million

Sterile gray walls and soft elevator music greet customers at this chain bookstore. While the store does not quite compare to more chic chains like Barnes and Noble, any store that calls its members, 'millionaires' deserves a chance. Here, discounts are abundant and the large magazine and newspaper section deserves ample perusing. **B-**

144 S Clark St
312.857.0613
BROWN LINE to QUINCY

Coconuts Music and Movies

If you're looking to buy some cheap DVDs for a weekend couch marathon, try this bargain-priced store. On the second floor you will find all sorts of items geared towards those with college humor, such as funny calendars and stuffed characters from the show Family Guy. While the prices are right, the neon lights and palm tree carpeting are somewhat obnoxious. **C**

26 E Randolph St
312.606.0899
BROWN LINE to RANDOLPH

The Gallery 37 Store

This little gallery features art created by local high school students through

66 E Randolph St
312.744.7274
BROWN LINE to RANDOLPH

'After School Matters,' an organization providing teens with hands-on training in the arts and positive relationships with adults. While the prices are a bit high, the paintings, sculptures and furniture are beautiful and unique. If you spot something you like, be sure to look at the tag: You may be surprised to see that the artist is only 14 years old. **B+**

Rock Records

Right out of the alternative scene of Wrigleyville, this music and movie haven is a dream come true for anyone in search of something a little left of center. The prices are similar to leading chain stores, but inside the walls are plastered with vintage posters and cutouts reminiscent of the days before MTV, iPods, and MP3s. Despite the eclectic look, Rock Records also offers modern hits within its diverse inventory. **B+**

175 W Washington St
312.346.3489
BROWN LINE to WASHINGTON

ArchiCenter Shop

After touring Chicago's best architectural sites, stop by the Chicago Architecture Center's shop. The shelves are lined with quirky stationery, huge photo books of Chicago, colorful figurines and nostalgic Frank Lloyd Wright souvenirs. It's usually filled with

224 S Michigan Ave
312.922.3432
PINK LINE to ADAMS

tourists fresh from the architectural tour of the city, but anyone can browse the shop for great gift ideas and Chicago mementos. Nothing is a steal, but the funky selection is worth a stop. **A-**

Symphony Store

Arrived a bit too early to the orchestra? Take a look at – and listen to

220 S Michigan Ave
312.294.3345
PINK LINE to ADAMS

– the variety of trinkets at the Symphony Store. The extensive collection of recordings is sure to have something to please your ear. For the music fanatic in your life, the store has great gifts: apparel, decorative items and stationery, all freckled with decorative treble clefs and quarter notes. **A-**

Graham Crackers Comic Books

Any comic book buff will love the variety of merchandise at Graham

77 E Madison St
312.629.1810
PINK LINE to MADISON

Crackers. In addition to trade publications, the store is stocked with back issues of older comics, action figures and, of course, Marvel comics to peak your interest. If you have any questions, the staff is knowledgeable and easy to talk to. **A**

Pay Half

Although it has its faults, like the sub par fitting rooms and the unfriendly

12 N Wabash Ave
312.364.9087
PINK LINE to MADISON

staff, Pay Half has great deals on trendy clothes for all occasions. Most women's tops run around $12, and jeans are about $25. The men's clothing is slightly more expensive, but still cheaper than most department stores. As you browse, keep in mind that you will get what you pay for. **C+**

Books in the City

Books in the City is a hot spot for DePaul, Roosevelt and Columbia students on

545 S State St
312.291.1111
RED LINE to JACKSON

the prowl for apparel, textbooks and school supplies in Chicago. If you're not a student, there's still a fun selection of home décor, but the selection is a bit meager. As is typical of most college bookstores, items here can be pretty pricey. **B-**

Brudno Art Supply

Brudno Art Supply is a valuable resource for local artists and college

29 E Balboa Dr
312.787.0030
RED LINE to JACKSON

students. Choose from a selection of drafting,

ABOVE: Polish Constitution Day Parade. COLETTE TAM • **LEFT:** Polish Constitution Day Parade. COLETTE TAM

LOOP

painting, drawing and photography supplies sure to meet any artistic needs. If you don't find what you're looking for in the store, Brudno has a catalogue with 20,000 products you can get delivered to the store or shipped directly to your home. Prices can be steep, but that's not uncommon in art supply stores. **A**

TOP South Water Kitchen, 225 N. Wabash Ave. COLETTE TAM • **MIDDLE** South Water Kitchen, 225 N. Wabash Ave. COLETTE TAM • **BOTTOM** South Water Kitchen, 225 N. Wabash Ave. COLETTE TAM

Cartridge World

Running low on ink? Bring your cartridge into Cartridge World. Rather

27 E Harrison St
312.428.4349
RED LINE to JACKSON

than throwing it out, you can have most major brands refilled in less than 10 minutes and for up to 50 percent less than the cost of a new cartridge. With this earth-friendly approach to recycling ink and toner, Cartridge World may very well be the future of the printing industry. **A**

Central Camera Co.

If you're a shutterbug, avoid this shop until the end of your trip. It's

230 S Wabash Ave
312.427.5580
RED LINE to JACKSON

heaven for the photography-obsessed, and you'll be quick to empty your wallet on all the goodies they have in stock. The store is long and narrow, and once you're inside, it may take days to find your way out. **A**

Loopy Yarns

Knit one, purl two. Despite being in the middle of the South Loop, this charming

719 S State St
312.583.9276
RED LINE to JACKSON

yarn shop feels like it belongs in a small town. The storefront isn't big, but it's packed from floor to ceiling with colorful yarns, needles of all sizes and knitting guidebooks. Inside, customers work on their own projects as employees help out between classes. Prices reflect the distinct nature of the shop, so dropping $9 on a skein isn't unusual. **A-**

Powell's Bookstore

Those who loathe Borders and crave a more authentic book shopping

828 S Wabash Ave
312.341.0748
RED LINE to JACKSON

experience should go to Powell's Bookstore. Venture downstairs to browse through shelves packed with every type of book imaginable, from contemporary fiction to oriental philosophy. The prices are incredibly low because the store buys most books as 'remainders' — those books that publishers have overstocked or don't need anymore. This store is great for perusing, and

true booklovers may lose themselves for hours between the dim stacks. **A-**

Prairie Avenue Bookshop

Even if the only architect you know is Frank Lloyd Wright, the Prairie Avenue Bookshop can give you a jumpstart on building your base of knowledge. Focused solely on architecture, this shop has everything from rare, out-of-print photos to huge coffee table books. It's the perfect place for someone on an architecture kick or for someone wanting to learn more about the Arts and Crafts movement [and willing to drop some cash on a thick volume]. **B+**

418 S Wabash Ave
312.922.8311
RED LINE to JACKSON

Utrecht Art Supplies

The passionate artist can find enough paints, brushes and canvases here to bolster their creative juices. The employees are knowledgeable about all of the ins and outs of oils, watercolors and temperas. With low prices, this store is a great choice for local art students. However, if you're just experimenting with art, you can probably find more useful supplies at a basic craft store. **B+**

332 S Michigan Ave
312.922.7565
RED LINE to JACKSON

Warehouse Liquors

Whether you're a wine aficionado or just looking for a drink to kick back with, Warehouse Liquors is a great place to shop. The store houses a wide selection of wine, liquor and beer to meet a variety of tastes. Although it may seem a bit overwhelming at first glance, don't be threatened by the sophisticated atmosphere. If you have questions, the staff is quite knowledgeable and very friendly. **A**

634 S Wabash Ave
312.663.1850
RED LINE to JACKSON

Zanzara Jewelry

In this hard-to-find jewelry shop, you will be dazzled with pieces made from pearls, crystal, turquoise and glass. These gaudy accessories are pretty cheap, but also a bit cheap looking. If you are looking for a big piece of jew-

333 S State St
312.431.1220
RED LINE to JACKSON

elry that will make a boring outfit stand out, you can definitely find a good necklace or bracelet. **B**

Atrium Mall

Housed in the James R. Thompson government building, the Atrium offers conveniences for the worker on the run, though no added delights. An abundance of fast food restaurants make up the majority of businesses, ideal for an employee's quick lunch. Remaining establishments include low cost clothing and shoe stores, a Post Office and a newsstand. The downtown employee will appreciate the convenience, but there is no real draw for the rest of the population. **C**

100 W Randolph St
312.346.0777
RED LINE to LAKE

Chicago Sports & Novelty

Any Bulls, Sox, Cubs or Bears fan will be happy to pay a visit to Chicago Sports. The store offers a wide selection of sports apparel and Chicago-specific gear sure to please both Chicagoans and visitors. Its convenient location on Michigan Ave. makes it hard to miss, and if you can't find what you're looking for in the store, a quick visit to the Web site will be sure to find you a great purchase. **B**

328 N Michigan Ave
312.641.6106
RED LINE to LAKE

Illinois Artisans Shop

Local artists shine at the Illinois Artisans Shop, which showcases the best handicrafts from the Illinois Artisans Program. These pottery, textiles, paintings, and knick-knacks have a unique flair that often represents the Chicago lifestyle. The store is perfect for a unique gift, a distinctive souvenir or a quality work of art that you couldn't find at a local mall. Prices range from reasonable mementos to pricey pieces with something for most every budget. **A-**

100 W Randolph St
312.814.5321
RED LINE to LAKE

KaBloom

Although small, KaBloom is a cool place to visit to pick up a bouquet of flowers sure to brighten any day. Just off Michigan

75 E Wacker Dr
312.726.4717
RED LINE to LAKE

LOOP

Wacker Dr. & LaSalle St. COLETTE TAM

Ave. and directly across from the Chicago River, this shop is in a great location for any Chicago urbanite looking to add a little color to an apartment or spice up an office space. Don't know what you're looking for? Don't worry; the florists are more than willing to help. **B+**

Mali Jewelry and Accessories

Mali Jewelry and Accessories houses truly unique jewelry and ornate

204 N Michigan Ave
312.263.0326
RED LINE to LAKE

handbags with moderate price tags. The jewelry is handcrafted using materials like semi-precious stones, freshwater pearls and even Swarovski crystals. If you're lucky enough to drop in during one of their sales, you are guaranteed to find a great deal. Overall, the helpful staff and convenient location make Mali a good stop on any Michigan Ave. shopping trip. **B**

Temptation II

Temptation II offers a wide range of accessories, including belts,

316 N Michigan Ave
312.920.0299
RED LINE to LAKE

bags, sunglasses, jewelry and even scrunchies. If you're looking for an inexpensive little something to add to an ensemble, this is a great stop. The quality is mediocre, however, and some items are reminiscent of a rainbow-colored accessory shop geared toward preteens dying to spend their monthly allowance. **C**

That's Our Bag

If you're looking for great deals on quality wallets, handbags, briefcases,

200 N Michigan Ave
312.984.3510
RED LINE to LAKE

luggage and more, visit That's Our Bag. The store is full of discounted merchandise by Ameribag, Timbuk 2, Samsonite and more. The overwhelmed sales staff is a noticeable flaw, but if you're willing to overlook that, you will leave the store with some great buys. **C+**

Bakers Shoes

If your wardrobe has been pleading with you for a pick-me-up, don't be

133 S State St
312.641.1203
RED LINE to MONROE

surprised if your feet lead you into this accessory enclave. A rainbow of flashy shoes — heels and flats alike — beg customers to be taken out for a night on the town. If you're more accustomed to a comfortable style, Bakers might not be your top choice, but the extensive sale selection may offer something that will catch even your eye. **B**

Designs by Rosa Inc.

If you have a loved one who you want to send flowers to in Chicago, call

140 S Wabash Ave
312.759.0607
RED LINE to MONROE

Designs by Rosa. At this family-run business, you will get the expertise of a florist who will make sure that your bouquet is made from quality, fresh flowers. Flowers can be ordered online or on location for delivery. Prices run high, but the floral creations are beautiful. **A-**

Nordstrom Rack

If you don't have tons of money to spend but like to appear otherwise, get acquainted with Nordstrom Rack. All the quality of Nordstrom merchandise at half the price, this department store offers customers racks of clothing, business attire, lingerie, shoes, handbags, jewelry and more. Although it's busy, don't let the crowds of people deter you. **B**

24 N State St
312.377.5500
RED LINE to MONROE

Reckless Records

True music junkies will appreciate the selection of vintage records, CDs, DVDs, cassettes and more at Reckless Records. With its edgy yet diverse vibe, this store attracts all types of music lovers, and the staff really seems to know its stuff. An extra bonus: Reckless will buy or trade any music or movies you're looking to exchange for something new or for a little extra cash. **A⁻**

26 E Madison St
312.795.0878
RED LINE to MONROE

Target

While Chicago has a vast shopping scene, sometimes all you want is a one-stop shop. For those times when you can't afford to spend the time or money scavenging State St. or Michigan Ave., head over to Target. Affordable and convenient, Target is easily one of Chicago's favorite chains. Whether it's music, accessories, clothes or furniture, you can always find something within this gargantuan store. **B**

1154 S Clark St
312.212.6300
RED LINE to ROOSEVELT

Filene's Basement

At Filene's, you will find racks of fashion's best finds at fashion's lowest prices. There are items from designers like Marc Jacobs, Calvin Klein and the Barney's collection for at least 50% off the original price. In the overwhelmingly-large store, you can also find great savings on shoes, jewelry, home goods and outerwear. Although it takes a while to find a quality item in the crowded racks, at least you'll leave with enough money for lunch. **A**

1 N State St
312.553.1055
RED LINE to WASHINGTON

LOOP

ABOVE: Oysy, 888 S. Michigan Ave. COLETTE TAM • **LEFT:** Oysy, 888 S. Michigan Ave. COLETTE TAM

NEAR SOUTH SIDE

IT'S THE MUSEUMS THAT DOMINATE

Ethnic culture beckons in the background but it's the museums that dominate in the Near South Side. This area has been shifting from a blue collar neighborhood to home of the wealthy and back in a near constant cycle. If it's booming culinary scene is any indication, this place is currently on an upswing. Gaze at mummies or meet Sue [the most complete Tyrannosaurus Rex skeleton] at the Field Museum of Natural History, where you should also check out the infamous and massive exhibit on evolution. Fly through space on a virtual tour of the cosmos in the Adler Planetarium. Maybe even march with the penguins, swim with the dolphins and beluga whales or play with the sea otters at the John G. Shedd Aquarium, the largest in the world. The Widow Clarke House is the oldest in the city and can be found among many other monuments to Chicago's elite of the 19th century in the Prairie Avenue Historical District. There's plenty to do outside museums though. Cheer on the NFL's Chicago Bears at Soldier Field or look at the beautiful Tiffany stained glass at the Second Presbyterian Church.

TO EAT

Gioco

Gioco, with its rich colors and authentic traditional Italian influences, offers an extensive wine list in addition to an award-winning menu. Highlights include Truffle Scented Scallops, Buffalo Ricotta Gnocchi and hand-made pastas. The restaurant takes its cue from its South Loop neighborhood location's sordid history: the back of the building is a 'speakeasy'

1312 S Wabash Ave
312.939.3870
GREEN LINE to ROOSEVELT

where one might expect to run into Al Capone himself. **A**

Grace O'Malley's

The classic Irish pub's exterior is as welcoming as the restaurant's friendly service and great food. Whether you are stopping in for a drink or a hearty bite to eat, this restaurant offers a variety of everyone's favorites, like onion rings, chicken tenders and a selection of grilled burgers. The restaurant also offers tempting sandwich options as well as

1416 S Michigan Ave
312.588.1800
GREEN LINE to ROOSEVELT

more than a dozen entrees, like Fish 'n' Chips or the Irish Blue Cheese-Crusted Pork Loin. **A**

Howie's

	1310 S Wabash Ave
	312.461.0944
	GREEN LINE to ROOSEVELT

Howie's, with its friendly staff and slightly mishmashed décor, is reminiscent of the mom and pop diners prevalent a few decades ago. The venue, which still uses the phrase 'soda pop,' packs charm, and diners can play arcade games or watch television. Howie's serves breakfast all day, and menu items are inexpensive. Enter at your own risk, as the smell of French fries filling the room will weaken any resolve against great diner food. **B**

Kroll's South Loop

	1736 S Michigan Ave
	312.235.1400
	GREEN LINE to ROOSEVELT

This South Loop diner has been serving good ol' American grub by the plateful since 1931. The décor features White-Sox and Bears paraphernalia and a long row of beer flags hanging from the ceiling. Each large-portioned entrée comes with a selection of classic side dishes ranging from whipped potatoes to applesauce. **C**

Ma & I

	1234 S Michigan Ave
	312.663.1234
	GREEN LINE to ROOSEVELT

Ma & I's slogan is a 'Thai dining experience,' and with the classy décor that inspires an intimate mood, it's clear that an experience will be had. While it's better to dine at Ma & I, it also offers delivery for the unfortunate few that can't make it in personally. Also, don't let the chic scene deter you – Ma & I is priced so that anyone can afford a dining experience. **A**

South Coast

	1700 S Michigan Ave
	312.662.1700
	GREEN LINE to ROOSEVELT

New on the Chicago scene, this sushi hot-spot is a great place to enjoy a delicious meal in the city. With an uptown swanky atmosphere accented by dimly-lit tables and dark navy décor, this restaurant boasts an impressive selection of sushi, as well as an assortment of appetizers, soups, salads and entrees like the Seared Tuna or Rib Eye. Prices are reasonable, with sushi roles ranging from $6-$13. **A**

The Chicago Firehouse Restaurant

	1401 S Michigan Ave
	312.786.1401
	GREEN LINE to ROOSEVELT

Built in 1905, this yellow-brick firehouse served Chicago's first families living on Prairie Avenue. Now, it's a first-rate restaurant serving savory steaks and seafood to Chicago's elite. During lunch, sleek BMWs pull up to the curb for valet service. The restaurant offers a range of steaks, and, for an additional $3, you can get your steak crusted [try the blue cheese]. For about $40, you can relish the taste of cedar plank roasted Dover sole. **A**

Panozzo's Italian Market

1303 S. Michigan Ave.
312.356.9966
GREEN LINE to ROOSEVELT

This deli's motto says it all: 'Eat. Drink. Live. Italian.' Perched on a corner near the Museum Campus, this little store feels authentically Italian. Customers are serenaded by the gentle strains of the accordion music as the tempting smell of basil and fresh bread wafts through the air. Even if you initially order only a small piece of lasagna, the friendly deli clerks, in true Italian style, will persuade you to eat more. The delicious sandwiches, ranging from $5 to $8, are a perfect lunch choice. There is no seating in the deli, but the lush lawns of Grant Park are just steps away. On the way out, pick up a baguette, a jar of marinara sauce, and some fresh mozzarella to create your own Italian delicacy at home.

Zapatista Cantina

This cantina on the Loop's South Side offers everything from traditional

1307 S Wabash Ave
312.435.1307
GREEN LINE to ROOSEVELT

fajitas and quesadillas to filet mignon. The outdoor patio is filled with flowers and is a great place to sit when the weather's fine, but inside the atmosphere is just as inviting. The menu also includes an extensive list of tequilas, and the breakfast menu's entrees will only cost you a five dollar bill. **A**

Carolina Carmel

This hip dessert bar allows patrons to indulge in tasty pastries while

1511 S State St
312.922.5007
RED LINE to ROOSEVELT

feeling as though they are seated in a trendy nightclub. On the weekends, Carolina Caramel turns into just that, with non-alcoholic beverages, sweet treats and a DJ that accepts requests. While the cake can get a bit pricey, the portions are hefty. This should definitely be a stop for those with a sweet tooth. **A**

Opera

Opera has a reputation for being a fancy, gourmet, Asian-fusion restaurant

1301 S Wabash Ave
312.461.0161
RED LINE to ROOSEVELT

for those of discerning taste, but don't believe it. While the appetizers and desserts are usually quite good, the entrées often range in quality from mediocre to terrible. It's easy to spend $100 on a dinner for two, and if you're going to spend that kind of cash, you might as well find a restaurant more deserving of your money. **C**

TO PLAY

12th Street Beach

Located at Northerly Island, 12th Street Beach is the perfect place to

1400 S Lynn White Dr
312.742.7529
GREEN LINE to ROOSEVELT

MAKING TRACKS ACROSS THE CITY: 'EL' TOURS

BY ELISABETH KILPATRICK

If you've ever ridden on the 'El,' your experience might have bordered on the mundane. You squeezed into a crowded car, got jostled all the way downtown and rushed off the train and out of the station. You may have even grumbled about the mysterious between-station delays or the less-than-desirable clientele (or smell). Well, it's time to take a deep breath and meet Chicago's transit system on much more friendly terms.

There's no better way to do it than to take the Chicago History Museum's 'Life Along the 'El'' tour, offered the first Sunday of every month. As one of the museum's four monthly tours, the Brown Line tour offers up a chance to see a new side of the city's train system. Sunday afternoons are the perfect time to enjoy Chicago's sights – and the 'El' – at a decidedly relaxed pace. The Brown Line itself, dubbed by many locals as the cleanest and prettiest of Chicago's seven train lines, helps the tour transcend from another daily commute into a leisurely, educational sightseeing trip.

Shepherding a group of tour-takers around the 'El' while giving them a sampling of Chicago culture takes patience and a thorough knowledge of the city. Luckily, Chicago History Museum's tour guides know their stuff. Groups can range from two or three people in the winter months to 25 or so in warmer weather, and lifelong locals appear as often as visitors. Tourists and residents alike are bound to walk away from the tour armed with more than a few new tidbits about

spend sunny Chicago afternoons. Unwind with a book on the beach or jump into the cool waters of Lake Michigan. A bike path and walkway also run through here, but if you're ready to get out of the sun, Adler Planetarium and Windy City Cafe are just steps away. Before you leave, though, watch boats set sail and dock at nearby Burnham Harbor. **A-**

Adler Planetarium

Space junkies unite at the Adler Planetarium to watch shows highlighting

1300 S Lake Shore Dr
312.922.7827
GREEN LINE to ROOSEVELT

the wonders of outer space. Those still yearning for more can venture outside to the Doane Observatory, where they are invited to peer through the lens of the largest public telescope in Chicago. Other highlights at the Adler include Rainbow Lobby, Sundial Plaza and America's Courtyard. General admission is $10 or less, but check the Web site for information on free admission days. **A**

Chicago Women's Park and Gardens

After touring the Prairie Avenue homes on a nice day, the Women's Park

1827 S Indiana Ave
312.744.1373
GREEN LINE to ROOSEVELT

and Gardens is an easy and relaxing break. Right in the midst of the historic Glessner and Clarke Houses, this garden commemorates some of Chicago's most famous women. A fountain, fragrant herbs, a rose garden, vegetables and rows of bright flowers make up this lovely city haven. **B**

Glessner House Museum

In the midst of Chicago's Prairie District, the Glessner House is a prime

1800 S Prairie Ave
312.326.1480
GREEN LINE to ROOSEVELT

example of late 19th century architecture and the site of a fun, historical tour. The home contains period artifacts from the Arts and Crafts era in which it was built. Go on a spring day to take advantage of the gardens and courtyard and take

NEAR SOUTH SIDE

both the 'El' system and Chicago.

The tour guides have a cheeky sense of humor, too. Greg Borzo, one of Chicago History Museum's eight 'Life Along the 'El'' guides, shared this 1897 quote from the New York Academy of Medicine about Chicago's 'El' trains, eliciting a chuckle from the group: 'The electrified elevated train system prevents normal development of children, throws convalescing patients into relapse, causes insomnia, exhaustion, hysteria, paralysis, meningitis and deafness.' [It has yet to be proven that this isn't true.]

Chicago's history is like the plot of a guilty-pleasure beach read: full of relationships, tinged with secrets and intrigue, and always revolving around money. After 115 years in existence, the 'El' train is literally the ideal conduit for exploring the city and its culture. The Brown Line's 10 miles and 28 stations provide a conversation starter into how

1892's World's Fair jumpstarted 'El' construction, why Chicago opted for elevated tracks instead of subways and which team played for decades at Chicago's Wrigley Field [here's a hint: it's not who you think].

There's a reason that so many Brown Line stations, from Kimball to Kedzie, are named after real estate developers [you can pretend you already knew that — just one of the many bits of cocktail-party trivia that the tour provides]. 'The 'El' and the neighborhoods grew together, hand in glove,' says Borzo. He's right. Coasting up through the northwest neighborhoods in the city along the Brown Line, it's beautiful to see the tiny rows of shops and restaurants that dot the blocks surrounding each 'El' station, spreading out as the blocks get farther away from the train line. The each station has its own particular flavor, whether it's the tree-lined quiet of Rockwell, the European-inflected boulevard at Irving Park or the

the combination tour to see Chicago's oldest building, the nearby Clarke House. **A**

National Vietnam Veterans' Art Museum

A surprisingly well-presented and touching gallery, the National Vietnam

| 1801 S Indiana Ave |
| 312.326.0270 |
| **GREEN LINE to ROOSEVELT** |

Veterans' Art Museum is home to art in various mediums created by Vietnam veterans. With a haunting dog tag sculpture in the main entrance called the Above & Beyond memorial, the first step inside will make you both appreciative and sad. This South Loop gallery is basic, understated and industrial, with an additional shop and café. **B+**

Northerly Island

When you live in the windy city, large expanses of green grass are hard to

| 1400 S Lynn White Dr |
| 312.745.2910 |
| **GREEN LINE to ROOSEVELT** |

come by, save for the 90-acre peninsula that is Northerly Island. Enjoy a picnic here after visiting the Planetarium or before catching a concert at the newly-constructed Charter Pavilion. Or, play a game of Frisbee while basking in the grandeur of the Chicago skyline. This is a perfect spot to spend a summer afternoon away from the crowded beaches and bustle of the Magnificent Mile. **A**

Coliseum Park

If you find yourself out and about along Museum Campus looking for

| 1466 S Wabash Ave |
| 312.747.7640 |
| **ORANGE LINE to ROOSEVELT** |

something fun for younger kids, check out this new park in the South Loop. Completely fenced in so little ones are safe from the hustle and bustle of downtown traffic, this colorful, kid-friendly playground provides Chicagoans a place to take a break as they plan their next adventure. **A−**

Shedd Aquarium

Dive into a great half-day adventure at the Shedd Aquarium and catch

| 1200 S Lake Shore Dr |
| 312.939.2426 |
| **RED LINE to ROOSEVELT** |

boisterous crush of businesses at Kimball. Spending a few moments looking out the window as the train travels to each station confirms one of the big truths about Chicago: it really is the city of neighborhoods.

One potential caveat to the tour is the unpredictability of the group that operates Chicago's 'El' trains itself, the Chicago Transit Authority. Ongoing construction on several of the train lines doesn't always make it easy to navigate the train system, and the occasional station closure can pop up. On one recent Sunday afternoon, the Brown Line was closed without warning from the Loop up to the Near North Side. No matter, though: tour guides handle these snags with quick thinking. The usual Brown Line tour was quickly adapted into a walking tour of the 'El' train's history in the Loop, followed by the normal 'El' tour along the operating

northern part of the Brown Line. The unexpected can even be part of the fun. While walking around the Loop, hidden gems, such as a chance to stand where the first 'El' station was built, made up for not starting the tour in its usual location.

Those who find that the Brown Line tour only piques their interest for more 'El'-related history are in luck. The additional Chicago History Museum 'Life Along the El'' tours all offer a different glimpse of the city. The Green Line South tour takes place on second Sundays, and in some months, there's a Green Line West tour on third Sundays and a Blue Line tour on fourth Sundays. And if you're a little skittish about taking all those sharp turns on the elevated tracks, rest easy. After serving 10 billion customers over the years with only a handful of accidents, the 'El' is the safest mode of transportation around.

glimpses of sea creatures from all over the world. You don't even have to be a fish lover to enjoy the cute sea otters and entertaining dolphin show. Watch out for large school groups and rambunctious kids, though; the shows and cafeteria can get overwhelming at times. **A**

The Field Museum of Natural History

What can be said about this world-renowned tourist hot spot? Housing one

| 1400 S Lake Shore Dr |
| 312.922.9410 |
| **RED LINE to ROOSEVELT** |

of the most remarkable collections of artifacts and exhibits, the museum is a visual tour through the past, without the bore of a high school history class. Walking in, you are greeted by Sue the T-Rex, worthy of the $7-$12 admission price alone. 'Visiting' exhibits should also remind Chicagoans that the museum isn't only a tourist spot. **A**

TO SHOP

Downtown Pets

This little pet store is rather dark and has that particularly unpleasant

| 1619 S Michigan Ave |
| 312.360.1619 |
| **GREEN LINE to ROOSEVELT** |

pet odor, even though it is mostly occupied by rows of saltwater and freshwater fish tanks. This is not the place to get a rhinestone collar and coat for little Tinkerbell, but basic pet supplies are abundant. Also, there is a large selection of rawhide dog treats. **C**

Heelz

Heelz offers the ultimate shopping experience for shoe lovers: friendly

| 69 E 16th St |
| 312.235.0467 |
| **GREEN LINE to ROOSEVELT** |

service, plush ottomans and, most importantly, rows of exquisite, breath-taking Italian shoes. The shoe-lined walls are a mosaic of beautiful florals, wild animal prints and metallics. Located on a gentrified South Loop side street, the store doesn't attract much walk-in traffic; its clientele is mostly in-the-know Chicago fashionistas. Casual shoe-shoppers beware: the prices range from $100 to over $1000. **A**

House of Sole

Hand-selected shoes and handbags are tastefully displayed in this modern

| 1237 S Michigan Ave |
| 312.834.0909 |
| **GREEN LINE to ROOSEVELT** |

European shoe boutique. Because the merchandise comes from interesting countries like Italy and Spain, everything has a unique twist to its design. But remember that the quality comes with a price, so be prepared to spend at least $100. **A**

Laughing Iguana Inc.

The Laughing Iguana is in an unlikely location in the south of Chicago, but this

| 1247 S Wabash Ave |
| 312.987.0995 |
| **GREEN LINE to ROOSEVELT** |

should not deter you from checking out its wide array of eclectic products. With bohemian-style clothing, good quality jewelry and a large gift section, The Laughing Iguana is worth a visit. The products are a bit pricey, but the sales rack will fit nicely with any budget. **B**

Paragon Book Gallery

Perhaps the reason Paragon is called a 'gallery' is because it's

| 1507 S Michigan Ave |
| 312.663.5155 |
| **GREEN LINE to ROOSEVELT** |

not quite a library and it's not quite a bookstore. Instead, it's a fusion of both. The Gallery houses an impressive collection of texts centered on every aspect of Asian culture. Open to the public for anyone who's just looking to browse, some of the books are also for sale. However, because many of them are highly-valued works, they're pricey. **C+**

Flaunt

Flaunt, located on a gentrified South Loop side street flanked by

| 75 E 16th St |
| 312.360.1000 |
| **RED LINE to ROOSEVELT** |

an upscale shoe store and beauty salon, is the perfect place to go if you are in need of a major makeover [and have some serious cash to drop]. In addition to fashion advice, owner Kim Turner offers image consultation, trunk shows and fitness seminars. This boutique mainly focuses on fashionable business attire. **B**

GRAFFITI

Named one of Business Week's 'up and coming' neighborhoods of 2007, East Garfield Park was once known for its vacant lots and deteriorating conditions, traces of which can still be seen. Riots in 1968 left many buildings burned and unusable; businesses left and residents fled. The area remained largely unchanged in the decades that followed. Now, due to its proximity to downtown and access to multiple mass transit lines, the area is seeing increased property values and new construction.

Photograph by Rachel Swenie

WEST

NEAR WEST SIDE

CHEAP MEXICAN FOOD AND CLASSIC FLEA MARKET BUYS

A culinary safari and many other delights lie in the Near West Side. The West Loop was once a sea of warehouses and industry but it has since transformed into one of Chicago's must see areas. Many of the city's hottest art galleries line the streets while posh, pricey restaurants and clubs light up at night. Union Station is here and Oprah too, at least her Harpo Studios where the show is shot. Maxwell St., where Chicago Blues began and a street market thrived, is also in the neighborhood. Much of that flavor has been lost due to rising housing costs but a visit to the New Maxwell St. Market on Sunday mornings still offers up cheap Mexican food and classic flea market buys. Little Italy, the birthplace of the Chicago-style pizza, beckons from Taylor St. Greektown on Halsted St. brims with restaurants and bars, many open 24 hours. The annual parade celebrates the Greek heritage but is there any better testament to a culture than a flaming piece of cheese? Afterwards, a trip to The United Center, home base for the Chicago Bulls and Black-hawks, offers a raucous night of sports and screaming for all.

TO EAT

G and G Restaurant

321 S Jefferson St
312.427.8226
BLUE LINE to CLINTON

Located just south of Union Station, G and G is the perfect place to satisfy an 'on-the-go' appetite. Almost every conceivable option is available, from omelets and donuts to fried chicken and home-made tamales. Nearly every item on the menu is priced under $5. Top off a filling meal with a milkshake, and you will walk away completely satisfied. **B+**

Lou Mitchell's

565 W Jackson Blvd
312.939.3111
BLUE LINE to CLINTON

Groovy booths and a bustling wait staff give this breakfast and lunch center its Hollywood prestige. Featured in several movies – including Ali – Lou's is the quintessential Chicago diner. Its specialties include fresh-squeezed orange juice, ice-cold melons, and double-yoked egg entrees. A 'Milk Dud' pancake is even available for kids or the otherwise sugar inclined. Serving the community at the same location since 1923, Lou's doesn't disappoint in

Chez Joel

1119 W. Taylor St.
312.226.6479
BLUE LINE to RACINE

This French bistro holds its own in a neighborhood dominated by Italian cuisine. Named after chef and owner Joe Kazouini, this sunny restaurant has become a critic's darling because of its exceptional service and great food. Entrees range from $15 to $25, but the food proves itself worthy of the price. Favorites of local patrons include steak frites [steak with fries], coq au vin [rooster with wine] and bouillabaisse [a classic fish stew from the port of Marseille, France], as well as apple tart, a smoked salmon appetizer and duck leg confit. Special care goes into making the meal enjoyable, including the plate presentation. While some other Little Italy restaurants bring Italy to Chicago, Chez Joel transports patrons to France. Talk about culture shock.

its advertisement as 'the best breakfast place on the planet.' **A**

Manny's Coffee Shop & Deli

Family-owned since 1942, Manny's Deli is one of few relics left over from the once thriving West Loop Jewish community. Manny's Deli is cafeteria dining – a bit unexpected for a restaurant that has been visited by many politicians. Grab a fiberglass tray, stand in line and watch as your sandwich is made in front of you. As Manny's is both a deli and a pseudo-historical landmark, expect a crowd. **B+**

1141 S Jefferson St
312.939.2855
BLUE LINE to CLINTON

West Loop Café

The macaroni and cheese colored stucco of the West Loop Café sets the

601 W Adams St
312.993.0222
BLUE LINE to CLINTON

taste buds in motion, and the delicious momentum doesn't stop at the door. Boasting a variety of flavors, the café serves food for any time of the day at any price range. Its healthy smoothies are well loved, and the marinated chicken sandwich also adds a new spin on a classic recipe. The café is open every day, except Saturday, from 7 a.m. until late afternoon. **A**

Moretti's

Sports fans flock to this casual dining spot that serves up barbecue and Italian dishes. Drink specials Tuesday through Thursday and free shuttle service to the United Center make this sporty restaurant an excellent alternative to tailgating before Blackhawks and Bulls games. Order up some baby back ribs and

1645 W Jackson St
312.850.0208
BLUE LINE to MEDICAL CENTER

LEFT Conte di Savoia, 1438 W. Taylor St. SARA STUBBLEFIELD • **ABOVE** Conte di Savoia, 1438 W. Taylor St. SARA STUBBLEFIELD

RIGHT: National Italian-American Sports Hall of Fame, 1431 W. Taylor St. SARA STUBBLEFIELD
• **BELOW:** National Italian-American Sports Hall of Fame, 1431 W. Taylor St. SARA STUBBLEFIELD

pizza, play a little pool or darts and then enjoy the game. **B**

Bar Louie

Friendly conversation and the light smell of beer waft out to the street,

> 1321 W Taylor St
> 312.633.9393
> **BLUE LINE to RACINE**

welcoming any who pass by the thick black over-hang of Bar Louie. A franchise bar, Bar Louie on Taylor St. offers the same mosaic-filled décor and soft lamp lighting as other locations, but it also offers unique dishes such as tortellini, macaroni and cheese, and crab cakes. Bar Louie accommodates groups of two to twenty, making it a casual spot for groups of any size. **B+**

Caffe la Scala

The cozy, carpeted dining room, rich wood, stain-glass accents and

> 626 S Racine Ave
> 312.421.7262
> **BLUE LINE to RACINE**

really generous portions make Caffe la Scala the perfect place to stuff yourself – and possibly lull yourself to sleep. Fill up with meatball Panini, caprese salad, white fish Vesuvio and chicken marsala. Dessert options include tiramisu, cannoli and tartufo. The typical crowd is a mix of UIC students, neighborhood regulars and United Center goers. Make a reservation for dinner so you are sure to get a table. **A-**

Scafuri Bakery

Trays of cookies and pastries displayed in glass cases invite passersby to

> 1337 W Taylor St
> 312.733.8881
> **BLUE LINE to RACINE**

peer in, but the smells of freshly-baked bread, apple strudel and pizzas cooling will keep a crowd inside for quite a while. The traditional white tile floor and a picture of a large Italian family on the back wall are as welcoming as the service. The store owner Annette takes care of

Café Ciao

939 W. Madison St.
312.850.2426
BLUE LINE to UIC-HALSTED

Open for less than two years, Café Ciao has gone a long way to establish itself in the West Loop community. This little corner of the world is certainly distinct. 'You can get a European meal and a glass of wine in the middle of the day, and just sit and linger,' said owner Julie Chung. The café draws people from all walks of life: college students, local residents and professionals. Nightly events such as wine and beer tastings, dance lessons, movies and live music are offered here. Chung looks forward to the addition of a karaoke system. The moderately-priced food items range from Panini sandwiches to flan and tiramisu.

her customers like family, but only if they listen to her advice to treat themselves. **A**

Stanley's on Racine

Opened in late 2006, Stanley's on Racine seems a bit out of place in its new neighborhood. Lack of drafts on tap and domestic macrobrews don't attract too many sports fans, but ample seating and a nice outdoor beer garden indicate that there is potential for this affordably priced eatery. In time, Stanley's should turn into one of the top neighborhood bars in the area. **B−**

324 S Racine Ave
312.433.0007
BLUE LINE to RACINE

Sweet Maple Café

The bright exterior of Sweet Maple Café soon gives way to a rustic dining room and the mix of UIC students and families who frequent this popular brunch spot. All dishes are under $8, and though the lunch menu may look appealing, nothing can compare to Sweet Maple's breakfast. Sweet Maple is best known for its omelets and biscuits, but it also offers grits, beef hash and eggs cooked to order. **A**

1339 W Taylor St
312.433.0007
BLUE LINE to RACINE

Taylor Made Pizza

This low-key pizza joint offers great Chicago-style pizza and a large television set to watch while eating or hanging out. A big plus is being able to view the chefs toss the pizza dough. The wait varies from 20 to 30 minutes, so either call for your order ahead of time if you're in a hurry or hang around and watch Wheel of Fortune in high-definition. **B+**

1220 W Taylor St
312.850.2000
BLUE LINE to RACINE

Union Park

This former near West Loop diner has been transformed into the quintessential neighborhood bar, complete with more than a dozen 40-inch TVs to watch every angle of the game. Daily food and drink specials make the already moderately-priced fare even more affordable. With the Chicago Police Academy just down

228 S Racine Ave
312.243.9002
BLUE LINE to RACINE

the street, don't be surprised by the number of cops. This 21-and-over bar is fine for a night out with the boys but not a Friday night dinner with the family. **B−**

Wings Chinese Food Carryout

Of all the Asian cuisine in Little Italy, this place is nothing special. A big disadvantage is that it is takeout only, so patrons cannot sit and eat. The food is inexpensive, with nothing priced over $8. Specialties include hot kung bao shrimp, satay beef and chicken hong sue. Quick and cheap, but pass it up if you are not on the run. **C**

1333 W Taylor St
312.243.0090
BLUE LINE to RACINE

Al's No. 1 Italian Beef

Celebrities and Chicagoans agree: Al's #1 Italian Beef is the best in Chicago. Picked as one of only 10 vendors to cater Hillary Clinton's 50th birthday party, Al's has grown from a roadside stand in Little Italy

1079 W Taylor St
312.226.4017
BLUE LINE to UIC-HALSTED

National Italian-American Sports Hall of Fame, 1431 W. Taylor St. SARA STUBBLEFIELD

Maui Wowi

850 W. Jackson Blvd.
312.738.3610
BLUE LINE to UIC-HALSTED

When asked to distinguish Maui Wowi from a host of other popular smoothie venders, owner Priscilla Taylor insists the 'quality of the products is so different that everything just tastes so much better.' Indeed, walking into this store is like walking right off the airplane; customers seem to be instantaneously transported to a Hawaiian island. The ambience is very relaxed, and the ingredients are all authentic, having arrived directly from the Hawaiian Islands themselves. In order to cater to the surrounding business district, Priscilla has even set up a large conference room with a projector available to rent for a small fee. The store is undoubtedly a destination, but there is an emphasis on healthy treats as well.

to 18 locations in the Chicagoland area. Unroll a greasy, gravy beauty from its wax paper and experience Al's distinctive sweet and Italian spices. Al's french fries only make the meal better. **A**

Artopolis Bakery and Café

As the menu describes, the Artopolis ['artos' meaning bread and 'polis' meaning town] 'complements … the unique-

306 S Halsted St
312.559.9000
BLUE LINE to UIC-HALSTED

Near West Side. SARA STUBBLEFIELD

ness of Chicago's Greektown.' Artopolis has a unique coziness, with seating available in various sections on the main floor and some in the upstairs loft. There are racks of imported wine, crates of Ouzo, and baskets of freshly-baked bread; however, the café is most famous for its 'Nescafe' coffee, which can be made cold with ice or served hot. **A**

Athena

At Athena, guests can sit outside on a large patio and toast to a skyline

212 S Halsted St
312.655.0000
BLUE LINE to UIC-HALSTED

view of the city. Blue and white chairs stay true to Greek national hues, and Doric columns in the courtyard reach up to the sky. Aside from the beautiful setting, Athena is in the heart of Greektown and serves an extensive array of authentic food for reasonable prices. **A**

Butter

Butter is the place to go for the occasional big spender. A creamy yellow

130 S Green St
312.666.9813
BLUE LINE to UIC-HALSTED

building just north of Greektown, it stands out and beckons to the affluently-minded. Daffodil arrangements on tables and decadent paintings of watermelon make for a cheery atmosphere. A three-course tasting menu is available for $52 a person. Such specialties as sheep's milk yogurt sorbet and caviar service make Butter a cut above the rest. **A**

NEAR WEST SIDE

LEFT: Capri Dolce Chicago Room. SARA STUBBLEFIELD
• **BELOW:** Tatsu, 1602 W. Taylor St. SARA STUBBLEFIELD

Byzantium

The classy black and gold trimmings of Byzantium sing to passersby of the establishment's utmost exclusiveness. Golden drapes hang in the windows, creating an aura that is entirely original. Only the most proper attire is allowed for a person seeking to gain entry; hats and tennis shoes are 'strictly forbidden.' Open from 6 p.m. to 4 a.m. daily, diners can feast on all the traditional Greek specialties – just be sure to make reservations in advance. **A**

232 S Halsted St
312.454.1227
BLUE LINE to UIC-HALSTED

Carm's Italian Beef

Started in 1929 as a grocery store, Carm's remains tucked between homes on a residential street. It is now run by second and third generations of the Carm family who use the same recipes as the original stand. Carm's offers hot and cold sandwiches, including ham and Swiss cheese subs and homemade meatball sandwiches, as well as Italian ice in a variety of flavors. **B**

1057 W Polk St
312.738.1046
BLUE LINE to UIC-HALSTED

Red Light

820 W. Randolph St.
312.733.8880
GREEN LINE to CLINTON

–Stacy Jacobson

Red Light offers a wide variety of unique, innovative dishes dominated by Chinese influences, but also inspired by Thai and French styles. The 'Asian inspired lavash pizza' [$14] comes with pesto, goat cheese, duck confit and greens tossed in a Thai chili scallion vinaigrette on flatbread. It tastes unlike anything you will try anywhere and for that reason alone is worth trying. Entrees range from fish to steak to chicken classics, with interesting twists like cranberry sauce with peking duck [$24] that is so tender it falls right off the bone. Some dishes, however, come with too much sauce. The interior and anterior of the restaurant are decorated with none other than red lights.

RIGHT: Parthenon Restaurant, 314 S. Halsted St. SARA STUBBLEFIELD • **BELOW:** Parthenon Restaurant, 314 S. Halsted St. SARA STUBBLEFIELD

Chicago's Busy Burger

Get a quick bite to eat in this black and white classic on Taylor St. The menu

1120 W Taylor St
312.226.7760
BLUE LINE to UIC-HALSTED

is all-American here, with Chicago-style hot dogs, salty fries and juicy burgers grilled to perfection. Because this place is so busy, the service tends to be a bit under par, but the low prices [$3 to $4] make it worth the trip. **B-**

Costa's Greek Mediterranean Dining

Live piano music and romantic lighting set the scene at Costa's, with

340 S Halsted St
312.263.9700
BLUE LINE to UIC-HALSTED

long-stemmed red carnations artfully placed at each table. The manager of this upscale Greek restaurant, Ari Petrov, is used to dealing with the press. 'Our lamb chops are the best in the city,' he said. 'Very thin-sliced.' Couple the chops with the signature appetizer – stuffed grilled calamari – and it's sure to be an exquisite experience. **A**

Demitasse

Reminiscent of an art gallery in a loft, this breakfast and lunch restaurant

1066 W Taylor St
312.226.7669
BLUE LINE to UIC-HALSTED

puts a chic spin on the typical American diner. The breakfast menu includes frittatas and stuffed French toast, and lunch features Panini and hummus plates. The atmosphere is cheerful and the extensive espresso bar is a plus; however, the

mediocre food and service hardly reflect the $7 to $10 price range. **B-**

Greek Islands

Every day is a busy day for the staff of Greek Islands. Pete Stasinopaulos, a

200 S Halsted St
312.782.9855
BLUE LINE to UIC-HALSTED

long-time server, declares it the 'cornerstone of Greektown.' The restaurant was started by four friends who came to Chicago in 1971; 3 were Greek and one was Italian, a ratio reflected in the menu. The Greek Isles is famous for its Arni Fourno [baked lamb], but the meatballs and lasagna are a favorite with kids. All of the restaurant's ingredients are imported from Greece. **A**

Greektown Gyros

As the lighted signs outside proudly declare, Greektown Gyros is

239 S Halsted St
312.236.9310
BLUE LINE to UIC-HALSTED

literally always open. In this quintessential gyros diner, the phone rings off the hook and the smells from the kitchen fill the building. How does it compare to Mr. Greek, the 24-hour gyros vender right across the street? A server grins and shrugs: 'Greektown Gyros, number one!' **A**

Hashbrowns

Hashbrowns of University Village offers one of the two best breakfasts in the

731 W Maxwell St
312.226.8000
BLUE LINE to UIC-HALSTED

city on this side of the West Loop. Hashbrowns

has a stylish, cozy atmosphere and a short – but impressive – menu. Pancakes and waffles come with sauces so good you can leave the maple syrup behind, and, of course, hash browns are the specialty. Try the sweet potato hash browns with a 'Maxwell St.' omelet. **B+**

Jak's Tap

Long a favorite for both students and professors, Jak's Tap boasts 40 beers

901 W Jackson Blvd
312.666.1700
BLUE LINE to UIC-HALSTED

on tap and a full dinner menu that more closely resembles a family-friendly chain restaurant than a bar. Though Jak's has a full bar with a wide selection of beers – microbrewers, stouts, lagers, porters, imported and domestic – it's time to try something new. The beer menu constantly changes so you never have to drink the same beer twice. **A**

Jamoch's Café

Known by UIC students as one of the best places to study, Jamoch's Caffe

1066 W Taylor St
312.226.7666
BLUE LINE to UIC-HALSTED

offers a comfortable setting to read, work or relax. Jamoch's offers breakfast and lunch, plus ice cream and shakes. For caffeine, try an iced mocha or flavored coffee. Games and magazines are available for anyone who wants to delay work just a little big longer. **B+**

Kabab Corner

There is no way for the owner of Kabab Corner to describe his restaurant's

760 W Jackson Blvd
312.906.9885
BLUE LINE to UIC-HALSTED

daily offerings. There's not a menu to present to customers because the selection is 'different everyday.' This is most definitely a good thing. The wonderful smells of Pakistani, Indian and Middle Eastern spices fill the open eating area of this mid-sized joint, and everything promises to be very authentic. **A**

Lalo's

Lalo's is a local, family-owned restaurant, though it looks and feels like a

733 W Maxwell St
312.455.9380
BLUE LINE to UIC-HALSTED

chain. Pricing also resembles a chain restaurant's; dinners run between $10 and $18 and the drink specials at the bar seemed a bit stingy. The 'authentic family recipes' are good, though the menu seems tailored to college students and urban professionals. **C+**

TOP Artopolis Bakery and Café, 306 S. Halsted St. SARA STUBBLEFIELD • **MIDDLE** Artopolis Bakery and Café, 306 S. Halsted St. SARA STUBBLEFIELD • **BOTTOM** Greek Islands Restaurant, 200 S. Halsted St. SARA STUBBLEFIELD

NEAR WEST SIDE

One Sixty Blue

1400 W. Randolph St.
312.850.0303
PINK LINE to ASHLAND

Located on the edge of Chicago's fashionable Market District, One Sixty Blue is a critically acclaimed, modern French restaurant that opened in 1998. The beautifully designed but comfortable space serves up mouth-watering specials from appetizers to desserts. Be sure to plan for a long dinner; patrons will want to savor ever bite at this trendy yet spacious eatery. Stop by on the last Friday night of every month for 'dust of the bottle night:' Four-course, prix fixe dinners are specially designed for a specific wine. Everything from the elegant décor and impeccable service to the abundant wine selection [in both half or whole bottles] and heavenly French-inspired desserts shouts sophistication and fun.

Massa Italian Café

Barbara's Bookstore customers don't even need to walk outside to enter

807 W Roosevelt Blvd
312.433.0123
BLUE LINE to UIC-HALSTED

Massa. When there isn't an event at Barbara's, the crowd tends to consist of UIC students at this small, cozy café. There's limited seating ideal for reading or studying, and the food is a typical Italian fare of panini and pizzas. The gelato is outstanding. **A**

Near West Side. SARA STUBBLEFIELD

Meli Café & Juice Bar

Open from 6 a.m. to 4 p.m. daily, Meli is the place in Greektown where it's

301 S Halsted St
312.454.0748
BLUE LINE to UIC-HALSTED

breakfast all day every day. Creative variations of typical breakfast items are offered for less than $10, including 'Cloud 9 Crepes,' sugared pecan pancakes and caramel banana pancakes. There is ample seating to accommodate its many customers, and sandwiches on the menu for those who feel weird eating a pancake any time after 11 a.m. **A**

Morgan's Bar and Grill

It's impossible to miss this University Village bar and grill. Morgan's

1325 S Halsted St
312.243.4800
BLUE LINE to UIC-HALSTED

resembles an average upscale sports bar tailored to a college crowd, but it hosts a wide selection of events. Expect to find both typical and unique nightly happenings; live bands play Saturdays and karaoke is on Thursdays, but watch for the off-beat events like Nintendo Wii night. The menu offers traditional bar fare with some surprises, like the amazing crab cakes. **A-**

Mr. Greek Gyros

Mr. Greek is a 24 hour community eatery very accessible for Greektown

234 S Halsted St
312.906.8731
BLUE LINE to UIC-HALSTED

new-comers looking for a quick taste of culture. Located at the corner of Jackson and Halsted in

LEFT: Harpo Studios, Near West Side. SARA STUBBLE-FIELD • **BELOW:** Near West Side. SARA STUBBLEFIELD

the self-declared 'heart of Greektown,' there's sure to be something to satisfy a hearty appetite. Diners can order the signature Gyros for less than $5 and Windy City fanatics can feast on a polish sausage in a sesame seed bun. **A-**

Pan Hellenic Pastry Shop

Athena Manolakos has been working in the Pan Hellenic pastry shop her
322 S Halsted St
312.454.1886
BLUE LINE to UIC-HALSTED

entire life. Her parents own the business, which was established in 1974. The Manolakos bakers are famous for their baklava, prepared with 'tender love and care.' Pan Hellenic has a homey feel and is quite inexpensive. Athena jokes that her dad is 'usually sitting at the front table playing backgammon.' Pastry lovers can choose from six different pastries, each available for a dollar and change. **A**

Parthenon

The uniquely pink stucco building that is the Parthenon creates
312 S Halsted St
312.726.2407
BLUE LINE to UIC-HALSTED

an initial intrigue that the restaurant does not fail to uphold. The bow-tied waiters on staff are ready and eager to tend to a diner's every need. With well over 100 items available on the menu, Parthenon defines the taste and hospitality that is Greece. **A**

Pegasus

Beautiful murals of Greek hillsides cover the walls of Pegasus. This fine dining
130 S Halsted St
312.226.3377
BLUE LINE to UIC-HALSTED

establishment has been open for more than twenty years, and it boasts a menu of specials that changes daily. In addition to its legacy of fine food, the restaurant features Greek music artists every Friday and Saturday night. **A**

Roditys

Manager Jim Kalas can rattle off the date of Roditys' founding like it's
222 S Halsted St
312.454.0800
BLUE LINE to UIC-HALSTED

his mother's maiden name: 'May 1, 1973.' As one of the original restaurants on Halsted St., Roditys works hard to defend its long-standing reputation. What distinguishes it from other fine dining in Greektown? 'All the restaurants are very good. But we're authentic,' said Kalas. He highly recommends the lamb dishes. **A**

Santorini

A vision of white greets guests as they enter Santorini, authentically
800 W Adams St
312.829.8820
BLUE LINE to UIC-HALSTED

mimicking the architecture of the actual Greek isle. This fine dining establishment has been a Greektown staple for over twenty years. Although known for its seafood, the restaurant also

serves traditional dishes such as spanakotiropita [spinach and feta cheese pie] and dolmades [vine leaves stuffed with meat]. **A**

Spectrum Bar and Grill

With live blues every Saturday, Spectrum is a true Greektown hot spot. Delicious appetizers such as fried zucchini and creamy spinach artichoke dip take this bar and grill beyond the caliber of the typical weekend hang-out. Order the steak sandwich house specialty for less than $10. If you're feeling adventurous, you can try the quail dinner for the same price. Located right under the New Jackson Hotel, Spectrum is open on Saturdays from 5 p.m. to 5 a.m. **A⁻**

233 S Halsted St
312.715.0770
BLUE LINE to UIC-HALSTED

Sushi Loop

It's hard to be a Japanese restaurant in Greektown, but Sushi Loop continues to provide an alternative cuisine with grace and ease. The colorful but mellow tones of the restaurant relax diners, and a bowl of Japanese candies at the front entrance adds an international flare. Try the 'Loop Bento' lunch special – a selection of tempura, teriyaki, Maki Mano and San Sali – for less than $12. **B⁺**

810 W Jackson Blvd
312.714.1234
BLUE LINE to UIC-HALSTED

Tatsu

Up-to-date young professionals and students fill this newly rehabbed, chic restaurant. Tatsu serves Thai food and stocks international beer and wine. It offers affordable sushi and is perfect for a date on a budget. Inventive rolls such as Sunset Maki – a combination of mango, salmon and eel – are among the most popular specials. The fish is always fresh, and a smiling staff will cater to your every need. **A**

1062 W Taylor St
312.666.8504
BLUE LINE to UIC-HALSTED

Thai Bowl

Plagued by rumors of bad service and dirty bathrooms, Thai Bowl tends to be hit or miss. Believing the food to be supreme, some prefer to order takeout to avoid Thai Bowl's pitfalls, while others swear off the place altogether. UIC students looking for a break from dorm food will probably appreciate the variety of dishes such as crab rangoon, sweet-and-sour chicken and Pad Thai. For anyone else, however, the trip may not be worth it. **C**

1049 W Taylor St
312.226.5865
BLUE LINE to UIC-HALSTED

The Che Café

Named after one of Cuba's most influential leaders, this charming

1058 W Taylor St
312.850.4665
BLUE LINE to UIC-HALSTED

cafe is a cheery oasis for those that crave a little Cuban flavor. The walls showcase different local artists every month, and seating arrangements include comfy couches and bayside window seats perfect for people watching. Menu items vary from the classic burrito to the chicken pesto focaccia sandwich. Coffee is $2 with unlimited refills, and affordable menu prices range from $1.75 to $7.75. Tip: try the potato salad. **A**

Tufano's Vernon Park Tap

1073 W Vernon Park Pl
312.733.3393
BLUE LINE to UIC-HALSTED

Located on the eastern edge of Little Italy, this family-run establishment has been frequented by such celebrities as Dolly Parton, Dan Marino and Tommy Lasorda. Photos of the stars line the walls of this cozy establishment that boasts two TVs, a selection of cigars behind the bar and great Italian food. Entrees range from $7 to $13. **B**

Tuscany

1014 W Taylor St
312.829.1990
BLUE LINE to UIC-HALSTED

Tuscany is best known for its fresh twist on northern Italian food in a setting quiet enough for conversation; it is the perfect spot for dining with family members, clients or long-lost friends. Tuscan street scenes painted on yellow walls complement the black attire of the staff, who tirelessly refill drinks and bread baskets. Tuscany's specialties include grilled sausage with sautéed onions and bell peppers, as well as pear ravioli. **B+**

Venus

820 W Jackson Blvd
312.714.1001
BLUE LINE to UIC-HALSTED

Venus invites visitors to indulge in a slightly different flavor. According to server Eva Stathopoulos, this Cypriot cuisine differs from traditional Greek cuisine because it incorporates more spices: "All the meat at Venus is slow-cooked at a low temperature so it's extra tender, and the meatballs and vine leaves are made with pork instead of beef. **A**

West Gate Coffeehouse

924 W Madison St
312.829.9378
BLUE LINE to UIC-HALSTED

'Coffee is great, early or late,' reads the exterior of this funky West Loop coffee house. An eclectic assortment of furniture provides ample seating room in this cozy getaway. Rifts of folk music linger in the air, adding to the low-key vibe. Customers looking for more than just a cup of joe can order an original curry chicken salad for a reasonable six dollars. Morning breakfast sandwiches are also very popular, as are the homemade treats. **B+**

Wow Café & Wingery

717 W Maxwell St
312.997.9969
BLUE LINE to UIC-HALSTED

Wow is yet another good restaurant that recently opened in newly-built University Village. It specializes in all types of wings and offers seventeen different sauces, from traditional buffalo sauces to the innovative Jamaican Jerk, Australian Taz Rasberry and Key West Citrus Salsa. Dollar beers are the perfect

NEAR WEST SIDE

Vivo

838 W. Randolph St.
312.733.3379
GREEN LINE to CLINTON

If you visit only one restaurant on Randolph St., make it Vivo. Vivo has survived 15 years in its location. As numerous new restaurants opened around it, Randolph St. transformed from a market district into a classy restaurant strip. Vivo, however, will always be able to claim its place as the first restaurant on the strip. Serving up Italian specialties like gnocchi gratinati and ossobuco, Vivo is pricy but delectably gourmet. Dining tables are very close to each other, so if you're claustrophobic, call ahead to request a private, more spacious dining area. Once inside, take note of the translucent bottles lining the walls in 'V' shapes.

beverage, and since Wow is located right by UIC, you won't be the only one drinking at noon. **B**

Zeus Restaurant

The black-and-white tiles of the vintage decades collide with the flavor

806 W Jackson Blvd
312.258.8789
BLUE LINE to UIC-HALSTED

of Athens in a very diner-esque setting at Zeus. Customers will find an interesting mix between Chicago and Greece here, with touristy pictures

TOP Greek Islands Restaurant, 200 S. Halsted St. SARA STUBBLEFIELD • **MIDDLE** Greek Islands Restaurant, 200 S. Halsted St. SARA STUBBLEFIELD • **BOTTOM** Greek Islands Restaurant, 200 S. Halsted St. SARA STUBBLEFIELD

of Mykonos and Santorini hanging below a wooden bust of the Chicago Bulls' mascot. This small establishment is primarily used during the day for takeout. Tasty Greek combos are available for under $5. **B**

@Spot

If you're wondering why @Spot looks much like the cold, sterile reception

2234 W Taylor St
312.226.9885
BLUE LINE to S WESTERN

area of an office building, it's because @Spot is owned by @Properties, a real estate company. A coffee shop that sells both coffee and property, @Spot doesn't deliver in either its menu or its atmosphere – the two most important elements in any coffee shop. **C-**

Lu-Lu's

The nearest restaurant to the west of the medical district, Lu-Lu's is every-

1000 S Leavitt St
312.243.3444
BLUE LINE to S WESTERN

thing a Chicago burger joint should be: A wise-cracking staff, Bulls and Bears sports memorabilia and a huge menu ranging from corndogs to ribs to pizza burgers. Lu-Lu's is a great place to stop for fast, cheap food in the area. **B**

Avec

Avec has the same owners as its sister restaurant, Blackbird, but boasts less

615 W Randolph St
312.377.2002
GREEN LINE to CLINTON

expensive prices and smaller plates. Popular small plate options include chorizo-stuffed medjool dates [$9] and marinated hangar steak [$11]. Large plates run from $14 to $20 and feature dishes like wood-fired pizza and focaccia. One wall is covered in empty wine bottles, while the rest of the deep, narrow room is decked with oak, cedar, and hickory . Overall, the establishment offers tasty dishes at reasonable prices. **B**

Blackbird

With its white and silver décor, Blackbird resembles the token trendy, modern

619 W Randolph St
312.715.0708
GREEN LINE to CLINTON

restaurant. The restaurant is situated in a slim but open room that looks like an old row house.

The Rosebud

1500 W. Taylor St.
312.942.1117
PINK LINE to POLK

Wonderfully old-fashioned Italian, The Rosebud's thirty-year success in Little Italy based on owner Alex Dana's philosophy 'keep it simple, keep it good, and keep it coming,' has turned the former grocery store into a key Chicago destination. The restaurant boasts visits from Jimmy Buffet, Frank Sinatra and Tony Bennett. Originally named Bocciola della Rosa, or bud of the rose, after Sicily's native flower, pronunciation troubles of American patrons convinced Dana to translate the name into English. The Rosebud's specialties include chicken vesuvio, pappardelle, [wide fettuccini noodles], sausage and peppers, baked clams and tiramisu. The glow of candlelit lamps on each table shines through the window shades, and the deep tones of the wooden floors, chairs and framed mirrors match the warmth of the excellent food and service. Entrees range from $20 to $30, but the higher price is worth the experience.

Blackbird offers upscale food, with entrees ranging from $25 to $35. The menu changes seasonally but always features unique dishes, such as rabbit and pork belly. An extensive wine selection is also available. **B**

Chicago Chocolate Company

Visit the Chicago Chocolate Company for an afternoon snack while strolling down Randolph St. or after dinner for delectable desserts. While the company specializes in all things chocolate [malt balls, turtles, toffee, fudge – to name a few], you can also enjoy soups, sandwiches, salads or coffee. Free samples are available at the counter, and individual chocolates such as 'amaretto meltaways' are available for purchase. For gifts, buy chocolates by the pound. Enjoy the aroma as you graze. **A**

847 W Randolph St
888.568.1733
GREEN LINE to CLINTON

Columbus

Columbus' owners call their establishment 'a fast food joint with a bar.' Though Columbus primarily offers diner options, it features the flat-screen televisions and sophisticated furniture of an upscale nighttime eatery. The menu has a wide selection of staples

651 W Randolph St
312.454.0148
GREEN LINE to CLINTON

that will satisfy any American. Its offerings range from pancakes for breakfast to Italian beef for lunch to soft serve ice cream cones and shakes for dessert. The restaurant delivers, but only within a one-mile radius. **B⁻**

Van Buren St. & Halsted St.
SARA STUBBLEFIELD

De Cero Taqueria

De Cero calls itself a 'modern day taqueria.' Its contemporary style

814 W Randolph St
312.455.8114
GREEN LINE to CLINTON

boasts a wooden interior and a bar within the dining room. The restaurant serves sophisticated Mexican fare. Tacos a la carte are about $3 to $5 and come with choice additives like avocado, skirt steak and shrimp. Entrees are more expensive, but desserts are only about $5. **B**

Downtown Gyros & Cafeteria

If you're looking for a place to grab a quick sandwich, burger or salad,

800 W Randolph St
312.455.5900
GREEN LINE to CLINTON

then go to Downtown Gyros. If you want quality, though, head elsewhere. Downtown Gyros offers expediency, good prices, and convenience, but the interior resembles – at best – a high school cafeteria. They deliver for free and are open 24 hours a day, Thursday through Sunday. **C**

Dragonfly Mandarin

A cascading staircase twists between the two floors of this trendy

832 W Randolph St
312.787.7600
GREEN LINE to CLINTON

Mandarin restaurant. Low lights and groovy pockets of space allow guests to chat and enjoy the new age artwork. According to the bustling wait staff, the most popular menu items include the Hunan steak and salt and pepper prawns. The bargain-hungry can get an appetizer, a cup of soup and an entrée for a lunch special of only $9. **A**

Extra Virgin

Extra Virgin offers delectable Italian food in the form of antipasti, small

741 W Randolph St
312.474.0700
GREEN LINE to CLINTON

plates and large entrees for reasonable, upscale restaurant prices. The cost of an entrée ranges from $13 to $25 and you can get anything from steak to pasta to chicken. Try the chicken marsala

Van Buren St. &
Halsted St.
SARA STUBBLEFIELD

for $16 or the filet gemellati [two twin filets] for $23. **A**

Fast Track

One block from the Clinton 'El' stop, Fast Track perches on its corner and holds its own.

629 W Lake St	
312.993.9300	
GREEN LINE to CLINTON	

A small burger and hot dog joint, Fast Track has indoor and outdoor seating, and its employees seem to take great pride in their grungy establishment. Prices are good: A cheeseburger costs $2.95 and a half-pound of wings costs $2.99. However, the inside could use a deep cleaning, and the outside is easily overlooked. **C+**

Holiday Neighborhood Grill & Bar

Holiday Neighborhood Grill & Bar is the perfect place to go for any meal,

740 W Randolph St	
312.207.0924	
GREEN LINE to CLINTON	

any time; this restaurant will make you feel good. The owner inherited the establishment from his parents and knows many of the sports bar's regular customers by name. Holiday offers 18 beers and inexpensive dishes, such as burgers for $2.50. **A**

Izurni

So many hip sushi places exist it's hard to distinguish between them.

731 W Randolph St	
312.207.5299	
GREEN LINE to CLINTON	

The Randolph St. district alone boasts a healthy selection. Izumi, a classic example of one these eateries, has a sushi bar manned by resident sushi chefs, and the requisite teriyaki dishes to match the fresh maki rolls. Dragon rolls [$13] are most frequently ordered, but Izumi says the lion roll with tuna, yellowtail, avocado, cilantro, jalapeño, and chili sauce [$11] is its specialty. **B-**

Jim Ching

Though college students often flock to late-night hotspots for greasy pizza

735 W Randolph St	
312.258.8800	
GREEN LINE to CLINTON	

or Chinese food, Jim Ching is not the answer. It provides the same style food and isn't worth the trip. Situated in a dinky dining room with an open kitchen and fewer than 10 tables, one can dine in, watch network television and enjoy Chinese staples like chicken with broccoli. **C-**

Jubilee Juice & Grill

From the outside, Jubilee looks like a dingy, over-the-counter lunch spot,

140 N Halsted St	
312.491.8500	
GREEN LINE to CLINTON	

but once inside, one realizes it boasts a large selection of fresh food, drinks and snacks for reasonable prices. Try any of five grilled fish sandwiches brushed in teriyaki or Greek sauce with a small salad for dinner [$9.95 to $10.95] or a simple Italian club sandwich for lunch [$5.75]. Sit down at one of the wooden booths, or order for delivery or carry-out. **B**

Marché

The only drawback to Marché is the maturity of its menu. Otherwise,

833 W Randolph St	
312.226.8399	
GREEN LINE to CLINTON	

the restaurant offers a wide variety of traditional and innovative French cuisine. Try the coq au vin [$19.95], or take a risk with braised rabbit chablis [$23.95]. The real treat in Marché is the décor; upside-down umbrellas dot the ceiling while a theatrical theme is present in the furniture and decorations. **A-**

Meiji

Meiji, a small sushi restaurant, houses a sushi bar in the back,

623 W Randolph St	
312.887.9999	
GREEN LINE to CLINTON	

a larger marble bar in the front, and two rows of individual tables. Its décor is Asian-themed, with dark lighting and colors, and it offers a fine selection of unique Asian fare. Teriyaki chicken [$18] and teriyaki salmon [$23] are staples of the menu, as well as Meiji's signature makimono rolls [$9 to $16]. **B**

Saxby's Coffee

Yes, Saxby's is a national chain, but Saxby's stands out as a fresh take on cof-

605 W Lake St	
312.463.0390	
GREEN LINE to CLINTON	

fee and comfort. With free Wi-Fi and a student

Gotham Grind

1311 W. Taylor St.
866.512.6642
BLUE LINE to RACINE

Owned by comic book artists and enthusiasts, Gotham Grind is part comic book shop, part coffee shop. Here you can buy a mainstream or independent comic book or borrow one from the bookshelf. Many of the comics that you'll find on the shelf are the employees' own, so expect to be asked for your opinion. Gotham Grind also supports local art talent by displaying art available for purchase, and they rent out the shop on Sundays for club meetings, film screenings and other events. The shop hosts a variety of events during the week, and you can count on Friday night movies.

discount, the chain appeals to shallow-pocketed youth looking for a place to chill. And Saxby's wide selection of drinks, including an array of sugar-free syrups in degrees of hotness and coldness, could please anyone. **A**

Sushi Wabi

Sushi Wabi resembles other token sushi bars, despite a strong fish smell

842 W Randolph St
312.563.1224
GREEN LINE to CLINTON

Near West Side. SARA STUBBLEFIELD

that penetrates the dining room. One difference is Wabi accommodates children too, as several are seated with parents without sticking out amongst groups of young professionals. Still, Wabi offers classics like California and spicy tuna maki, as well as nigiri and sashimi. **B-**

Teena Mia

Go to Teena Mia, just off the main stretch of restaurants on Randolph St.,

564 W Washington St
312.441.9577
GREEN LINE to CLINTON

for a quick, casual lunch. Thanks to its discrete location, it's not as busy as other area restaurants, but it's not worth a long trip. It's more of a local spot where you can eat if you don't want to get dressed for Marché or Vivo, or spend their high prices. **C**

Billy Goat Inn

Saturday Night Live's Jim Belushi brought the Billy Goat Tavern to America

1535 W Madison St
312.733.9132
PINK LINE to ASHLAND

with shouts of 'Cheezborger, cheezborger! No fries, chips! No Pepsi, Coke!' Established in 1934 in southern Chicago by a Greek immigrant, Billy Goat Tavern has expanded to eight locations, including this one near the United Center. Belushi might have exaggerated the no-frills menu, but one thing is for sure: Anything you order will clog some arteries. At least stop by for the Chicago history. **B**

NEAR WEST SIDE

Bombon Café

This Ashland bakery is truly a hidden treat. Pastries, breads, sand-

38 S Ashland Ave
312.733.8717
PINK LINE to ASHLAND

wiches and salads take on Mexican flavors in a small but cozy location just south of Union Park. Fans of Pilsen's famed Bombon Bakery will love the expanded seating and inexpensive but flavorful dishes served up by Luis and Laura Perea, Bombon's married owners and chefs. Bombon offers traditional south of the border fare such as tortas [Mexican sandwiches], tamales and quesadillas, as well as soups and salads. **A-**

Café Penelope

Near West Side residents can enjoy the American fare offered at this homey

234 S Ashland Ave
312.243.3600
PINK LINE to ASHLAND

restaurant. Ample seating and a quiet atmosphere attract locals for breakfast, lunch, dinner and late night dining. Patron favorites include homemade soups, sandwiches and thin-crust pizza. Dinner specials rotate daily, and weekend brunch, online ordering and specialty catering make this quaint establishment the perfect place any time of day. **B**

Cobra Lounge

If you've headed west on the CTA's pink or green line lately, you've seen the

235 N Ashland Ave
312.226.6300
PINK LINE to ASHLAND

big, flashy red neon sign for the Cobra Lounge. Don't expect to see a line of bars and restaurants – this side of Ashland is the old West Loop, and it seems fitting to have a metal bar and restaurant between warehouses and the 'El.' Rock and metal DJs spin when a live band isn't playing. **B**

Ina's

Chef Ina Pinkney scores with this homey neighborhood nook. Exposed brick,

1235 W Randolph St
312.226.8227
PINK LINE to ASHLAND

salmon-colored walls and sometimes Ina herself meet patrons upon entering. Breakfast, arguably Ina's specialty, features omelets and scrambled eggs while lunch and dinner are strictly traditional American: BLTs, roasted chicken and meatloaf.

No need to call ahead, but make sure to leave your cell phone at home or in the car: Cell phone use is strictly prohibited. **B+**

Jay's Amore Ristorante

Comfort food dominates the Italian-style menu at this Madison Ave.

1330 W Madison Ave
312.829.3333
PINK LINE to ASHLAND

establishment. A wide price range of entrees and wines makes Jay's perfect for a date, dinner with the family or a quick bite before a game at the United Center. The service is fast and friendly, and the location is convenient for Chicagoans far and wide. **A-**

La Lucé

Old World Italian flavors flow from this quaint West Loop bar and restau-

1393 W Lake St
312.850.1900
PINK LINE to ASHLAND

rant. The fare is just average for the moderately-priced entrees, and seating is limited in both the bar and dining areas. Weekend dinner specials and valet service are a plus, but countless other Italian restaurants in Chicago offer better tasting or less expensive dishes than this hole-in-the-wall on Lake. **B**

Palace Grill

Perhaps the quintessential Chicago diner, this little eatery attracts people

1408 W Madison St
312.226.9529
PINK LINE to ASHLAND

from all over, including a few Blackhawks from the United Center. Palace Grill offers a non-pretentious dinner: walk in, order, chat with other patrons, pay, walk out. Service is spotty though; George, the owner, is affable and chatty, but the wait staff gives a smart-aleck vibe that might keep first-time visitors from returning. **B+**

The Tasting Room

This trendy bar features a selection of more than 100 wines from around

1415 W Randolph St
312.942.1313
PINK LINE to ASHLAND

the world available by the taste, glass or bottle. Savvy sommeliers are found in each of the three sections – Randolph Wine Cellars, the retail wine store; the cozy downstairs lounge; and the upstairs lounge, which features a breathtaking view of downtown Chicago. A wide selection of artesian cheeses and desserts adds to this elegant yet comfortable West Loop wine bar. **B+**

BeviAmo Wine Bar

Stylish and sophisticated, BeviAmo is not a college bar. The trendy décor is appropriate for hosting monthly art shows, but the space is still small enough to serve as a neighborhood bar. BeviAmo has drink specials Sunday through Thursday, and the $25 wine tastings on Tuesday nights are recommended. BeviAmo offers a sophisticated night club atmosphere at a reasonable price. **A-**

1358 W Taylor St
312.455.8255
PINK LINE to POLK

Couscous

Couscous features foods from the Middle East and the Maghreb [an area of North Africa that includes Morocco, Algeria, and Libya]. The restaurant offers a clean, simple feel with green chairs, white paper tablecloths and beige walls decorated with flowers and trees. Try the ful medames, a dip of mashed fava beans, steamed semolina and coarsely ground durum wheat, a Maghreb staple. **B+**

1445 W Taylor St
312.226.2408
PINK LINE to POLK

De Pasada

The best Mexican restaurant in Little Italy, De Pasada offers both dine-in and takeout options. Known for its no-nonsense take on Mexican food, the restaurant cooks up tacos, burritos and flautas with lean, finely ground beef. Crisp taco shells and fresh ingredients such as tomatoes and salsa verde top it off. Nothing costs more than $8, making this place perfect for college students and money-conscious locals. **A-**

1519 W Taylor St
312.243.6441
PINK LINE to POLK

Francesca's on Taylor

Francesca's is a wonderful combination of a family-friendly Italian restaurant and a formal dining setting. Patrons dress in anything from cocktail dresses to khakis, and takeout is an option. The staff is very inviting, and you will soon feel at home. Most of the menu is hand-written by the chef, suggesting frequently-changing dishes. **A-**

1400 W Taylor St
312.829.2828
PINK LINE to POLK

Hawkeye's Bar and Grill Chicago

College students in the West Loop don't need to go to the north side

1458 W Taylor St
312.226.3951
PINK LINE to POLK

NEAR WEST SIDE

Greektown Music

330 S. Halsted St.
312.263.6342
BLUE LINE to UIC-HALSTED

▮In a building that used to be a Greek radio station and gift shop, two brothers-in-law hope to continue the tradition of Greek music. Pop tunes of a premiere Athens radio station drift through this small shotgun-sized store, streaming from a laptop computer. According to co-owner Giannis Morikis, Greektown Music is an important component of the neighborhood because 'it keeps everybody current as far as what's going on in Greece.' The brothers receive shipments of Greek newspapers three times a week, and all the top magazines come in once a week. In addition to news, CDs and DVDs, there are plenty of trinkets for touristy folk. Piles of souvenir shirts, children's books, miniature flags, key chains and general knick-knacks fill every cranny. The unique store caters to curious UIC students and is a regular haunt for members of the Greek community.

to get wild and crazy at a bar – they just go to Hawkeye's. With its huge crowds and noise loud enough to make the neighbors miserable, Hawkeye's seems like it should be near a party school instead. Drink and food specials like Monday's great 20-cent wings are college-budget friendly. **B+**

Illinois Bar & Grill

Whether you're a local or just want to feel like one, Illinois Bar and Grill

| 1421 W Taylor St |
| 312.666.6666 |
| **PINK LINE to POLK** |

feels a lot like a visit to a college buddy eager to fill you with alcohol. The food, of course, is a lot better, with huge meaty burgers and generous heaps of piping-hot chicken fingers. The place is small and cozy, with pool and darts in the back to escape the bustle near the bar counter. **A-**

Japonica

Japonica seems out of place in Little Italy; it serves sushi near Ashland

| 1422 W Taylor St |
| 312.421.3288 |
| **PINK LINE to POLK** |

Ave., where multicultural family-owned fast food restaurants dominate. The 20-seat Japonica split-level tunnel has a pre-packaged trendy feel, and the maki is nothing special. Japonica isn't necessarily a bad restaurant, but it isn't different from any other chic urban sushi place. **C**

La Vita Italian Restaurant

A bit more upscale than your usual family-style Italian restaurant, La Vita

| 1359 W Taylor St |
| 312.491.1414 |
| **PINK LINE to POLK** |

represents a more refined Italian dinner. A line of tables parallel to the bar offer seating options for a romantic date for two or dinner with the entire Italian family. The bar is clean and orderly, with a different cubby for each variety of wine. **A-**

Patio Hot Dogs

Patio Hot Dogs is definitely not worth the trip to Taylor St. when coming

| 1503 W Taylor St |
| 312.829.0454 |
| **PINK LINE to POLK** |

from far away, but locals craving a hot dog can watch as the Patio's staff prepares beef, hot dogs and french fries, and asks if you want salt or pepper on your food. Seating consists of stools along a dirty countertop, so take the food to go. **C-**

The Drum and Monkey

The Drum and Monkey delights in its Irish-themed fare in the middle of

| 1435 W Taylor St |
| 312.563.1874 |
| **PINK LINE to POLK** |

Little Italy. It showcases numerous shamrocks in the window and four Irish flags. The Irish pride extends to the pub's fish and chips, Shepherd's pie and chicken and brie sandwich. Co-owner Dominick O'Mahoney will point out the Belgium-made beer towers as the first to be installed in

ABOVE: Near West Side. SARA STUBBLEFIELD
• **LEFT:** Near West Side. SARA STUBBLEFIELD

NEAR WEST SIDE

Chicago. Both European and American beers are available. **B+**

who crave quick beauty breaks between classes; however, it can be quite busy, and you will not want to wait around for long in the small space. The prices are cheap, and students receive a 10 percent discount. The salon is most popular for eyebrow threading, a painful yet more effective alternative to waxing. **B+**

TO PLAY

Arrigo Park

Named for Victor Arrigo, an Italian American who served as an Illinois State Representative, this beautiful six-acre park showcases the statue of Christopher Columbus first exhibited at the 1893 World's Columbian Exposition. The statue was installed in Arrigo Park when the construction of UIC was causing huge changes within Little Italy. Play on the green or follow the deteriorating concrete trail around the park. Arrigo Park is a great place to study, relax or digest that Italian dinner. **A**

801 S Loomis St
312.746.5369
BLUE LINE to RACINE

Museum of Holography

Perhaps one of only a handful of museums devoted to holograms, the Museum of Holography offers a unique and inexpensive afternoon for parents and children. Discover how lasers create three-dimensional images at this artistic fun house, founded in 1976. Despite limited hours, the museum's high-tech laboratories, rotating exhibitions and courses at the School of Holography are worth a visit. **B**

1134 W Wash. Blvd
312.226.1007
BLUE LINE to RACINE

Our Lady of Pompeii

Our Lady of Pompeii has been part of the neighborhood since 1911, but historical value is not the only plus to visiting the church. Our Lady of Pompeii brings together members of Chicago's Italian-American clubs for networking, mingling and dancing in June and also hosts an annual festival of food and entertainment in August. **B+**

1224 W Lexington St
312.421.3757
BLUE LINE to RACINE

Wax On Wax Off

This small, family-operated salon has the best deals for UIC students

1039 W Taylor St
312.226.1473
BLUE LINE to UIC-HALSTED

Nar Hookah

Nar Hookah has a great idea: provide a relaxing environment for customers who want to relax. They offer 27 different flavors of hookah, a full bar, coffee, and will soon offer appetizers. Since no food is currently available, however, customers must subsist on lush maroon pillows and hookah flavors like jasmine mint mix. When Nar Hookah does acquire food options, its nice décor and the promise of a calm, soothing night will be much more appealing. **C**

806 W Randolph St
312.421.7007
GREEN LINE to CLINTON

Johnny's Icehouse

Seemingly out of place in the middle of Chicago's Near West Side, Johnny's is a great place to skate with the kids or some friends. The state-of-the-art facility complements a friendly staff at this hockey rink that offers lessons, clinics and hosts dozens of hockey teams. Newcomers and seasoned veterans alike will love Johnny's, which features heated indoor parking, ample seating, a fully-stocked pro shop, and a bar and grill overlooking the ice. **B**

1350 W Madison St
312.226.5555
PINK LINE to ASHLAND

Union Park

Set on thirteen acres in Chicago's Near West Side, Union Park offers residents recreational space all year long. An outdoor pool, baseball diamond, tennis and basketball courts, and playground are sure to attract kids, and the fitness center and walking trails will interest adults. The open field is the perfect spot to spend a lazy summer afternoon admiring its spectacular view of downtown Chicago's skyline. **B**

1501 W Randolph St
312.746.5494
PINK LINE to ASHLAND

National Italian American Sports Hall of Fame and Museum

Joe DiMaggio, Rocky Marciano, Mary Lou Retton and Ed Abbaticchio

1431 W Taylor St
312.226.5566
PINK LINE to POLK

are all honored in this museum in the center of Little Italy. A fun place to walk around, the single-room museum houses enough memorabilia to look at for several hours, though the volume of it all can be overwhelming. Pieces such as Rocky's 1952 heavyweight champion belt are of definite interest, and new athletes are added annually through the museum's induction ceremony. Admission is a $5 suggested donation. **B**

Taylor Street Tattoo

Little Italy's Taylor Street Tattoo attracts a lot of students from nearby UIC,

1150 W Taylor St
312.455.8288
PINK LINE to POLK

and you will not find a complaint among them. The tattoo artists have been featured in various tattoo magazines, and their professionalism shows in their craft and the cleanliness of their shop. Most of the tattoo artists' work seems to have an old-school, traditional flair. **A**

TO SHOP

Jazzy Flowers

Chicago's South Side residents are no longer the only ones who know about

35 S Racine Ave
312.421.7167
BLUE LINE to RACINE

Jazzy Flowers. This West Loop location opened in March 2006 and provides the community with flowers for any occasion. Despite high prices, customers can expect to find a wide variety of seasonal and traditional flowers in simple yet contemporary vase and basket arrangements. **C**

Athenian Candle Company

A beckoning fragrance reminiscent of the Mediterranean wafts

1125 S Western Ave
312.421.5048
BLUE LINE to S WESTERN

through the doors of the Athenian Candle Company. The candles here are made on site and distributed mainly to Greek Orthodox churches,

although owner Helen Paspalas promises there is something here even for browsers. 'We provide a lot of imported Greek products, but there are also multi-cultural, multi-religious and multi-ethnic items.' The business venture originated in Greece, and the shop has been family-owned and -operated for more than 80 years. **B+**

TOP Near West Side. SARA STUBBLEFIELD • **MIDDLE** Near West Side. SARA STUBBLEFIELD • **BOTTOM** Near West Side. SARA STUBBLEFIELD

Near West Side. SARA STUBBLEFIELD

Athens Grocery

An eclectic inventory lines the modest shelves of the Athens Grocery. There are

324 S Halsted St
312.332.6737
BLUE LINE to UIC-HALSTED

the typical necessities – raisins, Nescafe, bread, olive oil – but venture a little further and you'll find authentic Greek delicacies – tucked away boxes of freeze-dried herring, Greek cookies, blocks of imported cheese and an entire refrigerator case full of olives. This grocer has served the Chicago Greek community for over 100 years and receives daily shipments from Greece. **B**

Barbara's Bookstore at UIC

Located in the heart of University Village, Barbara's Bookstore

1218 S Halsted St
312.413.2665
BLUE LINE to UIC-HALSTED

has a selection most English professors would approve of, along with staff picks that never disappoint. The UIC location is the largest and has a secluded seating area in back for author readings. Visiting authors have ranged from Bill Clinton and James Ellroy to those brought by the UIC Program for Writers. No matter the event, it's always lively and fun. **A**

Breathe ... A Modern Clothing Lounge

Breathe's biggest disadvantage is the lack of similar clothing stores

1252 S Halsted St
312.997.2411
BLUE LINE to UIC-HALSTED

nearby; once you've tired of Breathe's selection, your shopping day is over. It looks and feels like a high-end fashion boutique, with a smaller selection and hangers spaced exactly two finger widths apart. However, unlike a fashion boutique, the designs are uninspired basics unworthy of the price. Sometimes when someone says, 'It's crazy to spend a hundred dollars on a plain T-shirt,' they're actually right. **C-**

Lush Wine and Spirits

Lush has one of the best selections of wine and beer in the city, and spe-

1306 S Halsted St
312.738.1900
BLUE LINE to UIC-HALSTED

cializes in lesser-known and international wine distributors. In fact, if a particular brand begins selling in large retail or grocery stores, Lush will stop selling it. Though it stocks an elitist selection, Lush has reasonable prices [$2 to $20 for beer, $10 and up for wine], and a knowledgeable staff is willing to help you sort through the unusual drink selection. **A**

Ralph's Cigar Shop

Dressed up with fedora hats and a wooden cigar-toting Indian, this Little

1032 W Taylor St
312.829.0672
BLUE LINE to UIC-HALSTED

Italy spot has the most affordable name-brand cigars in the area – prices range from $5 to $10 each. Ralph's has been family-owned and -operated for twelve years and is also a mini-lounge. Customers can drink coffee and bring movies to watch while they relax in lush chairs and sip beverages from the cooler. **A-**

Working Bikes

This is one of the few bicycle and bicycle parts shops in the city that has

1125 S Western Ave
312.421.5048
BLUE LINE to S WESTERN

a crowd waiting outside before the doors are unlocked. The shop attracts a mix of hardcore bicycle fanatics as well as those looking for a cheap ride since prices plunge well under $100. All bicycles at this shop were either donated or disposed of, and volunteers do a basic tune-up to make sure the bicycles are in decent condition. **A**

Primitive

If you're strolling through the Randolph St. neighborhood, be sure to stop in

130 N Jefferson St
312.575.9600
GREEN LINE to CLINTON

Primitive to look around. The eclectic multi-floor showroom features art, antiques and artifacts from all over the world. Primitive specializes in pieces from Asia and Africa, and takes special pride in its Buddha room, a replica of a Buddhist temple. Prices are hefty [one small statue costs $1,895], but stop in to browse. **B**

Salon Serene

Salon Serene offers standard hair and body care options, such as

625 W Lake St
312.441.0140
GREEN LINE to CLINTON

haircuts [$55-$70 for women, $55 for men] or eyebrow waxing [$20]. Prices are a bit steep for a salon that lines the Clinton 'El' station and is surrounded by fast food joints. Otherwise, Salon Serene is nothing special, but may be worthwhile if you live nearby. **B⁻**

Jan's Antiques

Flea market patrons and antiquing enthusiasts will love Jan's. Filled with

225 N Racine Ave
312.563.0275
PINK LINE to ASHLAND

massive church doors and pews, 100-year-old doorknobs, faucets and armoires, this shop has anything and everything. The best deals might not be that appealing, but there's no lack of selection – hundreds of rows of dust-covered antiques wait inside. Anyone looking to spruce up or redecorate should stop by Jan's, especially on weekends. **C⁺**

Conti di Savoia Italian Grocery and Deli

This Italian deli is definitely worth the trip to Little Italy. The family-

1438 W Taylor St
312.666.3471
PINK LINE to POLK

owned grocery has a long history in the area, and the deli itself is known for its Italian specialties. Walk down an aisle filled with olives or order a fresh sandwich with toppings from tuna to salami with provolone. **A**

Near West Side.
SARA STUBBLEFIELD

SOUTH LAWNDALE

BIG ON FAMILY AND COMMUNITY

Once home to a large Czech population, South Lawndale has become Chicago's largest Mexican neighborhood. The downtown – known as La Villita, or 'Little Village' – is the second largest commercial district in the city but has much more flair than Michigan Ave., the number one. Vibrant Hispanic music lines the streets. Enjoy the music while eating something delicious from one of the countless restaurants, bars and taquerias. The area of 26th St. hosts more than a thousand shops selling everything imaginable from jewelry to furniture, and usually at good prices. A far cry from its crime-ridden neighbor, North Lawndale, the largely residential neighborhood is big on family value and community. Every year, they host the 26th St. Mexican Independence Day Parade, one of the largest in the nation. The Little Village Arts Fest has many studios opening their doors and celebrating their ethnic art in October. On the outskirts of La Villita, you can find Apollo's 2000. A concert venue with as much for the eyes in the art deco architecture as it does on stage, Apollo's features mostly Mexican musical acts.

TO EAT

Nuevo Leon

Like the completely unrelated Nuevo Leon on 18th St., this restaurant serves up delicious food that exceeds the local drunken college student burrito joint. Barbacoa [shredded slow-cooked beef] and pico de gallo [fresh tomato salsa] are particularly delicious, as are the tortillas; homemade flour tortillas are uncommon at Mexican restaurants. Steer clear of

3657 W 26th St
773.522.1515
BLUE LINE to PULASKI

fish dishes though, as seafood here tends to be dry and overcooked. **A-**

Panadería Coral

Panadería Coral is a bit more expensive than nearby La Baguette, but it is much more friendly and upscale. While La Baguette resembles a slick, big box emporium, Coral has the vibe of Grandma's kitchen. Pastries are of a comparable quality, and it also offers breakfast, licuados [Mexican smoothies], coffee and tamales. **A-**

3807 W 26th St
773.762.4132
BLUE LINE to PULASKI

Taqueria La Justicia

3901 W. 26th St.
773.522.0041
BLUE LINE to PULASKI

Burritos and punk rock are a classic combination. At this roomy Little Village institution, you can find Mexican food and the South Side's finest punk bands under the same roof. The food is good and mostly focused on taqueria staples. Be sure to check this place out on a Friday night when the tables are pushed to the walls and a crowd of black leather and spiked hair arrives. Local Latino bands such as Condenada, I Attack and Sin Orden fill the always-packed room with extra short, extra fast and extra loud music not usually heard south of Madison St. You will not find ranchera or cumbia here, but La Justicia also hosts metal, ska and Spanish rock bands. Definitely one of the coolest spots in all of Little Village.

Dulce Landia

If you have a sweet tooth, welcome to paradise. This vibrantly-colored

3000 W 26th St
773.522.3816
PINK LINE to KEDZIE

candy store is packed to the brim with all kinds of sugary goodies, from traditional to exotic to difficult-to-find candy treats. Dulce Landia is fairly easy to navigate, but candy labels are sometimes difficult to follow; however, if you know what kind of candy you're after, you will probably find it here. **B**

El Chisme

This dine-in restaurant has a comfortable atmosphere with overhead lights that

3324 W 26th St
773.277.2533
PINK LINE to KEDZIE

set the perfect tone for lunch or dinner. El Chisme boasts of its 'authentic Mexican food,' and, while it is difficult to gauge whether this is the case, the food is certainly tasty and reasonably priced. The menu is a bit too traditional and limited, though overall this is a clean and classy establishment with better than average food. **B-**

El Fandango

This dark brick building is out of place on colorful 26th St., but the inside of

3331 W 26th St
773.762.1100
PINK LINE to KEDZIE

El Fandango is lively, bright and almost chain-like. The service is excellent, and the food is cheap but quite good. The menu tends toward standard but filling dishes. El Fandango's delicious salsa

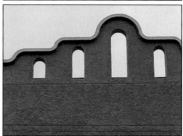

TOP Pink door, Kedzie St. RACHEL SWENIE • **MIDDLE** Mi Tierra Restaurant, 2528 Kedzie St. RACHEL SWENIE • **BOTTOM** House window, Albany Ave. and 25th St. RACHEL SWENIE

SOUTH LAWNDALE

roja is nutty and full-bodied with a peppery kick, but the refried beans are uninspiring. Traditional comfort foods like tamales and enchiladas are your best bet. **B⁻**

the walls. Confections such as tres leches cake, churros and pan dulce as well as more American cakes, donuts and rolls are priced around 50 cents each. **B**

La Baguette

La Baguette is an expansive bakery in an unattractive, family-friendly strip mall. However, make the trip for the huge piles of inexpensive Mexican pastries lining

3117 W 26th St
773.579.1873
PINK LINE to KEDZIE

Las Comales

This Mexican restaurant is part of a Chicago chain, and the 26th St. location is particularly popular. The menu is standard affair, and the service leaves much to be desired.

3141 W 26th St
773.247.0977
PINK LINE to KEDZIE

ESCAPING THE URBAN SPRAWL: THE NORTH BRANCH TRAIL
BY RYAN KING

For a large metropolitan area, Chicago offers a great deal of biking spaces and trails — both throughout the city and in the surrounding areas. Mayor Daley and his Bike Chicago campaign have helped create and maintain bicycle paths,

install the largest number of bike racks of any U.S. city and promote several large-scale city-wide bicycle events.

The North Branch Trail — one of the city's best — functions as the suburban artery to Chicago's Lakeshore bike path. It travels far enough away from the city to allow it plenty of expanses of prairie land and meandering river, yet close enough to be easily accessible. The trail starts at the corner of Caldwell Ave. and Devon Ave., located six miles from the lakefront, making it manageable to get there on bike. For those that are short on time, the trail can be reached via public transit as well. The CTA's No. 84 bus will get you there from the Bryn Mawr Red Line stop on the 'El,' where the Lakefront Trail ends.

The trail is a very easy bike ride on an entirely paved two-lane track with a dirt side path for joggers. The trail winds along the north branch of the Chicago River and ultimately finds its way to the Chicago Botanical Gardens. The entire trail can be completed in two hours at a leisurely pace.

Mile marker zero is a lightly wooded area that opens up onto grassy fields after a few twists and turns. There is a delicious little Filipino restaurant named Pampanga directly across the street. Dotting the winding trail are informational bulletin boards on forest ecology

SOUTH LAWNDALE

The atmosphere is decent: a clean establishment, but nothing remarkable. The food, however, is excellent, and customers have the options of dine-in or carry-out. **C+**

Taqueria Cuauhtemoc

At first glance, Cuauhtemoc doesn't seem like much, but this

2504 S Kedzie Ave
773.847.2263
PINK LINE to KEDZIE

humble, run-down restaurant is excellent for both food and sociology. Tortillas are tender with crisp

edges, and the birria [tender, spicy slow-cooked goat meat] is succulent and comforting. The majority of the clientele seem to be regulars, with interesting characters always at the counter. **B+**

Taqueria La Kermes

The graffiti on the windows does not make for the most attractive

3002 W 26th St
773.532.1666
PINK LINE to KEDZIE

or inviting display, but should you muster up the courage to try something different, you may

and conservation posted by the Forest Preserve District of Cook County.

Before you know it, you've reached the Caldwell Woods park area, home of the Jensen Toboggan Slides, making the trail fun even in the winter. There is parking available here and along the next few 'park areas.' On the other side of the trail is the huge Bunker Hill Park, a great place to people watch, as all types go there for kite flying, barbequing, volleyball, soccer, Frisbee, and the like. There are plenty of public restrooms available as well as covered picnic areas.

The only real downside to the trail is that it is broken up a bit. Every so often, you come to a major roadway that cuts across the trail and have to wait for traffic. Although it would be nearly impossible to have a bike path so close to an urban area without being interrupted, it's still a nuisance.

After passing through the first few park areas, the trail winds around several subdivisions, which is much less attractive than the unspoiled nature. Thankfully, in between a couple stretches of suburbs, lies one of the most beautiful and tranquil spaces on the trail. This area of open grassy expanse is known as the Miami Woods Prairie, and is truly a peaceful place and one the best spots of the North Branch Trail, as it really makes

you feel as though you are far from the big city.

The deer in the area are accustomed to the bike traffic, and will come right near you, allowing you a Snow White moment.

Things get rather confusing, however, when you reach Dempster St. The main road intersects the path, which zig-zags to accommodate it. There is a sign, but it's confusing. Don't go on Lehigh Ave., just continue on Dempster St. across the railroad tracks.

Once back on the trail, you will notice numerous walking paths

be pleasantly surprised by the quality of this taqueria's food. If you like Mexican food, then this will definitely appeal to your taste. In short: good food, very poor atmosphere. **C**

as roasted pumpkin seeds, mole sauce and several types of imported cheese. Various other funky Latin accoutrements such as candles and Day of the Dead paraphernalia fill out the shelves. This is an interesting little place to check out; it's a trip back in time to pre-Wal-Mart days. **A-**

TO SHOP

Cremería Santa Maria

In a word, La Cremería is eclectic. The name suggests an ice cream parlor, but this shop deals mostly in Mexican goods such

3424 W 26th St
773.277.1760
BLUE LINE to PULASKI

Yucca Texas Wear

For all you hipsters dying to sport cowboy boots, this is the place to get them cheap. 26th St. is teeming with Western apparel stores, but Yucca Texas Wear focuses

3600 W 26th St
773.277.2013
BLUE LINE to PULASKI

that branch off along the river. You can easily spend all day just exploring all the different nature trails. This is also where you begin to notice the horse trails. Somewhere around mile marker six, the trail passes the Glen Grove Equestrian Center, confirming that, yes, those have been horseshoe tracks that you have been spotting along the side of the bike path.

At mile 11, you will notice the following poem, unfolding in spray-paint as you ride:

'Roses are red
violets are blue
nothing would be better
than PROM with you – Joe'

This trail can be cute, real cute. There's no better low-cost date than a relaxing ride, exploring a new bike path, or revisiting an old favorite. You might as well put those picnic tables to use and pack a meal for two.

Just around the corner from mile 11 is a truly romantic spot where the trail opens up onto this huge body of water, part of the Skokie Lagoons. There are canoe rentals available, kayakers kayaking, and lots of space to fish. This is the final point on the southern trail. This is around where the southern half of the trail ends.

There's still plenty to see on the north half, which extends to the Chicago Botanical Gardens at mile 15.5. They go by rather quickly, with mostly wooded area.

The Botanical Gardens are gorgeous. Leave yourself at least half a day's time to explore the various themed islands, but don't forget to factor in the time it will take you to bike all the way back.

There are many reasons to visit the North Branch Trail, but it's most important draw is that it's relaxing and the air feels clean. It's a must-see for those who love the outdoors.

almost exclusively on cowboy boots. Of course, if you aren't interested in cowboy boots or gear, there really isn't much for you here. **C**

La Casa Bonita

	3507 W 26th St
	773.522.2570
	PINK LINE to CENTRAL PARK

Young women come into this quaint clothing store on a mission, sifting through the collection of reasonably-priced informal wear to separate the junk from the gems. There's not much to this shop, and some of the clothes [tops especially] verge on seeming tawdry, but a determined shopper could easily find a number of diamonds in the rough. Do not miss the accessories on the way out. **B-**

Velazquez Jewelers

	3544 W 26th St
	773.762.2969
	PINK LINE to CENTRAL PARK

If you're looking for the perfect set of earrings to match that gorgeous dress, you need to check out this charming jewelry shop. You can find everything here from the classy to the trendy, all of which is competitively priced. The more uniquely designed jewelry ranges from the stylishly creative to the 'what were they thinking?,' but there are plenty of great pieces for sale if you have the money to spend. **B**

Zemsky's Family Fashions

	3539 W 26th St
	773.522.1222
	PINK LINE to CENTRAL PARK

'Expect More, Get More!' is the mantra for this store. Zemsky's is far from trendy, though anyone looking for functional clothing will find a lot here for great prices. There are coats and school uniforms, a lot of simple casual items and an unhealthy preoccupation with the Dickies brand. You'll find plenty of clothes to sort through and may even come up with the occasional good buy. Just don't enter Zemsky's with your expectations too high. **C+**

Five Star Fashions

	3350 W 26th St
	773.762.3000
	PINK LINE to KEDZIE

Five Star is an urban clothing store with a Timberland boot focus right in the middle of the action of 26th St.. Prices are average, but the shop frequently has sales.

Five Star is a great locally owned alternative to giants like Foot Locker. It's a good place to pick up hip-hop fashions for cheap. **B+**

Gallery Fashion

	3400 W 26th St
	773.522.5365
	PINK LINE to KEDZIE

The store itself isn't much to look at, but who's got time to worry about that when there's such a wealth of colorful fashion available inside? Any young woman looking to make a splash at a formal dance would have no problem finding the perfect dress or skirt to meet the occasion and match her personality. Items are priced fairly, and the staff is very helpful. **B**

Mariano's Western Wear

	3259 W 26th St
	773.247.2300
	PINK LINE to KEDZIE

Unleash your inner cowboy in this expansive specialty shop. Vests, jackets, hats, boots and rugged jeans – this place has everything to complete the look. But be warned: The lack of mannequins and the vast, disorganized array of items can make exploring this store feel like you have landed in the Wild West. **B**

Modas Inc.

	3410 W 26th St
	773.277.9030
	PINK LINE to KEDZIE

If you're looking for the perfect evening gown or formal party dress, then look no further. This little store has high-end formal wear and enough classy jewelry to make your head spin. Everything looks expensive, and it probably is, so be careful not to visit unless you have some room to work with on that credit card. **B**

Ritmo Latino

	3701 W 26th St
	773.542.9007
	PINK LINE to KEDZIE

26th St. has an excellent selection of record stores specializing in Latin music. This one is a bit more polished than many of the other funky, eclectic places down the street. Ritmo Latino's selection runs the gamut of Latin genres, but its emphasis is on hip-hop and reggae. If you're into those genres, this is a good place to start. **B-**

BUILDING, REAR VIEW

This brick building stands near the area of McKinley
Park once known as Mt. Pleasant, a swampy site
adjacent to several steel and iron mills in the
working class neighborhood. In 1902, one year after
his assassination, Chicago's South Park Commission
opened an experimental park named for president
William McKinley. The park, meant to bring
green breathing space to residents of the filthy,
overcrowded tenement neighborhood, proved a huge
success and led to the development of a whole new
system of parks.

Photograph by Elizabeth Neurauter

SOUTHWEST

BRIDGEPORT

Home to large Irish-American, Croatian, Lithuanian, Asian and Hispanic populations, Bridgeport is one of the most ethnic areas of Chicago. Once an industrial heap, it is beginning its transformation into a residential community. It's located along a stretch of the Chicago River called Bubbly Creek due to the animal carcasses dumped there during the meat packing years which create a gaseous symphony as they decompose. The bubbles still persist but pricier homes have come in and notable landmarks still stand proud. Visit the Richard J. Daley House, childhood home of Mayor Daley, or play in McGuane Park. Visit the two stunning Polish Cathedral Style churches that dominate the skyline – St. Mary of Perpetual Help and St. Barbara – and marvel at the beautiful stained glass windows and painted ceilings. There's not too much in the way of shopping and fine dining but taverns and other dive joints quench the palate just as well. Bridgeport may not be glitzy but the down to earth atmosphere and historical buildings make it a nice place to live or visit for those looking for the less beaten path.

BRIDGEPORT

TO EAT

Freddie's Pizza & Pasta Parlor

Though the name of this restaurant suggests you take a look at the pizza and pasta choices, the beef sandwich should not be overlooked. However, judging by the satisfied looks on others' faces who ordered the namesake plates, they were not disappointed either. Portions are largle with reasonable prices and delivery is also an option. **A-**

701 W 31st St
312.808.0147
ORANGE LINE to HALSTED

Ace Bakeries

The tantalizing wedding and birthday cakes in the window are enough to make you go in, but the trays of homemade donuts, cannolies, cupcakes and pies are what make you sit down and stay for a while. Enjoy a delicious pastry at one of the few available tables or get a fantastic cake to go. The line is worth it. **A-**

3241 S Halsted St
312.225.4973
RED LINE to SOX-35th

Bridgeport Restaurant

Recognizable by the old-fashioned sign on the corner, this restaurant

3500 S Halsted St
773.247.2826
RED LINE to SOX-35th

holds Formica tabletops and ripped vinyl booths that have seen better days. The menu has a large array of standard diner fare and the daily specials are written on index cards attached to the menu with paper clips. The prices are moderate, but so is the service. **B-**

Healthy Food Lithuanian Restaurant

For authentic Lithuanian kugelis and blynai pancakes, this is the place to

3236 S Halsted St
312.326.2724
RED LINE to SOX-35th

go. The diner gives off a foreign spin with traditional artwork that accents the walls. The prices are reasonable and there are even a good number of vegetarian options. When you've finished your shake made from Lithuanian yogurt or your beet soup, you can buy classic amber jewelry by the front entrance. **A-**

Kevin's Hamburger Heaven

Open 24 hours, Kevin's Hamburger Heaven is the perfect place to go if

554 W Pershing Rd
773.268.5748
RED LINE to SOX-35th

you've got a burning desire for a hamburger in the middle of the night. They serve breakfast, lunch and dinner, which includes flapjacks, sandwiches, eggs, and burgers. As unfortunate as it is for credit-only customers, Kevin's only takes cash. Also, be sure to try their vanilla milkshakes, which are to die for. **B-**

La Mexicana Taqueria

A wrought iron entrance and inner brick walls make this spot cozier than your

815 W 35th St
773.890.1090
RED LINE to SOX-35th

average Mexican diner. The food is reasonably priced and the options are numerous. It also serves an extensive breakfast menu of omelettes,

THE CHICAGO CHIDITAROD

BY MATTHEW BIGELOW

On a bitter March day in Wicker Park, more than 200 would-be champions gather in a deserted lot eating sausages and guzzling Miller High Life for warmth and sustenance. Teams shuffle through the mix of snow, slush and mud waiting for the race to start.

A man in a bunny costume walks around screaming the lyrics to 'TNT' by AC/DC and beating a drum. Event organizer Devin Breen, wearing a leopard-print shirt and a cowboy hat, shouts over a bullhorn, advising the teams to do everything in their power not to get arrested.

Thirty-seven teams, five miles and one goal: first place in the 2007 Chiditarod.

'The Chiditarod is Chicago's urban Iditarod or shopping cart race, in the true spirit of the Alaskan Iditarod,' says Breen. 'Except instead of dogs we have people, instead of sleds we have shopping carts and instead of tundra, we have the frozen streets of Chicago.'

Team Zissou. The Cold Warriors. Pixies Revolt. All of them came out to vie for a shot at glory. The Buck Funnys drove all the way from Columbus to compete. One team even dressed up their cart as a replica of the Mystery Machine and donned Scooby Doo costumes.

But while the atmosphere may be one of extravagance, the race itself is simple. Four dogs and one musher push their cart just under five miles from start to finish. Along the way teams must hit four checkpoints [i.e. various Wicker Park bars] where they pause for a mandatory 20 minutes to 'water the dogs.' Drink specials and live bands attract fans to cheer on the teams.

burritos, and Mexican egg dishes. Sit at the counter for a shake, piña colada or Mexican soda. Bring a quarter for the gumball machine on your way out. **B**

Phil's Pizza

The mediocre pizza they serve up and the bland environment make this cash-only establishment fairly run of the mill. There are much better places to go in the area if all you are looking for is pizza. Even so, Phil's is reasonably priced and a reliable joint located in the Bridgeport neighborhood. **C**

3551 S Halsted St
773.523.0947
RED LINE to SOX-35th

Ramova Grill

Located close to Phil's, this is a great alternative if you enjoy the food

3510 S Halsted St
773.847.9058
RED LINE to SOX-35th

and atmosphere of old-school diners. Everything on the menu looks delicious, so this restaurant comes highly recommended. With traditional 1940's décor, the atmosphere goes along well with the diner cuisine, which includes breakfast, lunch and dinner options. **A**

TO PLAY

Bridgeport Tattoo Co.

This modish, clean tattoo parlor is a recent addition to the Bridgeport area.

3527 S Halsted St
773.533.8311
RED LINE to SOX-35th

The stylish staff is young and very personable. The hipster ambiance projected by the individuals who will be modifying your body is topped off with lime green walls, wood floors and leather reclining chairs spread throughout the room. **A-**

The first team across the finish line with at least 15 pounds of canned goods for donation brings home the trophy – a shopping cart wheel mounted on a block of well-polished mahogany.

DECEIT, MANIPULATION & TRICKERY

While the cause may seem altruistic, the Chiditarod elicits a stellar heat of competition. Teams strategized, formed alliances and teamed up on other teams to maximize their chances.

In the end, though, winning often isn't based on speed or dexterity, but cunning sabotage, a hallmark of the Chiditarod.

'A lot of people say that cheaters don't prosper,' said Brian Lauvray, captain of the winning team. '[But] the proof is right here, guys,' he said, hoisting the first-place trophy high above the competition's head.

Lauvray's team, the Corporate Dalliances, had been veritable bastards in order to ensure victory. They zip tied rival team's carts together, duct taped their

wheels and Lauvray even took off early from the starting line.

But that was nothing compared to the trick that won them Best Sabotage Award.

Gregg Sparks, the self-described 'lead dog' for Corporate Dalliances, sat at work the Friday before the race brainstorming different tactics while looking at the route on the Chiditarod Web site. 'Eureka,' he said to himself. While the boss wasn't looking, Sparks put in a little time on Photoshop and created a bogus map.

Before the race, Sparks walked around with a clipboard, shaking hands and distributing the map to the other contestants. A number of teams were sent scrambling across Chicago's West Side, hopelessly searching for the next check point.

'We were first coming in and then some sons of bitches taped our wheels and we got this fake map and then we were lost as shit and we started cursing at each other. We had a mutiny and

BRIDGEPORT

Daley Library

This small library is a bright and cheery place where you come to lose yourself in a book. The large windows, colorful ambiance and large selection of children's books make this a wonderful place to bring out the young bookworm in you. Take a seat amidst the shelves or at one of the computer stations to while away an hour. **A-**

3400 S Halsted St
312.747.8990
RED LINE to SOX-35th

TO SHOP

Augustine's Spiritual Goods

You'll think you stepped inside the world of Harry Potter once you open this shop's small blue door. The walls are lined with

3327 S Halsted St
773.843.1933
RED LINE to SOX-35th

potions and books on magic, spirituality and mysticism. Eclectic customers come here to buy everything from enchanted powders to voodoo dolls to four-leaf clovers. Don't pass this up, if only to experience the unique aura of this very 'charming' store. **A-**

Wendt Furniture

The owners here carry anything but furniture. More an open space than a store, this knick-knack paradise puts a new spin on the average 99-cent shop. The random offerings are separated into aisles of cardboard boxes on the floor. The items range from kids' toys to gardening tools to batteries to Chinese slippers. It's worth stopping in for cheap household items or to try your luck at finding cool flea-market-esque trinkets. **B**

3410 S Halsted St
773.927.9400
RED LINE to SOX-35th

---

now we're in sixth place,' said the captain of the team Pixie Revolts. [They ultimately finished in 19th place].

Despite the team's early successes, the Corporate Dalliances were not without tribulations of their own. Due to a miscommunication, half of the team left the third check point early [another major infraction] leaving Sparks and another teammate, Eric Porges, behind.

They were like a 'chicken running around without the proverbial feathers,' according to Porges.

To make up the time, Sparks borrowed a bike from a friend who was following the group and caught up with the rest of the team, leaving Porges to catch up on his own. This constituted a flagrant violation of the 'four dogs and one musher to one sled' rule.

Porges shrugged off the infringement. 'As long as our cart gets there and no one finds out about it until the race is over, we should be fine,' Porges said.

The lapse cost them, however, and at the last checkpoint they found

themselves in second place. After attempting to bribe the judges failed, the team stashed the first place team's cart in a snow bank in an alley behind the bar.

Poised for victory the team faced one last obstacle: one of their team members felt fatigued and feared she may slow the team down on their final leg. To compensate, she borrowed the bike and pedaled ahead, pausing before the finish line so the team could cross together.

From there on it was smooth sailing.

'THE BIGGEST HEARTS'
All told, the 2007 Chiditarod raises more than 2,000 pounds of canned goods each year. Although other cities boast similar events, such as New York City and San Francisco to name a few, the Chiditarod is unique because it is also a charity event.

'A lot of people talked about us not having the best cart or the best equipment. We had the biggest hearts though,' Lauvray said.

BRIDGEPORT

ARMOUR SQUARE

EXOTIC SIGHTS AND SMELLS ABOUND

On a tiny strip of land between the railroad tracks and the Dan Ryan Expressway, Armour Square is loaded with things to do for those not faint of heart. U.S. Cellular field is home to 2005 World Series Champion White Sox. While public urination makes a rowdy Cubs fan, Sox fans are known for their unabashed support for their team. 'The Joan,' as the field is nicknamed, has seen fans attack umpires and off-duty cops. The third largest Chinatown in the states, exotic sights and smells abound on the north end of Armour Square. Walking through Chinatown Gate and down Wentworth Ave., you'll find whole fried ducks strung up in storefronts and many Buddhist prayer rooms. For the shopper, there are gift shops a plenty carrying everything from Hello Kitty paraphernalia to faux designer bags to traditional Chinese brocade dresses. Attractions include Chinatown Square, which has large metal sculptures of the Chinese zodiac animals, and Chinatown Mural, celebrating Chinese immigrants. For a slower pace, Armour Square Park and Wentworth Gardens Park offer green in the city.

ARMOUR SQUARE

TO EAT

Aji Ichiban

The translation on the door – 'Munchies Paradise' – explains it all at this candy and snack shop. Milk candy, chocolate and fruit gummies in all shapes will satisfy any sweet tooth. More traditional snacks like preserved plums, ginger and dried fish are also in strong supply, many available for sampling. Buy as many or as few as you like, but be aware of the varying, and often high, prices on different types of treats. **A**

2117 S China Place
312.328.9998
RED LINE to CERMAK-CHNTWN

BBQ King House

If you can decode the menu, this combination takeout and sit-down style barbecue restaurant offers speed and convenience. The front half of the restaurant, with a full selection of roast ducks and chickens on display, is dedicated solely to takeout starting at 9 a.m. The traditional menu offers a wide selection, with lunch specials until 4 p.m. **B+**

2148 S Archer Ave
312.326.1219
RED LINE to CERMAK-CHNTWN

Captain Café and Bakery

Captain's Café and Bakery isn't a standout shop by any means, but it offers all the basics you would expect without the long line. For those wary of Chinese desserts, you'll be able to find all-American chocolate chip cookies and New York cheesecake alongside the pork buns and bean cakes. **B-**

2161 S China Place
312.791.0888
RED LINE to CERMAK-CHNTWN

Chiu Quon Bakery & Café

Satisfy your sweet tooth with a wonderful array of cookies, cakes and other Chinese confectioneries in this modest bakery. Their display case is stocked with traditional staples like mooncakes, curry beef puffs, egg custard tarts, and mango pudding, as well as Western-style fruit tarts and apple pies. If you get a chance, step into the back of this unassuming establishment where, without the wait of a long line, you will discover some quality dim sum for very little cost. **A**

2242 S. Wentworth Ave
312.225.6608
RED LINE to CERMAK-CHNTWN

Dragon King Restaurant

Dragon King serves Mandarin cuisine in an atmosphere that's a notch above the standard Chinatown restaurant. Dishes are a bit pricier, but still a deal with most dishes under $12 and 64 lunch dishes no more than $5.25 apiece. The second floor can also host a karaoke party for you and up to 149 of your closest friends. **A**

2138 S Archer Ave
312.881.0168
RED LINE to CERMAK-CHNTWN

Great Wall Restaurant

This no-frills lunch spot takes the difficulty of ordering a balanced meal off your shoulders with their preset family dinners for two to eight people. Dinners come with soup, rice and several dishes. If you come alone, there's a long list of $5.45 lunch specials served daily until 3 p.m. A separate BBQ King menu is also available, where you can order the ducks and chickens hanging in the window, or even special order a whole roast pig. **B**

2127 S China Place
312.808.9686
RED LINE to CERMAK-CHNTWN

Happy Chef Dim Sum House

Larger than most area restaurants, this one is good for a crowd. Do dim sum in the morning or come for a regular feast at dinner – they'll throw in an extra entree if you order three dishes off their preset list. If you just want two dishes, you still wind up with a free crab or lobster. The menu has no pictures and some unique options, so go with someone who can navigate Chinese cuisine. **A-**

2164 S Archer Ave
312.808.3689
RED LINE to CERMAK-CHNTWN

Hing Kee

Giant bowls of noodles, known as pho, take center stage at this Vietnamese and Chinese restaurant. If you're not in the mood for soup, take your pick from the fried noodles and other entrees section, most in the $6-$8 range. The basic menu without pictures can make choosing a pho daunting, so take along an adventuresome spirit or a knowledgeable friend. **B**

2140 S Archer Ave
312.808.9538
RED LINE to CERMAK-CHNTWN

Joy Yee's

This trendy and casual lunch and dinner spot in Chinatown Square is unique from other restaurants in the area. The brightly painted walls and modern furniture contribute to the festive atmosphere that attracts diners of all ages and backgrounds. You can scan the menu containing colorful images of an assortment of pan-Asian dishes [known for large portions] and specialty drinks. Tapioca lovers: be sure to save room for the refreshing bubble teas and fresh fruit freezes. **B+**

2159 S China Place
312.328.0001
RED LINE to CERMAK-CHNTWN

Ken Kee Restaurant

With more than 200 dishes to choose from, including a list of 'unique Chinese food' and specialty teas and smoothies, there's something for everyone on Ken Kee's extensive menu. Find your favorites, try something new like stir-fried duck tongue, or sample them both – every item on the menu sells for under $9. **B+**

2129 S China Place
312.326.2088
RED LINE to CERMAK-CHNTWN

ARMOUR SQUARE

KS Seafood

There's much more than seafood on the menu in this relaxed café. Most

2163 S China Place
312.842.1238
RED LINE to CERMAK-CHNTWN

regions of China are represented, and there are even a few Thai dishes if you look closely. Half of the takeout menu is in Chinese only though, so if you really want something authentic, take a guess and you might end up with a new favorite. **B**

Maxim's Bakery

This suitcase-sized bakery has your standard Chinese bakery delights. Large

2210 S Wentworth Ave
312.225.0205
RED LINE to CERMAK-CHNTWN

almond and sugar cookies baked daily are $0.50 each so your sweet tooth can be satisfied for a small price. It's easier to grab and go because there is little space to sit, let alone any room to stand in this mom and pop establishment. **C+**

Moon Palace Restaurant

A few steps from the Chinatown 'El' stop, Moon Palace is a modern,

216 W Cermak Rd
312.225.4081
RED LINE to CERMAK-CHNTWN

casual, family-friendly restaurant that substitutes soft lighting and jazz music for the traditional Chinese restaurant ambience. It attracts a variety of customers as it serves both Americanized and authentic Chinese food. Here, you'll find familiar favorites like orange chicken and fried rice, and plenty of choices for the more adventurous eater. For groups up to six that prefer to share, Moon Palace offers family style fixed-price options. **A–**

Mountain View Chef

The picture menu that doubles as an order sheet makes this an ideal place

2168 S Archer Ave
312.842.2168
RED LINE to CERMAK-CHNTWN

for dim sum beginners. Simply check the box next to the picture and description, and it will be delivered to your table momentarily. Each dish costs between $2 and $3, so you can try the curry mini octopus or chicken feet along with your dumplings, steamed buns and eggrolls. **A**

Penang

Located at the corner of the entrance to old Chinatown under the

2201 S Wentworth Ave
312.326.6888
RED LINE to CERMAK-CHNTWN

main gate, this Malaysian and sushi eatery offers a modern atmosphere and a wide selection of moderately-priced entrees, including plenty of seafood. For even the most indecisive diner, the a la carte sushi menu with single rolls for as low as $1.50 should suffice. **A**

Phoenix Restaurant

For delicacies like shark fin soup and Peking duck, Phoenix is the place to go.

2131 S Archer Ave
312.328.0848
RED LINE to CERMAK-CHNTWN

The upscale atmosphere, complete with a fully stocked bar and wait staff dressed to impress, only enhances the full-service menu of familiar and unique entrees. Before 3 p.m, the dim sum picture menu with more than 50 options is the best way to sample all Phoenix has to offer. **A**

Saint Anna Bakery and Café

Glistening pastries, buns and fruity cakes line the display case of this

2158 S Archer Ave
312.225.3168
RED LINE to CERMAK-CHNTWN

bustling bakery. They also sell an assortment of reasonably-priced iced drinks, smoothies and freezes, but faces stiff competition from Joy Yee's across the street. Credit cards aren't accepted, and a minimum $3 purchase per person is required if you want to sit down while you enjoy your treat. **B+**

Saint's Alp Teahouse

This hip hangout is an import from Hong Kong, and one of only two

2131 S Archer Ave
312.842.1886
RED LINE to CERMAK-CHNTWN

locations in the United States. You can order dim sum-style appetizers and a few entrées, but the main draw is the over 60 varieties of drinks. The menu is full of tantalizing beverages, with every kind of coffee, tea, milkshake and smoothie you can imagine – the worst part of your visit will be having to choose just one. **A**

ARMOUR SQUARE

Seven Treasures

Seven Treasures is a 'hole in the wall' restaurant that is anything but preten-

2312 S Wentworth Ave
312.225.2668
RED LINE to CERMAK-CHNTWN

tious. But even though the dine-in experience features only the barest essentials, you'll see plenty of customers return time after time to chow down on the most authentic Chinese foods. Their specialty drinks, which come in interesting flavors like avocado, honeydew, and red bean, are as satisfying as their eats. It's open late and the prices are cheap, so your stomach and wallet will thank you. **B**

Spring World

If you're into regional cuisines, Spring World is the place to go. The

2109 China Place
312.326.9966
RED LINE to CERMAK-CHNTWN

menu is divided into sections, so you can sample the specialties of Szechwan, Peking, Canton, Shanghai and even Yunan cooking. Seafood lov-

ers will find a wide variety, with everything from crab and shrimp to frogs and sea cucumbers. Another perk is the three hours of free parking while you dine. **B+**

Sunlight Café and Bakery

Expect to find a deal at this no-frills lunch spot. The simple menu offers

227 W Cermak Rd
312.674.1368
RED LINE to CERMAK-CHNTWN

Asian basics – lo mein, chop suey, and fried rice – with your choice of any meat. A few other traditional dishes round out the menu, and for those with room for dessert, a decent selection of pastries under $1 tempts diners from the display case. All lunches are $4.50-$5 and include a drink. **B**

The Noodle

Big bowls of Vietnamese Pho are the main attrac- tion at The Noodle, but

2336 S Wentworth Ave
312.674.1168
RED LINE to CERMAK-CHNTWN

BACHELOR'S GROVE: WHERE THE DEAD FIND NIGHTLIFE
BY MATTHEW STREIB

Just outside the Chicago city limits, nestled in the bosom of a forest preserve, is one of the most haunted places in the world. The Bachelor's Grove Cemetery, an old, abandoned patch of land, holds a modest array of graves and the hearts of many local ghost chasers. And if you're up for a discussion with the dead, it's certainly worth a visit.

Bad things have happened at Bachelor's Grove. The tiny, one-acre cemetery located in the sleepy town of Midlothian was established in the mid-1800s as one of Cook County's first cemeteries. Supposedly, it all started with the nearby lake, where a farmer drowned long ago when his horse dragged him and his plow under the water. During Prohibition, the mob allegedly used the site as a dumping ground for its marks, also drowning victims and their cars in the nearby lagoon.

there's something for everyone on the menu, which divides into categories 'For the Beginners,' 'Just Regular' and 'The Adventurer's Choice.' If the soup's not filling enough, order a few appetizers or an exotic fruit smoothie with tapioca in flavors like durian and jackfruit or strawberry and banana. Main entrees are $5-$6 and the smoothies will set you back another $2.95. **B+**

Three Happiness

At the original Three Happiness, it is common to see workers at a corner table near the kitchen and hear them laughing and speaking in Chinese. Their behavior sets up a 'grandma's kitchen' atmosphere for this small and unassuming restaurant in contrast to its more upscale counterpart across the street

209 W Cermak Rd
312.842.1964
RED LINE to CERMAK-CHNTWN

owned by the same family. The food here caters to authentic tastes and comes out in a flash. One thing to beware – when they say spicy, they mean spicy. **B+**

Three Happiness

Three Happiness has been a Chinatown favorite since its opening as a sister restaurant to 'the original' bearing the same name. With expansive upstairs and downstairs dining rooms this establishment is known for its savory dishes, full bar and late-night karaoke, but its main draw is dim sum served daily. You can order from the menu or directly from the circling carts, and, as is standard with any dim sum restaurant, the service is not as attentive as effective. **A-**

2130 S Wentworth Ave
312.791.1228
RED LINE to CERMAK-CHNTWN

Then, in the 1960s, authorities stopped burying people in Bachelor's Grove, and youths began frequenting the park, often to neck in secrecy. But in the 1970s, with the establishment of new roads, the cemetery was cut off from the highway, fenced in by the Forest Preserve District, and meant to be forgotten. Instead, it was vandalized. Gravestones

were knocked over, spray painted, or dumped in the lake. Many were stolen and appeared in police departments across the county. Even worse, many of the graves were dug up and the bodies desecrated for public view, and satanic groups held rituals in the cemetery, leaving the remains of sacrificed creatures behind.

For years, people have been seeing ghostly apparitions populating the grove, from benign orbs of white light to a two-headed creature rising from the lagoon. Red streaks have shot through the trees, a Victorian farmhouse has appeared and disappeared in a multitude of locations, a woman has been seen roaming the grounds with her infant, and a drowned farmer has plowed the ground with his horse. Best yet, terrible men in black hoods have chased visitors around the woods. Sounds like a great place for a vacation, no? I decided to spend the night.

It's really easy to get to Midlothian, which is near I-294, has a Metra stop, and is also only a half-hour bike ride from the 95th St. Red Line stop

Wan Shi Da Bakery

Find giant-sized youtiao, the traditional Chinese fried dough, at this otherwise non-descript bakery. There's a nice mix of sweet and savory buns and pastries, including a few elaborately decorated fruit tarts and chocolate cakes, and like most of the Chinatown bakeries there's an area in the back for enjoying your treats. This one is cleaner than most. **A-**

2229 S Wentworth Ave
312.225.1133
RED LINE to CERMAK-CHNTWN

Won Kow Restaurant

Atop a flight of stairs and behind two heavy glass doors is Chinatown's oldest restaurant. Since its opening in the late 1920s, Won Kow has been a popular dim sum destination [especially on weekends] and has gathered a loyal following. It offers everything a dim sum connoisseur craves, including shrimp dumplings, steamed buns, rice wrapped in lotus leaf and jasmine tea. Won Kow boasts numerous local awards and was recognized by The Tribune for its exceptionally mouthwatering pot stickers. **A**

2237 S Wentworth Ave
312.842.7500
RED LINE to CERMAK-CHNTWN

Franco's Ristorante

Franco's is an excellent choice if you're craving some homestyle Italian food before or after a visit to U.S. Cellular Field to see the White Sox. It is slightly more expensive than other area restaurants, but if you're willing to spend a few extra dollars, a visit to Franco's is well worth your while. **B+**

300 W 31st St
312.225.9566
RED LINE to SOX-35th

---

of the 'El.' We decided to bike it from the 'El,' but the ghosts of Bachelor's Grove didn't seem to want us to make it – I got a flat tire less than a block into the ride. But I was undeterred, and walked.

It was almost dark when I got near the abandoned cemetery, which can be hard to find in the daytime. But upon approaching the broken, barely attached chain-link fence, it was easy to see why the place was infamous. The cemetery had been utterly vandalized, both by hoodlums and by nature. Broken tombstones were nestled in waist-high grasses, the paths were almost indistinguishable, and a large tree had fallen in the center, destroying the cemetery's fence and probably covering some tombstones as well.

Obviously, people had been there recently. Each grave had been honored with a gaudy plastic flower. Most remarkable, however, was a tiny grave that sits near the back of the cemetery, marked 'Infant Daughter.' Apparently, the locals had adopted this child, leaving an array of old toys strewn about her grave

for her to play with. Soggy teddy bears stared out from the mud, surrounded by dried-out lip gloss and tattered dolls.

Staying the night was certainly a freaky experience. First, I was afraid that the police would come. Because of all of the vandalism, the police are supposed to patrol the area with some frequency, but rumor has it that they've kind of given up on the place.

What was really scary, however, were the cicadas of 2007. I mean, they were everywhere. Each blade of grass carries them, swollen-eyed, noisy, and ready to bite. They got in my tent, in my hair, and in my jar of peanut butter. If the ghosts of Bachelor's Grove weren't trying to frighten me off the property, they were certainly trying to gross me out.

I never saw a ghost while at the Grove. No lights, no apparitions, no men in black chasing me around. Judging by the trash can by the entrance overflowing with beer cans and vodka bottles, it seems like you need to have a little help to see the ghosts. But the aura was defi-

ARMOUR SQUARE

TO SHOP

AJ Housewares & Gifts

Look closely as you browse this variety store and you're bound to find a few surprises. The aisles are stacked floor-to-ceiling with trinkets, kitchen supplies and even [affordable] decorative fountains. Buy everything you need to cook and serve a meal from woks, plates, bowls and chopsticks, right down to the straws for bubble tea. Then follow your nose to the back corner, where you'll find a large stock of incense, candles and various other Buddhist effects. **A-**

> 2125 S China Place
> 312.567.9908
> RED LINE to CERMAK-CHNTWN

Chinatown Market

Stock up on all your favorite Chinese staples here – fresh fruit and veggies, every type of noodle you can imagine, sauces,

> 2121 S Archer Ave
> 312.881.0068
> RED LINE to CERMAK-CHNTWN

whole fish, candies, frozen buns and dumplings, and all sorts of tea await. The aisles are nice and wide for easy maneuvering. You won't have to walk far with your purchases, since parking in the adjacent lot is free. **A**

Evergreen Jewelry

If it's high-quality jade you're looking for, this is the place to go. Large and small bracelets, rings and pendants, including several renditions of the Buddha, are all on display here. There's plenty of gold to go around – many of the charms are unremarkable, but various Chinese gods, zodiac creatures and Chinese characters stand out from the rest. **B**

> 2263 S Wentworth Ave
> 312.808.0730
> RED LINE to CERMAK-CHNTWN

Fashion House

Bamboo and bonsai trees abound in this tiny earthy-smelling shop full

> 235 W Cermak Rd
> 312.326.1228
> RED LINE to CERMAK-CHNTWN

nitely creepy. I never saw anything, but I felt that I wouldn't be surprised if I had.

But, hell, you might be luckier than I, and you shouldn't leave Chicago without first taking a chance on seeing one of the most haunted sites in the world.

To get there: Once in Midlothian, find the Turnpike, which

intersects with Cicero Ave. Head west on the Turnpike until you hit a turn, where it will become 143rd St. On your right should be a park called the Rubio Woods Forest Preserve, and on your left should be a radio tower. Park in a nearby lot and just a bit off the tower should be a small, overgrown road which will take you to the cemetery.

of gift-worthy items. Depending on the size of the plant and quality of the pot, a live gift could set you back anywhere from $15-$100. For those less inclined to water their treasures, a variety of whimsical ceramic pottery decorations, glass figurines, wood carvings and even a few umbrellas dot the store. Gifts start at $1 and go up to around $200. **B**

Giftland

This combination souvenir stand, toy and candy shop and discount clothing

2212 S Wentworth Ave
312.225.0088
RED LINE to CERMAK-CHNTWN

store offers a wide variety of goods, minus some of the Chinatown charm. There are several aisles of Beanie Babies and other TY stuffed creatures, but the best part of this drugstore-like emporium is the wide selection of traditional men's, women's and children's clothing arranged by size all the way up to XXL. Get your slippers here for $6, and your Chinese costume is good to go. **B**

Gifts 'R Us

Compared to the neighboring gift shops, Gifts 'R Us feels strangely empty,

2220 S Wentworth Ave
312.328.9923
RED LINE to CERMAK-CHNTWN

but that's not necessarily a bad thing. The extra space makes for easier browsing of a quality collection that includes fountains, wall hangings and tile paintings. You won't feel as if you'll break something if you round the corner too fast, and the bubbling fountains create a soothing ambience. **B+**

Hoypoloi Gallery

Although somewhat of an anomaly in the midst of bustling Chinatown,

2235 S Wentworth Ave
312.225.6477
RED LINE to CERMAK-CHNTWN

this contemporary art gallery is definitely worth stopping by. More than 200 artists from around the United States display their work here in an eclectic collection of glass, 3-D paintings, metal work and even purses made from candy wrappers. Hoypoloi has been in this location nearly 12 years, and its plans for expansion will double the size of display area in the near future. **A-**

Ten Ren Tea and Ginseng Co. of Chicago

This shop features products from Ten Ren Tea Company, one of the

2247 S Wentworth Ave
312.842.1171
RED LINE to CERMAK-CHNTWN

largest and best known tea manufacturers of the Far East. Ten Ren promotes the 'art of Chinese tea to discriminating consumers worldwide.' It's a great place to buy high quality green, jasmine, oolong, black, and white tea, to name a few. Also, anyone curious about Chinese herbal medicine, including ginseng, will be readily welcomed by the friendly and knowledgeable staff. **A**

Woks 'N' Things

To recreate the fine food Chinatown has to offer, head to this cooking

2234 S Wentworth Ave
312.842.0701
RED LINE to CERMAK-CHNTWN

supply haven for everything but the actual food. Pick up a cookbook on your way in the door, then browse the woks lining one wall or the scattered sushi kits and bamboo steamers. Unique gadgets like vegetable 'cookie' cutters are sold here too, and the incense-enhanced atmosphere makes lingering to find them worthwhile. **A**

World Journal Bookstore

Unless you read Chinese, there's little in the way of reading material for

2116 S Archer Ave
312.842.8005
RED LINE to CERMAK-CHNTWN

you here, except for a few cookbooks or Chinese language textbooks if you're feeling particularly ambitious. But it's worth a quick browse, and you will find CDs, DVDs, cards, calendars and various other souvenirs for English and Chinese speakers alike. **B**

World Treasures Emporium

World Treasures Emporium is a nice one-stop shop if you want

2253 S Wentworth Ave
312.808.1818
RED LINE to CERMAK-CHNTWN

something more than a trinket. The second floor functions as a furniture showroom, while the main floor houses the more affordable treasures. Among the more unique finds are lantern light sets, money trees and bamboo shoots and spirals you can buy by the stalk to plant yourself. **B+**

ARMOUR SQUARE

LOWER WEST SIDE

NUMEROUS AND DIVERSE FESTIVALS MAKE IT A DESTINATION

While dashes of Italian flavor can be found in the Lower West Side, the area is mostly dominated by the Latin culture of Pilsen. Those looking for authentic Mexican cuisine need to look no further than 18th St. Taquerias, grocery stores and bakeries crowd the streets while exteriors and alleys are covered with colorful murals. A plethora of knick-knack shops fill up the spaces in between. 26th St., known as Little Village, is also a vibrant area with ethnic shopping galore. Though poverty and gang-violence has hit the area hard, the tight-knit community refuses to let that keep them down. Pilsen is home to the largest Latino cultural center in the U.S., The Mexican Fine Arts Center. The collection of nearly 2,500 pieces is stunning but numerous and diverse festivals make it a destination. The Polish Catholic Church, St. Adalbert's, provides a different ethnic flair but has since become dominated by the Mexicans of the area. To the west, in the neighborhood called Heart of Chicago, there are plenty of Italian restaurants for those seeking a different flavor.

TO EAT

Kristoffer's Café and Bakery

Named for the owners' son, Carlos and Christina Chavarria's café and bakery has become famous for its tres leches cakes. Kristoffer's multicultural menu includes everything from French toast, Southwestern omelets, roast-beef sandwiches, to Mexican or Mayan tamales. They often offer live music on Thursday evenings and Sunday mornings for enthusiastic guests. **A-**

1733 S Halsted St
312.829.4172
ORANGE LINE to HALSTED

Picante Grill

The Picante Grill is never crowded, though with great, reasonably-priced Mexican food and margaritas the size of your head, it really should be. The chef is constantly revising the menu to incorporate popular lunch and dinner specials into the mix. Daily discounts include half-off margaritas and $5 beer buckets, and the service is quick and always comes with a smile. **A**

1626 S Halsted St
312.455.8500
ORANGE LINE to HALSTED

Café Mestizo: Cultural Urban Coffee House

1646 W. 18th St.
312.427.5920
PINK LINE to 18th

Café Mestizo opened in the heart of the Pilsen community in 2003 with the goal of becoming a place 'where art, music & poetry come together over a great cup of coffee.' Since then the cafe has hosted countless open mic nights, art shows, musical performances and more. The self-declared 'cultural urban coffee house' also sells a variety of jewelry, art and apparel, such as shirts protesting the gentrification of Pilsen. In addition, they offer a varied menu, ranging from the coffee house classics like bagels to Mexican treats like tamales. Come in and enjoy some in Mestizo's deep purple interior.

Café Jumping Bean

1439 W 18th St
312.455.0019
PINK LINE to 18th

Considered the best café in the area, this small restaurant is the perfect place to bring a book or a good friend. The waiters serve coffee in large ceramic mugs perfect for huddling with when it's below zero outside. In addition to regular coffeehouse food, the café stocks a full menu of sandwiches, soups, and salads. Apparently writers, poets, and artists have been gathering in this establishment for the past 10 years with good reason. **A-**

Cuernavaca Restaurant

1158-60 W 18th St
312.829.1147
PINK LINE to 18th

Since 1970, Cuernavaca Restaurant has been serving up Tex-Mex food with style. Its terra cotta interior may seem kitschy at first – complete with chairs engraved with the word 'Mexico' – but it'll charm you in the end. Sit back and order a sizzling skillet of carne asada and enjoy the complimentary sopapillas, a sugary fried bread treat. Affordable and delicious, this eatery deserves a visit. **A**

Mundial Cocina Mestiza

1640 W 18th St
312.491.9908
PINK LINE to 18th

If Mundial Cocina Mestiza were located in downtown Chicago you'd probably pay twice as much for their Mediterranean Mexican creations. This BYOB establishment offers a selection of salads, crepes, entrees and more at reasonable prices. The Pilsen eatery pays careful attention to presentation; their crepa

TOP Temptation Chocolate Boutique. NICKY WATTS • **MIDDLE** Halsted St. and 18th St. NICKY WATTS • **BOTTOM** Light Exhibition, Pilsen Studio. NICKY WATTS

LOWER WEST SIDE

Skylark

2149 S. Halsted St.
312.948.5275
RED LINE to CERMAK-CHNTWN

With great beers like Great Lakes and DeKonick on tap, it's a shame that most people at the Skylark opt for the $2 Pabst. Situated at 2149 S. Halsted St. on the corner of Cermak, this nationally known bar draws the East Pilsen crowd – those anti-hipster hipsters who live and create art in Podmajersky-owned studios. Although the vegetarian fare like perogies and tater-tots are delicious, they're famous for their 'Skylark burger,' topped with spicy 'slaw, jack cheese, and beer-battered onion rings. The bartenders are friendly but don't mess around when they scream 'last call' over the music. Come prepared: the Skylark is cash-only and the ATM can be finicky.

del jardín is plated with a colorful selection of vegetables and warm, golden crepes. Come in for one of Mundial's homemade pumpkin tamales or sip a cup of cinnamon coffee in their sunny, casual atmosphere. **A**

Nuevo Léon Restaurant

1515 W 18th St
312.421.1517
PINK LINE to 18th

You can't miss Nuevo Léon with its bright, multi-colored exterior. A Pilsen hotspot for over 40 years, this eatery was opened by the Landin family, who came to Chicago searching for a better life. Sit down in the painted interior with murals adorning the walls and feast on Mexican favorites any time of the day. Nuevo Léon also caters. **A**

Pizza Nova

1842 W 18th St
312.666.3500
PINK LINE to 18th

If you don't feel like Mexican, you can pick up some Italian pies and sandwiches at Pizza Nova. Try their thin crust pizza, pan pizza, Pasta Nova, barbeque dinners and salads, or any number of other menu items. You can eat in or order delivery. Their pizza dough is made daily. **B**

La Fontanella

2414 S Oakley Ave
773.927.5249
PINK LINE to WESTERN

This cozy Italian restaurant is family-run and it shows. The atmosphere is charming, the waiters attentive, and the prices low compared with the quality of the food. An

Cardona's Mexican Restaurant, 1451 W. 18th St.
NICKY WATTS

LEFT: MBK Gallery, 1706 S. Halsted St.. NICKY WATTS • **BELOW:** MBK Gallery, 1706 S. Halsted St. NICKY WATTS

appetizer of artichoke hearts in lemon and garlic sauce alone makes it worth returning to La Fontanella, although the bland pasta with the otherwise delicious chicken is less appetizing. The tiny bar near the entrance is a gathering place for neighborhood Italians, and the dining area is perfect for a date. **B+**

paintings of Chinese emperors and an impressive 18th century imperial robe from the Qing dynasty] are superior to most local Chinese restaurants. Overall: a classy dining experience truly fit for an emperor. **A**

Emperor's Choice Restaurant

Emperor's Choice, located in the heart of Chinatown, serves excellent Cantonese cuisine, especially seafood. Try the prawns, steamed oysters or Maine lobster smothered in a variety of mouth-watering sauces. Dishes are a bit pricey, but the food, service, and atmosphere [the room is decorated with antique

> 2238 S Wentworth Ave
> 312.225.8800
> **RED LINE to CERMAK-CHNTWN**

TO PLAY

2nd Friday Gallery Crawls

On the second Friday of every month, Podmajersky Inc. opens its gallery doors from 6 to 10 p.m. All along Halsted Street the lights from Moka, Chicago Arts Department, the Listenbee Collection and others shine cheerfully through the windows. They offer free wine and

> 1915 S Halsted St
> 312.377.4444
> **ORANGE LINE to HALSTED**

LOWER WEST SIDE

Efebos

1640 S. Blue Island Ave.
312.633.9292
PINK LINE to 18th

Cozier than most internet cafés, Efebos is located in the heart of Pilsen. People come for their free Wi-Fi and BYOB policy and stay for the atmosphere. The menu features the typical café fare, but their drinks range from celery juice to cappuccinos to escamocha con salsa en polvo [a tropical fruit smoothie with spicy powdered salsa]. For a classical approach to coffeehouse-sitting, the bookshelves offer the works of Plato and Charles S. Pierce, Henry James and Faulkner novels, and the Norton anthologies of both poetry and short fiction. Or, if the mood strikes you, there's also a chess set.

snacks and the opportunity to talk to Chicago-area artists. Whether you're there for the art, booze, or both, the 2nd Friday Gallery Crawl remains one of Chicago's most exciting monthly events. **A**

4art Inc.

It's hard to miss 4art Inc.: big, loud, glowing. On the first floor of the 1932 S.

1932 S Halsted St
312.850.1816
ORANGE LINE to HALSTED

Halsted St. building, the spacious gallery typically displays more modern works, from painting to photography to sculpture. But don't be limited to the ground floor; all throughout the building

artists create and display their work. Be sure to make it all the way up to the fifth floor on 2nd Fridays and visit the studios of Robert Marshall and Ray Emerick. **B+**

Mexican Fine Arts Center Museum

Under a hum that mixes Spanish with English, groups of excited children

1852 W 19th St
312.738.1503
PINK LINE to 18th

shuffle through the brightly-lit museum. As the largest Latino cultural organization in the country and one of the largest collections of Mexican art, the Mexican Fine Arts Center weaves history

PILSEN: HEAVEN ON THE PINK LINE
BY ELIZABETH RYAN

On a quiet side street in Pilsen, a beat up minivan is parked with its windows open. A couple of old t-shirts are stretched over the front seats as slip covers, and in the cup holder on the dash, a fresh branch of lilac blossoms announces the arrival of spring in Chicago.

Pilsen lies on the Southwest side of the city, a short train ride away from the Loop on the Pink Line but a world away from the black business suits and take out sandwich joints that characterize downtown. Walking the streets of Pilsen, you see things you've never seen before. Life seems a little more magical here. On my first visit early May, I stepped off the Blue Island bus and two men in sombreros rode by on horseback.

For more than a century, this neighborhood has been the port of entry for immigrants, first as a home to Chicago's Bohemian community, who named it after a city in their native Czech Republic. In the 1960s the first Mexican families started moving into the area's square brick

worker's cottages and creating a unique aesthetic experience, best appreciated with a keen eye, an undirected stroll and a good conversationalist by your side.

Along the step-gabled brick buildings on 18th St., stores sell figures of Jesus, Mary and Joseph; Spanish music blares from CD stores and round-bottomed mannequins advertise tight polyester pants outside discount clothing shops. A

and culture among the works of art themselves. Their permanent exhibit contains over 5000 pieces, extending across all media including prints, sketches, folk art, photography, painting, sculpture, artifacts and textiles. **A**

the broken-down buildings into artists' studios, the alleyways into gardens. Now this area houses gallery openings for artists like Richard Pociask. A lovely space with a view of the alley garden, the Chicago Arts District comes as a surprise in this aging section of Halsted. **A**

TO SHOP

Chicago Arts District

These are the guys who brought you 2nd Fridays. Way back in the 1960s, John and Annelies Podmajersky began to convert

1915 S Halsted St
312.738.8000
ORANGE LINE to HALSTED

Dubhe Carreno Gallery: Contemporary Ceramic Art

A gallery entirely devoted to ceramics, Dubhe Carreño houses innovative and intriguing pieces by national and international artists. A sparse, white space smelling of

1841 S Halsted St
312.666.3150
ORANGE LINE to HALSTED

shiny red pickup truck with clean chrome hubs waits at a stop light. Men strut past the Western Union wearing ironed white jeans with cell phones clipped on their hip pockets. Little girls with long black hair tug their mother's hands at the friendly jangle of the ice cream carts, announcing tamarind popsicles and ice cream sandwiches.

Pastry shops with names like Nuevo Leon entice passersby with sparkling glass-shelved cabinets filled with fresh rolls, crispy pastries, smiley-

faced cookies and fluffy round breads, criss-crossed with crusted sugar. People walk between the rows, carrying metal trays and selecting golden sweet rolls to eat with coffee as an afternoon snack.

On a sidewalk off the beaten path, two women prepare burritos under a blue tarp tent. A plump elderly woman wearing a plastic hairnet scowls intently as she hacks cooked chicken with a cleaver, keeping one eye on the grilling meat and the other on a Latin version of 'Dancing With The Stars' playing on the television nearby. A younger woman ladles watermelon and pineapple juice from tall glass jars for $1 a cup; a man in a cowboy hat sits with his elbows planted on the long table, hunched over the tightly

sweet candles, this art boutique shows promise. The focus on ceramics prompts one to look closely at each piece. The only drawback to this Pilsen gallery is that few pieces are displayed, making it easily overlooked. **B**

The Watermark Gallery

Part of Pilsen's thriving new arts scene, the Watermark is a chic little

1839 S Halsted St
312.455.9696
ORANGE LINE to HALSTED

gallery showing bright, Warhol-esque art. Keith R. Evans owns the spot, and advocates sharing the artistic process. You can watch art being made in the working studio in the back. A clean, simple showing and working space, this is the place to come on a weekend afternoon for a look-around. **A**

wrapped burrito in his hands.

Pilsen is a feeling. Time seems to slow down and relax here. Cars stop in traffic to let jay walkers cross; people hang out on front porches. On summer evenings, elderly couples sit in lawnchairs on the sidewalk draped in thin blankets, watching the neighborhood's sleepy rhythms from the glow of the streetlight. Behind a gate in a communal alley, a man sits on a set of wooden steps singing along to the radio in his lap. A mother stands with an exhausted child in her arms, its head on her shoulder, its legs falling around her waist, as she rocks back and forth to the sound of Mexican folk songs and the smell of grilling meat waft-

ing through the balmy night air.

But Pilsen is also tiny moments of unexpected beauty. It's in the fence painted steel gray and bright pink. It's in the red geraniums planted in five-gallon pails on a rickety stoop. It's in the fruit truck parked on the street, selling bunches of bananas, green peppers and ripe tomatoes. And it's in the art that is everywhere, everywhere.

In addition to the trendy new galleries along Halsted St. and the National Museum of Mexican Art, Pilsen is covered in street art. Colorful paintings brighten the stairwells of the 18th St. train station with images of Jesus, indigenous Mexican symbols, mariachi musicians and the Mexican flag. The artwork continues into the streets, where sidewalk corners are inset with a bronze Aztec calendar and the area's brick buildings serve as canvases for hundreds of murals. Some murals record the cultural life of the community with scenes of families preparing tortillas for dinner and historical episodes the Mexican revolution, while others take a more direct political approach, depicting the dangers of factory farms and global warming.

Local muralist, Jose Guerrero started painting murals in the 1970's as a way to educate people about their history and galvanize them around important causes. Through his friendship with

Artesanias D'Mexico: Fine Mexican Folk Art

When you walk into this little store you won't know where to look first.

1644 W 18th St
312.563.9779
PINK LINE to 18th

Eliamar Loza's shop is filled front to back with art imported from Mexico. Cut paper flags of pink and red hang from the ceiling, and glass cases glitter with jewelry. Pick up a bright dress, a finely painted ceramic figurine or a set of handcrafted dishes and take home a piece of Mexico. **A**

Bombon

Husband and wife duo Luis Perea and Laura Cid-Perea own this little

1508 W 18th St
312.733.7788
PINK LINE to 18th

dessert shop. Stop in for fine Mexican cookies, intricate cakes and treats, and chocolate creations. Although it's a small shop, each pastry

local muralists Hector Duarte, Roberto Valadez, Roy Villalobos and John Weber, Guerrero painted murals on themes such as the struggle of the working class, the need for organized labor and the threat of gentrification. Like many South Side neighborhoods Pilsen is bracing itself against the forces of change that have transformed such corridors as Halsted St. near the University of Illinois Chicago into an alley of condominiums and franchise coffee shops.

Near the corner of 18th St. and Bishop St. is a mural Guerrero painted to call on the community to resist the forces of displacement. The mural features a large thunderbird eagle – the logo of the United Farm Workers -- with its wings outstretched, protecting a family unit. On the right hand side, people hold up signs that read, 'Stop Gentrification in Pilsen!' and 'This House is Not for Sale,' next to a large image of Cesar Chavez, the 60's-era labor organizer for the UFW. For Guerrero, art is a tool for maintaining the unique way of life that continues to flourish in the shadow of smokestacks, railroad tracks and other vestiges of Chicago's industrial past.

And as you wait for the train after a day spent basking in the energy of this community, you can't help but hope that his work succeeds in preserving the unique character of this hidden cultural gem.

Haro

2436 S. Oakley Ave.
773.847.2400
PINK LINE to WESTERN

Amidst traditional Italian restaurants, the northern Spanish flavor of Haro stands out – it may be the only Basque-style restaurant in all of Illinois. The restaurant is small and it gets crowded, so don't come here for quiet conversation, especially since Haro features flamenco, live bands, and Spanish poetry readings as often as possible. Original artwork and ceramic tiles give the restaurant an authentic look. With the huge selection of wine, you'll feel like you are in Spain. The pinxtos [a version of tapas] are delicious but a little pricey for the budget of a student or young professional. Go on a Wednesday to get $5 pinxtos at the bar.

case is filled to the brim with brightly-colored confections perfect for any occasion. One of the most high-class dessert stops in Pilsen, Bombon is worth a visit. Stop and smell the chocolate. **A**

Carniceria Rancho Alegre

This colorful little grocery store is well-stocked with fruits, veggies and hot peppers. Vendors often stand outside hawking treats and iced drinks. Come in and grab some local sweets, like Mari's Candy. Flavors include such tastes as Cachuate Estilo Japones from Mexico, which are Japanese-style peanuts. Also try Mi Yolis' extensive array of sweet treats, including corn-shaped lollipops. **A**

1759 W 18th St
312.733.0883
PINK LINE to 18th

Discoteca Rosy

Discoteca Rosy houses a truly eclectic collection of wares. Under a ceiling hung with CDs, you'll find Spanish language CDs, English language DVDs, teddy bears, purses, magazines and more. It's an aimless store whose outside is emblazoned with murals of Betty Boop and other characters. If you're looking for a particular CD it might not be the place to go, but it's worth a look nonetheless. **B**

1257 W 18th St
312.492.8837
PINK LINE to 18th

Libreria Giron

Librería Girón is one of four of Girón Books' Spanish language

1443 W 18th St
312.226.2086
PINK LINE to 18th

bookshops. Girón Books prides itself on its commitment to publishing and selling Spanish books, and with good reason. This tiny shop is full of children's books, cookbooks, history tomes, magazines etc. You can purchase the same books online, but coming in for a browse is far more enjoyable. **A**

Mestiza

A beautiful little shop in the heart of Pilsen, Mestiza's interior bursts with color. Frida Kahlo and other Mexican figures are the main focus here – adorning everything from earrings to handbags. Pick up a handmade journal, a bright t-shirt, a Mexican antique or a Che lightswitch. If you're looking for a gift, or just an addition to your wardrobe, Mestiza has you covered. You won't want to leave empty-handed. **A**

1010 W 18th St
312.563.0132
PINK LINE to 18th

Ochoa Sport

Ochoa Sport is full of products for everyone, even non-sports fans. The highlight of the shop is their vast array of colorful sneakers including brands like Puma, Adidas and Reebok. Even if you're not particularly athletic, you'll want to take home a pair. Pick up some bright red sneakers stitched with 'England' or 'Brazil' or a blue pair with sunshine yellow stripes. You'll be ready to cheer on your favorite team, or primed to go clubbing. **A**

1749 W 18th St
312.829.9310
PINK LINE to 18th

LOWER WEST SIDE

OMD

Although sparsely stocked, this uptown-style shop offers a nice selection of apparel and home goods. Snag one of their Chicago 'El' train tees [a big seller], or pick up some of their funky kitchenware. Frida-philes can even get their fix; OMD has several books on the artist. A little unfocused and still struggling, OMD promises to only improve its already eclectic stock. **B**

1419 W 18th St
312.563.9663
PINK LINE to 18th

Oxala

This brightly-colored shop is worth the long trip to Pilsen. Stocked with handmade jewelry, original art, candles, soaps and lotions, there's something for everyone at Oxala. The owner is on hand at all times to assist shoppers, offering to answer any question one might have about the handmade boxes and paintings. This is a store with Mexican flavor and a modern edge. **A**

1653 W 18th St
312.850.1655
PINK LINE to 18th

Revolver Records

Revolver Records is a Mecca for vinyl enthusiasts everywhere. The graffiti-covered walls house a selection ranging from punk to soul. Owner Marlon Hernandez will spin any record you choose on the turntables set up in the back, and in the summertime the party extends out to the street. Even if you don't own a turntable, stop by and browse through CDs, DVDs, and Revolver's custom-graffitied shirts. **A**

1524 W 18th St
312.226.4211
PINK LINE to 18th

Sanchez Sales

This little shop offers an array of clothing for men, women and children. Come in for a sports jersey or a cocktail dress. Looking for a pair of jeans or a top for clubbing? They've got it. This tiny boutique is stocked from wall to wall with inexpensive fashions. The clothing is nothing particularly special, but the selection is wide and varied. **C**

1647 W 18th St
312.733.9720
PINK LINE to 18th

Mural, Radio Arte Building, Pilsen Center. NICKY WATTS

LOWER WEST SIDE

NUCLEAR ENERGY

'Nuclear Energy,' by sculptor Henry Moore, was
unveiled at 3:36 p.m. on December 2, 1967, exactly
a quarter century after physicists achieved the first
controlled, self-sustaining nuclear chain reaction.
The twelve-foot-tall bronze piece sits on what used
to be the football field bleachers at the University of
Chicago's Stagg Field on the east side of Ellis Ave.
Beneath this spot is the site at which the experiments
took place under the leadership of Enrico Fermi to
whom the sculpture is dedicated.

Photograph by Christina Quintana

SOUTH

HYDE PARK

A HAVEN
FOR BOOK
SMARTS
AND STREET
SMARTS
ALIKE

Much like the book Dr. Jekyll and Mr. Hyde, Hyde Park is a neighborhood of two faces. It's a haven for book smarts and street smarts alike. Home of the University of Chicago, almost all its students and 60% of its faculty, it's an intellectual and cultural Mecca. Attractions include the Museum of Science and Industry and Frank Lloyd Wright's Robie House. In its independent bookstores, art galleries and used record stores along Harper Ct. and 53rd St., young intellectuals discuss everything from minimalism to game theory. The University brings world class classical music to The Court Theater. Every June is the 57th Street Art Fair, Chicago's oldest juried art show, which features more than 250 artists from across the nation. A primarily black, lower-income residential neighborhood makes up the other half of Hyde Park. The closeness between the families of the community keeps the area safe. Its ethnic diversity also makes it the place for Soul and Caribbean food. Carifete is an annual Caribbean carnival in August where colorful costumes, salsa and reggae mix for 12 hours. In addition, Hyde Park is the site of the Checkerboard Lounge, a club known for its live jazz.

TO EAT

Giordano's

Hyde Park's Giordano's offers deep dish pizza that's not entirely worth the wait or annoyances. The pizzeria is modest and tucked away, and the staff at the front counter is usually too distracted to promptly take care of its hungry customers. If pizza isn't your thing, Giordano's also serves pastas, salads and sandwiches, but there are plenty of other places that serve them with more consideration. **C−**

5311 S Blackstone Ave
773.947.0200
GREEN LINE to 51st

Hyde Park Gyros

A step up from a Vienna Beef stand but several steps below fine Greek dining, Hyde Park Gyros is impressive in name and convenience only. The value meal is reasonably priced and provides a gyro overflowing with meat, but the sloppy execution and unclean dining environment will make you regret even the few dollars spent. **C−**

1368 E 53rd St
773.947.8229
GREEN LINE to 51st

LEFT: Orly's Café, 1660 E. 55th St. CLAYTON FLYNN • **BELOW:** Aquarium, Orly's Café, 1660 E. 55th St. CLAYTON FLYNN

Lung Wah Chop Suey

This tiny carryout and delivery spot offers so-so suey at standard prices. Stay at home and pick up the phone because Lung Wah's dining area is more similar to a dining closet. Though the food is good enough to satisfy, the restaurant is easily trumped by even its neighborhood competition. **C**

1368 1/2 E 53rd St
773.324.0429
GREEN LINE to 51st

Nathan's

'For a Taste of Jamaica' … go somewhere else! The slogan doesn't quite fit at Nathan's, the tiny restaurant that offers a meager selection of authentic Jamaican food and an even smaller space for seating. Though the Jamaican Jerk Chicken dinner is appealing and the gyros are surprisingly tasty, Nathan's also provides an abundant selection of more common sandwiches for prices you'd expect. **C+**

1372 E 53rd St
773.288.5353
GREEN LINE to 51st

Rajun Cajun

Find authentic Southern cooking at this refreshing restaurant that will make you ask: 'Southern where?' Though the restaurant offers the interesting dichotomy of Indian and soul food, be prepared to find predominantly Indian offerings in both the ambience and menu. But really, where else can you get vegetable curry with a side of sweet potatoes? Not that you should. **B**

1459 E 53rd St
773.955.1145
GREEN LINE to 51st

Ribs 'N' Bibs

Follow the smoke to Hyde Park's premiere barbecue destination. Old West meets old school from the décor to the menu, which features mouth-watering burgers, shrimp and [of course] savory barbecue chicken and ribs. There are more than a few excellent deals on the menu, and the late hours are perfect for college students and hungry insomniacs. But be warned – it's carryout and delivery only, so stock up on Wet Ones and take those sizzlin' favorites home. **A-**

5300 S Dorchester Ave
773.493.0400
GREEN LINE to 51st

Veggies To Go

Check out the colorful cuisine of this 'alternative sub shop' on busy 53rd Street. Veggies To Go beats the standard sub chain by offering a wide variety of delicious sand-wiches, wraps, soups and smoothies. While the prices are a bit too high, the customizable menu choices and vegetarian-friendly atmosphere make this a fresh spot. **B+**

1375 E 53rd St
773.667.8344
GREEN LINE to 51st

HYDE PARK

Valois Restaurant

1518 E. 53rd St.
773.667.0647
GREEN LINE to GARFIELD

Valois is an 80-year-old edifice of the community, a throwback to Depression-era diners and a good crash course of everything Hyde Park. Since a mere 150 people can fit at a time, the line – a patchwork gathering of all parts of South Side society – snakes out the door most weekends. And then there's the food: Simple, filling and prepared at breakneck speed – and for cheap. Omelets, French toast, 'R-r-r-reubens' and ribs fly off the griddle right before the eyes of Valois loyalists. But don't get too lost in the skyline mural floating above your head or the perfection of the pancakes, because it's likely there are quite a few folks in line staring holes in your back, eyeing your seat.

Bonjour Bakery Café

1500 E 55th St
773.241.5300
GREEN LINE to GARFIELD

The food at this bakery is homemade and definitely done right. There isn't a huge selection, but from pastries to soup to sandwiches, Bonjour Bakery Café offers enough choices that it's difficult to choose. When the weather is nice, you can sit outside with your coffee and croissant. Otherwise you might have to battle your fellow customers for a seat or take your quiche to go. **A-**

Caffe Florian

1450 E 57th St
773.752.4100
GREEN LINE to GARFIELD

Despite the Italian name, Caffe Florian offers an unusual mix of items on its menu, ranging from wraps to guacamole. This small restaurant is quieter and less popular than its big brother, Medici on 57th, but with food that is just as good – and slightly cheaper. Their pizzas, both thin crust and deep dish, are top-notch. **B**

Cedars Mediterranean Kitchen

1206 E 53rd St
773.324.6227
GREEN LINE to GARFIELD

From the outside, Cedars seems a little dingy. But inside it's sharp-looking, authentic-feeling Mediterranean – and a good bargain, too. In the crucial hummus category it gets high marks, but vegetarians should be sure to double-check the meat content of any prospective order, as they feel the need to slip lamb into practically everything. And no matter what you go for – kebabs or couscous – be prepared to wait: The service doesn't always match the food's reputation. **A-**

Cholie's Pizza

1601 E 53rd St
773.684.8688
GREEN LINE to GARFIELD

So the service is iffy. So the lights are ugly. So it's not the cleanest-looking place, or the best decorated. So the pizza is greasy and a bit like cardboard. So what? It's cheap. And some people are in college, and this drives them to do things they wouldn't normally do and eat food they otherwise wouldn't. For a $1.50 large, entirely edible slice of pizza, that's all you really need to know. **C+**

Classics Café

1010 E 59th St
773.702.0177
GREEN LINE to GARFIELD

The sunny, antique atmosphere of this comfortable café lends itself well to conversations about your new favorite author or poet. Maybe its quiet ambiance will inspire your own great novel. With an excellent selection of drinks like delicious chai tea and some great baked goods, Classics is well worth the journey into the University of Chicago's slightly confusing Classics Building. **A-**

C-Shop

5706 S University Ave
773.834.1018
GREEN LINE to GARFIELD

Almost always crowded with students, the C-Shop offers Einstein Brother's Bagels and a nice selection of coffee drinks and

HYDE PARK

smoothies, as well as plenty of tables and booths to relax and get some work done. Windows lining the walls create an open atmosphere, and every Wednesday is 'Shake Day' where you can get tasty milkshakes in a variety of flavors. **A-**

Divinity School Coffee Shop

Known as the place where God drinks coffee, the bold entrance sign

1025 E 58th St
773.702.4806
GREEN LINE to GARFIELD

stating 'REPENT' is no surprise. Quirky irreverent religious and philosophical references abound in this relaxed coffee shop – complete with indie music and student artwork. But it can be overcrowded, especially at lunchtime, so grab a seat to enjoy some piping hot coffee and locally catered food. **B**

HomeMade Pizza Co.

Here, the pizza is taken home uncooked. The idea is to give you the freshest

1546 E 55th St
773.493.2000
GREEN LINE to GARFIELD

pizza possible, so they'll construct a pizza for you to your specifications and then tell you how to bake it when you're ready. Some of their suggested recipes include flavorful ingredients

like caramelized onions and sun-dried tomatoes, but staples like pepperoni and mushrooms aren't forgotten. **A**

Istria Café

Istria Café, located conveniently underneath the 57th St. Metra station,

1520 E 57th St
GREEN LINE to GARFIELD

offers typical Starbucks-era coffee and tea drinks at Starbucks-era prices. The only notable difference is it offers gelato. The light jazz soundtrack and large windows give the café a friendly, inviting atmosphere that attracts students and locals. Take advantage of the free Wi-Fi with any purchase. **B**

Kikuya

Kikuya may be the only choice for Japanese in Hyde Park, but it's not a

1601 E 55th St
773.667.3728
GREEN LINE to GARFIELD

bad one. Though the décor is more psychedelic than Japanese – 80s-reminiscent wood paneling with bright, colorful stripes – the food is tasty and reasonably priced. So groove to the J-pop in the background, let the friendly service take care of you and dig those chopsticks right in. **B+**

Unfinished mural, 55th St. Metra underpass.
CLAYTON FLYNN

HYDE PARK

La Petite Folie

La Petite Folie is one of the few options for fine dining in the area. This small French restaurant, located in the same mall as the Co-Op Market, offers a number of rich individual entrees as well as a prix-fixe meal. The wine list is extensive, and the small tables and lace curtains make for a cozy atmosphere. **A**

1504 E 55th St
773.493.1394
GREEN LINE to GARFIELD

Leona's

Leona's is proudly family-owned and operated, with a manager who boasts that he personally cleans the bathrooms before the customers arrive. The expansive Italian-American menu reads like the opening credits of Arrested Development, full of caricatures of Leona's family members, while the food, organic and made from scratch, gives the finger to typical comfort food. All this plus enormous portions and reasonable prices, and you'll be wishing Leona was your granny, too. **A-**

1236 E 53rd St
773.363.2600
GREEN LINE to GARFIELD

Medici Bakery

Like its parent institution Medici on 57th, the Medici Bakery is well-patronized by Hyde Park residents lured in by the smell wafting from the baking desserts, pastries and bread. The bakery is also pretty pricey, but the appetizing offerings are usually worth it. Stay for a while or take it to go. **A-**

1331 E 57th St
773.667.7394
GREEN LINE to GARFIELD

Medici on 57th

The Med is a staple of U. of Chicago life, so it's often busy, especially

1327 E 57th St
773.667.7394
GREEN LINE to GARFIELD

YOUNG DRINKERS TURN TO WINE FOR PANACHE
BY KELLY MAHONEY

On any given Saturday, The Bottle Shop in Wilmette props open its glass double doors, turns on soft music and invites the public in for a free glass of wine with friends. 'If you're going to drink wine, you need to taste it,' said owner Amy Lafontant. 'It's like getting to hear the music before buying the CD.'

Lafontant said between 30 and 50 people wander in during the tasting, which she also holds on Thursdays. The shop is just one of a plethora of wine shops springing up in the Chicago area to cash in on the idea that wine isn't just for special occasions.

'It goes better with dinner, with a meal,' said Wilmette enthusiast Danny Schuman, who began drinking wine in college and has introduced it to others. 'I can really have a good time sharing wine with my friends.'

The trend was sparked by prosperity, said Frank Molinaro, an employee at The Bottle Shop who serves up libations and knowledge at the tastings. 'For a while, wine really grew in popularity because people had more money,' Molinaro said. 'Wine is always looked on as a little more sophisticated than beer.'

La Petite Amelia in Evanston is catering to the trend. Richard Malphrus, the general manager at the sophisticated French bistro and wine bar, said the growth of wine can be traced back to a

on the weekends. Despite the wait, it has a wide selection of menu items, both classic and unique. The food, especially the pizza, is generally delicious though a little pricey. Some of the most exclusive items are the drinks, such as the Mexicana hot chocolate or the squeeze-your-own orange juice. Don't forget to carve your name into the table or wall to leave your mark. **A-**

Mellow Yellow

The ridiculously garish green-and-gold canopy is impossible to miss	1508 E 53rd St 773.667.2000 **GREEN LINE to GARFIELD**

– and hard to resist. The sign reading '#1 Chili in Chicago' may make it even harder, yet not everyone who gives in is glad they did. Recently under new management, the service may be a bit too mellow for some people. Yet the polyglot menu still impresses some, especially with Cajun food bumping up against Mexican tastes on the same nights. **C+**

Nile Restaurant

Chicagoans plodding through gray Hyde Park slush may find themselves	1611 E 55th St 772.324.9499 **GREEN LINE to GARFIELD**

needing Mediterranean food like they need air. They need look no further than the Nile. Hummus, baba ganouj, falafel, tabouleh and every other shade of Greek dish is available. While the service doesn't exactly inspire, with eyes closed it almost tastes like Athens. **A-**

Noodles Etc.

You can never have too much curry. And while that's not a hypothesis	1458 E 53rd St 773.947.8787 **GREEN LINE to GARFIELD**

that we would suggest testing, Noodles Etc.

---

change in perception. 'Starting in the '90s, there was a shift in American culture in that people started to become more educated about restaurants and wine as well,' Malphrus said. 'It's just so associated with good food.'

Schuman said he has been drinking wine for 15 years and has a simpler explanation for the trend. 'When you get older, you deserve it,' he said.

The Wine Manager of Un-cork It Chicago, Michael Kelly, said age may be part of a person's choice of beverage. 'I think it gives much more pleasure than a bottle of beer or a vodka,' Kelly said. 'It's a lifestyle choice; it's a little more mellow.' However, Kelly said at least a quarter of his clientele is young wine drinkers. The store holds Wine 101, a class focusing on teaching the basics, about every other month.

Kristy Lim, of WineStyles Evanston, said the chain store thrives in the neighborhood surrounding Northwestern University. 'We have a lot of people here who are well-traveled and they're taking what they've learned and bringing it back,' she said. 'It's a lot of Evanstonians from different walks of life.'

Lim said she thinks wine has become more approachable and a better value. 'People tend to like wines that are not from California and they like to keep it in the $10 to $15 range, which we can definitely accommodate.'

Lim's shop also offers wine tastings two times per week: a free session on Saturdays and a $10-admission session on Thursdays. 'The purpose of the tasting is to give people a chance to try wines they've never heard of,' she said in the dimly lit shop that stores various wines in stucco-textured cubby holes.

Lafontant said wine's biggest appeal is that it offers something different. '[Patrons] are sick of mixed drinks and beer,' she said. 'It offers more than just an alcoholic beverage.'

HYDE PARK

would be happy to let you try. This quick and clean restaurant serves up standard [read: amazing] Thai and snatches of Chinese. Though that's not enough to make it stand out in a neighborhood already overflowing with southeast-Asian options, enough curry should push out memories of the competition. Don't forget to top it all off with the savoriest of lychees. **B**

Orly's Café

Orly's is a tad confusing. It's a Chicago joint serving New York-style fare amidst Mexican décor that specializes in French pastries. And while this year it marks a quarter-century as a fixture in Hyde Park, that doesn't mean it can get away with so-so food. Many adore it for the early morning bagels, but

1660 E 55th St
773.643.5500
GREEN LINE to GARFIELD

LEARNING ABOUT WINE
BY KELLY MAHONEY

Richard Malphrus of La Petite Amelia in Evanston said there are some basic skills that can help curious beverage drinkers break into the wine realm. 'They're biggest pitfall is going after the label,' Malphrus said. 'Not what's written on it, but what it looks like.'

One of the basic principles of wine is the 75, 85, 95 rule for American-made concoctions. Of the type of wine, at least 75 percent of the grapes must be specific to the wine, 85 percent of the grapes must be from the geographic location listed and 95 percent of the grapes must be from the year listed.

According to Malphrus, European wine labels are also becoming easier to read because they generally are marked by region. As far as types of wine to try, Malphrus said there are some that are easier to start with. 'Part of it is going to be personal taste,' he said. 'If you're just starting to taste white wines, Riesling is a favorite.'

Riesling is a grape traditionally grown in Germany, Austria and France, although it is now grown in California, New York and Central America. The white wine produced from the grape is generally sweet and flavorful.

As far as red wines, Malphrus

Frank Molinaro of The Bottle Shop in Wilmette educates a patron about red wine at one of the store's biweekly wine tastings. KELLY MAHONEY

said he recommends pinot noir, one of the most popular wines in the world that has been made for thousands of years. 'It's difficult to get into really heavy reds right away,' he said. '[Pinot noir is] a good way to start to ease yourself into red wines.'

As far as Rosé, Malphrus said he has recommendations against certain types. 'Avoid the White Zinfandel at all costs,' he said. 'Seek out the good Rosé, it's out there.'

Malphrus said one doesn't need to invest much as some of his favorite bottles of wine cost less than $10. Instead, he said potential wine drinkers should cultivate an appreciation for the beverage. 'Somebody out there really loves what's going into this,' he said. 'A real wine aficionado understands that someone's heart and soul went into this.'

HYDE PARK

the entrées get mixed reviews. Hefty prices don't help either. **C+**

Piccolo Mondo Café

Nestled in the same building as a depressing-look-
ing rehab center, this café

| 1642 E 56th St |
| 773.643.1106 |
| GREEN LINE to GARFIELD |

is not in the most exciting part of the neighborhood. A glance at the Xeroxed menus and the
Coke machine buzzing in the corner doesn't get
your mouth watering either, but this piccolo
Ristorante has many devoted patrons who dig the
very quiet atmosphere and excellent Italian fare.
The reasonable prices only add to the amore. **B**

Pizza Capri

53rd is a haphazard
scene, so Pizza Capri
has no trouble coexist-

| 1501 E 53rd St |
| 773.324.7777 |
| GREEN LINE to GARFIELD |

ing with the gritty liquor store across the street
or the looming stone bank building next door.
This spot is moderately priced and has a warm
atmosphere, although a spick-and-span chain
restaurant feel. Expect fresh, hearty dough on the
pizzas, toppings ranging from basic to experimental, unassumingly friendly service and a giant
espresso machine on display that looks vaguely
like a robotic eagle. **C+**

Pockets

Is it fast food? Or just a
traditional restaurant?
It's hard to say. Pockets is

| 1309 E 53rd St |
| 773.667.1313 |
| GREEN LINE to GARFIELD |

an interesting hybrid of quick eating – one that
defies the stereotypes of fast food's plastic taste
and high dining's pokey speed. The place creates
addicts daily with its formula of wholesome,
speedy and relatively cheap food [especially the
vegetarian stuff]. Plus, it has delivery for those
ridiculously lazy days when you need a cheesed-
out calzone but can't work up the spirit to leave
your house. **B+**

Salonica

Salonica's main appeal is
its unfailing inexpensive-
ness: Though the food is

| 1440 E 57th St |
| 773.752.3899 |
| GREEN LINE to GARFIELD |

not always tasty, almost every item on the menu
is less than $8. The restaurant offers classic
diner fare, with an emphasis on Greek specialties
and a typical diner atmosphere, complete with
a counter. Another plus is the all-day breakfast
menu. **C+**

Sammy's Touch

Tucked away on the
perilous edges of the U.
of Chicago campus stands

| 5659 S Cottage G. Ave |
| 773.288.2645 |
| GREEN LINE to GARFIELD |

this Greek-American fast food powerhouse.
Extremely popular with both the University
students and other members of the community,
Sammy's provides quality burgers, gyros and
other greasy fare that will clog your arteries
without leaving your wallet starving. **B**

Seoul Corea

Tiny, plain and not the
least bit appetizing at first
glance, this mom and pop

| 1605 E 55th St |
| 773.288.1795 |
| GREEN LINE to GARFIELD |

restaurant nonetheless boasts an authentic menu
of cheap Korean eats. Enjoy unlimited appetizers in the Korean dining style and follow it up
with bulgogi and jap chae noodles. The food's
heavy on the spices but the owners are light
on the English, so don't set your heart on their
conversation. **B**

Siam Restaurant

College kids craving some
basil chicken, vegetarians
longing for some tofu

| 1639 E 55th St |
| 773.324.9296 |
| GREEN LINE to GARFIELD |

curry and many others wanting low-price yet
amazing Thai delights have a soft place in their
hearts for Siam. It may feel like eating in a broom
closet, but that's beside the point – this tiny, cozy
restaurant packs more flavor per square foot than
you may have thought possible. **A**

Thai 55th

Small and quiet, this
restaurant is a great place
to sit and talk over some

| 1607 E 55th St |
| 773.363.7119 |
| GREEN LINE to GARFIELD |

soup or a Thai iced tea. The wood paneling and
framed knickknacks give it a nice atmosphere,

HYDE PARK

RIGHT: Orly's Café, 1660 E. 55th St. CLAYTON FLYNN • **BELOW:** Museum of Science & Industry, 5700 S. Lake Shore Dr. CLAYTON FLYNN

though the '90s pop music on the radio seems a little out of place. Fast and helpful service sets Thai 55th apart from its neighbors – according to the waiter, 'all you have to do is enjoy!' **A**

The Snail Thai Cuisine

One of several Thai restaurants on the block, Snail stands out for the quality of its dishes. Silks and intricate woodwork line the walls, adding some ambiance to your curry. But when the décor disappoints you with its slight case of schizophrenia [what's impressionist about Thai food, anyway?], take a seat at a cushy banquette in either of two rooms and let that Pad Thai occupy your senses. **B–**

1649 E 55th St
773.667.5423
GREEN LINE to GARFIELD

Third World Café

Third World strikes the right balance between grimy and chic. Besides their delicious coffee, the shop has an impressive menu of vegetarian options and homemade goodies if you prefer sugar-overload. Settle down at this corner establishment to enjoy their expansive windows and free WiFi. But don't linger too long, Third World only houses their caffeinated evening patrons until 7:30. **B+**

1301 E 53rd St
773.288.3882
GREEN LINE to GARFIELD

TO PLAY

Drexel Fountain

Though a bit daunting stuck in the middle of a hectic intersection, the Drexel Fountain is worth a close look if you can dodge the traffic. A ring of four statues from various mythologies form the capstone of a man in modern dress leaning contemplatively on a tree stump. It makes for some oddly placed symbolism, but somehow effectively expresses the desire of early city planners to retain a natural outdoor spirit amidst the burgeoning urban sprawl. **C**

5100 S Drexel Blvd
312.744.6630
GREEN LINE to 51st

Japanese Spa Zen

And a gold star for offering Brazilian waxes for both genders. What Japanese Spa Zen lacks in elaborate luxury it makes up for with its subtle charms. The spa's humble space does not do justice to the variety of hair, beauty, wellness and massage services it provides. That said, the reasonable prices might be the most comforting aspect of your visit. **B+**

1380 E 53rd St
773.955.5353
GREEN LINE to 51st

Stamp'Lays Salon

The charm of Stamp'Lays Executive Salon is obvious from the first step inside. What at first seems like just a salon is also a spa and boutique that offers a wide variety of services ranging from hair and nail care to massages and facials. The salon also sells its own brand of makeup, designer clothes and jewelry amongst a beautiful décor with plenty of urban flavor. The tremendously friendly staff has truly got you covered from 'head to toe.' **A**

1371 E 53rd St
773.241.6200
GREEN LINE to 51st

Fountain of Time

Spend a moment with Father Time and friends at this 102-foot sculpture that took Lorado Taft 14 years to build. This stone outdoor piece is a must-see for fans of the medium who are a little sick of those 'museum things.' Casual observers will enjoy the free price but feel compelled to travel on through the neighboring parks. **B−**

5900 S Cottage G. Ave
312.744.6630
GREEN LINE to EAST 63rd

Midway Plaisance Ice Rink

If you've always wanted to ice-skate on the site of the 1893 World Fair Ferris Wheel, here's your chance. Admission is free on weekdays and skates rent for only $5, so bring your friends and hit the ice [hopefully not literally]. With broomball, ice-skating lessons, and the occasional movie or disco dance party on ice,

1130 N Midway Pl. Dr
312.745.2470
GREEN LINE to EAST 63rd

the Midway Rink offers a rare chance to conquer the dull Chicago winter with some outdoor fun. **C**

Midway Plaisance Park

If drawn to converging lines of trees in an idyllic setting, wander over to this horizontal gem in the southern part of the University of Chicago campus. The long, clear paths are ideal for activity fiends, but the vast lawns and open space will satisfy any visitor in need of outdoor relaxation. Just don't forget to bring your own food and amusement because there is not much else here. **B+**

1130 N Midway Pl. Dr
312.742.7529
GREEN LINE to EAST 63rd

57th St. Books

If you enjoy the semi-comforting claustrophobia of endless book stacks, take the stairs from street-level to this gem of an independent bookstore below. If the brick walls give you a cold shoulder, you can warm up the chill with a Chinese tea tasting. Cozy though it's not, whether you're looking for an obscure comic book or Danielle Steele's latest, its expert booksellers will help you navigate the nooks and crannies of the expansive basement collection. **A**

1301 E 57th St
773.684.1300
GREEN LINE to GARFIELD

Checkerboard Lounge

The Checkerboard moved to its tacky new Chucky Cheese-esque location last spring. At first, Hyde Parkers seemed to have reason to be excited. Local jazz royalty, including

5201 S Harper Ave
773.684.1472
GREEN LINE to GARFIELD

Osaka Japanese Gardens

5800 S. Lake Shore Dr.
773.702.9514
GREEN LINE to GARFIELD

Hyperventilating students from Hyde Park's University of Chicago and city-weary urbanites alike should stop by the Osaka Gardens every now and then. This deeply unusual and serene example of Japanese garden blooming in a concrete neighborhood is a refuge for many and a curiosity for others. The gardens closed in the 1940s after heavy vandalization and didn't reopen until several decades later. For this, anyone going for a romantic stroll over the graceful Moon Bridge will be thankful. Those capable of tuning out the traffic churning in the background may even be able to mentally transport themselves back to medieval Japan.

HYDE PARK

K.A.M. Isaiah Israel Temple

1100 E. Hyde Park Blvd.
773.924.1234
GREEN LINE to 51st

A sprawling, impressive building and a landmark of Chicago architecture, the K.A.M. Temple is the oldest synagogue in Chicago and claims to be the oldest in the Midwest. You can't help noticing its massive scale right away, but the winding structure begs to be explored for you to appreciate its details. The three huge oak doors at the main entrance are flanked by beautiful and intricately woven iron lamp-posts, Louis Sullivan-esque in their fusion of function and elegance. Even its gate-like series of front doors is rather inviting upon closer examination, capped with expert stone-carved Old-Testament iconography and flowering long hinges. The worship spaces inside are utterly breathtaking.

Fred Anderson and Hamid Drake, graced opening night. Since then, predictable, touristy blues has been the standard fare, and what little jazz goes on is unfortunately not your father's music. For that matter, it's not even your 25-year-old jazz aficionado friend's music. And the cover charge can be excessive. **C-**

Court Theatre

You won't find any stuttering amateurs here: Embedded in the U. of Chicago campus stands a surprising gem of a professional theatre company and one of Chicago's best cultural attractions. Its intimate auditorium hosts five plays per season, focusing on works with a classical resonance. Dubbed a designer's theatre, the Court's repertoire has an innovative flair and is known for its solid acting. **A-**

5535 S Ellis Ave
773.753.4472
GREEN LINE to GARFIELD

Mandel Hall

As the U. of Chicago's main auditorium, the hall hosts music department performances and concerts. The theater itself is a beautiful space; it was opened in 1903 and its wood paneling, stained glass windows, and ornate balcony give it a Victorian air. It is also the usual location for the U. of Chicago Presents Concert Series, which is open to the public and sometimes features chamber music. **A**

1131 E 57th St
773.702.8069
GREEN LINE to GARFIELD

Museum of Science & Industry

The Museum of Science and Industry comes at you like a hyperactive kid, its displays beeping, flashing and begging to be looked at. You can easily spend a day in the gigantic building. The potential for headaches after wandering for more than a few hours is high, but the experience is endearing. While some of the exhibits, like the magic of petroleum refining, fall flat, others, like the totally creepy, totally fascinating Body Worlds exhibit, are well worth the price. **B**

5700 S Lake Shore Dr
773.684.1414
GREEN LINE to GARFIELD

Noon Hookah Lounge

A café with free Wi-Fi during the day, the Hookah Lounge provides a cozy, charming hideaway at all times. At night, you may want to reserve an atmospheric private room – styled in red with draperies and cushions, these gorgeous spaces fill up quickly. Grab a cigar, play some checkers and try the Saudi Arabian apple hookah mix, 'rawah.' If you're feeling adventurous, you can even add a cinnamon flavor shot to the water. **A**

1617 E 55th St
773.643.1670
GREEN LINE to GARFIELD

Oriental Institute Museum

The outside of the Institute doesn't look very large, especially compared to the nearby Museum of Science and Industry.

1155 E 58th St
773.702.9514
GREEN LINE to GARFIELD

But inside are some of the most beautiful artifacts of ancient civilizations you will ever see, all for a suggested donation of just $5. Artifacts aren't obscured by a lot of outside 'packaging' like posters and kids' activities; they are generally placed in the open for visitors to look at along with helpful but short explanations nearby. Expect small crowds. **A**

Robie House

Know nothing about Frank Lloyd Wright? Take a tour with the friendly staff of the Robie House and emerge a convert to architectural geekdom. Even if your eyelids droop at the term 'fluid spaces,' the House will tickle your fancy for pretty art windows. Built in 1908, the impressively modern brick structure represents the cornerstone of Wright's prairie style. If you consider American architecture a synonym for lame, let the Robie House prove you wrong. **A**

5757 S Woodlawn Ave
773.834.1847
GREEN LINE to GARFIELD

Rockefeller Memorial Chapel

You don't have to blow the bank on plane tickets to Europe to appreciate Gothic architecture. Rockefeller Memorial Chapel's cushioned benches are the perfect spot to sit back and contemplate this limestone chapel's impressive stained glass windows and ornamental ceiling. Come on a sunny day to fully appreciate the brightly-colored lancet windows, and if that's not enough of a sensual experience, note the expansive schedule of music concerts held here throughout the year. **A-**

5850 S Woodlawn Ave
773.702.7059
GREEN LINE to GARFIELD

Seven Ten Lanes

The appeal of Seven Ten Lanes lies in its proximity and variety. Besides a nifty jukebox, it houses eight pool tables, a bowling alley and a restaurant – all adjacent to the U. of Chicago campus. The plasmas over the bar draw in the sports-inclined crowd. Beer ads, old photos and bookshelves line the walls, contributing to the cozy, laidback vibe. The menu strives

1055 E 55th St
773.347.2695
GREEN LINE to GARFIELD

to offer a step above comfort food with daily specials, but don't expect high dining. **B+**

Smart Museum of Art

University of Chicago's very own Museum of Modern Art, the Smart houses an impressive permanent art collection in addition to three exhibit spaces with work spanning 5,000 years. Fawn over the original furniture of Frank Lloyd Wright's Robie House, then move onto artifacts from the Chinese Bronze Age. Don't be fazed by the harsh concrete exterior – you will please your retinas with the visual hug inside. **A**

5550 S Greenwood Ave
773.702.0200
GREEN LINE to GARFIELD

The Renaissance Society

The 'not what you expect' on the brochure is right. Once you get past your sense of betrayal at its deceptive name, this tiny gallery of contemporary art has hardly enough material to justify the four-floor climb you'll take to get there. If you've got 10 minutes to spare for pretentiousness with a worldly flare though, this nook in Cobb Hall may just be the place. **C**

5811 S Ellis Ave
773.502.8670
GREEN LINE to GARFIELD

TO SHOP

Futons-N-More

What could have been the broke college student's dream is actually a cramped store with limited selection. For prices ranging from equal to or more expensive than those at a big box store, the futons come as a package deal with everything you need to make your friends' visits just slightly more comfortable. The store's fast delivery is at least a time saver if not a money one. **C**

1370 E 53rd St
773.324.7083
GREEN LINE to 51st

Hyde Park Records

If you can quote a record store movie by the end of this sentence or just have to have the new Ludacris on vinyl, this music lovers' paradise will hit the right note. The diverse

1377 E 53rd St
773.288.6588
GREEN LINE to 51st

HYDE PARK

selection beckons your index fingers in a laidback environment that's refreshingly free of pretension. Best of all, the friendly, often singing staff is always around to help with questions. **A**

The Freehling Pot & Pan Co.

Calling all potheads! This charming neighborhood store carries everything

1365 E 53rd St
773.643.8080
GREEN LINE to 51st

you need to stock your kitchen with the best pots, pans and utensils. Channel your inner homemaker and splurge on jams, spices and tea, or find linens and decorations for the Martha Stewart in your life. The prices are competitive with larger stores, but the staff's advice is free and friendly. **A**

Art's Cycle

No shiny, buffed-out mountain bike superstore here. Art's Cycle is a dingy

1652 E 53rd St
773.363.7524
GREEN LINE to GARFIELD

and shady-looking neighborhood bicycle repair shop with a few lonely models for sale. The mechanics have a reputation for good service, and if you can work up the courage to walk inside, you may fall in love with one of the stray two-wheelers on display. **B⁻**

Binny's Beverage Depot

Sometimes you need some booze and you need it now. An upscale joint,

1531 E 53rd St
773.324.5000
GREEN LINE to GARFIELD

Binny's understands this and does what it can to help out. This corner-front establishment stocks a way larger supply of fine liquor and wine than you would [hopefully] ever seek to drink and they even stock cigars. **B**

Bonne Sante' Health Foods

Soy milk, turkey jerky, tongue scrapers, and pills, pills, pills: This upscale

1512 E 53rd St
773.667.5700
GREEN LINE to GARFIELD

health food store has the best in holistic remedies and foods. Health nuts, new-age types and upstanding citizens just looking for some organic or vegan goodness adore the place, and it's easy to see why. Prices are probably higher than what your average college student can splurge on, but periodic sales on organic T.V. dinners are too good to be missed. Oh yeah, and they have pills. **A**

Cornell Florist

This little flower shop is conveniently located near campus for U. of

1645 E 55th St
800.324.1651
GREEN LINE to GARFIELD

Chicago students and offers the typical selection of bouquets and gifts for special occasions. A family business, it delivers for an additional fee. There isn't much that really sets this florist apart from others in the city, but the staff is welcoming and the store isn't overpriced, making it an obvious neighborhood choice for flower-worthy occasions. **B**

Museum of Science
& Industry, 5700
S. Lake Shore Dr.
CLAYTON FLYNN

What the Traveler Saw

1452 E. 53rd St.
773.955.5055
GREEN LINE to GARFIELD

Laurel Stradford, a half-Nigerian globetrotter and self-described gypsy, named this small Hyde Park boutique after a book she wrote for her mother. The book chronicles her many travels, which include crisscrossing Europe and Africa and visiting numerous countries on other continents as well. Setting foot inside of What the Traveler Saw is like seeing the whole saga of her travels before your very own eyes. Stradford collects the goods that interest her from each country, resulting in a colorful and fascinating mash-up of cultures and crafts. All products are handmade, Fair Trade certified and they all seem strangely like they belong together.

Cornell's Dollar Store Plus

Cornell's might be the funniest store in Hyde Park – and have the most useful things you'll never need. Inside the gritty brick exterior is a surreal whirlwind of water pistols, pots, pans, vats of aloe, wigs, 2-liter bottles of soda, Afrocentric paintings, and God knows what else. It may not all be a dollar, but it's all cheap and might come in handy someday. **C+**

1631 E 55th St
773.241.7410
GREEN LINE to GARFIELD

Dr. Wax

This rap- and soul-focused shop makes for a good twenty minutes of browsing through Wu-Tang records you forgot existed or Al Green gospel records you never knew existed. If you have a particular disc in mind they might have it, but anything you don't find can be ordered quickly, saving you cash on shipping. Don't expect smiles and small talk from the staff or go-get-'em customer service, but that oddly adds to the appeal. **B**

5225 S Harper Ave
773.493.8696
GREEN LINE to GARFIELD

Hyde Park Co-Op

The Co-Op is the default area grocery store and has its share of wonderful quirks. Aside from the typical grocery store offerings, you'll find a wall devoted to bulk grains and nuts and a bakery counter full of good stuff like cupcakes and fresh bread. They also serve food from local restaurants and have a small cafeteria,

1536 E 55th St
773.667.1444
GREEN LINE to GARFIELD

so it's worth a visit, even if you don't need to stock up on ingredients for your kitchen. **A**

Kilimanjaro International Art and Design

Looking for that perfect Kente cloth to wear around town, or perhaps just seeking out a headdress to go with the pearls for tomorrow night's party? This unique shop has clothing that people of all nations would feel sharp stepping out in, along with some truly fascinating art. Half the fun is discovering what's in the mixed-up racks. **B**

1456 E 53rd St
773.752.2940
GREEN LINE to GARFIELD

O'Gara and Wilson

O'Gara & Wilson is so authentic, you almost expect to see a lost Oxford don sitting in one of the wooden chairs among the shelves. Though the store is not large, it holds an impressive array of used and rare books. The best part, however, is the atmosphere: The store is filled with piles upon piles of leather-bound tomes and the charming smell of old books. **B+**

1448 E 57th St
773.363.0993
GREEN LINE to GARFIELD

Powell's Book Store

This institution is a charming jumble of thousands of scholarly and popular books, both new and used. Books at unbeatably low prices fill huge floor-to-ceiling shelves and sometimes lie in disorganized jumbles. The store

1501 E 57th St
773.955.7780
GREEN LINE to GARFIELD

HYDE PARK

focuses mostly on academic tomes with popular novels relegated to the basement. Powell's also has a large medieval studies section. **B+**

TOP Noon Hookah Lounge, 1617 E. 55th St. CLAYTON FLYNN • **MIDDLE** Noon Hookah Lounge, 1617 E. 55th St. CLAYTON FLYNN • **BOTTOM** Noon Hookah Lounge, 1617 E. 55th St. CLAYTON FLYNN

Reginald

It's a jacket. Or is it a shirt? No – it's a shawl! In this tiny room housing the collection of a Chicago-based designer, find classic, funky clothes that stand out for their versatility. The hangers are full of draping, clean pieces for all body types, and you can top off the outfit with original jewelry at reasonable prices. **B**

1648 E 55th St
773.288.2028
GREEN LINE to GARFIELD

Seminary Co-op Bookstore

Located in the dim basement of the Chicago Theological Seminary, this maze of a bookstore is completely packed with books covering the humanities and social sciences. It isn't a place to sit and flip through magazines, but you can definitely find some quality reads. If you get lost in the shelves, the staff can guide you towards what you are looking for and maybe you'll stumble upon something new in the meantime. **A**

5757 S University Ave
773.752.4381
GREEN LINE to GARFIELD

Shyne Silver Emporium

A family-owned shop, Shyne sells handmade jewelry and other original accessories by local designers, with the occasional Zambian piece thrown into the mix. It's also a rare jewelry store that isn't all about surfaces – the owners support local artists, musicians and designers, and even host events like record releases every month. **B**

1635 E 55th St
773.324.7204
GREEN LINE to GARFIELD

Style Central

Self-pronounced 'space stylers,' the proprietors of this beautiful establishment cater to your every decorative need. Though the price tags may prove too hefty and the pieces too chic for the dorm room, it's a pleasure just to stroll around ogling the dazzling stemware, intricate purses, and Oprah's favorite candle collection. If one trip doesn't clean out your wallet, drop by again for poetry readings and meditation workshops. Style Central is a one-stop aesthetic feast for all your Zen needs. **A**

5309 S Hyde Park Blvd
773.288.8930
GREEN LINE to GARFIELD

Toys et Cetera

Upon walking in the door, you'll notice Toys et Cetera is the most

1502 E 55th St
773.324.6039
GREEN LINE to GARFIELD

brightly-colored store in Hyde Park. The walls are covered with toys, games and stuffed animals. Displays throughout the crowded space show off cute puppets, tiny novelty items and the kinds of costumes you wish you had when you were a kid. Maybe you're looking for a present to send to your little sister, or maybe you just want to reminisce. Either way, et Cetera is fun. **A**

University of Chicago Bookstore

More or less the typical university bookstore, this shop is run by Barnes

970 E 58th St
773.702.8729
GREEN LINE to GARFIELD

& Noble and complete with a Starbucks café and plenty of University of Chicago key chains and sweatshirts. Though smaller than the usual model, it offers a nice selection of books by campus faculty not found in every large bookstore. Occasionally authors stop by to talk about their books and do signings, but this is more of a place to pick up necessities. **B**

Wesley's Shoe Corral

Located in a small strip mall, this well-kept shoe store is family-owned and

1506 E 55th St
773.822.9130
GREEN LINE to GARFIELD

has very friendly service. The variety of shoes is limited to a few choice brands, which include Birkenstock and Ugg. Wesley's is ideal if you are in search of some quality shoes for your treks around the city and you'd like to support a local business in the process. **A**

LEFT: 10th Church of Christ the Scientist. CLAYTON FLYNN • **ABOVE:** 10th Church of Christ the Scientist. CLAYTON FLYNN

▌APPENDIX: MAPS

EVANSTON

NORTH: Isabella Rd., four blocks north of Central St. **EAST:** Lake Michigan. **SOUTH:** Howard St. east to Chicago Ave. north to S. Blvd. east to Lake Michigan. **WEST:** McCormick Blvd. north to Golf Rd. northwest to Simpson St. east to Crawford Ave. north to Ridge Rd. northeast to Isabella Rd.

© Google Maps, 2008

ROGERS PARK

NORTH: Howard St. east to Chicago Ave. north to South Blvd. east to Lake Michigan. **EAST:** Lake Michigan. **SOUTH:** Devon Ave. extended east to Lake Michigan. **WEST:** Ridge Blvd.

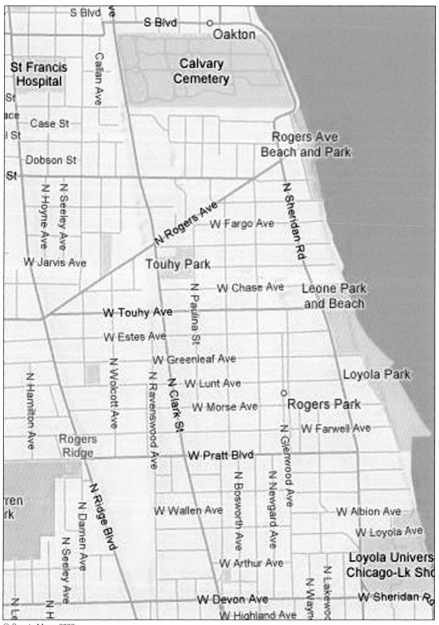

© Google Maps, 2008

▮ APPENDIX: MAPS

EDGEWATER

NORTH: Devon Ave. extended east to Lake Michigan. **EAST:** Lake Michigan. **SOUTH:** Foster Ave. extended east to Lake Michigan. **WEST:** Ravenswood Ave.

© Google Maps, 2008

UPTOWN

NORTH: Foster Ave. extended east to Lake Michigan. **EAST:** Lake Michigan. **SOUTH:** Montrose Ave. east to Western Ave. southeast to Irving Park Rd. extended east to Lake Michigan. **WEST:** Ravenswood Ave.

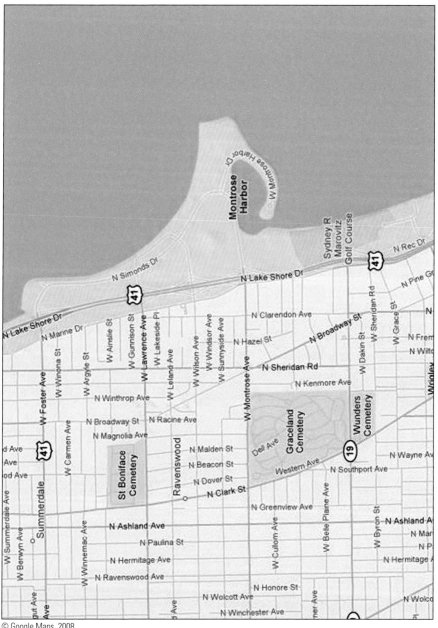

© Google Maps, 2008

▌APPENDIX: MAPS

LINCOLN SQUARE

NORTH: Bryn Mawr Ave. east to Western Ave. north to Peterson Ave. east to Ravenswood Ave. **EAST:** Ravenswood Ave. **SOUTH:** Montrose Ave. **WEST:** Chicago River North Branch.

© Google Maps, 2008

LAKEVIEW

NORTH: Montrose Ave. east to Western Ave. southeast to Irving Park Rd. extended east to Lake Michigan. **EAST:** Lake Michigan. **SOUTH:** Diversey Pkwy. extended east to Lake Michigan. **WEST:** Ravenswood Ave.

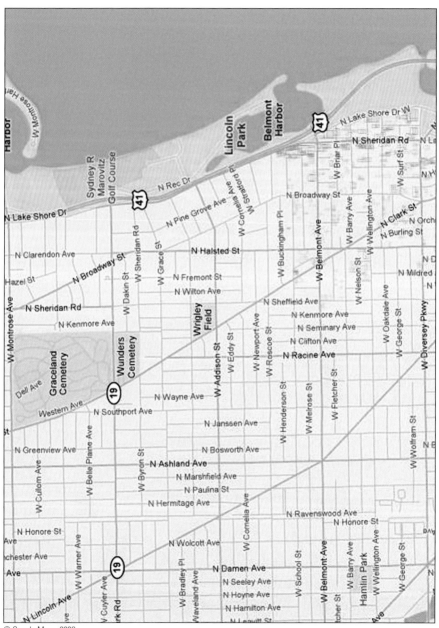

© Google Maps, 2008

LINCOLN PARK

NORTH: Isabella Rd., four blocks north of Central St. **EAST:** Lake Michigan. **SOUTH:** Howard St. east to Chicago Ave. north to S. Blvd. east to Lake Michigan. **WEST:** McCormick Blvd. north to Golf Rd. northwest to Simpson St. east to Crawford Ave. north to Ridge Rd. northeast to Isabella Rd.

© Google Maps, 2008

APPENDIX: MAPS

NORTH CENTER

NORTH: Isabella Rd., four blocks north of Central St. **EAST:** Lake Michigan. **SOUTH:** Howard St. east to Chicago Ave. north to S. Blvd. east to Lake Michigan. **WEST:** McCormick Blvd. north to Golf Rd. northwest to Simpson St. east to Crawford Ave. north to Ridge Rd. northeast to Isabella Rd.

© Google Maps, 2008

◀ APPENDIX: MAPS

LOGAN SQUARE

NORTH: Isabella Rd., four blocks north of Central St. **EAST:** Lake Michigan. **SOUTH:** Howard St. east to Chicago Ave. north to S. Blvd. east to Lake Michigan. **WEST:** McCormick Blvd. north to Golf Rd. northwest to Simpson St. east to Crawford Ave. north to Ridge Rd. northeast to Isabella Rd.

© Google Maps, 2008

WEST TOWN

NORTH: Isabella Rd., four blocks north of Central St. **EAST:** Lake Michigan. **SOUTH:** Howard St. east to Chicago Ave. north to S. Blvd. east to Lake Michigan. **WEST:** McCormick Blvd. north to Golf Rd. northwest to Simpson St. east to Crawford Ave. north to Ridge Rd. northeast to Isabella Rd.

© Google Maps, 2008

▌APPENDIX: MAPS

AVONDALE

NORTH: Belmont Ave. east to Pulaski Rd. north to Addison St. **EAST:** Chicago River. **SOUTH:** Diversey Ave. **WEST:** Kearsarge Ave. extended southeast to Diversey Ave. and northwest to Belmont Ave.

© Google Maps, 2008

NEAR NORTH SIDE

NORTH: North Ave. east to North Blvd. extended east to Lake Michigan. **EAST:** Lake Michigan. **SOUTH:** Chicago River. **WEST:** Chicago River.

© Google Maps, 2008

▌APPENDIX: MAPS

LOOP

NORTH: Chicago River. **EAST:** Lake Michigan. **SOUTH:** Roosevelt Rd. east to Lake Shore Dr. extended northeast to Lake Michigan. **WEST:** Chicago River.

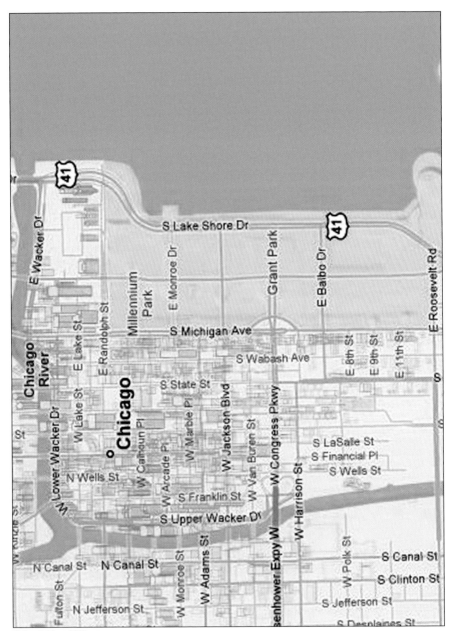

© Google Maps, 2008

NEAR SOUTH SIDE

NORTH: Roosevelt Rd. east to Lake Shore Dr. extended northeast to Lake Michigan. **EAST:** Lake Michigan. **SOUTH:** 26th St. extended east to Lake Michigan. **WEST:** Wentworth Ave. north to 18th St. west to the Chicago River.

© Google Maps, 2008

▮ APPENDIX: MAPS

NEAR WEST SIDE

NORTH: Isabella Rd., four blocks north of Central St. **EAST:** Lake Michigan. **SOUTH:** Howard St. east to Chicago Ave. north to S. Blvd. east to Lake Michigan. **WEST:** McCormick Blvd. north to Golf Rd. northwest to Simpson St. east to Crawford Ave. north to Ridge Rd. northeast to Isabella Rd.

© Google Maps, 2008

CHICAGO UNZIPPED

SOUTH LAWNDALE

NORTH: Isabella Rd., four blocks north of Central St. **EAST:** Lake Michigan. **SOUTH:** Howard St. east to Chicago Ave. north to S. Blvd. east to Lake Michigan. **WEST:** McCormick Blvd. north to Golf Rd. northwest to Simpson St. east to Crawford Ave. north to Ridge Rd. northeast to Isabella Rd.

© Google Maps, 2008

BRIDGEPORT

NORTH: The South Branch of the Chicago River. **EAST:** Dan Ryan Expy. southeast to Normal Ave. south to 28th St. east to Canal St. **SOUTH:** Pershing Rd. **WEST:** Chicago River extended south to Pershing Rd.

© Google Maps, 2008

ARMOUR SQUARE

NORTH: The South Branch of the Chicago River northeast to 18th St. **EAST:** Wentworth Ave. extended south to 35th St. east to LaSalle St. **SOUTH:** Pershing Rd. **WEST:** Canal St. north to 28th St. west to Normal Ave. north to the Dan Ryan Expy.

© Google Maps, 2008

◢ APPENDIX: MAPS

LOWER WEST SIDE

NORTH: 16th St. extended west to Western Ave. and east to the South Branch of the Chicago River. **EAST:** The South Branch of the Chicago River. **SOUTH:** Stevenson Expy. east to the South Branch of the Chicago River. **WEST:** Western Ave.

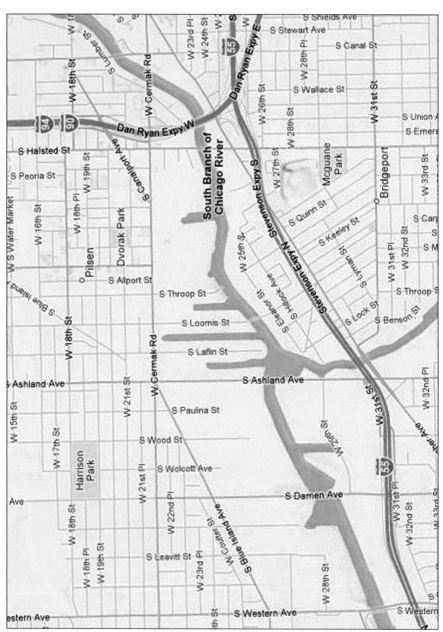

© Google Maps, 2008

HYDE PARK

NORTH: Hyde Park Blvd. **EAST:** Lake Michigan. **SOUTH:** 60th St. extended east through the East Lagoon to Lake Michigan. **WEST:** Cottage Grove Ave./East border of Washington Park.

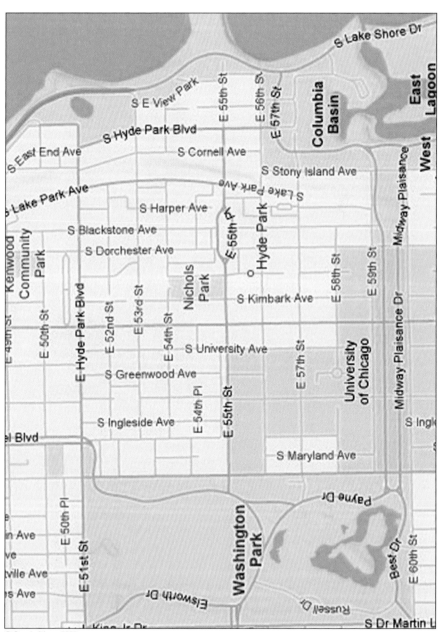

© Google Maps, 2008

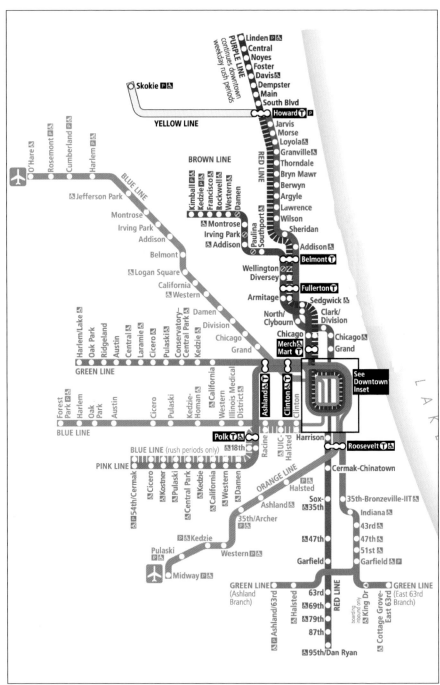

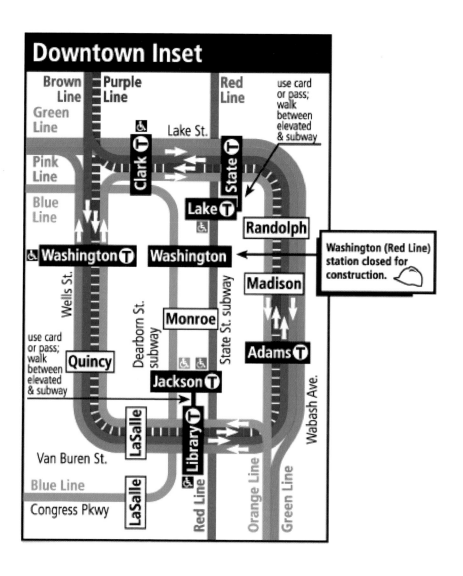

INDEX

Note: The 100 items in bold are editor picks.

INDEX

INDEX

INDEX

INDEX

INDEX

INDEX